Medieval History

General Editors

JOHN BLAIR   HELENA HAMEROW

Anglo-Saxon Farms and Farming

Anglo-Saxon farming made England so wealthy by the eleventh century that it attracted two full-scale invasions. In *Anglo-Saxon Farms and Farming*, Debby Banham and Rosamond Faith explore how Anglo-Saxon farmers produced the food and other crops and animal products that sustained England's economy, society, and culture before the Norman Conquest.

The volume is made up of two complementary sections: the first examines written and pictorial sources, archaeological evidence, place-names, and the history of the English language to discover what kind of crops and livestock people raised, and what tools and techniques they used in producing them. The second part assembles a series of local landscape studies to explore how these techniques were combined into working agricultural regimes in different environments. These perspectives allow the authors to take new approaches to the chronology and development of open-field farming, to the changing relationship between livestock husbandry and arable cultivation, and to the values and social relationships which underpinned rural life. The elite are not ignored, but peasant farmers are represented as agents, making decisions about the way they managed their resources and working lives.

A picture emerges of an agriculture that changed from an essentially prehistoric state in the sub-Roman period to what was, by the time of the Conquest, recognizably the beginning of a tradition that only ended in the modern period. Anglo-Saxon farming was not only sustainable, but infinitely adaptable to different soils and geology, and to a climate changing as unpredictably as it is today.

Debby Banham is a medieval historian who teaches in the Universities of Cambridge and London. During the 1970s she worked as an agricultural labourer, and when she arrived in Cambridge as a mature student, discovered that farming was the only thing she knew more about than the people who taught her. She has published *Monasteriales indicia: the Old English monastic sign language*, and *Food and Drink in Anglo-Saxon England*, as well as articles on Anglo-Saxon farming, diet, and medicine, and monastic sign language.

Rosamond Faith has taught medieval history at the universities of London, Cambridge, and Oxford, and is the author of *The English Peasantry and the Growth of Lordship* and many articles on English and French peasants, the rural economy, and the English landscape.

MEDIEVAL HISTORY AND ARCHAEOLOGY

General Editors
John Blair   Helena Hamerow

The volumes in this series bring together archaeological, historical, and visual methods to offer new approaches to aspects of medieval society, economy, and material culture. The series seeks to present and interpret archaeological evidence in ways readily accessible to historians, while providing a historical perspective and context for the material culture of the period.

ANGLO-SAXON FARMS AND FARMING

DEBBY BANHAM AND ROSAMOND FAITH

OXFORD

UNIVERSITY PRESS

OXFORD

UNIVERSITY PRESS

Great Clarendon Street, Oxford, OX2 6DP,
United Kingdom

Oxford University Press is a department of the University of Oxford.
It furthers the University's objective of excellence in research, scholarship,
and education by publishing worldwide. Oxford is a registered trade mark of
Oxford University Press in the UK and in certain other countries

First published 2014
First published in paperback 2020

Impression: 1

Published in the United States of America by Oxford University Press
198 Madison Avenue, New York, NY 10016, United States of America

British Library Cataloguing in Publication Data
Data available

Library of Congress Cataloging in Publication Data
Data available

ISBN 978–0–19–920794–7 (Hbk.)
ISBN 978–0–19–885550–7 (Pbk.)

Printed and bound by
CPI Group (UK) Ltd, Croydon, CR0 4YY

In memory of Joan Thirsk

Preface

This book has been a long time in the making. It arose from the authors' frustration at having no reading to offer our students when we told them that farming was the most important part of the Anglo-Saxon economy. Our original intention was to write a textbook to fill that need, drawing on the work of other scholars in a range of fields. But it soon became obvious that the scholarly community—even our corner of it—had not been directing its efforts to providing material for us to synthesize. We have therefore spent the intervening years grappling with the primary sources (including the landscape itself) in all their variety and with all their problems, as well as taking advantage gratefully of the work that has been done in the field by others, to attack a wide range of questions, some of which even we had not thought of when we began. The result has been a book much bigger than we originally intended, but we hope that its size, and the long wait, will be justified by its usefulness and interest, not only to students, but also to more senior scholars, and to readers outside academe. It should be even more useful now that modern agriculture is almost entirely divorced from the tradition that went back to our period, and many of our readers are unlikely to be familiar with farming of any kind.

We have tried to give an overall picture of farming in Anglo-Saxon England, as well as an idea of the variety it encompassed. In doing so we have drawn on the expertise of a large number of people, some of whom, to our regret, are no longer with us to be thanked. We are immensely grateful to them all, and apologize for not listing them all here.

Among those to whom we are especially grateful for help and discussion over the years are our series editors, John Blair and Helena Hamerow. We would also like to thank the anonymous readers for the press, who have improved the book considerably. Ruth Parr and a series of editors at OUP have patiently tolerated our queries and delays. We are particularly grateful to David Pelteret for his patience and expert advice.

We would particularly like to thank all those who have given us the benefit of their practical experience with crops and livestock, including the Grazing Animals Projects run by Natural England, the National Trust and several local wildlife and conservation bodies, David Nicholls, Virginia Bainbridge, Mary Castell, Richard Kitchin of Withill, Mr Eyre of Collaton, Bruce Garside of the Berkshire Pig Company, Gill Swanton of North Farm, Overton, the staff and wardens of the Essex Wildlife Trust, the Berkshire, Buckinghamshire and Oxfordshire Wildlife Trust, the Gloucestershire Wildlife Trust, Butser Ancient

Farm, Burnham Beeches and Stoke Row Nature Reserve, Crickley Hill Country Park, Dr Rachel Ballantyne, Dr Mim Bower, Dr John Letts, Simon Damant of the National Trust at Wimpole Hall, and the staff, past and present, of Bede's World at Jarrow.

Rosamond Faith has been lucky enough to have walked landscapes in the company of, and learned from, David Austin, David Siddle, Andrew Fleming, and Pete Herring, and two inspiring groups: Exploring Early Farming, and the West Oxfordshire Boundary Walkers.

We have both benefited from many hours of discussion at seminars and conferences we have attended over the years, notably those of the Medieval Settlement Research Group and the Medieval Diet Group, as well as various meetings organized by Dr Susan Oosthuizen. We are grateful to all the organizers and participants.

We would like to thank Kelly Walter and Frank Goodingham for valuable practical help. Cath d'Alton has created the maps and Jane Peart the landscape drawings.

The publication of this book has been made possible by a grant from the Scouloudi Foundation in association with the Institute of Historical Research. The Marc Fitch Fund generously assisted with the cost of the illustrations, as did the Department of Anglo-Saxon, Norse and Celtic, University of Cambridge. We are very grateful to both bodies, and to the Cassini Publishing Company for permission to reproduce its re-scaled First Edition Ordnance Survey maps free of charge, and to the Bodleian Libraries, the University of Oxford for permission to reproduce Cassini Historical Maps Old Series, 191. Copyright permissions for illustrations are acknowledged in the captions; while efforts have been made to trace the current owners of the copyrights of Zwemmer Publishing Ltd and West Air Photography, these have proved unsuccessful.

Most of all, we are grateful to each other for many stimulating and fruitful discussions over the years, and for extensive and helpful comments on each other's chapters. It is out of these debates that this book has grown.

We would like to dedicate this book to the memory of Joan Thirsk. Joan was a huge influence on us both, not only as a historian of agriculture, but also as a role model for female academics. We very much regret that Joan did not see the book completed, but we are glad that she knew it was to be dedicated to her.

Debby Banham and Rosamond Faith
Cambridge and Finstock, Oxfordshire

Contents

List of Plates

List of Figures

List of Tables

List of Abbreviations

ASC	Anglo-Saxon Chronicle
ASE	*Anglo-Saxon England*
CBA	Council for British Archaeology
DB	Domesday Book
EETS ss	Early English Text Society, Supplementary Series
EHR	*English Historical Review*
ER	East Riding (Yorkshire)
MGH	Monumenta Germaniae historica
NR	North Riding (Yorkshire)
ns	new series
ODan	Old Danish
OE	Old English
OED	*Oxford English Dictionary*
ON	Old Norse
OScand	Old Scandinavian
S	Sawyer, *Anglo-Saxon Charters*: all charters are cited by Sawyer number, either from the original publication, or from the revised online version <http://www.esawyer.org>
s.a.	*sub anno*
s.v.	*sub verbo*
WR	West Riding (Yorkshire)

Note on Periodization

Unless otherwise stated:
early Anglo-Saxon = fifth to seventh centuries,
middle Anglo-Saxon = eighth and ninth centuries,
late Anglo-Saxon = tenth and eleventh centuries.

For reigns of individual kings, see Simon Keynes, 'Appendix I: Rulers of the English, c. 450–1066', in M. Lapidge, J. Blair, S. Keynes, and D. Scragg (eds), *The Wiley Blackwell Encyclopedia of Anglo-Saxon England*, 2nd edn (Chichester, 2014), 521–38.

1

Introduction

Without Anglo-Saxon farming, the rest of English history would not have happened. The very earliest Germanic settlers in Britain had to provide themselves with food, as have subsequent generations in England ever since. The 'great men' of history, whether they built empires or composed masterpieces, could have done none of it if they hadn't had enough to eat. Their achievements have been celebrated in historical scholarship for centuries, but the people who produced the food have received much less attention. The vast majority of the population, in England as elsewhere, have been dependent until very recently on their own physical labour to ensure their supplies of food. This book, then, is about that most fundamental human activity, the provision of food, at the time when England's society, culture, and economy were coming into being.

Farming is usually counted as part of the economy: it produces wealth in its most basic form. While a good deal has been written about the early medieval economy in recent years, most of it has concentrated on the growth of trade and towns.[1] Agriculture has largely been taken for granted as the background against which commerce developed. In this book we attempt to illuminate that background by examining Anglo-Saxon farming as it worked at the most basic level: how did the 'average Anglo-Saxon' provide their household with food and other necessities, as well as producing a surplus to support those who did not feed themselves: the aristocracy, the Church, and, by the end of our period, a growing urban population?

In Part I of this book, we investigate the crops and livestock produced by Anglo-Saxon farming, and the tools and techniques used to produce them. In Part II, we explore in a series of landscape studies how these practicalities worked on the ground in different kinds of terrain. Our conclusions bring these two approaches together to provide a broad picture of Anglo-Saxon farming as a whole that is wide-ranging and comprehensive, as well as grounded firmly in detailed evidence. Apart from this chapter and the conclusions, we have not

---

[1] Naismith, *Money and Power*, is just one of many excellent books on the Anglo-Saxon economy that do not deal with production. Of the two recent blockbusters on the early medieval economy, McCormick, *Origins of the European Economy*, hardly looks at production at all, while Wickham, *Framing the Middle Ages*, does not 'drill down' to the basic practical level that concerns us here.

written any part of the book together, although we have each read every word the other has written: Debby Banham is responsible for Part I and Rosamond Faith for Part II. We have written in the first instance for our own pleasure, jointly and separately, as we discovered more and more about Anglo-Saxon farming, but we have always kept our readers in mind as we wrote. We imagine that most of our readers will either know about Anglo-Saxon England, but not about farming, or about farming, but not about our period. For the latter, we have provided a brief note on periodization (p. xv), and recommend the general books on Anglo-Saxon England listed in the bibliography, and for the former, a visit to a working farm will elucidate a great deal. For all our readers, we have provided a glossary of terms which seem to us to need explanation.

A FARMER'S VIEW OF ANGLO-SAXON ENGLAND

The vast majority of Anglo-Saxons were involved in farming. Agriculture formed the bulk of the economy: manufacturing as we know it hardly existed, and by our standards trade played a minor, if growing, role. Most forms of wealth, and many interactions between individuals or groups, were concerned with what we would consider to be farming matters. Theft, for instance, in Anglo-Saxon law is primarily theft of cattle. Commercial transactions are mostly concerned with livestock too. Rents, tithes, and probably many taxes were paid in foodstuffs. For the basic necessities of life—food, clothes, and shelter—Anglo-Saxon England was self-sufficient, and this was also true of virtually all individual Anglo-Saxons. The average Anglo-Saxon was a peasant, that is to say, the majority of people grew most of what they ate, and ate most of what they grew.[2] Even those at the top of the social scale, although they garnished their lifestyle with imported exotica such as spices and silks, relied for the basics on their own lands, from which they extracted products via food rents and other obligations. For the average Anglo-Saxon, staying alive depended on his or her own physical work, tilling the soil, and caring for livestock. People lived on their arable crops, enlivened by whatever animal foods could be produced, clothing came from the backs of their own sheep, and roofing and bedding materials from the fields. This book shows how Anglo-Saxons went about ensuring their own survival, producing their own food, clothing, and, to some extent, shelter.

Anglo-Saxon farmers were not living in an egalitarian society. As far as Anglo-Saxon political theory is concerned, society was divided into a simple two-tier hierarchy, *eorl and ceorl*, even though reality must have been more complex. On the one hand was an elite distinguished by birth, wealth, and, for

---

[2] Although Anglo-Saxon peasants were at the lower end of the social scale, we use the term to describe their economic *modus operandi*, not as a sociological category.

the men, office as *eorl*. On the other were all other free men, *ceorls*; most were farmers in one way or another, what King Alfred called 'people who work', an essential pillar of society alongside those who fight and those who pray. Most farmers were *ceorls*, but a good deal of the work of Anglo-Saxon farming must have been done by slaves.[3] The reader should bear in mind that, while our sources present society in masculine terms, we believe that, as always, women played a vital role in the rural economy. Free status gave the *ceorl* the obligations of paying tax, doing military service and so on, but also the right (and obligation) to participate in the public courts. But free status did not stop a *ceorl* being a peasant.

By the time of our earliest evidence in the seventh century, powerful people from the king down had rights over the land and the people who lived there. Their position entitled them to be supported by deliveries of goods and services, including food rents (OE *feorm*), from their estates.[4] The liability to supply these rested on peasant families who had a hide of land, or some fraction of it, so it was essentially an appropriation of peasant agricultural surplus.[5] Landowners might also establish an 'inland', an area generally near their central dwelling worked by slaves and very dependent labourers.[6] This is very much the situation described in the *Rectitudines* (see p. 8). But outside these inlands, substantial farmers had more in common with their socially more elevated neighbours. Farming was fundamental to the way Anglo-Saxon society was held together.

How did the world look to these farmers? The chapters that follow give examples of their capacity to initiate change. Yet they may often have remained reluctant to do so, whether because they had to take into account the interests of neighbours and kin, or simply because they were risk-averse. Thus 'progress', whether that meant adopting new tools or ways of doing things, might have taken generations to take hold, even within a restricted neighbourhood. To individual farmers, as a result, the world might look quite stable, even if particular changes intruded on their life and work. Nonetheless, farmers and farming must have been seriously affected by the dramatic events in Anglo-Saxon history. We do not know, for instance, how much of the population survived in areas taken over by Vikings, or how much reorganization was needed as a result. Major disasters caused by war and invasion are not the subject of this book, but must be borne in mind.

One change, if less dramatic than invasion, certainly did affect Anglo-Saxon farming. Even today, farmers are notoriously, and rightly, concerned with the

---

[3] For slaves, see Pelteret, *Slavery*.

[4] Robin Fleming describes this 'ranked' society as one in which 'individuals are unable to divert an inordinate share of the material resources and labour of their communities towards their own or their families' uses': *Britain after Rome*, 65–75, at 65. A similar argument can be found in Faith, 'Forces and relations of production' and her *English Peasantry*.

[5] Stenton, *Anglo-Saxon England*, 284–6; for food rents, see Banham, 'Food plants'.

[6] Faith, *English Peasantry*, 15–88.

weather. The early Middle Ages was a period, like our own, when the climate was in transition. In sub-Roman Britain, deteriorating climate probably aided the collapse of the Roman lifestyle and large-scale cereal production, but by the end of our period, England was well on the way to the 'little optimum', or Medieval Warm Period that preceded the Little Ice Age.[7] Recent intensive research activity on climate change has revealed that temperatures in the eleventh century may have been as high as in the early twenty-first, with the amelioration beginning as early as the seventh.[8] As at the present day, there were climatic fluctuations, some probably quite violent. Exactly how these might have affected Anglo-Saxon farmers we cannot be sure, but the effects could have been quite traumatic, possibly including the famines recorded in the Anglo-Saxon Chronicle. The overall improvement, however, must have facilitated many of the changes discussed in this book.[9]

SCOPE OF THIS STUDY

We have adopted a broad interpretation of the term 'Anglo-Saxon England', covering more or less the same area as modern England, and a period from around the beginning of the fifth century to the late eleventh. The term 'Anglo-Saxon' in this book usually covers anything or anybody within those territories and between those dates. It should not be taken as a 'racial' marker, unless it is explicitly contrasted with other ethnic terms such as 'British' or 'Scandinavian'. We do not normally use the term 'Anglo-Scandinavian' for later Anglo-Saxon England, but it should be remembered that its population was of mixed origin.

Our inclusive intention, both chronological and geographical, is, however, limited by the availability of information. Written sources only exist after the conversion of the Anglo-Saxons to Christianity, and those that deal with farming belong almost exclusively to the tenth and especially the eleventh centuries (the seventh-century laws of Ine of Wessex being a welcome exception). Some of our most useful information comes from documents that are not even pre-Conquest: the greatest compendium of data on Anglo-Saxon farming is Domesday Book, compiled twenty years after the end of Anglo-Saxon England. Fortunately, other forms of evidence are more evenly distributed across the period. Archaeological remains are particularly full for the time, largely pre-Christian, when the Anglo-Saxons buried their dead with grave-goods. Settlement sites, too, go back to the earliest Anglo-Saxon times. Landscape and

---

[7] For the broad trends, see Dark, *Environment*.
[8] See Burroughs, *Climate Change*, 252–6.
[9] For a suggestion as to how this might have worked, see Banham, 'In the sweat of thy brow'.

place-name evidence, though often hard to date, is not confined to the end of the period. But taking all our evidence as a whole, there is no doubt that we suffer from a bias towards the late Anglo-Saxon period, and earlier centuries are more difficult to penetrate.

Nor is the geographic spread of our information uniform: written evidence is much more abundant from the south of England than from the north (apart from the Venerable Bede). There are several reasons for this: the south and east were always the most prosperous parts of England, the dynasty that eventually ruled England came from the south, and the Vikings were more active in the north and east. Archaeological evidence has tended to cluster around universities and excavation units, but developer-funded excavation has also been more intensive in the south and east. Place-names and landscape evidence are fortunately immune from most of these problems, and of course securely located. Landscape history too is less affected by southern bias, but even so, our book, we have to admit, is stronger on the south of England and the West Country, than it is on the Northern counties.

We have not tried to simply 'push back into the Anglo-Saxon period' phenomena with which we are already familiar from the twelfth century onwards, or even later periods,[10] but to evaluate early medieval English farming as we found it. We have tried to avoid the implication that pre-industrial farming was 'timeless' and unchanging; indeed, our findings are concerned with change as much as with stability. We hope we have kept our minds open to the unexpected, as well as to practices that had a long afterlife. Our preconceptions have no doubt influenced our thinking more than we realize (other people's are always easier to see than one's own), but we have at least allowed for those we were aware of.

The term 'farming' is also interpreted broadly, to include both arable and pastoral operations. We deal mainly with food production, but also with that of textiles, especially wool, and also, to a much lesser extent, of building materials such as thatch. We have excluded horticulture and viticulture, and also forestry, which produced the major structural material, timber, but we have dealt with some woodland products used in farming, for instance as fencing and folds. Our focus is mainly on practicalities, but these are impossible to divorce completely from the organization of agrarian production, or indeed from the trade in agricultural products, especially in as far as it affects the ways they were produced. It is also hard to draw a line between production and processing, but we have concentrated on the former. Thus, cereal crops are pursued as far as the threshing floor, but not to the mill, still less the kneading trough. Dairy work is investigated to a greater extent, but mainly for what it reveals about how milk was produced in the first place. Generally speaking, we try not to stray too far off the farm and its resources. It has been well said that

---

[10] The phrase is from Dyer and Everson, 'The development of the study', 15.

a farmer is still farming when he goes to market, or even to the pub at lunchtime,[11] but we have not usually followed him or her.[12]

EXISTING SCHOLARSHIP ON ANGLO-SAXON FARMING

Given the importance of agriculture in the Anglo-Saxon economy, it is perhaps surprising that a volume with a title such as *Anglo-Saxon Farming* does not already exist. With a few honourable exceptions, Anglo-Saxonists have been content to take this basic aspect of Anglo-Saxon England for granted and focus on the interests of the more powerful and educated sectors of society. Even those that do deal with farming are not concerned primarily with the practicalities. H. P. R. Finberg's chapter on 'Anglo-Saxon England to 1042', in his volume in the great *Agrarian History of England and Wales*, ranges widely over Anglo-Saxon social and economic, and even political, history, but gives surprisingly little information about how farming was done. H. E. Hallam's chapter in the following volume has a more practical orientation, but its focus is the very end of our period, drawing particularly on Domesday Book.[13] The Domesday evidence is explored in exhaustive detail in H. C. Darby's Domesday Geography series, and synthesized in his *Domesday England*, but by its nature it is not concerned primarily with farming activities.

Archaeologists have devoted more attention to Anglo-Saxon farming than historians. Its recent study really began with Peter Fowler's 'Farming in the Anglo-Saxon landscape' (1980), and his more recent *Farming in the First Millennium* deals with many of the same issues as we do. However, his book deliberately eschews cultural divisions within Britain, or within the time-frame, in order to avoid preconceptions about 'Roman', 'Celtic', or 'Germanic' ways of doing things. As a result, it emphasizes continuities and commonalities, and does not highlight phenomena that were more specific in time or place, or indeed culture. Our book may be seen as complementing Professor Fowler's by concentrating on the specific farming practices of Anglo-Saxon time, place, and culture.

Archaeologists' willingness to engage with matters agricultural has been assisted by the growth in the second half of the twentieth century of scientific techniques that extract ever more information from biological remains. Some recent site reports, such as Gill Hey's on Yarnton in Oxfordshire, the series of volumes on Flixborough in North Lincolnshire, and the final report on Wharram

---

[11] By Pryor, *Farmers in Prehistoric Britain*, 20.

[12] Generally speaking, we assume we are dealing with farming *households*, and do not take a view on the gender of persons carrying out the work we discuss, except where there is specific evidence for this.

[13] Hallam, 'England before the Conquest'.

Percy in Yorkshire have been particularly useful in this respect.[14] Synthetic studies have also appeared in greater numbers in recent years, including the work of Pam Crabtree and Naomi Sykes on animal bones, and the surveys of zooarchaeology, archaeobotany, and other relevant topics in the *Oxford Handbook of Anglo-Saxon Archaeology*. All these have been extremely valuable to us.

Work on diet, by both archaeologists and historians, has also contributed to our knowledge. One of us began her research career in that area, and Ann Hagen has gathered a huge compendium of information, drawn from both archaeological and historical sources, in her *Second Handbook of Anglo-Saxon Food and Drink*. More recently, we have drawn upon the studies produced by the Medieval Diet Group.[15]

The work of Della Hooke on charter bounds, culminating in her *Landscape of Anglo-Saxon England*, and more recently her *Trees in Anglo-Saxon England*, deserves special mention. We have drawn not only information but inspiration from her publications: she is one of the few scholars who have really investigated conditions on the ground in Anglo-Saxon England. Margaret Gelling's work on place-names, too, has long been essential to any study of the landscape, and took a new and even more productive approach in her collaboration with the geographer Ann Cole. Their identification of the 'language of landscape', the immensely subtle and precise vocabulary used for particular landscape features, while not specifically concerned with farming, offers a way of seeing the world through Anglo-Saxon eyes, of distinguishing the various kinds of hills or streams or roads they knew and used.

One aspect of Anglo-Saxon farming that has received a thorough scholarly examination in the past is the early development of open fields. The standard work, and still very readable, is the Orwins' *The Open Fields*, but their views on origins have long been superseded. Tom Williamson's *Shaping Medieval Landscapes* presents a more recent perspective, and summarizes the history of open-field scholarship. The volumes on Anglo-Saxon landscape edited by Nick Higham and Martin Ryan contain some current contributions to the debate. But if our book does nothing else, we hope it will convince readers that there was much more to Anglo-Saxon farming than open fields.

Two recent studies, Professor Williamson's *Environment, Society and Landscape* and Susan Oosthuizen's *Tradition and Transformation*, also emphasize the Anglo-Saxon period as the cradle of agrarian developments that were of major significance in the later Middle Ages. Both authors have done much to stimulate our thinking over the years, and we hope that readers will find it useful to place our closer focus alongside their large-scale narratives. As we were going to press, Mark McKerracher was writing up his Oxford DPhil

---

[14] Hey, *Yarnton: Saxon and Medieval*; Dobney, Jaques, Barrett, and Johnstone, *Farmers, Monks and Aristocrats*.

[15] Woolgar, Serjeantson, and Waldron, *Food in Medieval England*.

thesis on agrarian change in mid-Anglo-Saxon England.[16] We are extremely gratified to see a young scholar investigating a topic so close to our own concerns. Perhaps Anglo-Saxon farming's time has come at last.

PRIMARY WRITTEN SOURCES

One of the reasons there has not been more work on Anglo-Saxon farming is undoubtedly the paucity of primary written evidence on the subject. Anglo-Saxon writers cannot be said to have taken a huge interest in how their food and other necessities were produced. Thus we have drawn, on a wide range of sources whose primary concerns are not necessarily very close to ours.

The estate management literature

The Anglo-Saxon estate management literature is not really a unified genre: it consists of two fairly theoretical prescriptive texts and one set of pretty informal records, all in Old English. The first two, the *Rectitudines singularum personarum* ('Rights of different people') and *Be gesceadwisan gerefan* ('On the prudent reeve', usually known simply as *Gerefa*),[17] appear together in Corpus Christi College, Cambridge, MS 383, but they probably have separate origins.[18] The *Rectitudines* lists, as its title implies, the rights and responsibilities of persons of different ranks, ranging from a thegn down to unfree peasants. The context in which these people and their relationships are envisaged is a rural estate, and thus many of their rights and responsibilities involve agricultural work and products. A number of them are specialist workers, such as shepherds and beekeepers, so the description of their duties gives useful detail. The *Gerefa*, on the other hand, is a handbook for a reeve or steward, listing the equipment he is responsible for and the work he must oversee at each season, as well as warning him repeatedly to put his employer's interests before those of the people subject to him. Doubts have been expressed about the *Gerefa*'s relationship to practical farming, chiefly because it clearly lifts batches of words from glossaries and other texts. It certainly needs to be used with caution, if only because much of its vocabulary is otherwise unknown. It was probably attached to the *Rectitudines* to supply a perceived gap in that text, which does not list a reeve among its *personae*.

The 'Ely Farming Memoranda'[19] consist of notes, jotted down at different times in the eleventh century, about goods, mostly agricultural, and money sent

---

[16] McKerracher, 'Agricultural Development in Mid Saxon England.'

[17] Both edited by Liebermann, *Gesetze*, i, 444–53 and 453–5.

[18] For the possible origins and purposes of the texts, see Harvey, '*Rectitudines singularum personarum* and *Gerefa*'.

[19] Edited by Robertson, *Anglo-Saxon Charters*, 252–6 (Appendix 2, no. 9).

from the refounded abbey at Ely to that at Thorney, as well as lists of livestock (including people) at Ely properties, and of rents owed in eels. They are practically unique as genuine Anglo-Saxon ephemera, intended no doubt to be kept for as long as the information had practical use, but not expected to have lasting value. The mention of money gives a rare insight into the market in agricultural commodities, which was probably only beginning to develop at the end of the period.

Laws

The *Rectitudines* and *Gerefa* are regarded as 'quasi-legal' texts, concerned as they are with custom, and found in a legal manuscript. CCCC 383 also contains the *Dunsætan* ('hill-dwellers'), an agreement between English and Welsh population groups living either side of a river and concerned chiefly with tracking cattle. The text is conventionally dated to the reign of Æthelstan (924–39), but only because it lists livestock values similar to those in the London trade regulations of that time.

Royal legislation from Anglo-Saxon England is much less concerned with agriculture. The law-code of Ine of Wessex (AD ?688 × 694)[20] concerns itself more with farming than any other Anglo-Saxon code, even the earliest ones from Kent, but it still leaves the vast majority of agrarian activities and concerns unlegislated for. This is in stark contrast with the early Irish law-codes which provided the basis for Fergus Kelly's magisterial study, or the Scandinavian ones examined by Annette Hoff.[21] The implication is that the Anglo-Saxon upper classes, especially later in the period, took a good deal less interest in how their lands were cultivated than their Irish or Scandinavian counterparts. Most Anglo-Saxon law-codes get no closer to the nitty-gritty of food production than cattle-rustling, clearly of serious concern to great land-owners as well as lesser people. The London trade regulations of Æthelstan's and Æthelred's reigns also give us a good deal of information about agrarian products, reminding us how rural a country England was, even at the end of our period.[22]

Charters

Like their legislation, the diplomas issued by Anglo-Saxon kings do not particularly focus on farming. The parties to these grants were concerned with the legal control of territory, not with how it was to be cultivated. However, they

---

[20] Edited by Liebermann, *Gesetze*, i, 88–123.

[21] Kelly, *Early Irish Farming*, Hoff, *Lov og landskab*.

[22] Æthelstan 6 and Æthelred 4, edited by Liebermann, *Gesetze*, i, 173–83 and 232–6 respectively. Derek Keene, who is editing the latter code for the Early English Laws project, would date it slightly later than Æthelred's reign.

were definitely interested in its boundaries, and it is usually in boundary clauses that Anglo-Saxon charters reveal information about crops, for instance, or the organization of land. As well as royal diplomas, the term 'charter' covers a more miscellaneous group of documents, often in Old English, such as gifts to ecclesiastical establishments, which may give more detail about crops and, especially, livestock.[23] Anglo-Saxon wills often list livestock, too, bequeathed either with landed property or separately.[24]

The literature of secular learning

A wide range of texts, all in some sense a product of the schoolroom, tell us something about farming, from the Venerable Bede's great textbook *De temporum ratione* (primarily concerned with calculating the date of Easter but incidentally revealing details of early agriculture recorded in the Old English names for the months)[25] to Abbot Ælfric's *Colloquy*, in which his pupils learn Latin by playing the part of adults in various occupations.[26] Some of the surviving Latin–Old English glossaries also help with the semantics of agricultural vocabulary, which, being so sparsely attested, is often obscure.

Charms and medical texts

Many surviving Anglo-Saxon charms concern farming in one way or another: there is a fair-sized group concerned with the loss or theft of livestock, including swarms of bees, a few dealing with veterinary medicine, and others intended to assure the success of arable operations, or the security of their products.[27] They attest to the implicit trust placed by Anglo-Saxon farmers (and others) in supernatural powers, which played a role analogous to that of 'science' at the present day. It has not been possible to do justice to that important topic in this book, but many of these texts also reveal practical details of Anglo-Saxon farming.

Narrative sources

No Anglo-Saxon narrative source is concerned primarily, or even secondarily, with farming, but those that relate episodes from everyday life often reveal details that would otherwise be lost to us. The Lives of St Cuthbert are

---

[23] Most of these 'miscellaneous' texts are edited in Robertson, *Anglo-Saxon Charters*, and Harmer, *Select English Historical Documents*.

[24] Whitelock (ed.), *Anglo-Saxon Wills*.

[25] Edited by Jones, *Bedae opera didascalica*, ii.

[26] Edited by Garmonsway, *Ælfric's Colloquy*.

[27] Banham, 'The staff of life' and Hollis, 'Old English "cattle theft" charms'.

particularly rich in this respect,[28] and even the Anglo-Saxon Chronicle, mainly concerned with kings and battles, lists famines and cattle-plagues among its events of national interest.

ARCHAEOLOGY

The Anglo-Saxon period, or much of it, is a 'proto-historic' one, in which very limited areas of life were informed by literacy, and thus even the most hard-core historian has to engage with non-written sources of information. As will be apparent already, farming scarcely came into the orbit of literate culture, and much of our evidence in this book is drawn from material sources.

Biological remains

Perhaps the most direct archaeological evidence for Anglo-Saxon farming comes from the remains of animals and plants themselves. Plants are represented by both pollen, the subject of a long tradition of scholarship, and macroscopic remains, mainly seeds, only studied more recently, mainly since the nineteen-sixties. Since that time, plant remains have also been used to study human activity, not just the natural environment. We usually assume that seeds found on settlements arrived there to be eaten, although we can only be sure they formed part of the inhabitants' diet if they have actually passed through the digestive system. We also assume they were grown nearby, unless they are clearly imported exotica. One way or the other, plant remains on settlement sites, or in burials, are part of culture, not nature.

The same applies to archaeological animal bone, which has been found from a larger number of sites. In this case, there are often enough bones to answer a wider range of questions. What ages were the animals when they died? Were there more males or females? Were they processed on the site? Were only the parts to be eaten brought to the settlement? Did the size or shape of the animals change over time, or differ from those at other sites? Comparison between different sites allow us to make generalizations about Anglo-Saxon England as a whole, as well as identifying change through time and sometimes regional variation.

Artefacts

Few of the tools used in Anglo-Saxon farming survive in archaeology, mainly because most of them were made of wood. A few such items were discussed by

---

[28] Edited by Colgrave, *Two Lives of St Cuthbert.*

Carole Morris in her two major compendia.[29] The iron parts of tools might be expected to be found more widely, but iron corrodes rapidly in the soil. Iron was also probably too valuable a material to be wasted and thus most of it would be recycled into further tools, weapons, or fittings. Nevertheless, a few ploughshares and coulters, for instance, do exist from the period, with the recent find of the latter from Lyminge of particular interest. Textile tools also supply information about wool production. Those tools that do survive are all the more valuable for their rarity, and may not survive by accident. They may be particularly significant items, deposited ceremonially for their symbolic value.

Landscape

For Part II of our book, the main source of information is the landscape itself. The way it has been used by previous generations has left a permanent impact on the countryside of the present day, sometimes changing its entire character in ways that are obvious to even the casual observer. But in many cases the marks are much more subtle, apparent only to the experienced eye. Indeed, it is not just the eye, but the whole body, that needs to experience the landscape in order to understand it. There is no substitute for close observation, and also for walking—and sometimes clambering—across a place, if one is to discover how it has been used in the past. It is perhaps unrealistic to expect that modern people can see the landscape as Anglo-Saxons did, but experiencing that landscape directly is our best hope of doing so.

Having said that, there is obviously a good deal of information to be derived from maps, especially old ones that show the landscape as it was before the major changes of the nineteenth to twenty-first centuries. Even modern ones can reveal patterns that are not apparent from the ground, and electronic mapping techniques offer even greater opportunities.

PLACE-NAMES AND LINGUISTIC EVIDENCE

Place-names can tell us a great deal about the character of different environments, land use, crops, and livestock management. 'Minor' names, such as field-names, especially, can help reveal the resources available to communities and individual farms. Perhaps surprisingly, place-names have enabled us to identify and visit farms whose buildings and fields have long disappeared but whose Anglo-Saxon names have survived. The etymology of words in the general language can also be revealing: the word 'barn', for instance, often meaning no more than a big shed at the present day, not even necessarily used to store grain, is etymologically a *bere-ern*, 'barley building', and points to the

---

[29] 'Anglo-Saxon and Medieval Woodworking Crafts', and *Craft, Industry and Everyday Life*.

much greater importance of barley in the early Anglo-Saxon period, in particular, than at the present day.

PRACTICAL FARMING EXPERIENCE

An invaluable source of information is the knowledge of those who work with traditional types of crops and livestock. These are not just traditional farmers—indeed, for crops, such traditional knowledge is all but lost—but also people working with plants and animals in new ways and for new purposes. The managers of native-breed sheep, pigs, and cattle, now used for conservation on marshland, wet meadow, high fells, and mountains, have a lot to tell us about the behaviour and diet of animals on traditional unimproved grazing. Clearly, Anglo-Saxon animals were not exactly like these 'traditional native breeds', but they shared important characteristics with them, including the ability to survive, and even thrive, in environments unsuitable for modern breeds. Similarly, experiments in growing types of cereals long considered 'obsolete' by commercial farmers yield information about how such crops grew, and how they differed from modern ones: the despised 'hulled' cereals, for example are more resistant to pests and diseases than the supposedly superior free-threshing ones. This type of information, while it cannot tell us how Anglo-Saxons farmed, can help us to understand a kind of farming that used resources and techniques no longer considered 'viable'. 'Ask the fellows who cut the hay' was George Ewart Evans' advice to anyone who wanted to learn about the work of the countryside, and people working there today still have a store of practical knowledge that rarely finds its way into books.

VISUAL EVIDENCE

Visual evidence consists, to all intents and purposes, of manuscript illustrations: the great variety of plant and animal motifs in Anglo-Saxon sculpture may be decorative, symbolic, or both, but they are not intended as accurate representations. The illustrations we have used come chiefly from calendar manuscripts and those containing biblical narratives. There are of course many problems with using these illustrations as historical evidence. The Harley Psalter (early eleventh century), which has many little farming scenes, is modelled on the Carolingian Utrecht Psalter, and the calendar pictures probably had a Continental exemplar, too, although it has not been identified.[30] However, the Harley illustrations depart from their exemplar in many details, which

---

[30] Catherine Karkov states that 'that model is now generally believed to have been Anglo-Saxon rather than Carolingian', but it is not clear why: 'Calendar illustrations in Anglo-Saxon England', 159.

may correspond to differences between Anglo-Saxon and Continental *realia*.[31] Thus we may be justified in using them as evidence for English equipment or practices. Even those illustrations which appear to be independent of Continental influence have to be interpreted with care: a biblical scene may show what the artist believed to be conditions in Palestine in Old Testament times, rather than Anglo-Saxon ones. Any manuscript is by definition made by an educated person, not personally involved in farming, and perhaps less familiar with real food production than with texts from far away. Nevertheless, these pictures do represent what some Anglo-Saxons thought farming looked like, and no Anglo-Saxon could be quite as cut off from the realities of rural production as most of us are today.

COMPARATIVE EVIDENCE

Even combining every conceivable source of information from within Anglo-Saxon England, we cannot answer every question we should like to ask about the farming of the period. We are often driven outside our own time-frame and geographical area for insights. Aware of the dangers of assuming that all 'pre-industrial' farming is the same, we have tried to avoid indiscriminate comparisons, but information about shepherding customs in early modern Europe, for instance, can help to explain Anglo-Saxon ways of doing things that otherwise make little sense. Scotland in the eighteenth and nineteenth centuries has proved a particularly rich source of such comparative material, having been well documented by educated travellers, antiquarians, and agriculturalists before it abandoned traditional farming practices. With all the necessary caveats, ethnographic analogy can save the historian from many a pitfall.

OUR APPROACH

As will be clear from the foregoing, we have drawn on a wide range of sources; this approach is characterized by Janken Myrdal, the Swedish historian of medieval agriculture, as 'source pluralism'.[32] This he distinguishes usefully from multi- or interdisciplinarity: although we draw on information from, for instance, archaeology and anthropology, we remain ourselves historians. Our training is historical, and so is our methodology. Like Myrdal himself, we do not have enough of the historian's traditional written source material to rely on it exclusively. Nor, we like to think, would we be so blinkered as to ignore other forms of evidence, even if we worked on a better documented period. Thus we

---

[31] Carver, 'Contemporary artefacts illustrated in late Saxon manuscripts'.
[32] 'Source pluralism and a package of methods: medieval tending of livestock as an example'.

hope to present as rounded a picture of Anglo-Saxon farming as possible, not confining ourselves to the restricted range of questions that can be answered from written evidence. Our aim is to bring to bear every available source of information, and let different kinds of evidence illuminate each other.

Nevertheless, the nature of our evidence means there will be many questions about Anglo-Saxon farming that we cannot answer definitively; inevitably there will be some gaps in our picture. One reason for such gaps is the social specificity of our written sources. All written sources of course come from the top of society; there is no evidence at all for literacy among the Anglo-Saxon peasantry, the people who actually did the farming. The sources for farming deal, most of them quite explicitly, with large complex estates, employing specialist workers and engaging in a market for agricultural commodities, at least to some extent. The operations of small farmers, doing all these jobs themselves, or with a small generalist workforce, may have differed in many ways, possibly quite significant ones. Some of these differences we may be able to work out, but others are likely to remain hidden from us. It is therefore important to remember that whatever evidence in these chapters comes from written sources may apply only to a minority of farming regimes.

But no one studying the early Middle Ages would refrain from asking a question about that period simply because they could not be sure of answering it: frequently, simply raising new questions is a way of creating knowledge. Even a partial or uncertain answer is better than no answer, and in what is in many respects a proto-historic, rather than a truly historic, period, often the best we can expect. Even if no real answer is forthcoming at all, light may at least be shed on related issues, or methodological insights may result. This is particularly true where, as so often in Anglo-Saxon history, we are trying to make the sources tell us about matters they were never intended to deal with. The Venerable Bede, for instance, despite the enormous range of subjects he wrote about, had little interest in agriculture. But farming formed the background to everything he did, like all Anglo-Saxons, and the alert historian can often pick up information let slip in passing by writers whose interests lay elsewhere.

Finally, it should be emphasized that, although our concern is explicitly with the 'nitty-gritty' of farming, this is not a 'how-to' book. Although there may be many advantages to Anglo-Saxon farming methods, compared with those in use at the present day, we are not recommending any particular practices. We cannot take responsibility for the success of anybody's crops, let alone the welfare of their livestock. For one thing, our sources often leave us frustratingly short of detail: should you sow your cereals in the spring, or the autumn? And for another, there can be no absolute certainty about the past, particularly a past as remote as the Anglo-Saxon period. Despite the years we have both put into this project, our information is still, at the end of it all, incomplete and often ambiguous.

PART I

2

Arable farming in Anglo-Saxon England

I: The crops

'and the broad barley crop
and the white wheat crop
and all the fruits of the earth'[1]

Here in Part I of our book, we explore what Anglo-Saxon farmers did, and how they did it, building up a broad but detailed portrait of Anglo-Saxon farming in practice. All Anglo-Saxon farming systems must, in fact, have been integrated ones, in which livestock and arable farming were indispensable to each other: arable crops depended on the manure and labour of animals, which in turn fed on the products of the arable, as well as on land not being cropped for the time being. The balance between the two elements must have varied widely between different geographical areas, some upland districts, for instance, being only marginally suitable for cereal cultivation. Nonetheless, since there was no significant market in agricultural products during most of our period, nearly everyone was dependent on what their land could produce: Part II will explore these issues in relation to particular landscape regions. Large landlords might require some tenants to specialize in producing certain crops or animal products (perhaps giving rise to place-names denoting peas, sheep, and so on), but the tenants almost certainly had to produce whatever else they needed for their own subsistence as well. Such specialization would in any case be impossible on the holdings of smaller landlords, let alone on those of independent farmers. For most people, if you wanted to eat it, you had to produce it. Thus all Anglo-Saxon farming regimes, whether on small farms or large estates, would in modern terms come under the heading of 'mixed farming'.

For purposes of analysis, however, it is more manageable to consider the two parts of the system separately. This chapter and the next will therefore deal with agriculture in the strictest sense, the cultivation of arable fields and

---

[1] *Æcerbot* charm, in Dobbie (ed.), *Minor Poems*, 116–18, at 118.

the production of crops. Livestock will inevitably appear in this discussion, especially the plough-oxen, without whose traction the cultivation of fields on any scale would have been impossible (see Chapter 3), but their lives away from the arable fields will be covered in Chapters 4 and 5.

In this chapter we examine which crops the Anglo-Saxons grew; in the next, we will look at how they grew them. What, then, was the staff of life for the Anglo-Saxons? Which were the staple crops without which life was unthinkable, and what other plants were grown in their fields? Our evidence for these questions consists overwhelmingly of plant remains from archaeological sites, mainly seeds, as other plant parts are rarely preserved.[2] Pollen studies also make a contribution, and our written sources, although not generally very interested in crop husbandry, nevertheless have some insights to offer.[3]

We will look at changes in the crops grown in England during the course of our period and at regional variations, in as far as these can be discerned. Even the question of change is not easy to tackle, however, due in part to the paucity of plant remains from the early part of our period.[4] In fact, fewer arable crops probably were grown in the early Anglo-Saxon period than in either the preceding Roman period or the following centuries, due to the post-Roman 'abatement' explored in Chapter 6. But it is the nature of the archaeological record that is responsible for our lack of archaeobotanical evidence from early Anglo-Saxon England: much of early Anglo-Saxon archaeology consists of burials, rather than settlement sites, while, even on those early settlements that have been excavated, refuse seems to have been dealt with differently than in the later Anglo-Saxon period.

CEREALS

Archaeobotanical remains from sites inhabited by Anglo-Saxons show, not surprisingly, that the greatest tonnage harvested from their fields, and consumed at their meals, consisted of grain crops.[5] This is true even allowing for other possible reasons for the predominance of cereal remains in archaeobotanical samples, such as the processes to which they were subjected, and where: most remains are preserved by charring, and therefore over-represent robust

---

[2] See Moffett, 'Food plants on archaeological sites', especially 347–8, for the nature of the evidence. The archaeological data discussed here (mainly macroscopic remains, but including some pollen records, from eighty-four sites) were originally gathered for Banham, 'Food Plants'. The more recent syntheses of Dark, *The Environment of Britain in the First Millennium*, Fowler, *Farming in the First Millennium*, and Moffett, 'Food plants', have also been consulted, along with other subsequent publications which add to the picture available in 1990.

[3] For a survey of palynological studies, see Dark, *The Environment*.

[4] Moffett, 'Food plants', 348.

[5] Moffett, 'Food plants', 352.

seeds, and those normally processed with or near fire, in both cases privileging cereals.[6] We begin then with grain crops.

Anglo-Saxon grain crops differed from modern ones in two main ways. The first concerns varieties. Although none of the cereal cultivars that exist today (even in seed banks) dates back as far as the Anglo-Saxon period, they do belong to the same species, and the types grown in early medieval England must have resembled the earlier varieties now known to a greater degree than those more recently developed. They will not have been stable cultivars in the modern sense, genetically almost identical and breeding true from seed. Instead they will have contained a good deal of genetic diversity, possessing as a result more resilience to variations in climate, soils, and cultivation than modern specialized varieties. Such genetic distinctiveness as they did have resulted from geographical isolation, both absolute, from the Continent, and relative, within Britain, so it would be more correct to describe them as 'landraces' than varieties in the botanical sense. Thus crops grown in the north of England are likely to have been more resistant to cold than those from the south, but there would be no sharp distinction between them, and those from the Midlands would probably be intermediate. Likewise, crops growing further west must have been better adapted to frequent rainfall, and those from the east to drought. Whether it was possible at the time to identify crops from different parts of England, or whether anyone noticed such differences as did exist, our sources do not reveal, but all crops must have looked a good deal less uniform than the ones we are used to today.[7]

The other difference is that medieval, and later, cereals had long straw, compared with what we see in English fields at the present day. For example, modern oats grown in 2013 measured 77 cm at harvest, compared with 97 cm for an old variety grown alongside them. It is only since straw ceased to be used on a wide scale for craft production and for animal feed and bedding, and since combine harvesters became the normal method of gathering in cereal crops, that modern short-strawed varieties have been developed. Today, old-fashioned long-strawed varieties are only grown for thatching and other specialist uses. No Anglo-Saxon straw survives at the present day, of course, but we can get some information from manuscript illustrations. The calendar pictures of harvesting do not show the standing crop very clearly, and the workers are hunched over, but the ears of the corn come to somewhere around their shoulders, that is to say, the straw is extremely long by modern standards (see Fig. 2.1). So we must envisage Anglo-Saxon cereals as much taller than those we are used to, and because of the genetic diversity of the crops, the appearance of an Anglo-Saxon cereal field will have been a lot more variable than the almost

---

[6] Among a fairly extensive literature on the taphonomy of plant remains, see for example Hillman, 'Ethnographic models from Turkey', and Jones, 'Ethnographic models from Greece'.

[7] See Moffett, 'The archaeology of medieval food plants', 47.

Fig. 2.1. August: harvesting, British Library, Cotton Julius A. vi, fo. 6v.

(© The British Library Board, Cotton Julius A. vi)

table-top evenness of modern ones (see also p. 36 for the possibility that crops were grown in mixtures, making them even less uniform).

With these points in mind, we can now turn to establishing which cereals were growing in Anglo-Saxon fields. Although the relative importance of the various grain crops changed during the Anglo-Saxon period, two were always grown and eaten more than the others: wheat and barley.[8] Oats and rye were never as common.

Wheat

The wheat the Anglo-Saxons grew included a wider range of species and varieties than we are familiar with today. In addition to our bread wheat (*Triticum aestivum* var. *aestivum*),[9] there was also club wheat (*T. aestivum* var. *compactum*), spelt (*T. aestivum* var. *spelta*), which had been the most important wheat in Roman Britain (see Fig. 2.2), and (more rarely) emmer (*T. turgidum* var. *dicoccum*) and (very rarely) einkorn (*T. monococcum*), both of which are generally regarded as prehistoric crops. Wheats, like other cereals, are divided into two groups, free-threshing and hulled. In hulled types, the innermost layer of chaff adheres tightly to the grain, and needs to be removed by heat, or by pounding or soaking, before the wheat can be ground into flour. Free-threshing wheats are ready to be milled once they are threshed, and do not need any intermediate processing, except perhaps drying (discussed in the next chapter).

---

[8] See Banham, 'Food Plants', 16–38.

[9] The classification of wheat species and varieties has changed a good deal in recent years. Here we follow the nomenclature of Feldman et al., 'Wheats'. Zohary and Hopf, *Domestication of Plants*, 18–53, count the sub-types as subspecies rather than varieties. It is rarely possible to distinguish archaeological finds of *T. aestivum* vars *aestivum* and *compactum*, but is likely that some records represent club wheat. There are also numerous records of wheat which could not be identified beyond genus level.

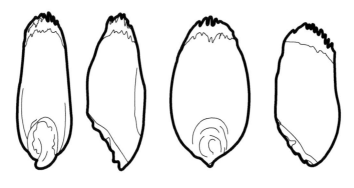

Fig. 2.2. Grains of spelt (left) and bread wheat.

(Drawing Debby Banham)

Of the types mentioned above, the first two, bread and club wheat, are free-threshing, and the last three, spelt, emmer, and einkorn, are hulled. Another type of wheat that may have been grown in England before the Conquest is rivet wheat, a free-threshing type of *T. turgidum*. This has been found on a number of medieval sites in southern England, but only one sample, from Higham Ferrers in Northamptonshire, has so far been firmly dated to the (mid-to late) Anglo-Saxon period.[10]

Of these, bread wheat is the most commonly found; hulled types are not found on more than 20 per cent of sites in any part of the period. It might seem surprising that these 'primitive' cereals were still in use at all, long after the introduction of 'modern' bread wheat, but the evidence, though sparse, cannot be dismissed. There is good evidence for spelt from middle and late Anglo-Saxon sites,[11] and at Bishopstone, in Sussex, a radio-carbon date was obtained from the chaff of spelt to confirm it was not a contaminant from an earlier period.[12] Thus we can see that, at least in some places, hulled wheats continued to be grown, probably throughout our period, and not only in places that might be 'forced' to grow them by unfavourable climate or terrain, or that might be expected to be late in adopting 'up-to-date' practices.

As far as we can tell, the Anglo-Saxons themselves did not distinguish as many kinds of wheat as we do. Apart from the general term *hwǣte*, there is only Old English *spelt* (from Latin *spelta*), which translates Latin *far* ('spelt, meal') four times in the mid-tenth-century Cleopatra Glossaries.[13] At the turn of the millennium, Abbot Ælfric translated *far* as *grǣg hwǣte* ('grey wheat'),[14]

---

[10] Moffett, 'Food plants', 350.
[11] Moffett, 'Food plants', 349.
[12] Ballantyne, 'Charred and mineralised biota', 170.
[13] Stryker, 'The Latin–Old English Glossary', 189, and Wright, *Anglo-Saxon and Old English Vocabularies*, ed. Wülcker, 273, line 20.
[14] Zupitza (ed.), *Ælfrics Grammatik*, 43.

which is an accurate enough description of spelt, but may suggest there was less need for a specific name for it by his time. It may be that *far*, and therefore both OE *spelt* and Ælfric's 'grey wheat', applied not just to spelt, but to other hulled wheats, which otherwise have no names in Old English; by the later Anglo-Saxon period, the 'prehistoric' hulled wheats, rarely grown, may not have needed individual names. The food rent at Hurstbourne Priors, Hampshire (c. AD 900), includes *hlafhwete*, literally 'bread wheat',[15] but probably meaning wheat fit for bread-making generally, rather than a particular type. The distinction may again be between hulled and free-threshing varieties, important in terms of the amount of labour needed to turn them into bread (see Fig. 2.3). Even if they had no vocabulary to distinguish them, however, Anglo-Saxon farmers presumably knew which kind of hulled wheat they were growing: both the grains and the plants are clearly distinguishable to the experienced eye.

Place-names denoting wheat are less common (twenty-three in what is now England up to the time of Domesday Book: see Table 2.1) than those for barley (see pp. 27–8). This may be interpreted in either of two opposing ways: most of these names may date from when barley was still dominant, or alternatively they were coined later, but wheat was by then so common as to be hardly worth mentioning. Nearly all are recorded from late in the period, but may have been in use earlier. We do not see *hwæte* used as a general term for cereals in the way that *bere* was. 'Wheat' names may indicate places where this crop was grown, or first grown, in mainly barley-growing areas, or where it was stored on a large estate or for commercial purposes. The furthest north are in West Yorkshire, and the furthest west in Somerset, which might represent the cultivation of bread wheat expanding from the more climatically favoured south and east.[16] However, 'barley' names cover roughly the same area.

The importance of wheat in the later period is shown by its appearance in the Anglo-Saxon Chronicle as an index of the cost of living. In 1039, the price of a sester of wheat reached *lv penega* (55 pence—unfortunately we have no information on its cost before then) and in 1043 'there was very great hunger across England, and corn as expensive as no one remembered before, and the sester of wheat went up to 60 pence, and even higher'.[17] Here wheat is clearly the corn that matters, certainly at Peterborough, where these entries were probably added, and no doubt among the privileged generally. It is likely that the peasantry had not been able to move to the more fashionable wheat as

---

[15] Robertson (ed. and tr.), *Anglo-Saxon Charters*, 206.

[16] See Banham, 'Food Plants', 20–1.

[17] Irvine, *MS E*, 77, 78. The size of the OE *sester* is not known for certain, but it is thought to have been considerably larger than the Roman *sextarius* (about a pint) from which it derives its name—perhaps roughly equivalent to a bushel. These pence are of course 'old' ones, at 240 to the pound.

Table 2.1. 'Wheat' place-names.

Modern name	County	Earliest form	First recorded
Waddon Hill	Worcestershire	Hwætedun	757
Waddington	Surrey	Whatindone	871 × 889
Wheathampstead	Hertfordshire	Hwathamstede	1060
Great and Little Wheatley	Essex	Wateleia	DB
North and South Wheatley	Nottinghamshire	Wateleia	DB
Whaddon (Rowley Hundred)	Buckinghamshire	Wadone	DB
Whaddon (Slapton)	Buckinghamshire	Wadone	DB
Whaddon	Cambridgeshire	Watone	DB
Whaddon	Wiltshire	Watedene	DB
Whatton	Nottinghamshire	Watone	DB
Whatcombe Manor	Oxfordshire	Watecvmbe	DB
Wheatley (Lower Straforth)	Yorkshire (WR)	Watelage	DB
Wheatcroft (Thorner)	Yorkshire (WR)	Watecroft	DB
Whaddon	Gloucestershire	Wadune	DB
Whatcombe	Berkshire	Watecumbe	DB
Whatcote	Warwickshire	Quatercote	DB
Whatborough	Leicestershire	Wetberge	DB
Wheatley	Lancashire	Watelei	DB
Whatfield	Suffolk	Watefelda	DB
Whatley (nr Frome)	Somerset	Watelei	DB
Whatley (Winsham)	Somerset	Watelege	DB
Wheatacre	Norfolk	Hwateaker	DB
Wheathill	Somerset	Watehelle	DB

Place-name evidence is drawn from the county volumes of the English Place-Name Society. Details of sources, etc. can be found in Banham, 'Food Plants', 16–38.

completely as the aristocracy or ecclesiastics; this was certainly the case later in the Middle Ages.[18] Even those who grew quite a lot of wheat might be paying all or most of it to their landlords or the Church, or (in the later period, when there was a developing local market in agricultural crops) they might do better to sell their wheat and live on less profitable crops.

[18] Stone, 'The consumption of field crops', 17–18.

Barley

When it comes to barley, there are two subspecies, six-row and two-row (*Hordeum vulgare*, subspp. *vulgare* and *distichum* respectively).[19] In two-row barley, only one of the three flowers at each node is fertile, and thus only two rows of symmetrical grains develop, and the ears look flat; in the six-row type, not only the two central rows appear, but four at the sides as well, making the ear look 'square'. Archaeobotanists can distinguish six-row barley by its diagnostic asymmetrical grains. The Anglo-Saxons grew both, but the six-row type was more common, and unambiguous examples of two-row barley belong mainly to the late Anglo-Saxon period.[20] Both hulled and free-threshing varieties exist, but all barley remains from Anglo-Saxon contexts are of hulled types, like those currently grown in Britain (see Fig. 2.3).[21] In prehistory, naked varieties were only common when barley was the dominant crop, and in the modern world they only exist where it is a major human food.[22] We might therefore expect free-threshing barley in the early Anglo-Saxon period, when the abundance of barley suggests it was eaten in large quantities, but it is not found. The

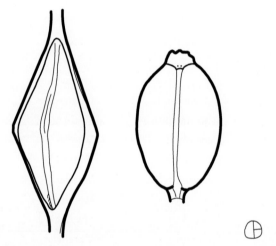

Fig. 2.3. Grains of hulled and naked barley.

(Drawing Debby Banham)

---

[19] This is the terminology of Zohary and Hopf, *Domestication of Plants*, 54–64; Harlan, 'Barley', does not give the two forms separate names.

[20] Moffett, 'Food plants', 351.

[21] Zohary and Hopf, *Domestication of Plants*, 58, say that two-rowed types are mostly hulled, while six-rowed barley includes both hulled and free-threshing forms.

[22] Harlan, *The Living Fields*, 92, table 4.1, and 103.

traditional 'bigg' or 'bere' still grown in northern Britain is also hulled. The relationship between naked barley and a major dietary role is evidently not straightforward in the British Isles.

The importance of barley in the early Anglo-Saxon period is confirmed by a law of Ine of Wessex (688–726): 'Mon sceal simle to beregafole agifan æt anum wyrhtan vi wæga' ('For barley-payment 6 weys must always be given for one worker').[23] What kind of payment is in question here, or who paid whom, is unclear, partly because *beregafol* did not survive into later Anglo-Saxon legislation, at least not under this name. It seems to be a relic of the time when barley was the major cereal crop in England; even by Ine's time it could have been paid in other corn, only the name reflecting the earlier situation. This scenario is supported by other linguistic evidence, where *bere*, 'barley' seems often to mean corn generally: a barn, for instance, is a *bere-ern*, a 'barley-building',[24] and the place name Barton, normally interpreted as meaning the place where the lord's cereal crops were either grown or gathered as food rents and stored, is *bere-tun*, literally 'barley-farm' or '-settlement'.[25] By 1086, it was opaque enough for Mulberton in Norfolk to be called *Molkebertuna*, literally 'milk barley-farm'. These elisions of meaning can only have arisen in a context where, as close to universally as made no practical difference, corn was in fact barley.[26] This makes *bere* place-names hard to interpret: if early, they should refer to corn in general, but, if late, they could denote places where barley retained its importance. None is recorded before the late Anglo-Saxon period, but it is impossible to tell how much earlier they may have originated (see Table 2.2).

In addition to these, Barton names are found in Bedfordshire, Berkshire, Buckinghamshire, Cambridgeshire, Derbyshire, Gloucestershire (2), Hampshire (2), Kent, Lancashire (2), Leicestershire, Lincolnshire, Norfolk (3), Northamptonshire (2), Nottinghamshire, Oxfordshire, Somerset, Staffordshire, Suffolk (2), Warwickshire, and Yorkshire NR (3); in other words, over most of England. Of these, the majority are first recorded in Domesday Book, but five appear before the Conquest, four in the tenth century (in Kent, Staffordshire, Suffolk, and Hampshire), and one in the eleventh (Norfolk). Berwick and similar names are less common, occurring in Kent, Lancashire, Norfolk, Oxfordshire, Shropshire (2), Sussex, and Yorkshire NR and WR. Only the first appears before Domesday, in 1035. Names in Barn- are found in Gloucestershire, Norfolk, Surrey, Sussex,

---

[23] Ine 59.1, in Liebermann, *Gesetze* (ed.), i, 116. According to Attenborough (ed. and tr.), *Laws*, 191–2, the wey of barley was in 1922 equivalent to 6 quarters.

[24] See *OED, s.v.* 'barn'.

[25] Smith, *Place-Name Elements*, i, 31.

[26] See Banham, 'Food Plants', 26–9.

Table 2.2. 'Barley' place-names, excluding Barton, Berwick, and names in Barn-.

Modern name	County	Earliest form	First record
Great Barford	Bedfordshire	Bereforde	DB
Barwythe	Bedfordshire	Bereworde	DB
Barcombe	Sussex	Bercham	DB
Barford Lodge	Northamptonshire	Bereford	DB
Barford St Martin	Wiltshire	Bereford	DB
Barford Park	Wiltshire	Bereford	DB
Barford St John/ St Michael	Cambridgeshire	Bereford	DB
Barford (Kineton Hundred)	Warwickshire	Bereforde	DB
Barford	Norfolk	Bereforda	DB
Barney	Norfolk	Berlei	DB

Warwickshire, and Yorkshire ER, NR, and WR. Only one (Yorkshire WR) is pre-Domesday, appearing *c.* 1030.

Hulled and free-threshing cereals

Within the Anglo-Saxon period, we can see a transition from hulled to free-threshing corn: free-threshing bread wheat emerged by the end of the period as the most popular of all the cereals, found on 73 per cent of sites in the tenth and eleventh centuries (up from 38 per cent in the fifth to seventh centuries, and 50 per cent in the eighth and ninth).[27] This may have been partly because the hulled wheats were grown less (20, 15, and 18 per cent in each successive phase), but this pattern is not very clear. However, barley also declined (88 per cent of sites in the fifth to seventh centuries, 64 per cent in the eighth and ninth, and 42 per cent in the tenth and eleventh). In the early part of the period, barley outnumbered all forms of wheat combined (which were found on 63 per cent of sites in the fifth to seventh centuries). It is likely therefore that wheat replaced barley as the main bread corn (and that bread replaced other types of cereal cookery to an increasing extent).[28] In late Anglo-Saxon England, the period that produced our main written sources for agriculture, more bread wheat was being grown in Anglo-Saxon fields than any other cereal. We might expect that

[27] There are of course many reasons why a particular taxon might appear on one site and not an-other, but, for cereals, the overall number of sites is sufficiently large (over eighty in Banham, 'Food Plants') that generalizations can be regarded as reasonably reliable.

[28] For this change, and the preferences that lay behind it, see Banham, *Food and Drink*, 14–20, and 'In the sweat of thy brow'.

everyone would still grow barley, for brewing and possibly animal feed,[29] as in later medieval, and indeed modern, agriculture. Barley was no doubt still being eaten by some people, too, in default of wheat. But in defiance of our expectations, barley is found on fewer sites as the Anglo-Saxon period draws to an end.

Over a longer time-scale, there was clearly a change in cereal preferences. In recent times, free-threshing cereals have been seen as self-evidently superior to hulled, presumably because they are easier to process into flour, and thus bread, as well as the greater palatability of bread from *T. aestivum*—hence the term 'bread wheat'. In present-day Britain, hulled cereals are grown almost exclusively for brewing and animal fodder; bread is only made from hulled cereals in niche traditions, such as Yorkshire oatcakes and Orkney barley bannocks.[30] In prehistoric and Roman Britain, by contrast, hulled cereals were predominant, although bread wheat was introduced in the Roman period.[31] Thus the changes in the Anglo-Saxon period represent a stage, and a crucial one, in a much longer-term trend.

Hulled cereals do have advantages over naked ones: in the field they are less vulnerable both to fungal disease and to predation by birds and other pests, and, being more resistant to damp, they store better, especially under less than ideal conditions.[32] In the damp British climate, resistance to moisture and therefore to fungi could have been crucial. The awns, stiff bristles projecting from the grains of 'bearded' varieties, also deter birds.[33] For animal feed, they can be given in the straw, and no threshing is required. For brewing, since the grain is not normally eaten, chaff adhering to it is not a problem. Hulled barley is preferred for malting because the germ survives harvesting much better than in naked varieties, and germination, the first stage in the malting process, is therefore much higher.[34] And even in cookery, if the grain is to be used whole, it may just need soaking first to remove the husks.[35] There are thus many reasons why hulled cereals may have been preferred to free-threshing ones in the early Anglo-Saxon period, but these reasons appear to have become less pressing, compared with the baking and eating qualities of bread wheat, as the period progressed.

[29] For the cultural importance of beer in Anglo-Saxon England, see Magennis, *Anglo-Saxon Appetites*, more or less *passim*.

[30] Mason and Brown, *Traditional Foods*, 270–1 and 228–9.

[31] Cool, *Eating and Drinking*, 69.

[32] Moffett, 'The archaeology of medieval food plants', 50.

[33] Moffett, 'Food plants', 351.

[34] Sally Francis and John Letts, pers. comm. Lisa Moffett suggests that hulled wheats were mainly grown for brewing, and bread wheat for baking: 'Food plants', 349.

[35] For other types of cookery, and Anglo-Saxon food uses of cereals generally, see Banham, *Food and Drink*, 13–25.

'Minor' cereals

Wheat and barley, then, were always the most important Anglo-Saxon cereal crops, but they were not the only ones. Rye (*Secale cereale*) and oats (*Avena sativa*) both appear in the Anglo-Saxon archaeobotanical record. It used to be believed that both of these originated as weeds of other cereals, before being domesticated in their own right,[36] and therefore that archeobotanical specimens might not represent cultivated plants. Now it appears that rye could have been the earliest cereal to be cultivated, but it still probably reached northern Europe as a weed, to be domesticated again north of the Alps.[37] Nonetheless, it is unlikely that rye was a weed in Anglo-Saxon fields; despite the fact that it is well adapted to growing in the British Isles, being winter hardy and able to grow on droughty soils,[38] it has not been found as a weed in Britain in recent times.[39] In fact, rye is mentioned as a crop in a very early written source, the laws of Wihtred of Kent (690–725), where it appears in the name of a month (possibly August), *Rugern*, 'rye harvest'.[40] It also appears in one food rent, from Westbury-on-Trym, near Bristol, dated between 793 and 796.[41] Its straw is mentioned in a medical recipe of the tenth century, and may have been valued for thatching and fuel.[42] Place-names mentioning rye are also reasonably widespread, suggesting that this was a crop of some importance when they were coined (see Table 2.3). These references, widely scattered as they are, show that rye was a familiar commodity at several dates and places in Anglo-Saxon England. In continental Europe, especially in the north, rye was the free-threshing cereal that replaced the hulled types during the early Middle Ages,[43] but in England that role was taken by bread wheat, as we have seen.

Oats probably came into their own as a crop as agriculture moved into northern Europe, and were certainly domesticated long before the Anglo-Saxon period.[44] However, they have wild relatives (*Avena fatua* and *sterilis*) which remain a serious arable weed in England, even in these days of chemical weed killers.[45] The grains of these wild oats are hard to distinguish in archaeobotany

---

[36] See Thomas, 'Oats', 134, and Evans, 'Rye', 167–8.

[37] Murphy, *People, Plants and Genes*, 48.

[38] Zohary and Hopf, *Domestication of Plants*, 64–5.

[39] Absent, in contrast to oats, from 'A list of common weeds of arable land', in Biffen, *Elements*, 257–60, drawn up before chemical herbicides became common.

[40] Liebermann (ed.), *Gesetze*, i, 12.

[41] S 146; this charter is tainted by the distrust generally attached to Heming's Cartulary, in which it appears, and may not be as early as the reign of Offa. It is not clear, however, whether these suspicions affect the food rent. For the text see Birch (ed.), *Cartularium Saxonicum*, ii, 380 (no. 273).

[42] *Bald's Leechbook*, II.72, para. 2, in Cockayne (ed.), *Leechdoms*, ii, 148, and Moffett, 'Food plants', 351.

[43] See Hamerow, *Settlements*, 135–6, for a useful summary and references.

[44] Murphy, *People, Plants and Genes*, 88.

[45] Clapham, Tutin and Moore, *Flora*, 636; Wilson and King, *Arable Plants*, Appendix 6, 'Some commonly occurring arable plants'.

Table 2.3. 'Rye' place-names.

Modern name	County	Earliest form	First recorded
Ryedown (Fyfield)	Berkshire	Rigedune	968
Roydon Drift	Suffolk	Rigendun	1000 × 1002
Roydon (nr Diss)	Norfolk	Rygedune	1035 × 1040
Ryhall	Rutland	Righale	1042 × 1055
Gt and Little Ryburgh	Norfolk	Reieburh	DB
Raydon	Suffolk	Reindune	DB
Reydon	Suffolk	Rienduna	DB
Riby	Lincolnshire	Ribi	DB
Roughton	Lincolnshire	Rocstune	DB
Roughton	Norfolk	Rustuna	DB
Roydon	Essex	Ruindune	DB
Roydon (nr Lynn)	Norfolk	Reiduna	DB
Ruyton	Shropshire	Ruitone	DB
Ryarsh	Kent	Riesce	DB
Rycote (Ewelme Hundred)	Oxfordshire	Reicote	DB
Ryhill	Yorkshire (WR)	Rihelle	DB
Ryton	Shropshire	Ruitone	DB
Ryton on Dunsmore	Warwickshire	Rietone	DB

from the cultivated forms (*A. sativa* and *strigosa*), unless the whole florets are preserved.[46] These can be told apart, and thus it can be shown that oats were an Anglo-Saxon crop, even if wild oats were also present as weeds. Oats are sometimes found in sufficient quantity to confirm their status as a crop, too,[47] and in the eleventh century the *kotsetla* (?cottage-dweller) in the *Rectitudines* was required to harvest them.[48] The paucity of oat place-names in England suggests either that they were not common, however, or that they were not generally thought worth commenting on (see p. 32). Oats did become more common as the period progressed (50, 45, and 79 per cent of sites, although the numbers at each site are never very large), and they are more common in Anglo-Saxon archaeology than rye (though considerably less so than wheat or barley). Both bristle and common oats (*A. strigosa* and *sativa* respectively) have been found, the latter by far the more common,[49] but

---

[46] As for instance as West Cotton, Raunds, Northamptonshire: Campbell, 'The preliminary archaeobotanical results', 69.

[47] Moffett, 'Food plants', 352.

[48] *Rectitudines* (Latin version only) 3, in Liebermann (ed.), *Gesetze*, i, 445.

[49] Moffett, 'Food plants', 351.

there is no evidence that Anglo-Saxons differentiated between them. Oats are a valuable crop where the climate is too wet for wheat,[50] and eventually they replaced barley as the main bread corn in many upland areas.[51]

There are no certain 'oat' place-names recorded before the Conquest: the lost *At leahe geat* (Worcestershire), which might have given a modern Oatley Gate, is recorded in the late tenth century, and there are two names which might contain Old Norse *hafri*, 'oats' (or alternatively Old English *hæfer*, a billy goat): Haversham in Buckinghamshire, *Hæfæresham* in 966 × 975, and Haverhill (Suffolk), called *Hauerhella* in Domesday Book. Whatever the implications of the relative abundance of 'barley' and 'wheat' names, the scarcity of 'oat' place-names must mean that the crop itself was not something Anglo-Saxons paid much attention to in the landscape.

Regional variation

The evidence offers some hints of regional variation in Anglo-Saxon cereal cultivation. This is, however, a hard question to deal with adequately, partly due to the general paucity of evidence, and partly to the distribution of archaeological work in England. It is true, for instance, that the majority of Anglo-Saxon records of rye come from sites in the east or Midlands of England,[52] but this is also true of wheat. The fact is that the overwhelming majority of archaeobotanical work has been done in the south and east of the country (in 1990, with the exception of York, nearly all the sites discussed in my dissertation were south and east of a line from the Bristol Channel to the Wash). This picture is beginning to change, however. Work by Jacqueline Huntley, for instance, shows that Northumbrians shared the southerners' preference for wheat,[53] despite the fact that it must have been more difficult for them to cultivate than in the south, and this is confirmed by a review of plant remains from northern England conducted by Huntley and Allan Hall.[54] Wheat is on the edge of its range in England, requiring warm and dry summers by local standards to produce a good crop.[55] A well-known story about St Cuthbert suggests that it was recognized as being difficult to grow in Northumbria in the seventh century: according to this episode, the saint could not produce a crop of wheat in his first year on Farne Island, but, with angelic assistance, he was able to harvest barley, even though he sowed it well past the time when it could be expected

---

[50] Francis, *British Field Crops*, 14.
[51] See Mason and Brown, *Traditional Foods of Britain*, 228–9, 264, 332.
[52] See Banham, 'Food Plants', 34.
[53] Huntley, 'Saxon–Norse economy'. She mentions a suggestion that wheat remains from Orkney and Caithness, even when accompanied by relevant weeds, represent crops imported from further south in the British Isles, but does not extend this to sites in northern England and southern Scotland.
[54] Hall and Huntley, *A Review*, 94–124.
[55] Biffen, *Elements*, 192.

to be successful.[56] Even without supernatural intervention, the use of barley as an insurance crop against the failure of wheat seems very plausible in northern England.

Changes

The story of Anglo-Saxon cereal growing represents an intersection of different trends, the pan-European replacement of hulled by free-threshing cereals, and the spread of Mediterranean practices under the influence of the Church.[57] In the early period we see a continuation of earlier practices: Roman spelt is still grown, together with some bread wheat, introduced to Roman Britain in emulation of Mediterranean tastes.[58] The 'prehistoric' hulled cereals, emmer and even einkorn, seem to have had a revival, too, after falling from favour under Roman 'civilization'. But barley was the most common of all. This is the period of 'abatement', when fewer arable crops were grown overall. In the middle of the Anglo-Saxon period, bread wheat, eventually the favourite cereal right across England, began its resurgence. Hulled wheats did not entirely die out, although it may only have been spelt that continued into the late Anglo-Saxon period. We also see the first signs of two previously unknown crops, rye and oats, which were to become much more important later in the Middle Ages. Of these, rye may have been introduced at a very early stage, perhaps by immigrant Anglo-Saxons coming from continental Germany,[59] although its heyday, even there, was later, and it never became a major crop in Anglo-Saxon England. Oats, although more common, were also a minor crop before the Conquest, even in parts of England where they were later the usual bread corn. Barley remained an important crop throughout the period, losing its pre-eminence to bread wheat, but always more common than the other cereals. By the Conquest, we see a cereal-growing regime recognizably like that of the later Middle Ages.

PULSE CROPS

After cereals, the next most common food crops in Anglo-Saxon archaeobotanical studies are the legumes, although they are less abundant than any of the cereals. Of the pulses, peas and beans are the most common, but lentils (*Lens culinaris*) have also been found on a few mid- to late Anglo-Saxon sites.[60]

---

[56] Colgrave (ed.), *Two Lives*, 220.
[57] See Banham, 'In the sweat of thy brow' for the links between the Church and changing cereal tastes.
[58] Cool, *Eating and Drinking*, 69.
[59] Moffett, 'Food plants', 351.
[60] Moffett, 'Food plants', 352.

Interestingly, the medieval English finds of lentil all belong to the ninth to thirteenth centuries, the 'Medieval Warm Period', and they come from rural sites in the south, the east, and the Midlands.[61] Thus it is possible that they represent a period when lentils were being grown in these favoured areas, rather than being imports, and we can count them as an Anglo-Saxon crop, if hardly a major one. The most common Anglo-Saxon legumes were probably the beans, although they are in fact less frequent in the archaeobotanical record than peas, possibly because, being such large seeds, they rarely survive whole, making them more difficult to identify.[62] The type of bean grown is now known as the field, horse, or Celtic bean (*Vicia faba* var. *minor*). It belongs to the same species as the familiar broad bean (*V. faba* var. *major*), but has not undergone the same breeding process to make the seeds bigger and more palatable for eating fresh.[63] As one of the common names implies, its main use today is as animal fodder, but in the Middle Ages, before broad beans were developed, field beans were food for people, too. Despite their rarity in archaeology, they were probably grown on a field scale in Anglo-Saxon England: sowing beans was one of the *Gerefa*'s spring tasks,[64] and money is listed for 'bean seed' in the Ely Farming Memoranda.[65]

Peas may have been a more specialized crop: the evidence of the medical texts suggests that they were thought of as rather 'delicate' food, suitable for invalids (whereas beans only appear in recipes for poultices).[66] Peas are also less robust plants than beans,[67] and there is some suggestion from place-names that slopes (presumably south-facing) were chosen for growing them: Peas Hill and the like appear quite commonly.[68] Their cultivation as a field crop may have been confined to more favourable soils or aspects, while they would have been easier to grow in the more protected environment of a garden. It has been suggested that peas were grown 'just outside the dwellings' to avoid unauthorized gleaning;[69] peas are certainly more palatable raw than field beans or cereals, so they may have been more vulnerable to such depredations.[70] By the later Middle Ages, they were a more common field crop than

---

[61] See Stevens, 'Lentils as climatic indicators'.

[62] Ballantyne, 'The charred and mineralised biota', 170. There are only seven records in Banham, 'Food Plants', 167, as against sixteen for peas.

[63] These are the terms used by Zohary and Hopf, *Domestication of Plants*, 106–10; those used by Bond, 'Faba bean', are less clear for our purposes. The 'varieties' familiar to growers are cultivars of these two varieties.

[64] Liebermann (ed.), *Gesetze*, i, 453.

[65] Robertson (ed. and tr.), *Anglo-Saxon Charters*, 252–7 (Appendix 2, no. 9).

[66] Banham, 'Food Plants', 176–8.

[67] Langer and Hill, *Agricultural Plants*, 269, for the climatic requirements of peas.

[68] Banham, 'Food Plants', 169. The Cambridge example, which is a market site (and flat at the present day), should not be taken as typical.

[69] Spencer, *British Food*, 25.

[70] In the 1960s, such predation was often by children, and this may also have been true in the Middle Ages.

beans,[71] but this may be the outcome of a development that was only beginning in our period. As for the type of pea grown, it must have been what we would now call the field pea (*Pisum sativum* var. *arvense*), with bicoloured flowers and seeds that dry to grey or brown rather than green, since the 'garden' pea (var. *sativum*)[72] was not developed until the sixteenth century.[73]

A further leguminous crop occasionally identified in (usually late) Anglo-Saxon archaeobotanical assemblages is vetch, *Vicia sativa*.[74] This could represent a weed contaminating other crops, but where it is found in substantial quantities, it is more likely it was being cultivated, probably as fodder for livestock rather than human food.[75]

Our evidence does not seem to support Lynn White's proposal that legumes, especially beans, played a large part in social and technological change in western Europe around the tenth century by improving the nutritional status of the population.[76] He believed that beans were a rare crop before a three-course rotation (in which one third of the land lies fallow, one third is sown in spring, and the rest in autumn) replaced the two-course version of open-field farming (in which cereals alternated with fallow) in the tenth century, and that legumes were not grown in the earlier system.[77] However, it is still uncertain when open-field farming became common in England (see Chapters 3 and 12), and it never became universal. The idea that the three-course variant was a later development from two courses has also been rejected.[78] Nor can we pinpoint a time when legumes became significantly more common as a crop than they had been before. As has been mentioned (p. 34), the archaeological evidence for beans is exiguous: none of it comes from the earliest part of our period, but overall numbers are so small that this is likely to be an accident of survival.[79] There is more evidence for peas, but still too little and too loosely dated to show a clear increase during the period. Peas certainly became more common later in the Middle Ages, but mainly replaced beans, rather than non-legume crops. It certainly cannot be shown, on the basis of evidence from England, that pulses became a major crop in or after the tenth century where they had not been before, nor that legume consumption increased. There is no evidence that

[71] Grown on 42 per cent of demesnes versus 17 in 1250–1349: Campbell, *English Seigniorial Agriculture*, 228 n. 151.

[72] Nomenclature from Zohary and Hopf, *Domestication of Plants*, 95.

[73] See Davies, 'Peas', 295.

[74] See Campbell, 'The preliminary archaeobotanical results', 75, for discussion of finds at West Cotton as well as other sites.

[75] Moffett, 'Food plants', 352.

[76] 'In the full sense of the vernacular, the middle ages, from the tenth century onward, were full of beans': White, *Medieval Technology*, 76.

[77] White, *Medieval Technology*, 71. In fact, the difference White saw in his sources may be between Mediterranean and northern European farming, reflecting the different climatic conditions in the two regions.

[78] Fox, 'The alleged transformation'.

[79] Banham, 'Food Plants', 167.

nutritional status improved significantly, and it would be unsafe to relate any other important changes to such developments. If there was an increase in legume cultivation, their importance was probably as an insurance crop that might survive when cereal crops failed for any reason.

MIXED AND MINOR CROPS

It is extremely likely that crops were grown in mixtures in Anglo-Saxon England, but it is hard to demonstrate this from pre-Conquest evidence. In the later Middle Ages, when local records were kept there is abundant evidence that mixtures of cereals, and of cereals and pulses, were grown in England. These included maslin (wheat and rye), dredge (spring barley and oats), and bullmong (oats, peas, and beans), to name only the most common.[80] None of these names go back to Old English,[81] and we have no local records from our period to reveal such practices on the ground. However, the only bread so far found in archaeology that might be Anglo-Saxon (in Ipswich, dating from the eleventh century) was made from mixed cereals, wheat and rye, which would be maslin in later terminology.[82] In archaeobotany, remains of barley and oats are quite often found together, occasionally where cereal remains are not more generally mixed, as at late Anglo-Saxon West Cotton.[83] One of the ovens at tenth-century Stafford also contained mixed cereals.[84] This does not of course mean that the cereals were necessarily grown together; they could have been mixed at any point after harvesting. Nevertheless, such finds do raise the possibility of mixed crops in Anglo-Saxon farming, and the reasons for growing them in the later Middle Ages (chiefly the need to salvage some kind of crop if the season turned out to be too wet, too cold, or even too hot and dry, for the preferred crop, or if it was hit by pests or disease) would presumably have had equal force before the Conquest.

Fodder crops

It is unlikely that any food crops apart from cereals and pulses were grown in the arable fields. The cultivation of brassicas and roots on a field scale for animal fodder is a later development, belonging to the 'agricultural revolution' of the eighteenth century,[85] and for human food, even more recent.[86] Later

---

[80] See the useful table in Stone, 'The Consumption of Field Crops', 13.

[81] The *OED*'s earliest citations are 1303, fifteenth century, and 1313, respectively, although such rural terms are likely to have flourished in the oral language for some time before being recorded in documents.

[82] Keith Wade and Peter Murphy (pers. comm.), and Banham, *Food and Drink*, 22–3 and Plate 5.

[83] Campbell, 'The preliminary archaeobotanical results', 69.

[84] Carver, *Birth of a Borough*, 70.

[85] Trow-Smith, *British Livestock Husbandry, 1700–1900*, 70–6.

[86] Farmers specializing in vegetables are still looked down on as 'market gardeners' by the 'cereal boys'.

medieval evidence suggests that cereals and legumes (by then including peas) were the only food crops normally grown as part of the open-field regime.[87] Some of the crops mentioned above may have been used for animal fodder, presumably mainly those types less favoured as food for humans; the use of barley bread in a remedy for a sick horse may be significant here.[88] Vetches, where they were grown, were presumably destined for fodder, since they are poisonous to humans, and this may also have been the use of lentils, which would be unreliable as a seed crop in England, even with the climate improving.[89] Those parts of any crop not eaten by humans, the chaff and straw, would also be valuable as food for beasts. The food rent in Ine's laws includes fodder (twenty pounds from ten hides), presumably for riding horses and pack-animals,[90] in addition to human food and drink. It might be only at this highest level of society that crops would be grown specifically as animal food (or crops fed to them that might be eaten by humans). A rare mention of fodder that explicitly concerns the peasantry is also found in Ine's code: 'Se ceorl se ðe hæfð oðres geoht ahyrod, gif he hæbbe ealle on foðre to agifanne, gesceawige mon, agife ealle; gif he næbbe, agife healf on fodre healfe on oþrum ceape' ('The peasant who has hired someone else's yoke [of oxen], if he has [enough] to pay all [the fee] in fodder, it should be ensured he pays it all; if he hasn't, let him pay half in fodder, half in other goods').[91] Here it is assumed that the hirer will have at least some fodder available, although this might simply mean grazing the oxen on his own pasture while he is using them. Either way, as in the food rent, it could consist of hay from meadows, or even plants collected from the wild, rather than arable crops (see Chapter 5, under 'Housing, feeding, and care' (pp. 124–6), for more on fodder; also Chapters 7 and, for tree fodder, 8). Even if no fodder crops were grown in the arable fields, this would not mean that arable land did not feed livestock. Animals must have grazed on the aftermath of crops grown for human consumption; although there is no explicit Anglo-Saxon evidence for this, it is inconceivable that the stubble would have been allowed to go to waste. They would also graze on fallows where these were part of the farming regime (see the next chapter), and on uncultivated headlands.

Fibre crops

The only non-food crops likely to have been needed in large enough quantities to be grown in fields are those used for textiles and cordage. Although the

---

[87] Orwin and Orwin, *The Open Fields*, 53–4.

[88] *Lacnunga* 165 (British Library, Harley 585, late tenth to mid-eleventh century), in Pettit (ed.), *The Lacnunga*, i, 114.

[89] Moffett, 'Food plants', 352.

[90] Ine 70.1, in Liebermann (ed.), *Gesetze*, i, 118–20.

[91] Ine 60, in Liebermann (ed.), *Gesetze*, i, 116.

majority of Anglo-Saxon textiles were woollen (see Chapter 5), flax (*Linum usitatissimum*) was spun and woven into linen, and hemp (*Cannabis sativa*) into canvas.[92] They were also the only plant materials suitable for making ropes and nets before jute was imported (though these could also be made from hide or gut). According to Penelope Walton Rogers, the two fibres were used more or less indiscriminately for textiles and cordage throughout the Middle Ages, presumably according to what was available locally. She records items made from hemp from the eastern counties only, whereas flax is found more widely.[93] At Flixborough in North Lincolnshire, the abundant evidence for textile manu-facture was attributed to woollen and linen production, although hemp seed, as well as flax, was found on the site.[94] There is no reason to believe that flax was grown for oil in Anglo-Saxon England: other than imported olive oil, needed for the liturgy and medicine, but much too expensive for anything else, vegetable oil seems to have been unknown.[95] Animal fats, especially lard, sup-plied the needs it fills today (see Chapter 5). There is some evidence that the seeds (linseed) were eaten,[96] and this may have been true of hemp seed, too, but textiles and cordage were certainly the main use of both plants. This would mean that flax could be harvested early in the year before the fibres became coarse, rather than waiting for the seed to ripen in high summer (though some seed would of course have to be saved for re-sowing). It would also mean that the type of flax grown would probably be tall, selected for its long fibres, rather than the shorter varieties developed for seed production.[97] Neither fibre crop, however, is likely to have been grown on anything like the scale of the cereals. Other 'economic plants' (dye-plants, medicinal herbs, fruit, and vegetables) would only have been needed in much smaller quantities, and some of them are quite tender plants, requiring a good deal of attention from those growing them, so that garden cultivation is much more likely than field production.[98]

CONCLUSIONS

We have already seen that the Anglo-Saxon period was one when the range of cereal crops grown in England was changing, as free-threshing cereals, espe-cially bread wheat, became more common than hulled ones (see pp. 28–9, under 'Cereals'). More legume crops may have been grown as well (this is certainly

---

[92] See Walton Rogers, *Cloth and Clothing*, 14–15.

[93] *Cloth and Clothing*, 14. She also records one item certainly and one probably made from nettle fibre, but this is extremely unlikely to have been cultivated.

[94] Jaques et al., 'The nature of the bioarchaeological assemblage', 43–4, table 4.5, and Dobney, Jaques, Johnstone, Hall, le Ferla, and Haynes, 'The agricultural economy', 116.

[95] Moffett, 'Food plants on archaeological sites', 355–6.

[96] Hall and Kenward, 'Setting people in their environment', 396.

[97] Francis, *British Field Crops*, 65.

[98] See Banham, '*Orceard* and *lectun*'.

true of lentils). At the same time, there was probably an increase in the overall volume of arable crops grown. After the 'abatement' of the post-Roman period (see Chapter 7), when former arable fields may have become pasture for live-stock, a gradual resurgence of arable farming seems likely. More cereals are found in middle and later Anglo-Saxon deposits than in earlier ones, to some extent due no doubt to the changing nature of the archaeological record (see the introductory remarks to this chapter). But where cereal remains grow more abundant at a particular site as the period progresses,[99] we may be seeing the process referred to in a continental context as 'cerealization', where arable farming becomes a more important element in the landscape compared with livestock husbandry.[100] In the Anglo-Saxon context, this may be a response to population growth, as more people can be fed on cereals than on animal foods from the same area of land,[101] but it may also be a case of changing fashions, with more 'up-to-date' practices spreading from the south and east to the north and west (for some of the changes, see Chapter 3). There is certainly a regional aspect to this: as we shall see in Part II of this book, our period saw arable crops grown in places where they have not been grown at any other period. It is hard to put a date on this 'arable revival': Helena Hamerow has placed it in the mid-Anglo-Saxon period,[102] and this is certainly the period when bread wheat starts to look dominant (see p. 33). However, much detail is lost by dividing the period up into broad 'early', 'middle', and 'late' phases (essential as this is for analytical purposes). No doubt changes began in some places before they are detectable in the archaeological record, even within the early Anglo-Saxon period: we know that East Saxon kings were already asking Bishop Mellitus for 'white bread' (almost certainly made from bread wheat) in the early seventh century.[103] But it is in the middle of the period that significant expansion in crop farming reaches the threshold of archaeological visibility, and the importance of arable continues to build during the later Anglo-Saxon centuries.

These changes, combined with changes in the choice of crops (certainly cereal crops), mean that by the end of the Anglo-Saxon period arable farming would look much more like its later medieval successor than had been the case at the beginning of the period. More of England would be under arable cultivation,

---

[99] This was remarked upon at Eynsham, Oxfordshire (see Pelling, 'Archaeobotanical remains', 440), and Hamerow, *Rural Settlements*, 147–8, lists several sites where either more cereal grains are found as the period progresses, or pollen analyses indicate increasing cereal cultivation.

[100] Bartlett, *The Making of Europe*, 152–3, sees cerealization as a component of colonization by 'Latin Christian', mostly Germanic, conquerors in continental Europe, but in England the conquerors were pagan, and Christianity was already established.

[101] It is estimated that arable crops could feed ten times the human population that could make a living off the same land by animal husbandry: Shiel, 'Science and practice', 14.

[102] *Rural Settlements*, 147–9.

[103] Bede, *Historia ecclesiastica* II.5, in Plummer (ed.), *Bedae Opera historica*, 91. See Banham, 'In the sweat of thy brow' for discussion.

and the familiar 'suite' of crops would be growing in the fields, dominated by bread wheat and, to a lesser extent, barley, with some oats and rye, along with legumes, predominantly beans and peas. Whether these were also divided into spring and winter crops, as in the later Middle Ages, we shall discuss in the following chapter, and the shape and management of those fields is explored there and in Part II.

3

Arable farming in Anglo-Saxon England

II: Tools and techniques

'My nose is downwards, I travel on my front
and dig in the ground, I go as he guides me,
the grey enemy of the woods, and my lord
travels bowed down, my guardian at my tail...'[1]

This chapter follows the processes that produced Anglo-Saxon arable crops, from the bare field to the threshing floor. Although agricultural work is cyclical, with preparations for the next year's crops beginning before the current year's are all gathered in, in the case of each individual crop there is a clear beginning, with the clearing of the remains of the previous crop and its weeds, or just weeds if the land has lain fallow, possibly manuring, and the opening of the first furrow. It is here that we shall begin.

CULTIVATION

Arable fields need to be prepared for growing crops. Ploughs are generally associated with fields and spades with gardens, but spades have been used to cultivate fields in Britain almost within living memory.[2] In the world as a whole, hand-tool agriculture, whether with spades, hoes, or digging sticks, has probably been as widespread as ploughing.[3] Given that a plough is a large and expensive piece of equipment, and needs large expensive oxen to pull it, there may have been many Anglo-Saxon farmers, especially those unable to farm in cooperation with neighbours, who could not use ploughs. There must also have been many fields that were unsuitable, too steep, for instance, or too wet, for ploughing, before tractors arrived. In a less thickly populated England than

---

[1] Exeter Book Riddle 21 (plough), in Krapp and Dobbie (eds), *The Exeter Book*, 191.

[2] See articles in Gailey and Fenton, *The Spade*; also Fenton, *Country Life*, 43–5, and Nicholson, *Traditional Life*, 60: 'the essential tool was the spade...[only] a few of the larger crofts had ploughs'. Also, for British settlers in North America, Hurst, *American Farm Tools*, 7.

[3] For a comparative study of a hoeing and a ploughing agriculture in otherwise similar societies, see Hill, *Dry Grain Farming Families*.

Fig. 3.1. March: digging and sowing, British Library, Cotton Julius A. vi, fo. 4r.
(© The British Library Board, Cotton Julius A. vi)

Fig. 3.2. January: ploughing and sowing, British Library, Cotton Julius A. vi, fo. 3r.
(© The British Library Board, Cotton Julius A. vi)

in recent centuries, much land that was unsuitable for ploughing was no doubt put to other uses, or even not used at all, but, again, individual farmers may not always have had the choice. Areas where this might have been the case are discussed in Chapters 9 and 12. So, although there is little firm evidence for spade cultivation of fields in Anglo-Saxon England, the men shown digging with spades in manuscript illustrations may have been meant to be cultivating fields as much as those depicted ploughing (see Figs 3.1 and 3.2), and they may represent a substantial minority.

Manuring

Until the Second World War, animal manure was the chief source of nitrogen for arable farming, vital in maintaining fertility where hungry crops such as cereals were grown repeatedly on the same land. From the later Middle Ages there is ample documentary evidence for manuring.[4] This is lacking before the

---

[4] Jones, 'Understanding medieval manure', 146.

Conquest, but the shepherd in the *Rectitudines* receives the dung of his charges for a short period as one of his perquisites (his lord no doubt getting the rest),[5] and one of the *Gerefa*'s summer tasks is 'taking out dung',[6] presumably not just to get rid of it, but for use. A low level of characteristic dung fauna from early medieval sites (even those with excellent preservation), compared with Roman and post-Conquest ones, suggests that dung was not normally stacked before use in Anglo-Saxon England,[7] but taken straight out to where it was needed. The lack of rubbish-pits and latrines on early Anglo-Saxon sites may mean that waste of all kinds was spread on the fields.[8] At Yarnton in Oxfordshire, however, a mid-Anglo-Saxon proliferation of the dungheap weed henbane (*Hyoscyamus niger*) suggested that there middening replaced direct removal of refuse.[9]

Scatters of medieval pottery in fields have been used to plot the distribution of manure by interpreting them as representing the contents of middens (manure mixed with domestic rubbish) spread on the fields to improve fertility.[10] Where these scatters are adjacent to their putative source, it is impossible to distinguish deliberate manuring from merely clearing out yards and byres, but where they lie at some distance from the settlement, manuring is the most likely explanation; medieval farmers would not move rubbish long distances just to get rid of it. Richard Jones (the doyen of medieval manure studies at the present day) has pointed out that pottery need not always equal manure, or vice versa: manure might not always be mixed with domestic waste, and pottery might even be deposited for its own sake, on the analogy of Roman sites, where pottery signals areas of raised fertility, giving rise to the belief it was itself responsible.[11]

For quite other reasons, the method may not work for the Anglo-Saxon period: in the first place, early Anglo-Saxon domestic pottery is notoriously hard to find in the field,[12] and, secondly, if middening was unusual before the Conquest, manure spread directly from folds and byres would rapidly become invisible. However, there can be no doubt that manure was produced in Anglo-Saxon England, and it must have been disposed of,[13] even if we cannot trace its use on the ground. This would undoubtedly have improved fertility. It seems likely in fact that Anglo-Saxon cereal crops were manured quite heavily: this would help account for high nitrogen levels in isotopic studies of Anglo-Saxon skeletons, including those of low-status individuals unlikely to

---

[5] *Rectitudines* 14, in Liebermann (ed.), *Gesetze*, i, 451.
[6] *Gerefa* 9, in Liebermann (ed.), *Gesetze*, i, 454.
[7] Kenward and Hall, 'Dung and stable manure', 86–7.
[8] Moffett, 'Food plants', 348.
[9] Hey, *Yarnton*, 49.
[10] The evidence and its interpretation have been reviewed by Jones, 'Signatures in the soil'.
[11] Jones, 'Manure and the medieval social order', 219 and 221–2.
[12] See comments by Hey, *Yarnton*, 49, for example.
[13] Although not necessarily outside settlements: Kenward and Hall, 'Dung and stable manure', 81.

be consuming large amounts of meat.[14] The availability of manure might also vary according to the other farming practices in use locally: where animals were mainly kept out on open grazing, away from settlements and arable fields, less dung would be available for those fields than where livestock grazed in enclosures close to home and were housed for at least part of the year (see Chapter 5 for animal housing, and Part II for various arrangements of grazing and arable). Farmers using ploughs would keep their traction animals near where they were needed, and thus have more dung at their disposal compared to those cultivating by hand, and those using heavy ploughs would need more animals to pull them than people ploughing with ards (see pp. 44–5 for different kinds of plough, and pp. 44 and 108–10 for animal traction). Manuring might therefore have become more widespread as the mouldboard plough came into common use.

Practical experience suggests that excessive nitrogen can be counterproductive in cereal cultivation as it reduces the natural competitive advantage that the crops have over weeds.[15] The effects of organic material on soil structure may have been as important as nitrogen, and manuring would also replace trace elements lost by cultivation. Anglo-Saxon farmers would not distinguish these effects, of course, but they would know that, where manure had been deposited, crops grew better. As well as manuring, fertility could be promoted by crop rotation, certainly practised in the later Middle Ages, ensuring that the same nutrients were not taken out of the soil year after year. Fallowing would rest the land periodically, as well as allowing weeds to be dealt with, and animals grazing on the fallows would add to its fertility. Legumes seem to have been a standard part of the Anglo-Saxon arable regime (see the previous chapter), and, although there is no evidence that they were recognized as improving soil fertility,[16] they may have been valued as less heavy feeders, taking less out of the land than perpetual grain cultivation.

Ploughs

Although it may often have been more practical to cultivate fields with spades, it is much less labour-intensive, at least for the humans involved, to use a plough. There must have been widespread variations in types of plough, but historians divide them into two main groups (shown in Figs 3.3 and 3.4): on the one hand the ard, or scratch plough, which has been described as a digging-stick turned over so that it can be pulled by an animal, and on the other the plough 'proper' (often known as the 'heavy plough'), which has, in addition to the share, a

---

[14] Hull and O'Connell, 'Diet: recent evidence', 677. See also Chapter 5.

[15] John Letts, pers. comm. This applies to 'primitive' cereals: modern ones have been bred to take advantage of high nitrogen availability.

[16] Stone, *Decision-Making*, 62–5, shows that their cultivation at fourteenth-century Wisbech can be associated with intensifying cereal production, but it is doubtful whether this association should be projected back before the Conquest.

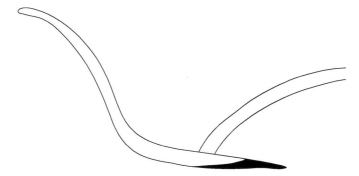

Fig. 3.3. An ard, or scratch plough.

(Drawing Debby Banham)

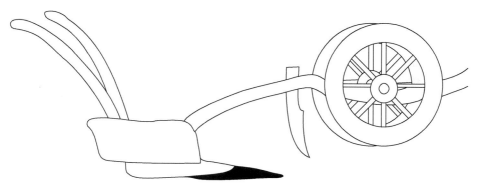

Fig. 3.4. A mouldboard plough, with coulter and wheels.

(Drawing Debby Banham)

coulter that cuts a line for the share to follow, and a mouldboard, which turns over the sod that the share has sliced. This is a much more substantial piece of equipment than the ard, and therefore usually has wheels to make it easier to pull. In practice, the distinction between the two is not quite so clear-cut: there have certainly been wheeled ards, and also ploughs, with or without wheels, which have either coulter or mouldboard, but not both. The crucial difference, however, is the mouldboard, which allows the plough to turn over the earth, thus burying the weeds and breaking the clods as they fall, rather than simply cutting into the soil as the ard does. The ard is capable of effective ploughing on most soils, with several passes in different directions to break up the land, but the weeds remain on the surface, and have to be removed by some other means. In this sense, the 'true plough' combines the advantages of the ard and the spade,[17] and changes in archaeobotanical weed-seed assemblages may reflect a change from ard to mouldboard plough (see p. 54).

[17] Orwin, *A History of English Farming*, 5.

The introduction of the 'true plough' to England is no longer attributed to 'our Anglo-Saxon ancestors', but its story is not yet certain. In the first place, it seems to have been in use in Roman Britain,[18] before Germanic settlers started arriving in what was to become England. Secondly, until recently, the heavy plough was believed to be unknown in early Anglo-Saxon England. However, a large (6 kg) iron coulter has now been found in a sealed seventh-century context at Lyminge in Kent,[19] much earlier than any previously known evidence for heavy ploughs in medieval England. This suggests that, in this most prosperous kingdom of early England, the 'heavy' plough was either continuously in use between the Roman and Anglo-Saxon periods, or was reintroduced at an early date. The coulter was in extremely good condition, clearly not a worn-out piece of equipment that had been thrown away. In fact, it seems most likely that this was a 'special', or indeed ritual, deposit, which may mean that a coulter, and probably the plough it belonged to, was a special object, even in Kent, at this time.[20] This is part, albeit an exceptional part, of an increasingly clear phenomenon involving the deposition of agricultural equipment in special ways, almost certainly implying ritual. The well-preserved ploughshares from Bishopstone in Sussex and Flixborough in north Lincolnshire, both dated to the ninth century, are also part of the same phenomenon, although mouldboard ploughs might have been more common by this time.[21]

The physical remains of Anglo-Saxon ploughs are few in number, probably because iron was too valuable a commodity not to be reused under normal circumstances. In addition to the finds discussed above, only a few shares survive, and a couple of coulters.[22] These latter may indicate the existence of mouldboards too, but, as we have seen, the two do not inevitably go together. In Ireland, the transition from ard to mouldboard plough has been traced in the changing size of ploughshares, but no such progression can be observed in England, especially since complete Anglo-Saxon shares are extremely rare.[23] Nor is it clear that mouldboard ploughs always have larger shares than ards. The rarity of wood in Anglo-Saxon archaeology means that no certain examples of the wooden parts of ploughs survive, either.[24] The most likely is the tenth-century 'ploughman' burial at Sutton Hoo, containing what look like the remains of an ard, apparently made entirely of wood.[25]

[18] See Applebaum, 'Roman Britain', 83–7.

[19] See Thomas, 'Ploughs, Kent, and the Anglo-Saxon conversion'. We should like to thank the director of the excavations, Dr Gabor Thomas, for discussing this find with us in advance of further analysis and definitive publication.

[20] See Hamerow, 'Special deposits'.

[21] For the Bishopstone hoard, see Thomas, 'The symbolic lives of late Anglo-Saxon settlements', and, for Flixborough, Ottaway, 'Agricultural tools'.

[22] For discussion and illustrations, see Hill, '*Sulh*', and Astill, 'Archaeological approach', 201–2.

[23] See Brady, 'Labor and agriculture'.

[24] Carole Morris reports possible fragments of a plough from Anglo-Scandinavian York in *Craft, Industry and Everyday Life*, 2323, but none in 'Anglo-Saxon and Medieval Woodworking Crafts', an earlier survey of the whole of England.

[25] Burial 27: Carver, *Sutton Hoo*, 322.

Table 3.1. Anglo-Saxon illustrations of ploughs

MS	date	p./folio	type of plough	no. of oxen
Bodleian, Junius 11	s. x/xi	p. 54	wheeled with coulter	2
		p. 77	wheeled, prob. with coulter	2
British Library, Harley 603	s. x/xi or xi in.	21r	ard	2
		51v	ard	2
		54v	ard	2
		66r	ard	2
British Library, Cotton Julius A. vi	s. xi in.	3r	wheeled with coulter	4
British Library, Cotton Tiberius B. v, pt 1	s. xi 2/4	3r	wheeled with coulter	4

For Oxford, Bodleian Library, MS Junius 11, see Ohlgren, *Anglo-Saxon Textual Illustration*, and the Bodleian Library website, <http://image.ox.ac.uk/show?collection=bodleian&manuscript=msjunius11>, and for British Library, Harley 603, Ohlgren and the British Library website, <http://www.bl.uk/catalogues/illuminatedmanuscripts/record.asp?MSID=18402&CollID=8&NStart=603>, both accessed 20 January 2014.

The tendency to attribute innovation to newcomers has also led to the heavy plough being associated with Scandinavian settlers, but again the evidence is far from clear.[26] By the eleventh century, however, pictures of such ploughs appear in Anglo-Saxon manuscripts (Table 3.1). Given the complexities of transmission associated with manuscript illustration, it would be possible to dismiss these as simply copies of continental exemplars. However, the calendar pictures, which show coulters, mouldboards, and wheels (see Fig. 3.2 and Plate 1), appear to draw on a continental tradition, including the Stuttgart Psalter (Württemberg-ische Landesbibliothek Stuttgart, Bibl. fo. 23) and the computistical collection, Vienna, Österreichische Nationalbibliothek, Cod. 387 (both ninth century), in which an ard is shown. Following Martin Carver's rule of thumb, namely that where Anglo-Saxon illustrators changed the details of objects copied from their exemplars, these changes were based on objects the illustrators saw around them, this should mean that mouldboard ploughs were familiar in England by the eleventh century.[27] The calendar illustrations (but not all Anglo-Saxon plough pictures) do look accurate enough to suggest the artist was familiar with the real thing and how it worked, not just representations of it. There are also

[26] See Banham, 'Race and tillage', 181–7.
[27] See Carver, 'Contemporary artefacts'.

Fig. 3.5. Psalm 36 from the Harley Psalter, British Library, Harley 603, fo. 21r. A figure can be seen ploughing with an ard, centre foreground.

(© The British Library Board, Harley 603)

clear depictions of ards (in the Harley Psalter, Fig. 3.5), however, so if we are going to take these pictures as representing the ploughs in use in late Anglo-Saxon England, we have to recognize that these were various and that some farmers were 'still' using ards. It is always worth remembering that farming does not generally change fast, however manifestly more efficient new methods may seem to outsiders.

Two written sources (also from late in our period), Ælfric's *Colloquy* and the *Gerefa*, mention the same parts of a plough: the share and the coulter. In Ælfric's *Colloquy*, the ploughman has to equip his plough with *uomere et cultro* ('sceare 7 cultre' in the Old English gloss) before starting work,[28] no doubt because these valuable metal parts might be stolen if left in the field overnight. This is presumably the reason why they are listed among the *Gerefa*'s equipment, too: the peasantry could be trusted with the cumbersome and less valuable wooden parts, but the reeve needed to look after the iron ones. We are thus left in the dark as to whether the two writers envisaged their plough as having a mouldboard; this would be among the wooden parts (hence the name, even though modern ones are metal—see Fig. 3.6), permanently fixed to the frame, or indeed part of it. The coulter, which is mentioned in both sources, usually goes with a mouldboard, but, as has been already mentioned, it is certainly not the case that they never exist separately.[29]

---

[28] Garmonsway (ed.), *Ælfric's Colloquy*, 20.
[29] Indeed, Comet, 'Technology and agricultural expansion', 22–3, believes that the 'ard-with-coulter' was a stage in the development of the 'plough proper'.

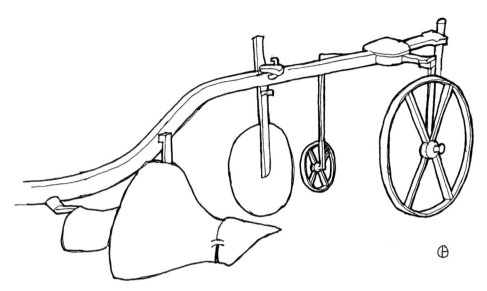

Fig. 3.6. Nineteenth-century plough showing mouldboard (left) joined to, but not combined with, share, wheel-shaped coulter, and land-side and furrow-side (right) wheels.

(Drawing Debby Banham)

The only text that makes the presence of a mouldboard absolutely clear, despite not mentioning it explicitly, is Exeter Book Riddle 21, quoted at the head of this chapter, and dating from some point in the second half of the tenth century. Allowing for all the usual caveats attached to using literary texts as historical evidence, not to mention the deliberate ambiguity of riddles as a genre, the following lines leave no doubt that the plough is envisaged as turning the sod, as well as having two 'points', share and coulter:

> 'as I go there is green on one side of me
> and, my track clear, black on the other;
> driven through my back there hangs underneath
> one skilfully made point, another at my head,
> firm and moving straight ahead. It falls to the side,
> what I tear with my teeth...'[30]

Another source of information about types of plough, at least potentially, consists of the marks left in the soil by ploughing. Normally these are obliterated by the next ploughing, or even before, but if, for instance, an earthwork is erected over the field, as at Hen Domen in Montgomeryshire, or it is buried by a sand-blow, as at Gwythian in Cornwall, they may be preserved to be found by archaeologists. This has happened on only a few sites that belong to our

---

[30] Krapp and Dobbie (eds), *The Exeter Book*, 191, lines 9–14; my translation.

period. Of these, Hen Domen, Gwythian, and even Sandal Castle, West Yorkshire, are not in core Anglo-Saxon areas, while the marks at West Stow, Suffolk,
are uncertainly dated: they could be as late as the thirteenth century.[31] Since the
type of plough that might have produced these marks is a matter of such
interest, this is usually commented upon, but recent work on soil profiles has
cast doubt upon earlier identifications.[32] Plough-marks thus remain currently a
problematic type of evidence, as well as an exiguous one, but new work should
provide valuable information in the future.

   All this evidence together suggests that the ard was the typical, if not the
only, plough in the earlier Anglo-Saxon period, with the mouldboard plough
becoming more common as the period progressed, but never superseding the
ard completely. The reasons for the persistence of the ard could be various: in
many places (some of them discussed in Chapters 9 and 12), the terrain may
have been too broken for the mouldboard plough, and in others people may
not have had the resources to adopt such a large and expensive piece of equipment. Whereas the ard uses a maximum of one metal part, namely the share or
shoe, the heavy plough normally requires two, the share and the coulter, a
much bigger investment (as well as requiring more animals to pull it) than an
ard. The heavy plough might thus have been more practicable in more prosperous parts of England, even by the end of our period when prosperity was
increasing generally.

Ploughing

Fields cultivated with ards must have needed to be ploughed several times
before they were ready to be sown (although it may have been mainly on
lighter soils, where the difference would not be so great, that ards continued
in use). This would mean that more time and labour would have been needed
to cultivate the same amount of land than where the heavy plough was in use.
On 'light', that is, well-drained, land, the field could be ploughed several
times in quick succession, to give the weeds as little time as possible to re-
grow, but on heavier soils, longer intervals in order to allow the action of rain
and frost to break down the clods before ploughing again would produce a
better tilth. Heavy land might in any case be waterlogged in the winter, and
thus unworkable for much of the time between harvest and sowing (see
pp. 56–7 for more on waterlogging and drainage). The schedule must also
have varied with the season as well as the terrain, but a farmer using an ard
might spend more or less the whole winter ploughing, whenever conditions
allowed, starting as soon as the previous year's crops were cleared. With the
heavy plough, there could still be more than one ploughing, the first perhaps

[31] See Astill, 'Fields', 74.
[32] See Lewis, 'Characterization and Interpretation of Ancient Tillage Practices'.

soon after harvest and another as the time for sowing approached, to bury the weeds that had grown in the meantime, but it would also be possible to pack the ploughing operations into a shorter time.[33] This would facilitate the cultivation of winter cereals such as bread wheat and rye (see the previous chapter). Animals could also be folded over the winter on the aftermath of crops on drier ground, which need only be ploughed when it was about to be sown. Thus the new plough might make more feed available for livestock, although, as it used more animal traction, it would also increase demand (see pp. 36–7 and Chapter 5).

Traction

Animals did not only contribute their manure to arable production: they made it possible by pulling the plough. Traction in Anglo-Saxon England was the responsibility of oxen, pulling against a yoke (see p. 53); horses did not yet play a major part (see Chapter 4). In Domesday Book, the standard plough team consists of eight oxen,[34] but in manuscript illustrations of the Anglo-Saxon period and later, such large numbers are never seen yoked to one plough at the same time. Various explanations can be adduced for this discrepancy. It may be that the illustrators ran out of space, or tired of drawing oxen; the audience, after all, would know what was intended. On the other hand, it may be that the whole Domesday team was never in fact working at once, or that the team at least sometimes consisted of fewer than eight animals.

All illustrations, of whatever type of plough, show animals in pairs. In fact the usual number in Anglo-Saxon manuscripts is two (one pair), both in the Harley Psalter, where the plough is always an ard, and in Junius 11, where it has wheels and a coulter (see Table 3.1). Only the calendar illustrations show two pairs of oxen. There are of course many problems with using these illustrations as historical evidence, as has been discussed above, but, if we ignore the Junius pictures (where the ploughs do not look as if they would have worked and the oxen are tiny), the illustrations depict one pair of oxen pulling an ard, two a wheeled plough. Early Irish sources seem to regard six animals as the full complement, with four actually pulling at once;[35] four was also the 'normal ploughing team' until recently in Shetland.[36] Farmers must always have had to train young animals, and the 'full team', whether in Domesday Book or elsewhere, probably included bullocks not yet working at full capacity. This might explain why some Domesday tenants are said to possess half a plough, or some

---

[33] See Tom Williamson's proposal for the origins of cooperative ploughing: *Shaping Medieval Landscapes*, 141–59.
[34] See Darby, *Domesday England*, 125–6, for discussion.
[35] Kelly, *Early Irish Farming*, 49 and 474–7.
[36] Nicholson, *Traditional Life*, 61.

other fraction.[37] With four oxen, or even two, they might in fact have been perfectly able to plough, even though they lacked replacement animals. Thus the ideal full team and the number of animals yoked to the plough at any one time might differ considerably.

The few Old English references to plough teams unfortunately fail to tell us how many animals were involved; perhaps it was too obvious to need stating. In the laws of Ine of Wessex, we read of a farmer hiring his neighbour's *geoht* (yoke) of oxen, and paying in fodder,[38] but we are not told whether these animals pulled the plough on their own, or together with the hirer's own *geoht*. At this period, the plough was likely to be an ard, and therefore one pair of oxen might suffice. Later we meet a different collective term for oxen. In a Worcester lease of the first half of the eleventh century, among the equipment supplied to the lessee was *ii. gesylhðe oxan*, 'two plough-teams of oxen'.[39] This term (minus its prefix) also appears in the will of Bishop Ælfwold of Crediton (AD 1008 × 1012): 'He geann godrice...an sylhðe oxna' ('He bequeaths to Godric...one team of oxen').[40] Derived from *sulh*, 'a plough', *(ge)sylhð(e)* might be translated 'a ploughing', or 'a ploughful'. There can be no doubt that it means 'enough oxen to pull a plough'. These references come from the end of the Anglo-Saxon period, so the plough is probably a 'heavy' one, with a mouldboard. The drafters of these documents, like the Domesday clerks, assume that a fixed number of oxen goes with each plough, but the only evidence for that number being eight comes from the will of the reeve Abba (*c.* 835), who left his brother half a *swulung* (the Kentish term for a ploughland, from *sulh*), along with stock including four oxen.[41] This might mean that the standard plough team had been eight since the ninth century, but it could equally represent a tradition local to Kent,[42] or simply a coincidence.

Ards could perhaps have been pulled by a single animal,[43] and this would mean that, although more time and manpower were needed for ploughing, fewer oxen were called for. The whole ploughing outfit was thus accessible to farmers who could not afford a mouldboard plough and its accompanying large team, or who did not have neighbours near enough to share one (peasants in Domesday Book rarely have a whole plough, or team, each).[44] This might help account for the persistence of the ard in the late Anglo-Saxon

---

[37] See Higham, 'Settlement, land use and Domesday ploughlands', for discussion of anomalous numbers of ploughs and oxen in Domesday Book.

[38] Ine 6, in Liebermann (ed.), *Gesetze*, i, 116.

[39] S 1421; Robertson (ed. and tr.), *Anglo-Saxon Charters*, 154.

[40] S 1492; Napier and Stevenson (eds), *Crawford Charters*, 23.

[41] S 1482; Harmer (ed.), *Historical Documents*, 3–5 (no. 2), at 3.

[42] Kent is of course where the Lyminge coulter was found, and may have been in the forefront of agricultural change (see p. 44, under 'Ploughs').

[43] Like the Orkney 'stiltie-ploo'; see Fenton, *Country Life*, 37 and Fig. 19c.

[44] See Darby, *Domesday England*, 125, for examples of sokemen (relatively high-status peasants), who did not all even own a whole ox.

period. It might also mean that designs of plough varied with the nucleation (or dispersion) of settlement, that is to say, the proximity and availability of neighbours. There is no point having a plough that requires four oxen if the rest live a day's walk away (oxen do not move fast). Settlement nucleation is of course associated with an open-field, that is, a cooperative, system of agriculture (see pp. 68–72), and the need to assemble plough beasts might be the reason for this association.[45]

The Julius version of the January calendar picture (Fig. 3.2) shows a yoke between the leading pair of oxen; in the Tiberius manuscript (Plate 1) it is not at all clear how they are attached to each other or to the plough. The Julius yoke is a straight piece of timber, but is not attached to the horns of the oxen, so it is presumably a withers yoke, pushed with their shoulders, rather than a head yoke, which they would have to pull.[46] A withers yoke normally has ox-bows around the animals' necks, but these are not seen in the Julius picture. No other harness is visible, so we should probably imagine some quite straightforward means of connecting the plough to the yoke. Columella, writing in first-century AD Italy, says that the withers yoke allowed oxen to pull a heavier plough,[47] so it is possible that this was part of a new 'suite' of technology that came in with the mouldboard plough and free-threshing wheat (see p. 33).

Oxen can only plough for a relatively short day; it is heavy work, and they need to rest, drink, and, being ruminants, chew the cud, even if they are not fed until they return to their housing.[48] In the winter, when much ploughing took place, the hours of daylight would also limit the time spent working. A day's ploughing might only occupy a few hours, the rest being taken up with feeding and watering, maintenance, and travelling between housing and field.[49] The standard day's ploughing was probably an acre, as in later periods (in fact the acre as a measurement may have originated as the amount a team could plough in a day).[50] Ælfric's ploughman regarded even this as demanding: 'omni die debeo arare integrum agrum aut plus' ('every day I have to plough a whole acre or more').[51] Thus, the amount of ground worked, even with the heavy plough, would have seemed very limited by modern standards. Each team might have worked for, say, half the year (October to March inclusive), less Sundays and

[45] See Higham, 'Settlement, land use and Domesday ploughlands'.

[46] Watts, *Working Oxen*, 23.

[47] *De re rustica* II.23, in Ash (ed.), *Columella*, 122.

[48] Manolson and Fraser, 'Cattle', 187, recommend two widely separated working periods of four hours apiece, but this would be hard to achieve in winter, especially if there was a long walk morning and evening.

[49] In 1970s Lincolnshire, a semi-retired farm-worker, who had been a horseman in the 1920s, stated that he used to walk the horses five or even seven miles before starting work, and back again at night (pers. comm.). The distance Anglo-Saxon oxen walked to work would be limited by their speed.

[50] See *OED*, *s.v.* 'acre 2(a)'.

[51] Garmonsway (ed.), *Ælfric's Colloquy*, 20.

holidays, which would amount to less than 150 acres in a season. The Domesday ploughland seems to have varied between about 60 and 120 acres.[52] This would have limited the amount of arable that each household or community could cultivate, no matter how much theoretically high-quality arable land was available to them.

Productivity

It is usually assumed that the mouldboard plough improved agricultural productivity. Presumably its immediate appeal to Anglo-Saxon farmers was that it made it easier and quicker to work the land they were already dealing with, and still produce the same amount of crops. This would allow them to expand their arable area, and thus to increase their yield of crops, if they had the labour and the inclination—but these are big 'ifs'. Winter cereals, which might have been a major motivation for changing to the mouldboard plough (see pp. 56–7), would give a better yield overall than spring ones simply by being in the ground for a longer growing season. It is also believed that the mouldboard plough improved productivity by suppressing weeds, but evidence to demonstrate this, let alone quantify it, is rare. At Yarnton in Oxfordshire, the abundance of perennial weeds declined markedly during the mid-Anglo-Saxon period, vis-à-vis annual species.[53] This was, in the report, interpreted as representing a transition to more intensive cultivation with a mouldboard plough, but it is not clear whether the overall weed burden declined. Annual weeds would, however, be less of an obstacle to cultivation than perennials (see pp. 60–1 for more on weeds and weeding).

The nearest thing we have to an Anglo-Saxon cereal-yield figure comes from a schedule of payments due to the church at Lambourn in Berkshire: 'of ælcere hide geneatlandes…oenne æker to teoþunge oðhe an hundred sceafa on hærueste' ('from each hide of *geneat*'s land…one acre towards the tithe, or a hundred sheaves at harvest').[54] There are a number of difficulties here, most immediately the size of both the acre and the sheaf, but also the date of the document, which was only written down in its current form in the thirteenth century. Nor should it be taken to mean that the authorities believed every acre, or any particular acre, would produce exactly a hundred sheaves every year. But it does indicate a rule of thumb which may have been more widely recognized. Since the earliest possible date for the document is the early eleventh century, the rule probably applies to cultivation with a mouldboard plough,

---

[52] See Darby, *Domesday England*, 95–120 for discussion. His map of 'Conjectural arable in 1086' (Fig. 43) is based on 100 acres per team.

[53] Greig et al., 'Environmental evidence', 362–4.

[54] Robertson (ed. and tr.), *Anglo-Saxon Charters*, 240. See Blair, *The Church*, 449, for discussion. This figure must represent a beneficial assessment, otherwise it would suggest only ten acres of arable to the hide.

and so still leaves us without any figures for ard cultivation, or any sense of change (up or down) through time.

The fundamental desire for food security constitutes a strong motivation to increase yields. A full barn at the end of harvest is the most satisfying thing a farmer can see, but the amount of food most Anglo-Saxons could store would be limited (see pp. 63–4). The desire for security is always counterbalanced by the need to conserve energy: if they could produce the same amount of food more quickly, Anglo-Saxons might prefer to do something less strenuous in the time saved.[55] There might be pressures, perhaps from landlords or markets, to produce more, but we can only speculate about the effects these might have had. It is normally assumed that levels of food production, and thus population, did rise during the Anglo-Saxon period.[56] The idea is that more 'efficient' methods such as the mouldboard plough allowed more food to be produced, and a greater population to be supported, both in the sense that more children would survive childhood to have children of their own, and of a growing urban population who, even if they grew some of their own food in town fields, made part of their living from craft production or trade, and thus had to get some of their food from elsewhere, presumably by buying it. In the absence of reliable figures for population or crop yields, however, let alone firm dating for the agricultural developments we have been discussing, such trends, however plausible, remain largely hypothetical.

Advantages of the mouldboard plough

Why would an Anglo-Saxon farmer take up the mouldboard plough in the first place? The modern view that it is simply 'better' than the 'primitive' ard may not have been obvious to farmers who had always got on perfectly well with ards, like their fathers before them and everyone else they knew. One possibility has already been touched upon: it might enable farmers to complete their ploughing quickly in the autumn, ready to sow winter cereals such as rye and bread wheat. This might not be the only connection, however, between the mouldboard plough and winter crops.

In the traditional narrative of Anglo-Saxon settlement, 'heavy' ploughs allowed farmers to move from 'light' soils to 'heavier' ones,[57] and the role of soils has once more been brought to the fore by Tom Williamson's work on the origins of open fields.[58] This perspective can be extended to the adoption of the mouldboard plough. The expansion of wheat cultivation must have involved

---

[55] For the theoretical debate on such issues, see Ellis, *Peasant Economics*, especially 'The drudgery-averse peasant', 102–18.

[56] See Faith, *English Peasantry*, 141–2, for a discussion which links population growth with farming practices.

[57] See for instance Stenton, *Anglo-Saxon England*, 285.

[58] In his *Shaping Medieval Landscapes*.

growing it in some areas where conditions were less than ideally suited to this crop, as explored in Chapters 6, 9, and 12. In England, such conditions would include soils that were too wet or heavy, as well as weather that was too cold or wet, or a growing season that was too short. If wheat was a winter crop and barley a spring one, as in the later Middle Ages, a major obstacle to expanding wheat production would have been winter waterlogging.[59] Of the European cereals, only spelt will tolerate standing in water for any length of time,[60] and yet numerous English fields, or parts of them, are even now saturated in the winter.[61] This was an acute problem in 2012–14, but is common even in much drier seasons. Before subsoil drainage became widespread in the nineteenth century,[62] it must have been much more so.

When subsoil drains were first introduced, in the seventeenth century, 'the draining away of superabundant water' was regarded as 'the chief difficulty of English agriculture'.[63] There must have been some existing, if less effective, means of making heavy soil fit to grow winter crops. Once such was ridge and furrow. This does not mean the single furrows produced by the plough, with ridges left between them, but ridges up to several yards wide, produced by ploughing several passes inwards towards the first furrow, covering each individual furrow with the next pass of the plough, and leaving a double furrow between ridges (see Fig. 3.7) The ridges provide a raised, and therefore warmer and drier, growing area for the crops, and the furrows act as a drainage channel.

Such an arrangement cannot be achieved with an ard, since that does not turn the soil, but merely cuts into and stirs it. A mouldboard plough, however, lifts and turns the soil in one direction (traditionally to the right) and thus ridges can be created if, instead of steadily ploughing across the field like a tractor, the ploughman follows what is effectively an elongated spiral. This type of ridge and furrow is relatively common as a relict landscape feature in

Fig. 3.7. The formation of ridge and furrow.

(Drawing Debby Banham)

---

[59] Stone, *Decision-Making*, 56, has examples of fourteenth-century winter crops being lost to flooding.

[60] For a rather extreme demonstration of this, see Bottema et al., 'An agricultural experiment'.

[61] Known in Lincolnshire during the 1970s as 'black holes', and believed to swallow tractors.

[62] See Phillips, *The Underdraining of Farmland*, esp. 2–3 and 14.

[63] Lavergne, *The Rural Economy of England*, 182. Although there was undoubtedly an element of propaganda in such statements by proponents of drainage, they cannot have been entirely unrelated to agricultural reality. See Phillips, *The Underdraining of Farmland*, esp. 5–7.

England today, wherever medieval arable was put down to grass immediately it was enclosed, and has not been ploughed up since.[64] It can be distinguished from more modern examples, and similar features such as spade-built 'lazy-beds' (actually very hard work), by its sinuous appearance in plan ('the aratral curve'). It is however impossible to date with any precision, and no single example can be proven to be of Anglo-Saxon origin. Nevertheless, it provides a plausible motivation for taking up the mouldboard plough, despite the greater investment involved, in that it would allow the expansion of wheat cultivation into areas of poor drainage.[65]

Workers

The ploughman did not have to deal with the long, heavy mouldboard plough and its team on his own. In Ælfric's *Colloquy*, the 'ploughman' says that he has a boy to drive the oxen with a goad, who is hoarse with the cold and shouting ('Habeo quendam puerum minantem boues cum stimulo, qui etiam modo raucus est pre frigore et clamatione').[66] Presumably he shouted to encourage the oxen, in case the goad was not enough. The calendar pictures, too, show the plough and its oxen accompanied by two humans, one behind, guiding the plough, and one in front, leading (or dragging or prodding) the oxen. This must be why the ploughman in the *Rectitudines* is designated the *folgere*, or 'follower'.[67] Paul Harvey offered this identification very tentatively,[68] but it is confirmed by Exeter Book Riddle 21, quoted at the head of this chapter. This depends on the paradox of the one in charge ('hlaford min', the ploughman) walking behind his subordinate (the speaker, the plough), showing that this was a familiar idea to Anglo-Saxons.[69] In Domesday Book, David Pelteret has shown that two men per plough was the normal complement; he suggests that increasingly heavy ploughs required two adult workers, rather than the Anglo-Saxon man and boy.[70]

Sowing and 'minor' cultivations

No Anglo-Saxon source tells us when farmers sowed their seed. The *Gerefa*'s list of seasonal tasks omits this vital procedure; presumably everyone knew when arable crops needed to be sown: their lives depended on it, after all. The calendar illustrations show a sower following the plough (see Plate 1 and

---

[64] See Liddiard, 'The distribution of ridge and furrow'.
[65] As argued in Banham, '"In the sweat of thy brow"'.
[66] Garmonsway (ed.), *Colloquy*, 21.
[67] *Rectitudines* 10, in Liebermann (ed.), *Gesetze*, i, 450.
[68] '*Rectitudines* and *Gerefa*', 14.
[69] Krapp and Dobbie (eds), *The Exeter Book*, 191.
[70] Pelteret, *Slavery*, 194–200.

Fig. 3.2); this is a perfectly plausible procedure (see p. 59), but it cannot be right for January (when the calendars show it), a month too cold to sow anything in the British Isles. The only evidence we have to go on is later medieval practice: in the Midland System of open-field farming (see pp. 68–72), one field was sown with spring and one with winter 'corn'. Wheat and rye fell into the latter category, and barley and oats (with beans and peas) into the former.[71] As we have seen, wheat and rye, the free-threshing cereals, were ousting hulled types of corn right across northern Europe in our period (see Chapter 2). But this replacement of hulled by free-threshing corn might also have involved winter cereals superseding spring-sown ones as the primary staples. If it was spring sowing that originally made farming possible in northern Europe, by avoiding the harsh winter weather, it might have been the development of hardier winter cereals, or new techniques for growing them, that made the desirable free-threshing species available in these areas.

Immediately before sowing (whether this was immediately after ploughing or months later), the fields may have been harrowed to break down the remaining clods and drag out any weeds that survived the plough or that had grown since ploughing. The Bayeux Tapestry has a picture of a harrow pulled by a horse,[72] but pre-Conquest evidence for the harrow is rare. It is not shown in any manuscript illustration. The *Gerefa* lists egeðgetigu, 'harrow gear' among the equipment the reeve should have at his disposal (although this part of the list has the appearance of an afterthought).[73] There is a possible reference to harrows in the Ely Farming Memoranda: '7 iii. ege[ðan þr]eora orena wyrþa' (and three ?harrows worth three ora).[74] The square brackets enclose the editor's interpretation of an illegible section of the document, so this is not incontrovertible evidence. A Peterborough list of stock at Yaxley, Huntingdonshire, dating from AD 963 or later, includes *an egþwirf*, interpreted as meaning 'part of the tackle of a harrow', although the second element of the compound resembles Old English *hwyorf*, '(domestic) animal' (see Chapter 4).[75] Before manufactured metal harrows became common, they traditionally consisted of branches of trees such as hawthorn, so perhaps we should not expect a specialist tool. As all three documentary citations belong to the later part of our period, harrows proper possibly became more common towards the Conquest.

Sowing would of course be done by hand, as shown in the calendar pictures of both ploughing and digging (see Figs 3.1 and 3.2). This is now known as

---

[71] See Orwin and Orwin, *The Open Fields*, 55 and 142–3.
[72] See Chapter 5 and Wilson, *Bayeux*, Plates 10 and 11.
[73] *Gerefa* 17, in Liebermann (ed.), *Gesetze*, i, 455.
[74] Robertson (ed. and tr.), *Anglo-Saxon Charters*, 252–6, at 252, line 19.
[75] Robertson (ed. and tr.), *Anglo-Saxon Charters*, 74 (text) and 329 (note). This list is almost certainly a later addition to the list of gifts of Bishop Æthelwold to Peterborough, to which the date 963 properly belongs, but it is unclear how much later. The manuscript is mid-twelfth century.

broadcast sowing, in contrast to sowing in rows, which only became practicable in the eighteenth century.[76] The sower walks forward at an even pace, casting the seed alternately to left and right with each step, or else to one side only, taking care to achieve an even coverage.[77] The calendar illustrations may be accurate in showing the sower working in the field with the plough-team or diggers. Exeter Book Riddle 21 has the plough speaking of someone who 'sows in my tracks'.[78] There are good reasons to sow directly into the furrow or onto the harrowed tilth: the soil has no time to dry out, providing a good moist seedbed, nor is there an opportunity for weeds to germinate and get ahead of the crop. The plough or harrow could also go over the seed once it was sown. In the digging illustration, a man with a rake is shown, who may be preparing a seedbed or covering the seed, or both.

At Butser Iron Age Farm in Hampshire, the late Peter Reynolds described broadcast sowing without harrowing afterwards as 'an extravagant way of feeding the birds'.[79] Even with such cultivation, losses to birds and other pests must have been huge by modern standards. In recent experiments at West Stow Anglo-Saxon village, Suffolk, whole sowings of broadcast cereals disappeared while drilled ones immediately adjacent remained untouched.[80] Some means would then have to be adopted to keep birds off the growing crops during the year: possibly something moving noisily in the wind to frighten the birds, or dogs, or the traditional children throwing stones, as shown on the Bayeux Tapestry and in the earlier eleventh-century Old English Hexateuch (see Fig. 3.8).[81]

Weeding

The other task that went on more or less throughout the growing season would have been keeping the crop free of weeds. In the absence of chemicals or mechanical hoes, there would be more weed growth, but this might be reduced by repeated ploughing, or by what would now be regarded as suboptimal nitrogen levels (see p. 60). In a previous set of West Stow experiments, the amount of weed material in the harvested crop was negligible.[82] Cereals shade out weed growth, and broadcast sowing would not have left spaces between rows for weeds to grow in. Long-strawed crops would overtop even those weeds that did grow, and fast-growing annual weeds die down before harvest time.

---

[76] Orwin, *A History of English Farming*, 68.

[77] Seymour, *Self-Sufficiency*, 137.

[78] 'saweþ on swæð min', line 6, in Krapp and Dobbie (eds), *The Exeter Book*, 191.

[79] Reynolds, *Iron Age Farm*, 63.

[80] Rachel Ballantyne, pers. comm.

[81] Wilson, *Bayeux*, Plate 11; the West Stow experiments found a scarecrow (even wearing a reproduction Anglo-Saxon helmet) ineffective.

[82] Mim Bower, pers. comm. This was also true in very small-scale experiments at Newnham College, Cambridge, in 2013.

Fig. 3.8. Abraham scaring birds, British Library, Cotton Claudius B. iv, fo. 26v.

(© The British Library Board, Cotton Claudius B. iv)

However, archaeobotanical samples, as well as later medieval farming manuals,[83] show that in practice weeds were not excluded entirely from traditionally farmed cereal crops.

It is not clear how much weeding was in fact carried out, as it appears very infrequently in our sources. A *weodhoc* appears among the *Gerefa*'s tools, and Bede identifies August as *Weodmonath*,[84] but no detail is given about the kind of weeds encountered, or how they were dealt with. The only information we have about weed types comes from the Old English versions of the gospels, which variously translate the Vulgate's *zizania* as *coccel*, 'corncockle' or *ate*, 'oats', where the Authorized Version has 'tares'.[85] Corncockle (*Agrostemma githago*) and wild oats (*Avena fatua*) were thus regarded as weeds in Anglo-Saxon England. Corncockle is now extinct in the wild in Britain,[86] but wild oats remain a serious contaminant of cereal crops. It would certainly be desirable to exclude both from the harvested crop, as neither can be removed by sieving or winnowing, having seeds of similar size and weight to cultivated grains.

It may be that weeding, being a tedious job that was never definitively finished, was carried out by women and children, as in other times and places; this might account for its absence from even those written sources that do concern

---

[83] See for instance Tusser, *Five Hundred Points*, 63 and 102–3.

[84] *De temporum ratione*, ch. 46.

[85] Matt. 13:25–30, in Skeat (ed.), *Holy Gospels*, [Matthew], 112–15.

[86] Wilson and King, *Arable Plants*, 82.

themselves with farming (which were undoubtedly produced by men). Or it may be that the problem was not as great as we, with assumptions formed by modern chemical and mechanical farming, have supposed.

HARVESTING, STORAGE, AND PROCESSING

The evidence for Anglo-Saxon harvesting techniques is exiguous. The calendar pictures show reaping with sickles (see Fig. 2.1), as was the practice until the nineteenth century, when scythes with cradles came in.[87] Sickles, like other agricultural tools, are rare in Anglo-Saxon archaeology, but two were found at Bishopstone in Sussex.[88] The better preserved of the two, of ninth-century date, shows the characteristic curved blade, as shown in the calendar, and the remains of a wooden handle. The calendar reapers are cutting the stalks fairly low, but not right down at ground level. This agrees with practical experience of reaping with the sickle, and would exclude low weed growth.[89] However, with so little evidence, we cannot estimate the 'usual' height at which Anglo-Saxon cereals were cut, or how much variation resulted from different subsequent uses of the crop and its straw,[90] or differing local tradition.

Once cut, cereals would be bound into sheaves and stooked in the fields to dry, as remained the practice until harvesting by hand finally went out in the early twentieth century.[91] References to sheaves are relatively rare, but the Lambourn church-dues use them as a standard unit (see pp. 54–5, under 'Productivity'), and the mythical hero Scyld Sceafing, 'Shield son of Sheaf', or 'protection descending from abundance', who appears in the prologue to *Beowulf*, shows that 'sheaf' could stand for cereals, and hence for prosperity in general, in long-established Anglo-Saxon tradition.[92]

Experience would be required to judge when the crop was ready to be cut, as ripe as possible without shedding valuable grain onto the ground, and how long to leave it to dry in stooks before carting it to the farmyard for stacking. Wheat is the quickest to dry, but can itself take three weeks.[93] In southern Scotland, eight days were traditionally allowed for wheat, two weeks for oats, and

---

[87] Morgan, *Harvesters and Harvesting*, 17 and 27, for the change from sickle to scythe. The scythes shown in the Harley Psalter, fo. 21r, are being used to cut hay, as is apparent from the text below, Ps. 36(37):2.

[88] Ottaway et al., 'Cultivation, crop processing and food procurement', 130.

[89] Simon Damant, pers. comm.

[90] Letts, *Smoke Blackened Thatch*, shows that thatching straw was cut with the ears in the later Middle Ages.

[91] Morgan, *Harvesters and Harvesting*, 18 ff. See his Appendix A, 'On Shocking Corn', 195–6, for various regional styles of stooking (or shocking).

[92] Line 4, in Klaeber (ed.), *Beowulf*, 1. See Neidorf, 'Scribal errors' for the latest argument for an early date for the poem.

[93] Seymour, *Self-Sufficiency*, 139.

three for barley.[94] Further south, wheat might be ready in a few days, but oats should stand in the stook for 'three Sundays'.[95] Oats and barley, which retain more moisture in their stems than wheat, used to be swathed and turned, like hay, before being stooked.[96] To protect these slower-drying crops from wind and rain, they have also been made into 'mows', small stacks in the field, more secure than stooks but allowing more drying than full-sized stacks in the yard or barn.[97] There is no evidence for either practice in the Anglo-Saxon period, but farmers' climatic calculations must have been as fine then as in later centuries, and practice as varied.

The harvest would probably involve people who did not normally work in the fields: more recently, it has been the one time in the year when everyone from small children to grandparents was drafted in to help.[98] The weather in August and September is hardly reliable in the British Isles, so a speedy harvest is always desirable, but in Anglo-Saxon England harvesting may not invariably have consumed all the available labour in the same way as it did later. In the eighteenth and nineteenth centuries, some villages in Scotland and the islands grew only small amounts of cereals, and were inhabited only by adult males at harvest time, the women and children being at the summer pastures with their animals,[99] and this may also have been true in the Anglo-Saxon period in some upland regions (see Chapter 6).

It is unlikely, too, that the 'traditional' division of labour at harvest, with men cutting the standing corn and women and children binding the sheaves, goes back very far. Although the scythe has been regarded as a 'man's tool if ever there was one',[100] the sickle was by no means a male preserve. In late nineteenth-century Oxfordshire, the sickle, already obsolete for harvesting, was still used by women 'who cared to go reaping', while most of the harvest was 'mowed' by men with scythes.[101] Both the Luttrell Psalter (second quarter of the fourteenth century) and Stephens' *Book of the Farm* (1844) show women reaping with sickles while a man follows behind binding the sheaves.[102] Both

---

[94] Fenton's figures are for Midlothian in the eighteenth century: *Country Life*, 71.

[95] Morgan, *Harvesters and Harvesting*, 21.

[96] Morgan, *Harvesters and Harvesting*, 21.

[97] See Seymour, *Self-Sufficiency*, 150–1, for instructions.

[98] See for example Evans, *Ask the Fellows who cut the Hay*, 137, or Morgan, *Harvesters and Harvesting*, 23–6. However, Morgan casts doubt on the applicability of this picture to periods before the nineteenth century: *Harvesters and Harvesting*, 14 ff.

[99] Fenton, *Country Life*, 124, 131.

[100] Seymour, *Self-Sufficiency*, 138.

[101] Thompson, *Lark Rise to Candleford*, 223, also 49. The differential use of the verbs 'reap' and 'mow' shows that the scythe was still remembered as originally a haymaking implement. Morgan, *Harvesters and Harvesting*, 17, associates the sickle in the mid-nineteenth century with the 'conservative' Irish.

[102] Backhouse, *Luttrell Psalter*, 23; Stephens, *Book of the Farm*, Fig. 262. According to Fenton, *Country Life*, 54, the sickle was traditionally a female tool because 'women are said to be physiologically better adapted to bending'. This sounds like masculine justification to the present authors, especially the one who worked on the land in the 1970s and has had intermittent back trouble ever since.

show three women reaping side by side (although one is giving her back a rest in Luttrell) while one man binds for them all, so the nineteenth-century method may go back a long way. Of the Anglo-Saxon calendar illustrations, Tiberius too shows one binder to three reapers (in Julius, there are only two reapers: Fig. 3.1), but all the workers in both manuscripts are male. This is clearly unrepresentative of the Anglo-Saxon rural population, but it leaves us uninformed on the gender division of labour at harvest time.

More recent customs suggest that some kind of ceremony surrounded the cutting of the last sheaf, although it would be dangerous to suggest that any known customs go back to before the Conquest (still less to pre-Christian fertility rituals, though some such must have existed).[103] In the *Rectitudines*, workers received drinks or feasts at both harvesting and corn carrying.[104] As in later periods, the removal of the last load or sheaf might have signalled that the harvest field was open for gleaning. This is not attested in the Anglo-Saxon records, but it is hardly likely that the grain which fell to the ground during reaping and carting would be allowed to go to waste, or to the birds.

Storage

The word 'barn' (*bere-ern*), as we saw in Chapter 2, goes back to the time when barley was the main bread corn in England. However, the physical evidence for barns and granaries in Anglo-Saxon England is extremely thin on the ground.[105] Insect remains from York show that Anglo-Saxon cereals were not stored on the same scale as in the Roman period, or after the Norman Conquest, when the grain pests found in Roman Britain reappear abruptly.[106] This probably means that cereal crops were usually stacked outside. Once 'all was safely gathered in', stacks could be thatched to protect the harvested grain from the weather, and perhaps decorated to invoke supernatural protection.[107]

Even where crops were stored under cover, their safety was not assured, as revealed by a fragmentary charm in Old English and Latin from the eleventh century:

'…long feather-edged [*or* four-edged] sticks, and write on each edge of either stick…one Our Father to the end, and then lay…one on the floor of the barn, and the other on…on top of the other stick, so that there is the sign of the cross in them [*or* on it], and take four pieces of the blessed bread that is blessed on Lammas day and crumble it

---

[103] See Roud, *The English Year*, 377–9; Fenton, *Country Life*, 70; and Banham, 'The staff of life'.

[104] Two separate celebrations were held in later centuries, too; see Porter, *Cambridgeshire Customs and Folklore*, 122, for some relatively recent examples.

[105] Hamerow, 'Timber buildings', 145, and *Rural Settlements*, 61–2. This was also true in contemporary, and much damper, Ireland: Brady, 'Food production', 141. For the lack of such evidence from medieval Europe more generally, see Groenewoudt, 'The visibility of storage'.

[106] Hall and Kenward, 'Setting people in their environment', 399 and 424, and Kenward and Whitehouse, 'Insects', 187.

[107] See Banham, 'The staff of life', 298–9, for what little evidence there is on this matter.

in the four corners of the barn. This is the blessing that belongs to it: So that rodents do not spoil the crops, say these prayers over the sheaves and hang them up without having spoken: "In the city of Jerusalem, where rodents neither live nor have power, nor collect grain, nor enjoy corn." This is the second blessing: "Lord God almighty, who has made heaven and earth, you bless this fruit, in the name of the Father and of the Son and of the Holy Ghost, Amen. Our Father." '[108]

Here the sheaves (*garbas*, although this can mean crops more generally) were stored in a building, rather than being stacked outside. Rodents must have been a major hazard to stored crops, whether indoors or out: zooarchaeological evidence shows that both mice and rats were present in Anglo-Saxon England.[109] In 1972, 10 per cent of annual food production was lost to rodents worldwide, and almost 50 per cent in India.[110] Cats and dogs would provide further (and arguably more effective) protection (see concluding remarks to Chapter 4).

Threshing and winnowing

Winnowing and threshing (*uentilare et triturare*) are two of the manual tasks cited by Bede as evidence for the humility of Abbot Eosterwine of Jarrow.[111] The calendar pictures for December show grain being threshed with flails (see Fig. 3.9), as was traditional in England until threshing machines and then combine harvesters replaced manual methods. There is no Anglo-Saxon evidence

Fig. 3.9. December: threshing, British Library, Cotton Julius A. vi, fo. 8v.

(© The British Library Board, Cotton Julius A. vi)

---

[108] British Library, Cotton Vitellius E. xviii, fos 15v–16r. See Ker, *Manuscripts containing Anglo-Saxon*, 300, for text. The ellipses (…) represent about six letters missing at the beginning of each line on fo. 15v. Square brackets enclose uncertain or supplied readings. The translation is my own.

[109] Hall and Kenward, 'Setting people in their environment', 409; O'Connor, 'The house mouse', 132; Rielly, 'The black rat', 140–2.

[110] Van Doesburg, 'Archaeological evidence for pest control', 199.

[111] Bede, *Historia abbatum*, 8, in Plummer (ed.), *Bedae Opera historica*, 371.

for threshing by, for instance, walking animals over the harvested plants. The flail in the Anglo-Saxon pictures resembles nineteenth-century examples,[112] consisting essentially of two sticks of approximately equal length, held together firmly with strips of something flexible, usually hide, in such a way as to allow free movement. One stick is held in the hands and the other, the swingle, beaten against the pile of cereal ears, knocking out the grain. The flexible attachment, the souple, means that the swingle can hit the ears with substantial force, increased by lifting the flail high to maximize the arc of approach. In nineteenth-century Scotland, 'an average to good barnman' could thresh 48 to 108 sheaves in a day.[113] Whether Anglo-Saxon threshers could achieve such daily rates, we do not know, but they had the technology.

The calendar illustrations do not give any indication of the threshing floor (*odene*) mentioned in the *Gerefa*. Whether indoor or out, a threshing floor must have a smooth surface, and this is probably what the area of 'hard standing' adjacent to the tenth-century drying kilns at Stafford was for.[114] The December illustration in both calendars shares the undulating ground-line seen in the other months, which must therefore be purely conventional. They do show a man holding a winnowing basket, if not actually winnowing. He is bending over, and grain is shown below the basket, so perhaps he is tipping out a basketful before receiving the next from the threshers. In both pictures, another man stands behind the winnower, holding a stick that does not look like a flail, as there is no joint. He is perhaps an overseer (the *gerefa*?) with a tally-stick: in the Tiberius picture, horizontal lines are shown on the stick, probably not shading, as they are not present on the flails or other objects in the illustration.

If the harvest was dried in the fields and then stacked, whether outside or under cover, it could be threshed straight from the stack, as it was in England for many centuries during the later Middle Ages and early modern period, and might not need further drying before it was used. Corn driers are known from the Roman period in Britain,[115] but seem to have gone out of use afterwards.[116] However, a recent survey by Helena Hamerow has shown that they were a common feature of the later Anglo-Saxon crop processing regime.[117] At West Cotton in Northamptonshire, a late Anglo-Saxon structure, which had clearly had a fire in it, yielded both sprouted and ungerminated grains, and was associated with a mill; in other words, it had been used for malting, but also for drying or parching for some other purpose, most likely milling.[118] Driers have

---

[112] See for example the drawing in Hill, 'Prelude', 20.
[113] Fenton, *Country Life*, 79.
[114] Carver, *Birth of a Borough*, 66–72, Figs 4.8 and 4.9.
[115] See Reynolds and Langley, 'Romano-British corn drying oven'.
[116] See Monk, 'Post-Roman drying kilns'.
[117] Hamerow, *Rural Settlements*, 151–2.
[118] Campbell, 'The preliminary archaeobotanical results', 69.

long been in use in other parts of Britain,[119] and the *Gerefa* mentions a kiln (as well as an oven and an oast) at the threshing floor.[120] At Stafford, where there were two different types of oven adjacent to the area of 'hard standing', we may have a kiln and oast (or some other combination of these three structures) at an *odene*.[121]

Lisa Moffett has pointed out that the excavated ovens or kilns of Anglo-Saxon date are too small to dry an entire harvest prior to storage; if they were used for drying, this is much more likely to have taken place immediately before milling.[122] There are more recent parallels for this from within the British Isles,[123] and experimental work shows that drying makes cereals much easier and quicker to grind in hand querns (although these were probably becoming less common when driers reappeared). Kilns might be expected to be associated with hulled cereals, which cannot be ground unless they are treated first to remove the innermost layer of chaff (see Chapter 2). At Stafford, most of the cereal remains were oats.[124] But the majority of excavated examples come from later in the Anglo-Saxon period, when free-threshing wheats were becoming increasingly common. They are probably to be associated with larger-scale crop processing as cereal production intensified; water mills started to replace hand querns, too, from the ninth century.[125] In the earlier period, when hulled cereals were more common, they must have been processed in ways that leave no obvious trace in the archaeological record, such as parching over a domestic fire,[126] pounding, or soaking.

ENCLOSURES AND FIELDS

The Old English *feld* means open country, not an area for arable cultivation; presumably it changed its meaning in response to the vast unenclosed open fields discussed on p. 71. But many, perhaps most, Anglo-Saxon arable crops were grown in enclosures—OE *croft*, *tun*, or *æcer*—especially in the early period, when arable farming probably occupied relatively small areas compared with livestock.

---

[119] Fenton, *Country Life*, 94–7.
[120] *Gerefa* 11, in Liebermann (ed.), *Gesetze*, i, 454.
[121] Carver, *Birth of a Borough*, 67–72, Figs 4.8 and 4.9.
[122] Moffett, 'Ovens/kilns', 61.
[123] See Nicholson, *Traditional Life*, 63.
[124] Moffett, 'Ovens/kilns', 62–3. Scottish kilns (Nicholson, *Traditional Life*, 63, and Dixon, 'Of bannocks and ale', 160) were also used for oats.
[125] Hamerow, *Rural Settlements*, 152–3. In Ireland, both corn driers and water mills are associated with an expansion of cereal cultivation at a similar period: Brady, 'Food production'.
[126] As practised in seventeenth-century Scotland: Dixon, 'Of bannocks and ale', 160.

Enclosures

Boundaries, preventing trespass on the arable by both humans and livestock (whoever these belong to), are necessary in any mixed farming regime.[127] The term *æcertyning* ('field-fencing') implies it was normally the arable, not the pasture, that was enclosed in Anglo-Saxon England,[128] and that animals were otherwise allowed to roam free. This is likely to have been the case since the origins of farming in Britain, there being no call to fence grazing land as long as there was plenty of it.[129] During the course of the Anglo-Saxon period, however, livestock would increasingly need to be enclosed as the population (of humans, but also of livestock as a result) grew, meaning more animals were kept in proximity to the arable, and pressure on grazing increased (see Chapters 5 and 7).

The laws of Ine of Wessex (seventh century) and the *Rectitudines* (eleventh) both deal with the problems of keeping crops and livestock separate.[130] In Ine's laws, anyone who neglects fencing his own meadow or arable is responsible for any damage done to other people's crops (as well as his own) as a result, unless the animal intruder is a persistent breaker of hedges or fences, in which case the owner of the fencing is entitled to kill it. In the *Rectitudines*, the hayward (responsible for hedges or fences, not hay), has his arable nearest the pasture, so that his are the first crops to be damaged if he neglects his duties. It seems that the *Rectitudines*, and presumably widespread custom by this date, has institutionalized a solution to the problem described in Ine's code. At both Hurstbourne Priors and Tidenham, fencing was part of the services performed by the people living on the estate.[131]

Many Anglo-Saxon settlement sites have no visible fencing or ditches, but some enclosures must have existed, even in the early period.[132] Many Anglo-Saxon boundaries were probably too flimsy to leave remains visible to archaeology: as well as temporary hurdle structures, they may have included ditches that did not extend below the topsoil, and hedges, either quick or dead (see further, Chapter 7). Live hedges might leave ditch-like traces behind, or they might be invisible as physical remains.[133] Some postholes interpreted as buildings may also have belonged to outdoor enclosures, either to keep livestock in, or out. At Yarnton, Oxfordshire, it was thought that Roman field boundaries might still have been in use in the early Anglo-Saxon period.[134] Certainly many banks and ditches going back to prehistory are visible at the present day, and it is always

---

[127] For a wider discussion of Anglo-Saxon enclosures, see Hamerow, 'Overview: rural settlement', 122–3.

[128] In the survey of Tidenham, Gloucestershire: Robertson (ed. and tr.), *Anglo-Saxon Charters*, 204–6 (no. 109). For more on this text, see Faith, 'Tidenham', as well as Chapter 7.

[129] Pryor, *Farmers in Prehistoric Britain*, 82.

[130] Ine 40–42.1 and *Rectitudines* 20–20.1, in Liebermann, *Gesetze* (ed.), i, 106–8 and 452.

[131] Robertson (ed. and tr.), *Anglo-Saxon Charters*, 206 (nos 109 and 110).

[132] See Chapter 10 for some 'enclosure' features in charter bounds.

[133] See Pryor, *Farmers in Prehistoric Britain*, 85.

[134] Hey, *Yarnton*, 43.

easier to work within existing earthworks rather than alter them, even with present-day earth-moving equipment. Where existing boundaries became over-grown, however, unless they were very substantial, they might soon become invisible, and be further damaged in the process of clearance.[135] In areas with plenty of stone, 'prehistoric' traditions of walling, and indeed the boundaries themselves, no doubt continued in use. The lower courses of walls still in use today might be Anglo-Saxon, or even older.

Open fields

One feature of Anglo-Saxon farming that has received a good deal, not to say a disproportionate amount, of scholarly attention is the destruction of enclos-ures, that is to say the reorganization of arable land into open fields.[136] This was by no means a uniform development across England; as discussed else-where in this book (especially Chapter 12), it may not even have been the most common way of rearranging arable fields. Areas where arable was reorganized may not have been in a majority either. Many parts of England, mostly in the west, never had open fields, and in others, such as East Anglia, they remained a minor element of the agricultural landscape.[137] In this light, it is perhaps sur-prising how much ink has been spilt over the origins of the open fields.[138] Their interest is increased, however, by their association with the formation of vil-lages, which also took place, at least in some areas, before the Conquest.[139] If open fields were created by a wholesale reorganization of communities' arable landholdings, this would be easier where the community's houses were clus-tered together, rather than scattered across the land. Living close together would also make working together easier, but the relationship between settlement nucleation and arable reorganization is far from certain.[140] Since many general-izations about medieval arable farming are based on the better documented period when open fields were common, it is worth examining the evidence for their existence before the Conquest, and for their operation as an agricultural system.

Origins Many writers regard the establishment of open fields as essentially a feature of arable expansion in the high Middle Ages.[141] It has not been believed

[135] Rippon, *Beyond the Medieval Village*, 166–7.
[136] For this bias in the scholarship, see Rippon, 'Landscape change in the "long eighth century"', esp. 42–5, and, for a work which does a great deal to redress the imbalance, his *Beyond the Medieval Village*.
[137] See maps assembled by Williamson, *Shaping Medieval Landscapes*, 4.
[138] See Rowley (ed.), *The Origins of Open-Field Agriculture*, for a range of views.
[139] See Hamerow, 'Settlement mobility and the "Middle Saxon Shift"'.
[140] See Oosthuizen, 'Medieval field systems', for one proposal.
[141] The main proponent of a late origin was Joan Thirsk; see, for instance, her 'The origins of the common fields'.

for a long time that they were introduced by 'our Anglo-Saxon ancestors' when they arrived from their continental homelands,[142] but there is evidence for something resembling open-field farming before the Conquest.

One early source, frequently cited, is the law-code of Ine of Wessex (AD ?688 × 694):

'Gif ceorlas gærstun habben gemæne oððe oþer gedalland to tynanne 7 hæbben sume getyned hiora dæl, sume næbben, 7 etten hiora gemænan æceras oððe gærs, gan þa þonne þe ðæt geat agan 7 gebeten þam oþrum þe hiora dæl getynede hæbben, þone awerdlan þe ðær gedon sie; abidden him æt þam ceape swylc ryht swylce hit kyn sie.'[143]

'If peasants have a common paddock or other shared land to fence, and some have fenced their part, some haven't, and [animals] have eaten their common fields or grass, then those who are responsible for the gap should go and make amends to the others who have fenced their part for the damage that has been done there; they should seek from the livestock such justice for themselves as is appropriate.'

This is part of a section on fencing: it follows clause 40, on the fencing of individual peasants' holdings. This clause clarifies responsibility where several people are involved, and 42.1, which follows, deals with cattle which break down fences. Here we see that *ceorl*s might hold land in common (*gemæne*) in the eighth century, or in shares (*gedæl*). A *gærstun*, literally 'grass enclosure', is the type of land most likely to be involved, but other land is also covered, and later parts of the clause make it clear that this includes arable. The peasants evidently do not work together on fencing, since some might have completed theirs while others have not, and it is not clear if cultivation is cooperative. Most importantly, we are not told how the land is laid out, but we are talking about a plot small enough to fence, not the huge expanses of open fields. The mere existence of shared or common landholding does not have to mean open fields.

The number of places where open fields certainly existed before the Conquest is very small. A few charters have bounds which zigzag around or between divisions of arable land, and others describe the land granted as 'lying acre under acre', or some similar expression.[144] Although neither of these is watertight evidence for open fields, the easiest way to visualize what they describe is as large fields divided into strips and furlongs. On the other hand, the occurrence of features such as headlands (OE *heafod, heafodland*, and possibly *forierth*) and gores (OE *gar*, literally 'spear(-head)', but evidently already 'triangle') need not indicate open fields. Headlands also exist in enclosed fields, as at Himbleton, Worcestershire: 'to hryancroft ondlong þæs croftes heafodlondes þonne to þam oþran heafodlonde of þæm heafodlonde þæt to bercroft' ('to the rye croft, along the

---

[142] See Finberg, 'Anglo-Saxon England to 1042', 397–9, for earlier stages of the debate.
[143] Ine 42, in Liebermann (ed.), *Gesetze*, i, 102.
[144] See Hallam, 'England before the Norman Conquest', 42–3; Fox, 'Approaches to the adoption of the Midland system'; and Hooke, *Landscape of Anglo-Saxon England*, 126–7.

headland of the croft, then to the other headland, [then] to the barley croft').[145] Triangular pieces of land occur wherever rectangular fields cut across features on a different alignment, such as earthworks or Roman roads. Likewise, OE *æcer* need not refer to a strip in a divided arable field; the shape is never specified, and it is sometimes simply a measurement, applied to meadow as well as arable.[146] Nor does 'every third acre' necessarily imply rows of strips: in one case it refers to a wood,[147] and it is paralleled by, for instance, 'every third pig'.[148] What is distinctive about the holdings granted in these charters is not that they (necessarily) lie in open fields, but that they consist of small parcels of land, not whole estates, and thus have to be described largely in terms of agricultural features, or else in measurements. This may be evidence for a growing land market in Anglo-Saxon England, but need not indicate changes in the way land was managed.

Most scholars' views on the origin of the open fields depend on what they consider plausible in terms of more general social and economic change during the relevant period. Here we would like to focus more closely on farming and the concerns of farmers. We have seen in Chapter 2 that there was a substantial increase in the amount of wheat grown in England during the Anglo-Saxon period. This change is likely to have been driven by an appetite for wheat bread, not only lighter and more palatable than other bread available at the time, but favoured by the Church, and, probably increasingly, the secular elite. This preference existed quite early, certainly from the time of the conversion, and probably spread down the social scale as it became more realistic. So what was it that allowed the preference for wheat to be gratified increasingly in the later Anglo-Saxon period? The mouldboard plough cannot explain it. The mere existence of technology does not automatically lead to its widespread use; there must be other factors encouraging people to adopt it. As we have seen above, this kind of plough not only allowed land to be ploughed more quickly for autumn sowing, but also enabled the draining, and thus cultivation, of heavy wet land. This would allow bread wheat to be grown in new areas of England, encouraged by the improving climate.[149] Both mouldboard plough and ridge and furrow are easier to use in an open-field layout, and thus the taste for wheat bread could ultimately be responsible for open-field farming.

Open fields and ploughs In the Orwins' classic account of open-field farming (which remains the basis of current ideas), the crucial feature is not just that the fields are large and unfenced, but they are divided into furlongs, each in turn made up of long narrow strips (often of about an acre each) running in the same

---

[145] S 1373; Robertson (ed. and tr.), *Anglo-Saxon Charters*, 116.

[146] It measures both in S 1280; Robertson (ed. and tr.), *Anglo-Saxon Charters*, 88.

[147] In the will of Leofgifu (1035 × 1044), Whitelock (ed.), *Anglo-Saxon Wills*, 76–8, at 76.

[148] Harmer (ed.), *Anglo-Saxon Writs*, 344–5. This expression is also implied in Ine's law-code; see Chapter 5.

[149] For more on how these factors may have interacted, see Banham, '"In the sweat of thy brow"'.

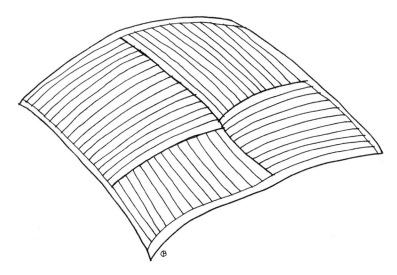

Fig. 3.10. Furlongs and strips in an open field.

(Drawing Debby Banham)

direction (see Fig. 3.10).[150] These strips are fundamentally units of landholding, but they may coincide with units of ploughing, and it is the mechanics of working with the mouldboard plough, and the oxen pulling it, which determines the long thin shape. The basis of this idea is that the plough, with its traction animals, was long and thin, and heavy and difficult to turn, and therefore the best way of working with it would be to plough for as long as possible in one direction before turning. Turning would also need a lot of space, so long thin strips would enable more land to be used for growing crops and less for turning. Each furlong usually had a headland at each end for turning, at right angles to the plough-strips. Although there are many 'woulds' here, it is hard to see how else this arrangement of arable land in strips arose. Open fields without the strips are unknown, so the most economical explanation is that the plough required the strips, which in turn entailed the creation of the open fields.

On the other hand, the heavy plough and open fields are not inextricably linked. The mouldboard plough existed in Roman Britain, but fields were not divided into long thin strips; in Scandinavia, open fields were cultivated with ards.[151] Within England, ridge and furrow, presumably made with a mouldboard plough (see pp. 46–51), can be found in small enclosed fields, and there are large areas with open fields but no ridge and furrow. There are also strips without open fields, as discussed in Chapter 12. It is perfectly possible to plough with a mouldboard plough without producing ridge and furrow, and on well

---

[150] Orwin and Orwin, *The Open Fields*, 30–52, esp. 35–6.
[151] See Myrdal, 'The agricultural transformation of Sweden'.

drained soils there would be no need for them. Thus we cannot assume that, because the heavy plough existed in Anglo-Saxon England, there must have been either ridge and furrow or open fields. Surviving examples of ridge and furrow can only be dated by their morphology: the 'aratral curve' takes us back to when oxen, rather than horses or machinery, were used for ploughing, but that need not mean before the Conquest. Thus we cannot be certain that any example of ridge and furrow is Anglo-Saxon.

Field layout and arable management In 'classical' open-field farming, the arable was divided into either two or three 'courses' (often involving a larger number of physical fields, despite the terms 'two-field' and 'three-field system'). One would be fallow each year, so that animals could graze the aftermath, eat the weeds, and fertilize the land.[152] In a two-course system, half the land would be fallow, and all the arable crops grown on the other half. With three courses, the division was between winter crops (mainly wheat), spring crops (mainly barley), and fallow. The surviving open fields at Laxton, Nottinghamshire, are worked as three courses, although the 'fallow' is now used for fodder crops.[153]

A Worcester lease of 904 has been cited as evidence for a pre-Conquest two-field system:[154] it lists land at Barbourne, Worcestershire, with sixty acres of arable north of Barbourne, and 60 to the south, temptingly similar to the common North and South Fields of many later medieval systems. But Barbourne is named from a stream, so the land (clearly not the whole estate) may be on either side of the watercourse, rather than of the village.[155] It is often supposed that three-course rotations superseded two as population growth required more food to be grown on the same land, but at Barbourne there was a two-field system long after the Conquest, so that was not the sequence there.[156]

Other Anglo-Saxon evidence for either a two-course or a three-course system is lacking. Rotation is first recorded in any detail in manor-court records of the thirteenth century, and even then, modified versions operated in places where open fields did not occupy all the arable. As we have seen, there is no evidence that open fields were common even in the eleventh century, and standard management regimes may have been a long way off. Ine's law-code shows that in the eighth century some tasks might be undertaken in cooperation, and some land could be held communally or in shares, but that need not mean that other aspects of the system must also have existed. Many agricultural tasks may have

---

[152] Orwin and Orwin, *The Open Fields*, explain this in much greater detail than is possible here, and surprisingly little of their explanation has been superseded by later scholarship.

[153] See Beckett, *Laxton*. A visit to the village does a great deal to elucidate the 'classic' system: <http://www.laxtonvisitorcentre.org.uk> (accessed 13 September 2013).

[154] Dyer, *Lords and Peasants*, 27; S 1280, Robertson (ed. and tr.), *Anglo-Saxon Charters*, 36.

[155] As pointed out by Finberg, 'Anglo-Saxon England', 904.

[156] See Fox, 'The alleged transformation'.

been undertaken by farmers working together, as they were more recently, so cooperation is not evidence for any particular arrangement.[157] Ine's laws also show that farmers could use each other's oxen without ploughing together.[158] Nor do the various charters tell us much about management. Nonetheless, it cannot be ruled out that something like the 'classic' two or three courses existed before the Conquest.

More common than open fields must have been some version of the more flexible 'infield–outfield' arrangement (see Chapters 9 and 10). The land (usually) nearest the settlement is cultivated every year, and manured regularly, while the rest is mainly used as pasture, but parts of it (usually adjacent to the infield) are taken into cultivation as required, and returned to pasture when fertility declines. Probably even more common than either 'system' was something that would look much less systematic to an outsider, but would make perfect sense in the light of detailed knowledge of the local terrain. One field might grow excellent barley crops, but never produced good beans, for no apparent reason; another might catch the wind coming up the valley early in the year and thus could not be used for young stock; and so on. Holdings like this might be managed in ways that could never be represented in a diagram, or even several paragraphs, with cropping sequences of different lengths, incorporating different crops and different lengths of grass leys, in different fields, or livestock movements that took advantage of odd flushes of growth in odd places. In practice, even operations that can be reduced to diagrams must have been much more variable in detail, with the choice of spring crops in a three-course rotation, for instance, varying not only between fields or even parts of fields, but between years in the same field, taking account of variations in the weather, or even a family wedding months before that had put everything behind all season. Such details are of course inaccessible to us now, but could have been just as significant to the people dealing with them as the larger-scale patterns that we can perceive.

CONCLUSIONS

In arable farming, the Anglo-Saxon period can thus be seen to be one characterized by change. At the beginning of the period, agriculture in lowland Britain seems to have reverted from introduced Roman practices to something like the *status quo ante*, with much less intensive cereal farming. During the following centuries, some of those introduced practices seem to have been reintroduced,

---

[157] In 1970s Lincolnshire, for instance, three smallholders harvested their cereals in succession, using the combine harvester belonging to one of them, and the tractors, trailers, and labour resources of all three.

[158] Ine 6, in Liebermann (ed.), *Gesetze*, i, 116.

or perhaps spread from places where they had been continuously practised. Some farmers and communities moved to a more arable farming regime from a more pastoral one (see Chapter 10), and some adopted new equipment and methods of cultivation, such as the mouldboard plough and ridge and furrow. The greater numbers of plough oxen required may have led to more arable land being fenced, and would also have allowed more of it to be manured. Some communities may have reorganized their arable land completely. And more people built kilns or ovens to dry their corn. Since all these changes in cereal production happened over roughly the same period of time, and coincided with the change from hulled to free-threshing (and probably autumn-sown) cereals, discussed in the previous chapter, it is likely that they were all related. Alongside them was a major technological change which does not strictly belong to the realm of farming, but must nevertheless have been closely connected, the introduction of mechanical mills, driven by water or oxen, relieving women of the labour of grinding by hand.[159]

Although it is hard to say how far or how fast most of these changes proceeded, it seems likely that, at the end of the Anglo-Saxon period, more land in England was under arable cultivation than at the beginning, more land was being ploughed and manured, more mouldboard ploughs were in use (and possibly fewer ards as a result), more arable land was ridged up to improve its drainage, and more of it, if not yet much, was arranged in large unfenced open fields (although more, paradoxically, may also have been fenced, against the greater numbers of livestock now kept close to settlements). Such novelties may have been quite slow to take hold, and several of them still relatively insignificant by the end of our period. But some of them were Anglo-Saxon innovations: ridge and furrow and open fields had not existed at all at the beginning of the Anglo-Saxon period. And taken as a group, these changes represent a quite new way of doing things: greater emphasis on arable cultivation, and more intensive methods of going about it. Whatever happened on individual holdings, across England as a whole arable production is likely to have increased considerably.

---

[159] See Banham, 'Food Plants', 39–70, and for additional archaeological evidence, Hamerow, *Rural Settlements*, 152–5.

4

Animal husbandry in Anglo-Saxon England
I: The Livestock

There can be no doubt that the Anglo-Saxons valued animals more than plants. Livestock appear in Anglo-Saxon legislation far more than crops, and Anglo-Saxon landowners, who generally took little interest in how their food was produced,[1] nevertheless thought it worthwhile to bequeath animals in their wills. Horses are the only ones mentioned individually, but substantial numbers of oxen, cows, sheep, and pigs appear too, whereas crops never feature in wills (nor do poultry or goats). It is of course unsafe to extrapolate from ruling-class to peasant attitudes, but people who look after livestock make a considerable investment in the animals they depend on, especially the larger, longer-lived species, and they put considerable effort into caring for them. The same kind of physical and emotional investment is extremely unlikely to have been made in crops: most of them live only a single season, hundreds if not millions of individual plants are involved, and they make little appreciable response to either the labour or the sentiment bestowed on them by humans. Hence we should not be surprised to find far more livestock than crops in Anglo-Saxon texts that are not concerned primarily with food production or supply.

This does not necessarily mean, however, that animals were more important in terms of calories, or even tonnage, in their contribution to human diet at the time. It requires far more land, especially, and labour to produce the same number of calories from animals than from plants. If the object is simply to feed the maximum number of people from a given area of land, plant foods are much more efficient.[2] But acreage is unlikely to have been the limiting factor in Anglo-Saxon farming, especially in the early period. It seems likely that the population was considerably less dense than it had been in Roman Britain, and

---

[1] See Banham, 'Race and tillage', 165–6.

[2] In 2010, livestock husbandry used 83 per cent of the agricultural land in Britain, but produced less than 30 per cent of the nutritional value derived from British farming as a whole: Wexler and Harper, 'The lay of the land', 14; see also Shiel, 'Science and practice', 14.

thus it may have been labour that was at a premium, making intensive production of either plant or animal foods difficult (and probably unnecessary).[3] There
may therefore have been large areas of land occupied, albeit sparsely, by livestock kept as envisaged in Chapter 10: left to themselves for much of the time,
and rounded up only when needed for eating or trading, or in the case of sheep
for shearing. Such low-input systems are not apparent in our written sources
(but see 'Pigs' on pp. 97–100); but these sources come chiefly from near the end
of the Anglo-Saxon period, when the human population was probably growing
appreciably, and more intensive production methods had become both more
necessary and more practicable as a result.

In any case, Anglo-Saxon diet was not purely functional, merely a means of
keeping body and soul together: it could demonstrate wealth and status (as
well as a host of other qualities), just as modern diet does.[4] Eating large animals, or offering them to others, showed that one controlled both the land on
which they had been reared and the labour necessary to care for them and turn
them into food. Animal foods also provided concentrated nutrition: protein,
which is in short supply in a purely vegetable diet, and fat, which contains
more calories, weight for weight, than other nutrients. Thus access to livestock
made people feel well fed and comfortable, both physically and socially. In
Anglo-Saxon England, even slaves received meat sometimes.[5] For most people,
though, most of their diet, most of the time, came from plants, and a quite
limited range of plants at that. Animal foods were a treat, and livestock in the
field were a promise of future security and enjoyment.

In terms of acreage occupied, the importance of livestock is likely to have
diminished as more cereals were cultivated. But this may not mean that the
numbers of livestock decreased; if 'cerealization' was a concomitant of population growth, the demand for animal foods must also have been increasing,
especially if prosperity was improving as well.[6] This would presumably have
been accommodated by more intensive production methods; higher stocking
ratios, for instance, and fattening on more concentrated feedstuffs. 'Ranch'-
type regimes might be replaced by operations with greater labour inputs. Large
areas of pasture, previously available to anyone living close enough to make
use of it, might be divided up among settlements or communities, as proposed
in Chapter 12. It is difficult to find evidence for such changes in documentary
sources, for nearly all our written evidence about livestock husbandry comes

---

[3] It is impossible to be more definite about population numbers, either before or after the Anglo-Saxon
aduentus, or indeed about the survival of the British population, who are likely to have been enslaved
by the settlers. If there were large numbers of such slaves, labour would have been less of a limiting
factor. For various opinions on the survival question, see Higham (ed.), *Britons in Anglo-Saxon
England*.

[4] See now Gautier, 'Cooking and cuisine', and references cited there.

[5] *Rectitudines* 6.8, in Liebermann (ed.), *Gesetze*, i, 449.

[6] Bartlett, *The Making of Europe*, 152–3, and see the discussion at the end of Chapter 3.

from the end of our period. Archaeology, however, covers our period more evenly.[7] Such evidence as we do have for the numbers of individual species, and changes in such numbers, as well as the balance between species, is discussed later in this chapter.

Despite the commendable efforts of various 'living history' organizations, most notably Bede's World at Jarrow,[8] it is impossible to find animals today that are exactly like those kept in Anglo-Saxon England, or even to be certain what those animals looked like. To tell how medieval livestock of any species differed from their modern counterparts, the best guide is provided by the efforts of animal breeders in the intervening period. They have wanted bigger animals, thus medieval ones were smaller, as confirmed by the zooarchaeological remains.[9] They have wanted faster-growing ones, thus medieval animals grew more slowly. They have wanted more productive animals, thus medieval ones produced less of whatever people get from them: milk, eggs, wool, meat. They have wanted poultry that lay all year round, and mammals that milk continuously, without going dry in the winter. Until recently, they wanted pigs as fat as possible.[10] Medieval farmers valued most of these qualities too, but their ability to engineer them in their livestock was much more limited, and thus their livestock represents an early stage in a process of which modern farm animals are the result.[11] Anglo-Saxon livestock would be counted as 'primitive' by modern standards, and thus surviving 'primitive' breeds probably resemble them most closely. Some appropriate comparisons are considered in the following sections of this chapter.

Anglo-Saxon farm animals did not belong to carefully selected, genetically uniform, and stable breeds such as we find in modern farming.[12] Before the eighteenth-century 'improvements' of breeders such as Robert Bakewell began,[13] there was much more variation within any population of livestock, and less between populations. These 'landraces' owed such genetic distinctiveness as they possessed to relative isolation from other geographical populations, and adaptation to their local terrain.[14] Stock from the hills would be recognizably different from lowland animals ('thriftier', smaller), and so would the tougher animals

---

[7] Terry O'Connor points out, however, that the age-at-death data do not suggest that pastoral production was under stress: 'Animal husbandry', 373.

[8] See Grocock, '"To eat, to wear, to work"'.

[9] Rixson, *History of Meat Trading*, 89, Fig. 5.5, has a handy drawing of Anglo-Saxon-sized livestock standing in front of their modern equivalents.

[10] Albarella, 'Pig husbandry', 72.

[11] They are not necessarily the final result, however. Recent demand for leaner meat has meant selection for characteristics neglected by earlier breeders, and not only in pigs.

[12] See Sykes, *The Norman Conquest*, 50. Information about the degree of genetic variation among Anglo-Saxon livestock populations should soon start to become available, as biomolecular techniques improve: O'Connor, 'Animal husbandry', 373.

[13] See Trow-Smith, *British Livestock Husbandry, 1700–1900*, 45–69.

[14] For the distinction between modern breeds and pre-modern geographical variants see Clutton-Brock, *Natural History*, 41–4, esp. 44, and for the consequent futility of trying to establish ancient origins for existing breeds, Wiseman, *The Pig*, xii–xv.

from cold or wet areas compared with those in sunnier parts of England. Some of this variation would be due to natural selection, as in wild populations, but human intervention played a part, too.[15] Farmers would choose to breed from the most productive animals (in terms of carcass weight, milk or wool yields, or progeny), resulting in flocks and herds sharing characteristics that fitted them to thrive in the local environment. At Flixborough on the Humber, as at Yeavering in Northumberland, cattle of two separate size ranges may have come from different geographical populations.[16] The existence on one site of animals with different lengths of horn, outside the range of normal sex differences, also suggests that selection had taken place: an example is James Street in London (a mid-Anglo-Saxon assemblage), where four short-horned and three medium-horned cattle were identified.[17] Such breeding efforts could only operate, however, within the limitations imposed by nature and by contemporary understanding of inheritance. Some concept of family characteristics and their transmission was no doubt current, in relation to livestock as well as people, but ideas like bloodlines and pedigrees lay far in the future. It is also worth bearing in mind that the characteristics that we can identify in zooarchaeological remains, such as horn length, may not themselves have been the most important to Anglo-Saxon breeders, but could be by-products of selection for other more or less utilitarian properties.

Domestic animals show much more diversity in appearance than their wild counterparts,[18] so variations in coat colour and markings will have been a feature of Anglo-Saxon livestock. Some animals may have been deliberately selected for colour (see pp. 82–3 and 93 for likely examples, notably horses and sheep), but this could not have been done on the systematic scale that produced modern breeds with their standard colouration or markings (Red Poll, or Belted Galloway, for example). Herds of closely related animals could therefore contain numerous colour variations and markings. Selection for size is likely to have been more widespread, but many factors would modify its success; as already indicated, most Anglo-Saxon farm animals were much smaller than their present-day counterparts, as the zooarchaeological remains show (see the various sections of this chapter for individual species). Overall, any Anglo-Saxon flock or herd would contain considerably more genetic variation than a modern one, and much of that variation would be visible to the casual observer.

The following sections discuss the species of livestock that were kept in Anglo-Saxon England. The way in which they were kept and the products for which they were raised will be the focus of the next chapter.

---

[15] See Ryder, *Sheep & Man*, 31, for the relationship between natural and artificial selection in domesticated animals.

[16] Dobney, Jaques, Johnstone, Hall, la Ferla, and Haynes, 'The agricultural economy', 164; Higgs and Jarman, 'Yeavering's faunal remains', 332.

[17] Armitage, 'The Animal Bone', 30.

[18] Because such mutations are not suppressed by natural selection, and may even be encouraged by humans; see Anderson, 'The molecular basis for phenotypic change during pig domestication', 43, for an explanation.

HORSES AND OTHER EQUIDS

'Sometimes, the brave in battle let their fallow mares gallop, run in competition...'[19]

The horse (*Equus caballus*)[20] was an important animal in Anglo-Saxon England: the first leaders of the English are said to have been called Hengist ('stallion') and Horsa.[21] In the London guild regulations of King Æthelstan's reign (924–39), the compensation for a stolen horse was the same as for a slave, half a pound (of silver, 120 pence).[22] Its importance was largely due to the association between horses and the aristocracy, and the latter's favourite pastime, hunting, as well as horse-racing, and the more serious pursuit of warfare.[23] The Ætheling Æthelstan left a stud to his huntsman in his will (1015), and one Thurstan excluded a deer-park and a stud from the bequest of woods at Ongar to his servants (or young men) in his will of 1043 × 1045, presumably to keep these assets within his family.[24] The ætheling also left to his relations and close associates six individual horses, two described by the colour of their coats, along with other prized possessions, such as weapons.[25] Equestrian burials like the one in Sutton Hoo (Suffolk) mound 17 confirm the value placed on horses and their association with powerful male figures.[26] But the *Rectitudines* shows that people well below the rank of aristocrat also owned horses: the *gebur*, whose heavy week-work obligations emphasize his low status, did not have to perform labour services himself while his horse was engaged on his lord's business.[27] Thus we can envisage horses existing in fairly large numbers in the Anglo-Saxon countryside.

The 'business' envisaged in the *Rectitudines* is carrying (*aferian*, probably of both messages and goods), but the important question here is whether horses also did farm work. John Langdon has shown that horses were used increasingly for traction in England during the twelfth century.[28] Before that, their

---

[19] *Beowulf*, lines 864–5, in Klaeber (ed.), *Beowulf*, 33.

[20] The terminology employed here for domesticated animals follows Corbet and Clutton-Brock, 'Appendix: Taxonomy and nomenclature', 436, though without the inverted commas that the authors recommend.

[21] Bede, *Historia Ecclesiastica* I.15, in Plummer (ed.), *Bedae Opera historica*, 31. Bede regarded this as no more than a tradition (*feruntur*, 'they say').

[22] Æthelstan VI, 6.1, in Liebermann (ed.), *Gesetze*, i, 176.

[23] Bendrey, 'The horse', 16, and Fern, 'The archaeological evidence for equestrianism', 67. For a comprehensive survey of Anglo-Saxon written references to horses, see Keefer, '*Hwær cwom mearh?*'

[24] S 1503; Whitelock (ed.), *Anglo-Saxon Wills*, 56–63 (no. 20), at 60, and 80–5, at 82.

[25] Two were stallions: Whitelock (ed.), *Anglo-Saxon Wills*, 58, 60. Contemporary Irish sources also associate horses closely with men of high rank and fancy riding gear; Kelly, *Early Irish Farming*, 88–9. See Keefer, '*Hwær cwom mearh?*', 125–7, for a fuller listing of horse bequests.

[26] Carver, *Sutton Hoo*, 115–37; Fern, 'The archaeological evidence for equestrianism' and 'Early Anglo-Saxon horse burial'. Horses in cremations are also associated with males: Bond, 'Burnt offerings', and Williams, 'Animals, ashes and ancestors'.

[27] *Rectitudines* 4, in Liebermann (ed.), *Gesetze*, i, 446.

[28] See Langdon, *Horses, Oxen*, esp. 48–51.

employment is thought to have been limited by the difficulty of pulling heavy loads with the types of harness available before the horse-collar was introduced.[29] No Anglo-Saxon illustration shows a horse pulling either a cart or an agricultural implement (but see p. 83, under 'Donkey'), and the late ninth- or early tenth-century author of additions to the *Old English Orosius* thought it remarkable that the Norwegian Ohthere ploughed with horses: 'þæt lytle þæt he erede he erede mid horsan'.[30] The Bayeux 'Tapestry' shows a horse pulling a harrow, and in the twelfth century horses were particularly associated with this light implement, which could be pulled without a horse-collar.[31] The 'Tapestry' does show a collar, however.[32] This type of harness is thought to have arrived in western Europe in the ninth century, but the 'Tapestry's' depiction would be the earliest English representation. The 'Tapestry' may represent a Norman innovation here, or, as there are signs of repairs to this section, it may have been altered later.

If horses were not used for agricultural work before the Conquest, they were bred and kept on something like a farm. In addition to the two studs already mentioned, the Old English *stod* is not uncommon in place-names, and it may be that such establishments were relatively common in the countryside.[33] Between 975 and 1016, one Ælfhelm left a stud at Troston, Suffolk, to his wife and 'my companions who ride with me'.[34] There may have been a stud at Wolverton Turn, Milton Keynes, where horse made up a high proportion of the animal bones (11 per cent), and was represented by very young, as well as older, animals.[35] Large numbers of horses, both 'tame' and 'wild', are also bequeathed in some aristocratic wills, presumably indicating large-scale breeding, or at least training, enterprises.[36] The compiler of the *Rectitudines* does not include a 'horse-herd' among the large specialist staff of his (presumably hypothetical) estate, however, so it may be that studs were normally run separately from general

---

[29] Langdon, *Horses, Oxen*, 9–10. For more on these various types of harness see Kelekna, *The Horse in Human History*, esp. 161–2.

[30] 'What little he ploughed, he ploughed with horses.' The main point was that he and his compatriots did little ploughing of any kind, and lived chiefly on hunting, trading, and their livestock: Bately (ed.), *Old English Orosius*, 15.

[31] Langdon, *Horses, Oxen*, 58–9, but see also Clutton-Brock, *Horse Power*, 71–2. The single *hercerarius* ('harrowing animal') listed in the *Inquisitio comitatus Cantabrigiensis* is believed to be a horse; see Darby, *Domesday England*, 164.

[32] Wilson, *Bayeux*, Plates 10 and 11.

[33] Stodmarsh, Stoodleigh, Studall, Studham, Studland, and the various Studleys; see Mills, *Dictionary of English Place-Names*, s.vv. There are also OE compounds, *stodhors* and *stodmyre*, 'brood mare', but no equivalent terminology for other domestic species; see Keefer, 'Hwær cwom mearh?', 128.

[34] S 1487; Whitelock (ed.), *Anglo-Saxon Wills*, 30–5 (no. 13), at 32.

[35] Sykes, 'The animal bone'.

[36] Untamed horses in the will of Wynflæd and one hundred wild horses and sixteen tame geldings in Wulfric's (S 1539 and S 1536; Whitelock (ed.), *Anglo-Saxon Wills*, 10–15 (no. 3), at 14, and 46–51 (no. 17), at 50). There are also 1,372 *siluestres* or *siluaticae* mares in Domesday Book and its satellites: see Darby, *Domesday England*, 164. These were not necessarily living in wooded areas; the terms simply mean 'wild'.

farming operations, however large and complex. The lack of neonatal horse remains on most Anglo-Saxon sites probably means that horses were too important
to be raised in the same way, and at the same sites, as ordinary livestock.[37]

The livestock listed in Domesday Book and associated documents include
only 4,756 horses, clearly a very incomplete figure, even for the few counties
covered. High-status riding horses are probably not counted; 3,008 are *runcini*,
working horses of some kind, but they need not have been working in agriculture.[38] Their main use may have been as personal and household, or even
commercial, transport (Old English *hwyorf* may be the equivalent: see pp. 83–4,
under 'Donkeys and mules').

The uses of horses in Anglo-Saxon England did include eating, as butchery
marks on some archaeological horse bones demonstrate.[39] Some cut marks
may be associated with skinning for leather manufacture, or other crafts,[40] but
where, for instance, long bones have been split to extract marrow,[41] parts of the
animal at least were being consumed. Meat not considered fit for human consumption may have been fed to dogs, so butchery marks do not necessarily
mean that horses were eaten by people.[42] Nevertheless, the general avoidance
of horsemeat in modern England need not be ancient, and should not prevent
us from recognizing that horses represented a potential food resource for the
Anglo-Saxons. In prehistoric Britain, although 'not a regular part of the diet',
there is no doubt that horses were eaten on occasion,[43] and this may have been
the situation in Anglo-Saxon England, too.

It is often stated that the consumption of horseflesh was a pagan custom suppressed by the Church.[44] In fact, ecclesiastical authorities in these islands seem
to have been fairly relaxed about this issue; the Penitential of Pseudo-Theodore
states: 'The horse we do not forbid, but it is not the custom to eat it,' and most
early medieval penitentials contain a similar statement.[45] It does seem, however, that the use of horses as meat declined after the conversion,[46] and, as

---

[37] Bendrey, 'The horse', 14–15.

[38] Figures from Darby, *Domesday England*, 164. He thought the *runcini* were packhorses. See also
Langdon, *Horses, Oxen*, 34 and 296.

[39] For example at West Stow, Suffolk (fifth to seventh centuries): Crabtree, *West Stow*, 104. Hagen,
A Second Handbook, 189, lists other sites with butchered horse bones.

[40] See Cameron and Mould, 'Devil's crafts and dragon's skins?' for leather and Riddle and Trzaska-
Nartowski, 'Chanting upon a dunghill' for bone, etc.; also Albarella, 'Tawyers, tanners'.

[41] At Flixborough, butchery marks were more frequent on horse bones than on other domestic mammals, especially in the latest phase (tenth to eleventh centuries): Dobney, Jaques, Barrett, Johnstone,
Carrott, and Hall, 'Patterns of disposal and processing', 103–4 and 115, Fig. 6.42.

[42] See, for instance Hey, *Yarnton*, 342, where this possibility is discussed.

[43] Bendrey, 'The horse', 12.

[44] See Hagen, *A Second Handbook*, 188–9.

[45] *Paenitentiale pseudo-Theodori* xvi.17, in Wasserschleben (ed.), *Die Bussordnungen*, 566–622, at
603; my translation. The chapter is translated and discussed by Meens, 'A penitential diet'. For other
penitentials see Flechner, 'The making of the Canons of Theodore', 140 and 143.

[46] In Ireland, it was certainly associated with 'pagan' ceremonial (see Kelly, *Early Irish Farming*, 353),
but this is less clear for England.

hippophagy was already in decline in the Roman Empire,[47] this may be a Mediterranean trend transmitted to northern Europe by the Church (like the taste
for bread wheat, or unaccompanied inhumation).[48] Ann Hagen has argued
plausibly that it was advantageous to those who valued horses for riding to
discourage their use as food.[49] In 893 eating horses was seen as exceptional,
even for the heathen and notoriously savage Vikings: 'they were oppressed by
lack of food, and had devoured the greater part of their horses, and the rest [of
the horses?] had died of hunger'.[50] If horses were not a normal part of the diet,
this may explain why they were not raised in the same way, or at the same establishments, as other domesticated mammals.

Appearance

Anglo-Saxon horses would have looked like ponies to the modern eye: the
majority were around 13 hands when adult, with some as small as 11.2, and
the largest only just reaching 14.[51] Free-living horses such as New Forest
ponies are sometimes said to be 'original English' types, without overseas
influence, but this valued species has probably been subject to human manipu-
lation from an early stage.[52] Roman military horses are believed to have been
imported into Britain,[53] so their descendants would be part of the Anglo-Saxon
gene pool, and horses of oriental origin may also have been introduced during
the Anglo-Saxon period.[54] Horses imported to improve Irish stock in the early
Middle Ages are thought to have come mainly from Britain, presumably
including England,[55] implying selective breeding, and possibly importation
from the Continent, in order to produce larger, stronger, faster, or otherwise
more desirable animals.

The colour of horses is rarely mentioned in Anglo-Saxon sources. In Ireland,
white horses were the most highly valued, presumably because they were
uncommon, as well as for symbolic reasons.[56] The ætheling Æthelstan's will
(cited on p. 79) also mentions a white horse, as well as a black stallion, and

---

[47] Bökönyi, 'Horse', 167.

[48] Bishop George of Ostia, the papal legate to England, condemned the practice in 786 on the grounds
that 'none of the Christians in the East does it': Haddan and Stubbs (eds), *Councils*, iii, 459.

[49] Hagen, *A Second Handbook*, 188–9.

[50] ASC A, *s.a.* 892/3: 'þa wæron hie mid metelieste gewægde 7 hæfdon micelne dæl þara horsan
freten 7 þa oþran wæron hungre acwolen', in Bately (ed.), *MS A*.

[51] Fern, 'The archaeological evidence for equestrianism', 65.

[52] DNA studies have shown that even the 'wild' Exmoor pony is closely related to other modern
British breeds: Yalden, 'Conclusion', 191. See Bendrey, 'The horse', for prehistoric human influence on
horses in Britain.

[53] Clutton-Brock, *Natural History*, 110.

[54] Keefer, '*Hwær cwom mearh*?', 124–5.

[55] Kelly, *Early Irish Farming*, 90–1.

[56] Kelly, *Early Irish Farming*, 92.

another stallion with some kind of variegated markings: 'anes fagan stedan'. In *Beowulf*, horses are described as *æppelfealuwe*, 'apple-fallow'.[57] These were of course all valued aristocratic mounts, whose nomenclature may have been as artificial as present-day equine terminology, and which, in any case, are more likely to have been selected for colour. The appearance of less prestigious horses may not have been so important to their owners; such selective breeding as they practised was probably for more practical qualities, but their animals were no doubt smaller, slower, and generally less impressive than those of the aristocracy.

Donkeys and mules

The evidence for asses and mules in Anglo-Saxon England is very small. The Old English Hexateuch depicts donkeys (*Equus asinus*), calling them in Old English *assan*, where the Latin text has *asini*, showing that Anglo-Saxons could translate the Latin term, and the illustrator knew what the animal looked like (see Fig. 4.1). In the same Bayeux 'Tapestry' scene as the horse and harrow mentioned earlier, there is a plough apparently being pulled by an ass or mule.[58] However, the ass, though hardy in the sense of being able to survive on very poor feeding, is not happy in a cold and wet climate, and is regarded as being at the edge of its range in Britain, so it is unlikely to have been common in Anglo-Saxon England.[59] Mules are more adaptable, but, since they are hybrids between ass and horse, can only be bred where donkeys are available.[60] Both donkeys and mules were known in Roman Britain, although numbers were small, but there is virtually no zooarchaeological evidence for donkeys or mules in Anglo-Saxon England.[61] The single animal recorded, found near the Thames, could well have been an import.[62] A very small number of mules and asses (three and sixty-two, respectively) are listed in Domesday documents, far fewer than any other species.[63] It is possible that both donkeys and mules died out in Britain after the Roman period, and were reintroduced by the Normans. New techniques for differentiating the bones of equids in archaeological assemblages should help clarify this situation in the near future.[64]

The evidence from written sources and illustrations is certainly not strong enough to contradict this archaeological absence. It has been suggested that the Old English word *hwyorf* means a donkey: in the *Dunsæte* regulations, it

---

[57] Line 2165, in Klaeber (ed.), *Beowulf*, 81.

[58] Wilson, *Bayeux*, Plates 10 and 11.

[59] Epstein, 'Ass, mule and onager', 174, and Johnstone, 'Donkeys and mules', 17. The donkey's later ubiquity in Ireland is attributed to poverty, not to the animal's suitability for the climate.

[60] Epstein, 'Ass, mule and onager', 181.

[61] Johnstone, 'Donkeys and mules', 22–5.

[62] Baxter, 'A donkey (*Equus asinus* L.)'.

[63] Darby, *Domesday England*, 164.

[64] Johnstone, 'Donkeys and mules', 25.

Fig. 4.1. Donkeys from the Old English Hexateuch, British Library, Cotton Claudius B. iv, fo. 49v.

(© The British Library Board, Cotton Claudius B. iv)

denotes an animal ('wilde weorf') which has to be compensated for at a rate of twelve shillings, where a horse is worth thirty shillings and an ox thirty pence.[65] It seems extremely unlikely that a feral ass would be valued higher than an ox (let alone so much higher), and much more plausible therefore that this is an untrained horse or pony.[66] *Hwyorf* may refer to a working horse, like Latin *runcinus*, or it may have been a general term for a beast of burden. In the Antwerp–London glossary (eleventh century), *hwyorf* glosses *iumentum*, 'a beast of burden'.[67] If donkeys were absent from Anglo-Saxon England, however, it is much more likely to have referred to horses of various kinds, or even to cattle.

CATTLE

'Then I saw a creature of the weaponed kind
greedy with the joy of youth; the life-giver allowed him
as tribute four streams shooting brightly, flowing on demand.
Someone spoke, who said to me
"This creature, if he survives, will break the hillsides;
if he's taken apart, he'll tie up the living." '[68]

---

[65] Liebermann (ed.), *Gesetze*, i, 374–8. The etymology of *hwyorf* is obscure, usually interpreted as a compound of *orf* ('cattle', 'property'; see pp. 86–7) with an unknown first element.

[66] If the shilling is calculated at the traditional Anglo-Saxon rate of five pence, the *weorf* is worth twice as much as an ox.

[67] Porter, *The Antwerp–London Glossaries*, 58, line 495; later in the glossary (60, line 511), *iumentum* is paired with *pecus* and glossed 'ælces kynnes nyten' ('any kind of livestock').

[68] Exeter Book Riddle 38, in Krapp and Dobbie (eds), *The Exeter Book*, 199.

The significance of cattle (*Bos taurus*) in early medieval Ireland is well known: they played a major role in mythology; kings demonstrated their vigour by leading cattle-raids on neighbouring kingdoms; and cattle were not just a measure of wealth, but a unit of exchange.[69] We do not have such evidence from England, but the importance of cattle to the Anglo-Saxons almost certainly goes back into prehistory, and probably to their pre-Christian religion.[70] In the seventh-century royal burial at Sutton Hoo in Suffolk (mound 1), a pair of drinking-horn mounts was found which are too big for the horns of domestic cattle,[71] but would have fitted the aurochs (*Bos primigenius*), the wild ancestor of domestic cattle, which was extinct in Britain long before the Anglo-Saxons arrived.[72] These horns must thus either have been heirlooms, brought over from the Continent by the ancestors of the king buried in mound 1, or else imported nearer the date of the burial. Either way, they were clearly of great value, although it is impossible to be certain if they had supernatural meaning. No other explanation, on the other hand, accounts for the heap of cattle skulls in building D2 at the royal site of Yeavering in Northumbria.[73] This is where Bede set his story of the mass baptism of Northumbrians in 627 following King Edwin's conversion, complete with a pagan priest and temple,[74] but he makes no mention of any ritual involving cattle. Where he does mention cattle, however, is in explaining the Old English name for November, *blodmonath*, and he may have had Yeavering in mind when he spoke of slaughtered cattle being dedicated to heathen deities.[75]

A recent discovery suggests that cattle could sometimes be valued as individuals, like horses (see p. 79). A whole cow was buried with a woman of fairly high status in the mid-sixth century at Oakington in Cambridgeshire.[76] This looks like a parallel to the horses buried with wealthy men, and there are also two horse burials at Oakington, but this is a cemetery with an unusually high proportion of female (and infant) burials, and a very high incidence of food offerings, so it is hard to interpret the cow burial at present.[77]

There is in any case no need to invoke ritual to explain the value of cattle; there are good practical reasons, too. They are 'expensive' animals: being large, they take several years to reach maturity (and, in the case of oxen, to train), and thus more goes into a cow, ox, or bull than a sheep or pig, in terms of feed, and also of human labour. Thus ownership of cattle was evidence of prosperity,

---

[69] Kelly, *Early Irish Farming*, 27–8 and 57–66.

[70] For the relationship between the ritual and utilitarian value of cattle in African traditional societies see Ryder, *Sheep & Man*, 69–70.

[71] Bruce-Mitford, *Sutton Hoo Ship-Burial*, 55–7 and figures 42–3.

[72] The latest remains from Britain date to the Bronze Age: Legge, 'The aurochs and domestic cattle', 32–4.

[73] Hope-Taylor, *Yeavering*, 98–100, 325–32, and Plate 83.

[74] Bede, *Historia Ecclesiastica* II.13 and 14, in Plummer (ed.), *Bedae Opera historica*, 111–15.

[75] *De temporum ratione*, ch. 15, in Jones (ed.), *Opera didascalica*, ii, 329–32.

[76] Pitts, 'Britain in archaeology', 8, and anon., 'Archaeologists find "cow-woman"'.

[77] Duncan Sayers, pers. comm.

and of control over labour. It is a commonplace of the scholarship that 'property' and 'cattle' were closely related concepts in Anglo-Saxon thought (see p. 87). Thus people might want to own cattle just because they were valuable, much as people like having money in the bank today. But cattle did also fulfil the Anglo-Saxons' needs. They are a multi-purpose animal, providing food, traction, and hides, and their bones and sinew, as well as their horns, were also valuable materials.[78] As a meat animal, their large size makes them good value: more flesh and fat is returned for the labour of feeding, management, slaughtering, and butchering than from smaller livestock. Nonetheless, it does seem that they were valued to an extent that cannot be explained purely by their role in industry and food-production.

The value of cattle, then, was in a sense incalculable, but it was calculated, sometimes to the minutest degree. The laws of Ine of Wessex (seventh or eighth century) list the value of cattle, and of parts of them, in hard monetary terms: a cow's horn is worth two pence, but that of an ox ten pence. This five-fold ratio is out of proportion to the relative size of cattle horns, so symbolism of some kind must be at work. Tails and eyes appear to be worth the same in either cow or ox, five pence (one shilling).[79] These are large sums (though much smaller than those paid for human injuries): a whole ewe plus her lamb was also worth a shilling in Ine's laws. Only cows and oxen are mentioned, not bulls, which, though obviously essential to the continuing use of cattle, do not themselves directly produce their economic value, and must have been much rarer. The emphasis on horns may be to protect the animals; a bull is much more difficult to steal or injure than cows or oxen, hence the challenge of bull-fighting. Nonetheless, bulls are equally rare in other Anglo-Saxon sources: it was oxen and cows that figured largest in people's minds. An ox was the most valuable animal after the horse, worth thirty pence in Æthelstan's reign (a quarter the value of a horse), compared with twenty for a cow, and ten and five for a pig and sheep respectively.[80] Large sums are also paid for mill-oxen in the Ely Farming Memoranda.[81]

Evaluating the importance of cattle is complicated by ambiguities in the vocabulary, in both Old and modern English.[82] 'Cattle', 'chattel', and 'capital' derive from Latin *capitalis*, and hence from *caput*, 'head'. In Old English, both *feoh* and *orf/yrfe*, can mean either 'cattle' or 'property, wealth'.[83] The will of

---

[78] At Flixborough, the possibility of vellum production was also explored: Dobney, Jaques, Barrett, and Johnstone, 'Zooarchaeological evidence', 234. Cf. Grocock, '"To eat, to wear, to work"', 92.

[79] Ine 58–9, in Liebermann (ed.), *Gesetze*, i, 114–16.

[80] Liebermann (ed.), *Gesetze*, i, 176. In *Dunsæte*, the values are 30, 24, 8, and 5 pence (a shilling) respectively, whereas a horse is worth the huge sum of 30 shillings: Liebermann (ed.), *Gesetze*, i, 378.

[81] Robertson (ed. and tr.), *Anglo-Saxon Charters*, 252–7 (Appendix 2, no. 9), at 254.

[82] See de la Cruz Cabanillas, 'Shift of meaning', for discussion.

[83] Charles-Edwards, 'The distinction', regards *orf* and *yrfe* as separate words, meaning 'cattle' and 'wealth, inheritance', respectively, but in practice they are often used interchangeably, for instance in *Dunsæte*.

Ealdorman Ælfred (871 × 889) includes a bequest of land 'mid cwice erfe 7 mid earðe' (with [literally] live stock and with crops/arable).[84] *Feoh* is cognate with 'fee', 'fief', and 'feudal', but, in Old English seems specific to moveable wealth.[85] OE *ceap*, 'goods, bargain', which gives us 'cheap', is also used to mean cattle, even in non-commercial contexts. In Ine's laws, for instance, it is *ceap* that might eat the grass or crops if peasants neglect their fencing. When laws on theft refer to *ceap*, *feoh*, or *orf*, are we dealing with moveable wealth in general, or only the kind that moves on four legs?[86] Occasionally, there are clues to indicate that the four-legged kind is intended, but it is frequently impossible to be certain whether livestock or goods in general are in question. Such a situation can only have arisen in a context where, for all practical purposes, cattle were moveable wealth and moveable wealth was cattle, and therefore it was unnecessary to distinguish between them. Jewellery and fancy swords might have displayed wealth more impressively, but wealth must overwhelmingly have consisted of livestock.

It is even more difficult to establish when *feoh*, *orf*, or *ceap* mean 'cattle' in the sense of livestock generally, or of *Bos taurus* in particular. For Old English to tolerate such ambiguity must mean that normally it made little difference if an Anglo-Saxon thought cows and oxen were meant when in fact livestock in general was intended, or vice versa. This was not because most Anglo-Saxon livestock were *Bos* (see the next section), but because of the greater importance attached to bovines.

Numbers

Naomi Sykes has shown that, throughout the Anglo-Saxon period, on well over half of all archaeological sites the bones of cattle are more numerous than those of sheep (both are always more numerous than any other species).[87] This contrasts markedly with the Domesday evidence, which gives much larger figures for sheep than cattle at the end of our period, more than ten to one (over 285,000 to rather under 24,000) in the counties for which livestock are recorded.[88] However, these numbers exclude the plough-teams of these counties, at eight oxen per team, and there are clearly other problems with the figures: only 456 cows are recorded for the eight counties, and only one bull (in Cornwall). If these numbers were even approximately accurate, cattle would have died out in England before the end of the eleventh century. It is unlikely that such a substantial difference is due to a mere accounting error, or to the processes that

---

[84] S 1508; Harmer (ed.), *Historical Documents*, 13–15 (no. 10), at 13.

[85] See Hollis, 'Old English "cattle-theft charms"'.

[86] The late Patrick Wormald was of the opinion that nearly all Anglo-Saxon theft laws referred primarily to cattle (pers. comm.).

[87] Sykes, 'From *cu* and *sceap*', 58, Fig. 5.1, confirming the findings of earlier studies: Sykes, *The Norman Conquest*, 28.

[88] Darby, *Domesday England*, 164.

produced Anglo-Saxon bone assemblages, although the large, robust bones of cattle are undoubtedly overrepresented in comparison to smaller species.[89] The way species frequencies are calculated also has a bearing: raw fragment counts (NISP) usually exaggerate the importance of cattle, while estimations of minimum numbers (MNI) tend to suggest higher levels of sheep/goat and pig.[90] Jacqui Mulville estimated that cattle numbers at Eynsham were exaggerated by about 5 per cent as a result.[91] Due to the methodological difficulties of producing minimum numbers, however, most studies have stuck to NISP, and syntheses have to proceed on the same basis.[92] Against these factors, most zooarchaeological records come from settlement sites, where the animals were consumed, so the bones of plough oxen might be underrepresented, as well as bones used for craft production. Either way, the bones found in archaeology do not represent the relative numbers of animals grazing in Anglo-Saxon fields in a straightforward way. Nonetheless, the percentage of sites with more cattle increases from just under 60 in the fifth to seventh centuries, to over 70 in the mid-ninth to mid-eleventh, so there were certainly more cattle, relative to sheep, in later Anglo-Saxon England than had been the case earlier, even if they did not outnumber them in absolute terms. As well as larger numbers of plough oxen, a growing taste for beef, or for cows' milk, may be involved, or an increasing ability to indulge it (see Chapter 5). As with cereals (see Chapter 2), the dietary preferences of the ruling classes probably spread down the social scale.

Surveys do suggest that it is mainly high-status and urban sites ('consumer sites') which have more cattle, while villages ('producer sites') tend to have more sheep.[93] This implies that cattle were more highly valued for food, while sheep might be kept in greater numbers primarily for their non-meat products (see the next chapter). The relative scarcity of the meat-bearing bones (as opposed to heads and feet) of cattle on later Anglo-Saxon rural sites suggests that the best eating was being sent to urban consumers or landlords.[94] Cattle would no doubt be preferred to sheep as providing more meat per carcass,[95] as well as for their prestige.

Appearance

There is less evidence for the appearance of cattle in early medieval England than in Ireland, where great value was placed on white cows, especially those with red ears, which seem to have had magical associations, while it is likely

---

[89] See O'Connor, 'Animal husbandry', 364.

[90] Sykes, *The Norman Conquest*, 28.

[91] Ayres et al., 'Mammal, bird and fish remains', 345.

[92] Sykes, *The Norman Conquest*, 9. For an evaluation of both NISP and MNI, see Gautier, 'How do I count you?'.

[93] Crabtree, 'Animal exploitation in East Anglian villages', 43; Sykes, *The Norman Conquest*, 37–9, Fig. 38.

[94] Sykes, *The Norman Conquest*, 38–9.

[95] 7.3 sheep to a single 'cow', according to one calculation: Dobney, Jaques, Johnstone, Hall, la Ferla, and Haynes, 'The agricultural economy', 123.

that black cattle were in fact most common there.[96] However, an Old English medical recipe which calls for the milk of a cow of one colour (*anes bleos cu*)[97] suggest that this was unusual, some kind of patterned coat being the norm. The markings of breeds have only been standardized quite recently, and it is likely that the coats of Anglo-Saxon cattle, even if closely related to each other, varied a great deal. No markings are shown on the coats of cattle in manuscript illustrations, perhaps reinforcing the idea that a single colour was valued over variegation. The oxen shown in the Tiberius calendar have plausible red-brown coats (see Plate 1), and a variety of shades is shown in the Hexateuch (see Fig. 4.2).

The oxen shown in manuscripts look extremely small alongside the men working with them. This is to some extent artistic convention, but Anglo-Saxon cattle really were small in comparison to their modern counterparts, a shoulder height of 113 cm being regarded as typical.[98] Cattle sizes declined gradually during the Middle Ages across the whole of Europe.[99] This has been attributed to loss of Roman breeding expertise, or to climatic deterioration, but Terry O'Connor suggests that there was no incentive to select for larger size: 'even a small ox…would yield a quantity of meat requiring well organized and prompt redistribution, salting, and smoking.'[100] It would also be more manoeuvrable in the field; a larger animal is always more challenging to manage. At Bede's World, Dexter oxen, with a shoulder height up to 107 cm for a cow,[101] were chosen for ploughing experiments, being the closest among modern breeds to the size of Anglo-Saxon cattle.

Naomi Sykes found that the size of cattle in England actually rose between the early and middle phases of the Anglo-Saxon period (fifth to seventh and seventh to ninth centuries, respectively), and then fell off again later (ninth to eleventh centuries).[102] However, her mid-Anglo-Saxon samples come largely from urban or proto-urban sites, so the apparent peak in this period may be due to trading centres sucking in the best animals from the countryside. This idea is supported by data from Flixborough, on the Humber, where a new, larger type of cattle appears in the ninth century.[103] Cattle of this size, rare on Anglo-Saxon sites, do appear at early medieval ports on the other side of the North Sea, so it was suggested these animals were imported. There is other

---

[96] Kelly, *Early Irish Farming*, 31–4.

[97] *Lacnunga* CLXIII, in Pettit (ed.), *Anglo Saxon Remedies*, i, 114, and London, Wellcome Library, MS 46, no. 5, in Napier, 'Altenglischen Miscellen', 326.

[98] O'Connor, 'Animal husbandry', 367. At West Stow the range was 100–120 cm and at Eynsham and Yarnton all measurable early to mid-Anglo-Saxon specimens fell between 105 and 135 cm; eleventh-century specimens at Eynsham ranged from 100 to 107 cm: Ayres et al., 'Mammal, bird and fish remains', 351 and 369. See also Dobney, Jaques, Johnstone, Hall, la Ferla, and Haynes, 'The agricultural economy', 167, Fig. 7.46.

[99] Bökönyi, 'The development of stockbreeding'.

[100] O'Connor, 'Animal husbandry', 367.

[101] Dexter Cattle Society, <http://www.dextercattle.co.uk> (accessed 16 August 2012).

[102] *The Norman Conquest*, 50–1 and Fig. 47.

[103] Dobney, Jaques, Johnstone, Hall, la Ferla, and Haynes, 'The agricultural economy', 187.

Fig. 4.2. Cattle from the Old English Hexateuch, British Library, Cotton Claudius B. iv, fo. 49v.
(© The British Library Board, Cotton Claudius B. iv)

evidence for trade on the site at this time, and the large cattle do not persist into later phases of the site, so they probably represent imports rather than new stock introduced into Anglo-Saxon farming.[104] Sykes attributes the later Anglo-Saxon decline in cattle stature to a drop in quantity and quality of grazing,[105] which seems plausible in the context of a growing human population. Another factor may have been warfare: the later Anglo-Saxon period was also the Viking period.[106] The level of disruption that raiding and conquest occasioned in the Anglo-Saxon countryside is unquantifiable,[107] but could have been sufficient to wipe out any success earlier farmers had had in improving the size of cattle.

We might expect a difference in size between oxen and cows, as castrating bull-calves makes them continue growing beyond the normal size of an adult animal. However, the only zooarchaeological assemblage where the dimensions of cattle seemed to cluster at two separate points is the one from Flixborough.[108] This extremely large collection of bones might be expected to reveal variations not apparent in smaller assemblages, but the investigators decided that these two clusters represented different types of cattle (see the previous paragraph), rather than sexual dimorphism.[109] The lack of similar data from elsewhere probably means that the stature of the sexes overlapped, the biggest cows being larger than the smallest oxen.

[104] Dobney, Jaques, Barrett, and Johnstone, 'Evidence for trade and contact', 214.
[105] This she associates in turn with the beginnings of open-field farming, but we see the effects of this as minimal.
[106] Sykes suggests war as an explanation for the drop in cattle stature after the Conquest, but not before: *The Norman Conquest*, 52.
[107] See Banham, 'Race and tillage'.
[108] Dobney, Jaques, Johnstone, Hall, la Ferla, and Haynes, 'The agricultural economy', 151.
[109] Dobney, Jaques, Johnstone, Hall, la Ferla, and Haynes, 'The agricultural economy', 160.

Present-day cattle are divided between dairy breeds, with 'a wedge-shaped body, the thin end of the wedge at the front',[110] and more rectangular beef breeds.[111] Cattle bred chiefly for traction (see the next chapter) need hefty shoulders, and are deeper-bodied at the front,[112] like the modern British Longhorn.[113] Specialist breeds did not exist in our period, however: no Anglo-Saxon cows would have had the enormous udders of modern dairy animals. Sykes's figures suggest greater diversity of cattle sizes in the later Anglo-Saxon period than before, probably due to selection for different characteristics, but it is not possible to identify any particular types, let alone their specific conformation.[114] The oxen in the Tiberius ploughing scene look particularly well muscled, while the Julius ones are more lightly built.

It is likely that all Anglo-Saxon cattle had horns. As the aurochs, from which domestic cattle are descended, was horned,[115] polling (the absence of horns) must be a post-domestication development, and it may be that polled cattle were not yet known in England in our period. All the cattle in Anglo-Saxon illustrations are horned. We have seen that horns were a valued commodity, probably for symbolic as well as practical reasons.[116] From a livestock management point of view, there are advantages and disadvantages to horns. The current threatened status of the modern Longhorn breed is attributed to the danger of injury to other animals if they are reared in confined conditions,[117] and people, too, are at risk of goring, especially by bulls or by cows with calves.[118] On the other hand, horns allow animals to defend themselves against predators and thieves, and they provide useful handles for the attachment of head-yokes, and for tethering. They can be blunted, or capped, to avoid accidents.[119]

SHEEP

'A sheep must go with its fleece until midsummer.'[120]

The sheep, *Ovis aries*, never seems to have the same significance in human society and thinking as cattle. In cultures across the globe, men who boast about the number of cattle owned by their families may profess to have no idea of

---

[110] Williams, *The Backyard Cow*, 13, and Biffen, *Elements*, 520.
[111] Biffen, *Elements*, Plate V.1, facing p. 514.
[112] Biffen, *Elements*, 517, and Alderson, *A Chance to Survive*, 14.
[113] Epstein and Mason, 'Cattle', 17.
[114] *The Norman Conquest*, 51, Fig. 48.
[115] Epstein and Mason, 'Cattle', 8.
[116] Leahy, *Anglo-Saxon Crafts*, 60.
[117] Alderson, *A Chance to Survive*, 138.
[118] In Ireland, the owner of a cow could not be held responsible for any injury she inflicted while her calf was up to three days old: Kelly, *Early Irish Farming*, 37–8.
[119] See Wade-Martins, 'Oxen ploughing'.
[120] Ine 55, in Liebermann (ed.), *Gesetze*, i, 114.

sheep numbers.[121] In Anglo-Saxon England, too, sheep seem to have been taken for granted, compared with cattle. They are absent from Old English literature, apart from biblical and preaching texts,[122] and there is no sign that supernatural, or much other, significance was attached to them. Their value was placed consistently at a shilling (four or five pence), considerably below that of cows (twenty or twenty-four pence) or oxen (thirty pence), and below pigs (ten pence or eight pence), too. And yet the sheep is an extremely useful and versatile animal. Its unique contribution to human well-being is of course its woolly fleece, which provided the vast majority of Anglo-Saxon textiles (see Chapter 5), but, like other domestic vertebrates, its body provides meat at the end of its life, and, while alive, it supplies food in the form of milk; indeed, it may have been the major dairy animal in Anglo-Saxon England. It is this triple use which must have made it so valuable to the Anglo-Saxons, especially the poorer ones. Those who could not afford to keep large, expensive, and hungry cows would be able to supply the same needs from sheep, which can thrive on much less lush pasture (Chapter 5). This very thriftiness, however, means that the sheep, an animal that any peasant can afford to keep, is rarely a status symbol.

Numbers

Naomi Sykes shows that cattle (*Bos*) bones outnumber those of sheep on a majority of sites throughout the Anglo-Saxon period (see pp. 87–8), but documentary sources frequently mention sheep in larger numbers than cattle. The *Rectitudines* regards six sheep, two oxen, and one cow as the basic requirement for a peasant holding.[123] The reeve Abba left five cows and fifty ewes in his will (835) to Lyminge, and ten cows and a hundred ewes to Folkestone.[124] In Domesday Book and its satellite documents, sheep also outnumber cattle by over ten to one overall. There are clearly problems with these figures (see p. 87), but the huge preponderance of sheep over cattle must bear some relationship to reality.

The counties with Domesday animal data may not be typical of England as a whole, however. There clearly was regional variation, although it is hard to interpret: zooarchaeological evidence from West Stow (Suffolk) shows that sheep were more common there in the early Anglo-Saxon period than on most sites in England,[125] and East Anglia was also sheep country in the later Middle Ages. In the late Anglo-Saxon period, however, Sykes shows that sheep were more common in the south and west of England than in the east and north.[126] At Eynsham in Oxfordshire, sheep were more common than cattle throughout the

---

[121] See Hill, *Dry Grain Farming Families*, 154–5, 164–5.
[122] For preaching, see DiNapoli, *An Index*, 58 and 79.
[123] *Rectitudines* 4.8, in Liebermann (ed.), *Gesetze*, i, 447.
[124] S 1482; Harmer (ed.), *Historical Documents*, 3–5 (no. 2), at 3.
[125] O'Connor, 'Animal husbandry', 367. This is not true of all East Anglian sites, however.
[126] *The Norman Conquest*, 29.

period.[127] Sykes suggests that areas settled by Scandinavians were slower to move to a regime with more sheep than the rest of England. Increasing numbers of sheep may be associated with the growing wool trade (see the next chapter), and this could mean that there really were more sheep in 1086 than before the Conquest.

One reason for larger numbers of sheep than cattle is of course their smaller size:[128] more sheep than cattle will be needed to provide a given weight of meat.[129] This also makes them more economical to 'run'. Someone who did not have enough pasture or feed for a cow or ox might easily manage a couple of sheep. Sheep are 'thriftier': at the present day, upland areas of Britain are often dismissed as 'only fit for sheep', but these despised animals have kept the populations of those areas in food and clothing for centuries, where cattle might have starved. These are also areas with little level land suitable for ploughing. In our period they are much more likely to have been cultivated with the ard, or even spades, than the heavy plough with its large team of oxen, and so fewer cattle would be needed for traction (see Chapters 3, 5, and 12).

Appearance

One of the consequences of domestication in sheep has been an almost complete replacement of their natural variegated colour pattern (still seen in the 'primitive' Soay from St Kilda) with a uniformly white skin and fleece.[130] Humans have generally preferred white sheep to black, or any other colour, no doubt because of their attractive fleece, and its amenability to dyeing. In Ireland, a greater value was attached to white than to coloured sheep, but black and brown ones were more common.[131] There is no such evidence for differential valuation in England, suggesting that white fleeces were not in short supply, and Anglo-Saxon illustrations show white sheep (see Plate 5 and Figs 4.3 and 4.4). Ryder proposed that the Herdwick, with its greyish fleece, was a Scandinavian introduction of the late Anglo-Saxon period,[132] but elsewhere there may have been more white sheep.

Most Anglo-Saxon sheep probably had horns. Hornless (polled) sheep are rare in the wild, and Ryder believes this remained the case in domestic stocks until the later Middle Ages.[133] A study of the evidence for polling in later medieval sheep suggested two types, one in which both sexes were horned, the other with polled ewes. However, a type in which some ewes were horned, some

---

[127] Ayres et al., 'Mammal, bird and fish remains', 344–6, tables 10.1 and 2, and 363, table 10.16.
[128] O'Connor calls sheep the 'small change' of Anglo-Saxon farming: 'Animal husbandry', 367.
[129] There could be ten times as much meat on a cattle carcass as a sheep: Sykes, 'From *cu* and *sceap*', 57.
[130] Ryder, *Sheep & Man*, 16–17.
[131] Kelly, *Early Irish Farming*, 70.
[132] Ryder, *Sheep & Man*, 192–3. Current work on DNA will shed more light on when various types of sheep arrived in the British Isles.
[133] Ryder, *Sheep & Man*, 37–8.

Fig. 4.3. May: tending sheep, British Library, Cotton Julius A. vi, fo. 5r.

(© The British Library Board, Cotton Julius A. vi)

Fig. 4.4. Sheep from the Old English Hexateuch, British Library, Cotton Claudius B. iv, fo. 49r.

(© The British Library Board, Cotton Claudius B. iv)

polled, such as the modern Soay, would also account for the evidence.[134] A (probably) polled ewe is shown being suckled in the calendars (see Fig. 4.3), but most sheep in Anglo-Saxon art are horned, and archaeological work also shows that, at least at some sites, both sexes were horned.[135] At two sites in York, there were sheep with two pairs of horns, a feature now confined to 'primitive' breeds; York as a whole showed a variety of horn sizes and shapes, suggesting several types of sheep.[136]

[134] Armitage and Goodall, 'Medieval horned and polled sheep'.

[135] This was the case at mid-Anglo-Saxon James Street in London: Armitage, 'The animal bone', 32. See also Ryder, *Sheep & Man*, 186–7.

[136] O'Connor, 'Animal bones from Anglo-Scandinavian York', 433.

Early medieval sheep were smaller overall than modern ones: a shoulder height of 56 cm is considered typical for Anglo-Saxon England,[137] and their size declined during the period.[138] Terry O'Connor has shown that 'improvement' of sheep results in reduced size, but increased robustness (that is to say, the diameter of long bones becomes greater in proportion to their length), and Naomi Sykes shows robustness increasing throughout the Anglo-Saxon period, from a level equivalent to present-day Orkney sheep, through 'Hebridean' figures, to something comparable to the modern Shetland breed.[139] Thus Anglo-Saxon sheep would look more slender than modern ones, but stockier than the most 'primitive' breeds known today. Robustness, however, is probably not what Anglo-Saxon sheep breeders were aiming at: greater milk yield and an increased quantity and quality of fleece are more likely (see the next chapter). Anglo-Saxon sheep probably looked increasingly woolly as the period progressed, although less so than modern breeds. Wethers (castrated males) usually grow bigger and produce more wool than ewes, but the very large assemblage from Flixborough revealed no sexual dimorphism.[140] The size ranges of Anglo-Saxon ewes and wethers must have overlapped too much to be differentiated in the statistics.

GOATS

The goat (*Capra hircus*) was undoubtedly much less numerous in England throughout the Middle Ages than the sheep, or indeed cattle or pigs. Just how many there were in relation to sheep (or indeed in absolute numbers) is, however, hard to establish, due to the notorious difficulty of sorting the sheep from the goats in zooarchaeological assemblages.[141] The two animals are very similar in appearance, and most of their bones are much the same shape. Only a few skeletal elements can be distinguished readily, in particular the skull,[142] which is not often found in food-waste deposits. The horns are distinct (see Figs 4.4 and 4.5), but these are usually found separately, due to their industrial uses.[143] However, studies of distinctive elements, supported by the historical evidence, show that sheep were much more common than goats, and thus the designation of most

---

[137] O'Connor, 'Animal husbandry', 367. The range at West Stow, Eynsham, and Yarnton was 58–68 cm, suggesting rather larger animals at these sites; The eleventh-century specimens at Eynsham were all over 58 cm, but only three were involved: Ayres et al., 'Mammal, bird and fish remains', 351 and 371. See also Dobney, Jaques, Johnstone, Hall, la Ferla, and Haynes, 'The agricultural economy', 172, Fig. 7.51.

[138] Sykes, *The Norman Conquest*, 52, Fig. 50; O'Connor found a decline only in the second half of the period: 'Animal husbandry', 367.

[139] Sykes, *The Norman Conquest*, 53, Fig. 51, and see also 54 and 63, Fig. 52, for a study of a much smaller number of frontal bones that supported these findings.

[140] Dobney, Jaques, Johnstone, Hall, la Ferla, and Haynes, 'The agricultural economy', 166–71.

[141] See O'Connor, 'Animal husbandry', 364.

[142] Mason, 'Goat', 85–6, and diagram; Ryder, *Sheep & Man*, 6, Fig. 1.1 (d) and (e).

[143] O'Connor, *Bone Assemblages*, 114–15.

Fig. 4.5. Goats from the Old English Hexateuch, British Library, Cotton Claudius B. iv, fo. 49r.

(© The British Library Board, Cotton Claudius B. iv)

'sheep/goat' bones as 'probably sheep' is unlikely to result in a major distortion of the true picture. In those counties where Domesday Book or its satellites list livestock numbers, even partially, sheep outnumber goats by between 6.9 and 91.2 to one.[144] Clearly no precise significance should be attached to these numbers, but the overall picture of substantially more sheep than goats seems reliable. The impression that numbers varied considerably from place to place, although probably an artefact of uneven recording, is no doubt correct, too. Although zooarchaeological remains are relatively widespread, they do not show even coverage across the country, or similar abundance at all locations.[145]

Goats are browsers rather than grazers, eating material too tough or sparse for sheep or cattle,[146] and they cope with rocky terrain that other animals avoid.[147] They were probably kept where conditions for one reason or another did not allow other livestock to thrive.[148] Christopher Dyer's survey of place-names shows that goats were often associated with 'inaccessible and inhospitable' locations, rough grazing, and woods, while names mentioning them are less common in the central lowlands.[149] Their enterprising attitude to human attempts to confine or control them also makes goats more suitable for open range than small areas of pasture close to houses and gardens.[150] Only small

---

[144] Dyer, 'Goats', 25, table 1, drawing on figures from Darby, *Domesday England*, 164.

[145] Summarized by Dyer, 'Goats', 21.

[146] Mackenzie, *Goat Husbandry*, 22–3.

[147] Mason, 'Goat', 86.

[148] At Yarnton, Oxfordshire, the positive identification of goat bones was taken as an indication of the presence of scrub: Hey, *Yarnton*, 43.

[149] Dyer, 'Goats', 22–3.

[150] Mackenzie has a whole chapter on 'The control of goats' (*Goat Husbandry*, 99–118).

numbers could be tethered to prevent damage to crops or buildings, and would still need some human supervision.

Goats do not appear frequently in Anglo-Saxon documents. Forty-seven feature in the Ely Farming Memoranda's list of livestock from Hatfield,[151] and a charter of Ceolwulf of Mercia in 822 mentions them among livestock that might be pastured in the Weald of Kent.[152] The *Dunsæte* regulations for Anglo-Welsh border relations give a standard value for a goat, 'II p' (half the value of a sheep), at the end of the list.[153] The *buccan* mentioned in the provisions for a funeral feast at Bury St Edmunds were probably goats, too.[154] Goats appear more frequently in charter boundary clauses[155] and place names, showing that they were more familiar than the documents' reticence suggests, but they were probably never common. Dyer shows that goat numbers fell from 1066 onwards,[156] and this may not have been a new trend: already in the Anglo-Saxon period, they may have been increasingly concentrated in localities unsuitable for other livestock.

Appearance

The 'Old English' goat, despite the name, is not an Anglo-Saxon breed. Being derived from feral animals,[157] it is relatively free from the effects of modern breed selection, but it is unlikely that Anglo-Saxon goats resembled it particularly. Another old breed, the Bagot goat, isolated possibly since the fourteenth century,[158] is a small animal, probably similar in size to medieval goats, and possibly in its black-and-white colouring, too.[159] Anglo-Saxon goats were probably left to organize their own breeding, so may have varied a good deal in appearance. Like other livestock they would have been small by modern standards.

PIGS

'I'm bigger and fatter than a mast-fed pig, a grunting boar, a dark rooting creature that lived pleasantly in the beech-wood.'[160]

The Anglo-Saxon period has been described as 'the heyday of swine husbandry' in England.[161] Pigs, or at least boars, clearly featured in the imaginative

---

[151] Robertson (ed. and tr.), *Anglo-Saxon Charters*, 256.
[152] S 186; Kemble, *Codex diplomaticus*, i, 272–3 (no. 216).
[153] *Dunsæte* 7, in Liebermann (ed.), *Gesetze*, i, 378.
[154] Robertson (ed. and tr.), *Anglo-Saxon Charters*, 252 (Appendix 2, no. 8).
[155] Dyer, 'Goats', 24.
[156] Dyer, 'Goats', 26–7.
[157] Alderson, *A Chance to Survive*, 45.
[158] Alderson, *A Chance to Survive*, 53 and 118–19.
[159] It most closely resembles the Valais breed from Switzerland, and may possibly derive from that area: Sambraus, *A Colour Atlas of Livestock Breeds*, 118.
[160] Exeter Book Riddle 40, in Krapp and Dobbie (eds), *Exeter Book*, 203; my translation.
[161] Albarella, 'Pig husbandry', 73.

Fig. 4.6. September: hunting and pigs at mast, British Library, Cotton Julius A. vi, fo. 7r.
(© The British Library Board, Cotton Julius A. vi)

life of the Anglo-Saxons: depictions of them on, for instance, the shoulder clasps from the Sutton Hoo (Suffolk) royal burial (mound 1) and the Benty Grange helmet from Derbyshire (both of the seventh century), associate them firmly with aristocratic warriors, no doubt on account of their fierceness.[162] Pigs were high-status animals in the early Middle Ages, found in greater numbers on 'elite' Anglo-Saxon sites than elsewhere.[163] Giving no 'secondary products' (other than offspring) during their lifetime, pigs are a long-term investment, recouped only after slaughter.[164] Even 'rangy' medieval pigs provided protein associated with more fat, and therefore with more calories, than any other domestic mammal.[165] Huge herds, exploiting the fecundity of pigs, as well as their dietary versatility, were kept by aristocratic landowners in the large tracts of woodland over which they had rights (see the next chapter). This must have been mainly a commercial operation, not for home consumption, although the storage potential of preserved pig products means that they could be consumed over a long period. They might also be used for large-scale ceremonial feasting, as most famously in Papua New Guinea,[166] but descriptions of Anglo-Saxon feasts never tell us which species were eaten.[167] All this is clearly well outside the capacity of a peasant farmer, but less exalted Anglo-Saxons did nevertheless keep pigs: the *geneat* in the *Rectitudines* (equivalent to the Domesday *uillanus*) paid one every year for pasture rights, his *gærsswyn*.[168] The humbler *gebur*, on the other hand, paid for his grass in ploughing.[169]

---

[162] See Pluskowski, 'The archaeology of paganism', 770 and, for illustrations, Webster and Backhouse, *The Making of England*, nos 14 and 46.

[163] Sykes, *The Norman Conquest*, 42, where she also summarizes the debate about their status. See further Dobney, Jaques, Barrett, and Johnstone, 'Zooarchaeological evidence', 222 and 238–40.

[164] Ervynck, et al., 'The transition from forest dwelling pigs to farm animals', 173.

[165] Grigson, 'Culture, ecology and pigs', 99.

[166] See, among a large literature, Sillitoe, 'Pigs in the New Guinea Highlands'.

[167] See Magennis, *Anglo-Saxon Appetites*, for discussion.

[168] *Rectitudines* 2, in Liebermann (ed.), *Gesetze*, i, 445.

[169] *Rectitudines* 4.1b, in Liebermann (ed.), *Gesetze*, i, 446.

The value of a pig in various Anglo-Saxon sources placed it between cattle (twenty to thirty pence) and sheep (a shilling), as befits the relative sizes of these animals. A pig (presumably fully grown) was worth a maximum of 10d in Æthelstan VI, and 8d in the *Dunsæte* regulations.[170] In a fragmentary will from Bury St Edmunds, a pig is worth seventeen pence.[171] This animal would already have been fattened for the table: a herd of eighty pigs in the Ely Farming Memoranda was only worth a pound and a half, 4½d each, presumably for animals of all ages, and another herd of thirty was valued at 6d (each, presumably).[172] The average pig in the larger herd, whose value was by no means certain of being realized either in money or in food, was the only one worth less than a sheep (at five pence to the shilling).

Numbers

Pigs were domesticated in Europe from the local population of wild boar,[173] which were still present in Britain in the early Middle Ages.[174] This means that pig bones found on Anglo-Saxon sites could in theory be either wild or domestic, but, as with most species, domestic pigs are smaller,[175] and the large numbers found are much more typical of domestic than wild species. There is no clear trend in pig numbers within the Anglo-Saxon period: they are consistently higher than in the later Middle Ages,[176] although lower than sheep/goat numbers,[177] and therefore lower than cattle as well (see pp. 87–8). This despite the huge numbers in Anglo-Saxon wills, for instance the two thousand left by the ninth-century *dux* (ealdorman) Ælfred.[178] In Domesday Book, on the other hand, pig numbers are consistently much lower than sheep (but higher than goats and cattle).[179] These figures may exclude the large herds 'at mast' in the woods (see the next chapter), clearly still a flourishing operation at the time of Domesday,[180] but numbers are higher in Essex than in neighbouring Norfolk and Suffolk, possibly reflecting the greater area of wood-pasture in Essex.[181] Wicken Bonhunt in that county produced a mid-Anglo-Saxon zooarchaeological

---

[170] Liebermann (ed.), *Gesetze*, i, 176 and 378.

[171] Robertson (ed. and tr.), *Anglo-Saxon Charters*, 252 (Appendix 2, no. 8).

[172] Robertson (ed. and tr.), *Anglo-Saxon Charters*, 252–6 (Appendix 2, no. 9).

[173] Larson et al., 'Current views on *Sus* phylogeography', esp. 35 and Fig. 2.1.

[174] Alabarella, 'The wild boar', 63.

[175] See Dobney, Ervynck, Albarella, and Rowley-Conwy, 'The transition from wild boar to domestic pig'; Grigson, 'Culture, ecology and pigs', 83–4; and Rowley-Conwy and Dobney, 'Wild boar and domestic pigs', esp. discussion at 141.

[176] Albarella, 'Pig husbandry', 74 and table 6.1.

[177] Albarella, 'Pig husbandry', 76 and Fig. 6.1.

[178] S 1508; Harmer (ed.), *Historical Documents*, 13–15 (no. 10), at 15.

[179] Darby, *Domesday England*, table on 164.

[180] Indeed, most of the evidence for Anglo-Saxon pannage comes from Domesday Book: Darby, *Domesday England*, 172–5 and Fig. 60.

[181] Albarella, 'Pig husbandry', 81.

record dominated by pig bones, something quite anomalous among Anglo-Saxon bone assemblages generally, so Essex may have specialized in pig-rearing at that time.[182] Pigs also seem to have been more common south of the Humber than in the north.[183] Overall, it seems likely that, apart from the large herds kept (at least for part of the year) on wood-pasture, smaller numbers of pigs were kept on Anglo-Saxon farms than sheep or cattle.

Appearance

It might be expected that the difference in lifestyle between pigs fending for themselves in the woods and those fed, and inactive, in sties would be reflected in physical differences,[184] but a study of pig bones and teeth from medieval Flanders failed to demonstrate any clear distinction.[185] The zooarchaeological remains from Anglo-Saxon England do not suggest two divergent forms either.[186] The pigs in the calendar pictures, which are feeding in woodland, look small in proportion to the men and dogs alongside them, and certainly lack the magnificent bellies of modern swine. In the Tiberius version, one looks pink, but the others have the ginger colouring of the modern Tamworth (see Fig. 4.6 and Plate 2). Although Tamworths may not be a very old breed, their long snouts and prick ears show that they are relatively free of the influence of Chinese stock introduced in the eighteenth and nineteenth centuries.[187] Tamworths are lean by modern standards, and Anglo-Saxon pigs were probably equally thin, if not more so, as well as small. The size of Anglo-Saxon pigs does not seem to have varied much across the period,[188] the shoulder height of about 75 cm calculated for mid-Anglo-Saxon London sites being fairly typical.[189]

POULTRY

'Often the broody hen, even though she clucks painfully, she spreads
her feathers and warms up the chicks.'[190]

---

[182] For Wicken Bonhunt, see Crabtree, 'Production and consumption', and for a comparison with other sites, O'Connor, 'Animal husbandry', esp. table 20.1.

[183] O'Connor, 'Animal husbandry', 366–7.

[184] Clutton-Brock, *Natural History*, 96–7.

[185] Ervynck et al., 'The transition from forest dwelling pigs to farm animals'.

[186] Sykes, *The Norman Conquest*, 54–5, Figs 53 and 54.

[187] Epstein and Bichard, 'Pig', 152; Grove, 'Current views on taxonomy', 24; Anderson, 'Phenotypic changes during pig domestication', 50.

[188] O'Connor notes only one clear trend in stature across the period, in sheep: 'Animal husbandry', 367. Sykes did find some reduction in size, but attributed this to the decline of wild boar: *The Norman Conquest*, 45.

[189] Armitage, 'The animal bone', 31, table 5.

[190] 'Oft seo brodige henn, þeah heo sarlice cloccige, heo tospræt hyre fyðera and þa briddas gewyrmð': Byrhtferth, *Enchiridion* II.1, lines 225–7, in Baker and Lapidge (eds), *Byrhtferth's Enchiridion*, 68. Byrhtferth may have been thinking of Matthew 23:37, 'quemadmodum gallina congregat pullos suos sub alas', but the hen's painful clucking and the warmth she offers her chicks are his own additions.

Very little importance seems to have been attached to poultry by the Anglo-Saxons. As Dale Serjeantson points out, this disdain has been shared by the published scholarship,[191] but her recent monograph goes a long way to remedying that situation.[192] Apart from a riddle (see p. 102) and Byrhtferth of Ramsey's vignette above, chickens are absent from Old English literature. Nor do they make frequent appearances in documentary sources. No doubt the Anglo-Saxons took poultry for granted, except when it got under their feet, as their successors continued to do until the industrialization of poultry production.

But this does not mean there were no changes in English poultry in all that time. For centuries, chickens, ducks, and geese have been the familiar farmyard poultry in Europe, but it seems unlikely that ducks had been domesticated by the Anglo-Saxon period.[193] Geese and hens appear regularly together in Anglo-Saxon food rents, but ducks are absent.[194] Since domestic ducks are descended from the native mallard (both *Anas platyrhynchos*), it is not possible to distinguish the bones of wild from domesticated birds (apart from the large modern breeds),[195] but at West Stow, although duck is listed with domestic birds in the bone report, it actually appears in the small numbers typical of wild species rather than domesticated ones.[196] This is true at most Anglo-Saxon sites.[197] Naomi Sykes found that, although more common in Anglo-Saxon than in post-Conquest assemblages, duck bones appeared in very small numbers compared with goose or, especially, chicken.[198] It is not until the later Middle Ages that duck bones resembling mallard, but of a larger size, appear in England.[199] Wild mallard (and other native ducks) would of course have been plentiful in Anglo-Saxon England, and possibly attracted to farmyards. They might have been encouraged by Anglo-Saxon humans, intent on eating them or their eggs:[200] ducks are described as 'commensal' (sharing food sources) with humans before domestication,[201] and this was probably the situation in Anglo-Saxon England.

It has been suggested that the importance of poultry (in the general sense) in the Anglo-Saxon diet, and therefore in the farming of the period, has been

---

[191] Serjeantson, *Birds*, 267 and 285–6; see also Sayer, 'Eggs, an underesearched topic', and cf. O'Connor 'Animal husbandry'.

[192] Serjeantson, *Birds*, especially chapters 11 and 12.

[193] See Clayton, 'Common duck', 336, and Harper, 'Tardy domestication.'

[194] For instance in grants by Ealdorman Oswulf (?806) and Lufu (843 × 863) (S 1188 and S 1197) to Christ Church, Canterbury, Harmer (ed.), *Historical Documents*, 1–2 (no. 1), at 1, and 7–8 (no. 4), at 7, respectively.

[195] Serjeantson, *Birds*, 301.

[196] Crabtree, *West Stow*. It also appears much less in Irish texts than chickens or geese; see Kelly, *Early Irish Farming*, 107.

[197] Ayres et al., 'Mammal, bird and fish bones', 356.

[198] Sykes, *The Norman Conquest*, 28.

[199] Serjeantson, *Birds*, 301.

[200] Mallard have a higher nutritional value, attributable to their high percentage of fat, than either goose or chicken: Serjeantson, *Birds*, table 10.2.

[201] Serjeantson, *Birds*, 300; for a definition of commensality see O'Connor, 'Making themselves at home', 271–2.

underestimated,[202] but Naomi Sykes shows that poultry bones from archaeo-logical sites remain in small numbers, compared with post-Conquest finds, throughout the Anglo-Saxon period.[203] This means a lower level of consumption of poultry as meat during the Anglo-Saxon period than later in the Middle Ages, but their eggs may have been more significant (see the next chapter).

Unlike geese and ducks, whose wild ancestors are native to the British Isles, domestic fowl or chickens (*Gallus gallus*) are descended from Asiatic jungle fowl,[204] and must therefore have been introduced to Britain by humans. It is thought that in most parts of the world they were first kept for fighting, their use as food being adopted with various degrees of rapidity thereafter.[205] The Romans are credited with popularizing domestic fowl in western Europe,[206] and in lowland Britain chicken bones become common during the Anglo-Saxon period.[207] Naomi Sykes' data show them making up a greater percentage of the total poultry bones in the later than in the early to middle part of the period,[208] indicating a rise in their numbers. At Flixborough, clearly an anomalous site, 'vast quantities' of chicken bone were found in the earliest, seventh-century phase, where chickens alone outnumbered pigs; only in the latest phase, tenth to eleventh centuries, were overall poultry numbers lower than pig.[209]

The Old English runic riddle 'Cock and hen',[210] like Byrhtferth's hen and chicks, shows that chickens were a familiar sight in Anglo-Saxon England. Their ubiquity is confirmed by the obligation on the lowly *gebur* to render two *henfugelas* at Martinmas,[211] and evidence that they were raised in substantial numbers comes from the London trade regulations of Æthelred's reign, where a toll of one hen or five eggs is taken from baskets of (unspecified numbers of) hens or eggs.[212]

Domestic geese are descended from the native greylag goose, *Anser anser*, and indeed the two interbreed at the present day.[213] Greylags breed in captivity,[214] and thus Anglo-Saxons could have taken native geese in from the wild to build up their stocks. Birds may have moved in and out of domestication quite readily, as they did until recently.[215] It is thus hard to distinguish the bones of

[202] Hull and O'Connell, 'Diet', 677.

[203] *The Norman Conquest*, 27–8.

[204] Crawford, 'Domestic fowl', 298–300.

[205] Crawford, 'Domestic fowl', 300.

[206] In Britain there are some remains from the pre-Roman Iron Age: Yalden and Albarella, *History of British Birds*, 101 and table 5.1.

[207] Serjeantson, *Birds*, 272.

[208] *The Norman Conquest*, 28.

[209] Dobney, Jaques, and Johnstone, 'Pastoral strategies', 87, and Jaques et al., 'The nature of the bio-archaeological assemblages', 48, table 4.7.

[210] Exeter Book Riddle 42, in Krapp and Dobbie (eds), *The Exeter Book*, 203–4.

[211] *Rectitudines* 4, in Liebermann (ed.), *Gesetze*, i, 446.

[212] IV Æthelred 2.11, in Liebermann (ed.), *Gesetze*, i, 234.

[213] Serjeantson, *Birds*, 292.

[214] Crawford, 'Goose', 347.

[215] Serjeantson, *Birds*, 292–3.

domesticated from wild birds when they are found in archaeological contexts,[216] but at early Anglo-Saxon West Stow, for instance, their numbers suggest domestic or tame birds rather than wild ones, and this also true on six middle and late Anglo-Saxon sites, where they were ten times as common as ducks.[217] At James Street in London (mid-Anglo-Saxon), the size of a goose sternum was slightly larger than in wild greylags, suggesting selection for greater weight of meat.[218] The bones of the wing and leg became shorter during the Middle Ages, as breeding emphasized weight in the torso, and husbandry kept the animals sedentary.[219] These changes may already have begun in the Anglo-Saxon period, but systematic investigation has yet to be undertaken. At Flixborough, DNA studies of goose humeri successfully distinguished domestic from wild birds, and showed that the majority were domestic.[220] There is no mention of geese in Æthelred's trade regulations (see p. 102), so they may still have been a less common species at this time, in contrast to the vast numbers driven to London in the early modern period.[221] Among poultry recorded in food rents, hens outnumber geese (twice as many in the grants noted on p. 101), but geese, being so much bigger, might still provide more meat.[222]

There is no evidence that domestic doves (*Columba livia*), from which today's feral pigeons descend, were kept in Anglo-Saxon England. Across western Europe, pigeons are rare in zooarchaeology before the eleventh century, and only feature in written records after that.[223] The raising of squabs in dovecotes appears to be a post-Conquest innovation in England, although known to Pliny the Elder in the first century AD.[224] However, the rock dove, now confined in Britain to the Highlands and Islands,[225] may have been more widespread in the Middle Ages,[226] and thus pigeons might have been available to, and even encouraged by, Anglo-Saxons. The large round building at Yarnton (see the next chapter), provisionally identified as a poultry run, was also compared to later dovecotes, but lacked the diagnostic juvenile pigeon bones in its floor deposits.[227]

Appearance

Selection of distinct forms of poultry is unlikely to have advanced very far in early medieval England. Chickens, hardly counted as livestock in the Middle

---

[216] Serjeantson, *Birds*, 295.
[217] Crabtree, *West Stow,* and Albarella, 'Alternate fortunes?'
[218] Armitage, 'The animal bone', 33.
[219] Serjeantson, *Birds*, 296.
[220] Dobney, Jaques, Johnstone, Hall, la Ferla, and Haynes, 'The agricultural economy', 178–80.
[221] Wilson, *Food and Drink*, 130.
[222] Serjeantson, *Birds*, 295.
[223] Serjeantson, *Birds*, 307.
[224] Hawes, 'Pigeons', 354.
[225] Hawes, 'Pigeons', 353.
[226] Dovecotes were restocked from wild colonies in thirteenth-century England: Serjeantson, *Birds*, 305.
[227] Serjeantson, *Birds*, 309.

Ages, were no doubt left to their own devices as far as breeding was concerned. Evidence for selection is rare: at Eynsham, two distinct size ranges of domestic fowl indicate either strong sexual dimorphism or two different types of chicken.[228] The chickens in *The Wonders of the East*, illustrated in Plate 4, are described in the text as 'like ours at home, red in colour',[229] but this was not of course written in England, and they were certainly unlike 'ours at home' in causing serious burns to anyone who touched them. The (Old) English Game Fowl is the closest of the European chicken breeds to the wild ancestor,[230] and thus probably the oldest British breed now in existence.[231] They cannot trace their ancestry to the Anglo-Saxon period, but, bred for fighting,[232] and more recently for show, they preserve traits of wild chickens which have been bred out of other types. Like 'Old English' fowl, Anglo-Saxon chickens were probably lightly built and long-legged compared to the heavy meat and laying breeds of today.

At Flixborough, DNA studies showed that domestic geese belonged to two distinct types, resembling the two main modern breeds.[233] Anglo-Saxon geese may have had white plumage; this is one of the most common features of domestic breeds, presumably because humans find it attractive to look at.[234]

BEES

'Settle down, victory women, sink to the earth,
do not fly wild to the woods,
be as mindful of my goodness
as everyone is of food and home.'[235]

Eva Crane, the authority on honeybees (*Apis mellifera*), regards them as native to the British Isles, although this view is not universally shared.[236] There is, however, no doubt that bees were kept in Anglo-Saxon England: their products were highly valued (see the next chapter). Many Anglo-Saxon crops also depended on bees, although it is unlikely that the role of honeybees in promoting the setting of fruit was understood.[237] Literary sources often describe bees flitting from flower to flower, but it is the honey they collect

---

[228] Ayres et al., 'Mammal, bird and fish bones', 355.

[229] Orchard, *Pride and Prodigies*, 176 and 186; my translation.

[230] Serjeantson, *Birds*, 273.

[231] Hams, *Old Poultry Breeds*, 16–18.

[232] Serjeantson, *Birds*, 326. She found no Anglo-Saxon evidence for cockfights, however (325–31), despite their clear popularity in the Roman period and later Middle Ages.

[233] Dobney, Jaques, Johnstone, Hall, la Ferla, and Haynes, 'The agricultural economy', 90.

[234] Serjeantson, *Birds*, 297.

[235] 'Charm for a swarm of bees', in Dobbie (ed.), *Minor Poems*, 125; my translation.

[236] See Crane, *Archaeology of Beekeeping*, 14–15.

[237] According to Crane, *World History of Beekeeping*, 473–4, the role of bees in pollination was first described in 1750.

(usually as a metaphor for knowledge) that is emphasized, not the effect on the flower.[238]

Actual Anglo-Saxon bees are rarely found in excavation, no doubt due to the fragility of their remains. However, they were a relatively common discovery in the waterlogged deposits of Anglo-Scandinavian York, including two finds at Coppergate dense enough to represent whole hives. At three other sites in York, there were enough bees to suggest hives nearby.[239] Nowhere else has produced the same numbers, but charred fragments of twenty-three bees were found at James Street in London, along with a good deal of other burnt material.[240]

The swarm charm cited at the beginning of this section suggests that bees were well respected in Anglo-Saxon England, but they may not have been valued quite as highly as they were in Ireland. The Anglo-Saxon Chronicle does not list mortalities of bees as the Annals of Ulster do,[241] nor do we have a whole legal text devoted to bees like the seventh-century Irish *Bechbretha*.[242] This might be because, after the conversion, England was in closer touch with the Continent than Ireland, and thus had better access to wine, which to some extent replaced mead, made from honey, at the top of the hierarchy of alcoholic drinks.[243] However, in the eleventh century, the *Rectitudines* still discussed beekeepers in much the same terms as swineherds, showing their importance to the local economy, despite their low status as people. Similarly, honey continues to be mentioned in food rents right up to Domesday Book (see the next chapter).

CONCLUSION

In terms of species, then, Anglo-Saxon livestock consisted of the same animals we are used to seeing today, apart from ducks. But the way some of them were thought of differed very markedly; horses, for instance, were conceived of as individuals, associated firmly with upper-class male warriors, and, most importantly for us, were not used in agriculture and not normally eaten. Cattle (*Bos taurus*) were the most highly valued of the farm animals, and the most favoured for meat. They and sheep were both more numerous than other species, although there is conflicting evidence as to which of them existed in the

---

[238] For instance the *Colloquia difficiliora* of Ælfric Bata, 7 and 11, in Gwara and Porter (eds), *Anglo-Saxon Conversations*, 186 and 188–90, or Aldhelm, *De uirginitate prosa*, iv–vi, in Ehwald (ed.), *Aldhelmi opera*, 231–4. Until *c*.1800, it was believed that bees collected honey ready-made from flowers; see Crane, *World History of Beekeeping*, 564.

[239] Hall and Kenward, 'Setting people in their environment', 397.

[240] Robinson, 'The charred honeybees', 38.

[241] Kelly, *Early Irish Farming*, 214. These are of course mass mortalities; individual insects are not accorded obits.

[242] Kelly, *Early Irish Farming*, 108.

[243] See Kelly, *Early Irish Farming*, 113, for the status of mead in Ireland. For wine in England see Banham, *Food and Drink*, 48–9.

greater numbers. The number of assemblages dominated by cattle bones increases during our period, indicating a growing taste for beef, and probably a growing number of plough oxen, too. But in some parts of the country, there is also a move to a regime involving more sheep, probably associated with growth in the wool trade. During the period sheep also grow more 'robust', more like modern than 'primitive' breeds. Evidence for different types shows that effort had been invested in selecting both cattle and sheep. Pigs were in third place numerically overall, but enormous herds were kept in some places. Goats were a minority species, only kept in certain areas. Poultry numbers are impossible to quantify: written documents rarely mention them, and bird bones are almost certainly underrepresented in the material record. But chickens were certainly more numerous than geese. Bees are probably the species whose status has changed the most: far from being a minority hobby, as at the present day, the frequent occurrence of honey in food rents shows that bee-keeping played an important role in the culture and economy of Anglo-Saxon England.

Dogs and cats have not been mentioned, because they were not producers of food and other useful materials, but they were certainly kept by the Anglo-Saxons.[244] Their importance in food production should not be overlooked; both played vital roles in protecting crops and livestock from theft and predation. Thus cats really belong to the previous chapter, and dogs to the next one, which discusses the management of livestock.

[244] Domestic cats were present in Roman Britain, and probably slightly earlier: Kitchener and O'Connor, 'Wildcats, domestic and feral cats', 92. Remains of both species are found in small numbers on Anglo-Saxon sites, for instance at Eynsham in Oxfordshire, where gnawing of animal bones also suggested both animals were present: Ayres et al., 'Mammal, bird and fish remains', 354 and 401. At Flixborough, a possible dog coprolite was identified, as well as gnawed bones, and there were cat bones: Jaques et al., 'The nature of the bioarchaeological assemblages', 45, table 4.5, and 51. At York, there was evidence for different sizes of dog, and some were given individual burials, in contrast to the cats: O'Connor, 'Animal bones from Anglo-Scandinavian York', 439–40.

5

Animal husbandry in Anglo-Saxon England

II: Livestock products and production

Here we look at the ways animals were managed—housing, feeding, herding—and the products for which they were raised, a major factor in deciding how they were kept. For instance, if animals are to be milked, they have to be kept near where people live or, if they are to be sent to distant pastures, people have to go with them. If they are kept primarily for milk, there will be 'surplus' male animals, which may be culled at a young age; if meat is the main aim, they may be raised to full size, but not allowed to grow old and tough. Male animals are larger and stronger, better for traction, meat, or wool production, but only a few are needed for breeding.

WHAT ANIMALS DID FOR PEOPLE

At the present day, the main reason for keeping almost any farm animal is to eat its flesh. But meat, in most societies, is a luxury, and livestock can offer many other goods and services. An animal carcass provides many products apart from meat (see Chapter 4), but, perhaps more importantly, living animals are even more productive, and in some cases for many years.[1] It would be profligate to raise animals purely for slaughter without first allowing them to provide, variously, milk and dairy products, eggs, or wool. Recent isotope studies show that there was more protein in the Anglo-Saxon diet than the excavated animal bones would account for: the gap must have been filled largely by 'secondary products', such as eggs and, in various forms, milk.[2] A transition from husbandry aimed primarily at these 'secondary products' to one concerned chiefly with meat production has been located at the end of the Middle Ages in England, using age-at-death data from archaeological animal bones.[3] The only

---

[1] See Rixson, *History of Meat Trading*, 13–20, for post-mortem non-meat products; also Dobney, Jaques, Johnstone, Hall, la Ferla, and Haynes, 'The agricultural economy', 117.

[2] See Hull and O'Connell, 'Diet: recent evidence', esp. 677.

[3] Albarella, 'Size, power, wool and veal', esp. 27–8 and table on 27.

animal unaffected by this change was the pig, but even pigs, with no 'secondary products', will produce many litters in a lifetime if they survive.[4] In addition to these physical products, livestock provide pulling power, both for transport and, more important on a farm, for tillage. Before agricultural machinery became widespread, arable as well as pastoral farming was, as we have seen in Chapter 2, dependent on animals.

Traction

In the previous chapter, we saw that neither horses nor other equids were important traction animals in Anglo-Saxon England. On Anglo-Saxon farms, both ploughs and carts were pulled by oxen (and probably also by cows).[5] Though slow compared with horses, cattle are big, hefty animals, well endowed with both strength and stamina. An Old English riddle from the Exeter Book (*c.* AD 1000) shows how closely cattle and ploughing (as well as leather and milk) were identified in the Anglo-Saxon mind:

> 'I journey on feet, I pierce the earth,
> green fields, while I'm carrying my spirit.
> If I lose my life, I tie firmly
> dark slaves, sometimes better people.
> Sometimes I give a precious drink
> to a man from my bosom…Say what I'm called,
> I who plunder the land in life
> and after death serve humanity.'[6]

This is the most basic level of human experience: the ox will confine you if you lose your freedom, or it will stop you dying of hunger. 'Mortalities of cattle' are reported in the Anglo-Saxon Chronicle alongside such nationally important events as battles and royal succession,[7] not just because cattle were valuable, or people got fond of old Daisy, but because without cattle, people would be unable to plough, and would have no bread the following year. The death of cattle meant that people would die, too.

All Anglo-Saxon illustrations of ploughing show oxen (see Chapter 3), and the status of the ox as the normal traction animal is confirmed by their appearance

---

[4] Pigs may be a prestige animal in a subsistence economy precisely because they are raised purely for meat; see the previous chapter.

[5] Ethnographic studies show that the role of draught cows has been underestimated, especially in small-scale agriculture: Isaakidou, 'Ploughing with cows'.

[6] Riddle 12, in Krapp and Dobbie (eds), *The Exeter Book*, 186; see also Riddle 38, quoted in Chapter 4, p. 84.

[7] ASC *s. aa.* 89(5–)7 (A): 'great pestilence among cattle and men'; 986 (C, E): 'the great pestilence among cattle first came to England' and presumably lasted some time; 1042 (E): 'more cattle died than anyone remembered before, both through various diseases and through bad weather'; 1046 (C): 'no man alive … could remember so severe a winter as that was, both through the mortality of men and mortality of cattle', in Bately (ed.), *ASC MS A*, O'Brien O'Keeffe (ed.), *MS C*, and Irvine (ed.), *MS E*.

Fig. 5.1. Oxen pulling carts (partly redrawn) from the Old English Hexateuch, British Library, Cotton Claudius B. iv, fo. 67r.

(© The British Library Board, Cotton Claudius B. iv)

pulling carts, in both calendar pictures (Fig. 2.1) and the Old English Hexateuch (Fig. 5.1). Anglo-Saxon carting would be on unmade tracks, or across open country, so the same qualities (strength and sure-footedness) would be needed for pulling both carts and ploughs. The contribution of cattle to manuring (see Chapter 3) might not be confined to their dung, either: a pair of oxen can pull about 250 kilos, eight times as much as a woman can carry on her back.[8]

Assembling and maintaining a plough-team was a major undertaking for most farmers, not only because of the size of oxen and the expense of feeding them, but also because they take a long time to reach maturity, and to train.[9] In Welsh law, an ox was assumed to start work in its third year, when it would be fully grown, although training might continue for longer.[10] Practical experience shows that, to work yoked together, oxen have to be trained in pairs, getting used to their partner and to their own side of the yoke,[11] and all Anglo-Saxon illustrations show oxen in pairs (see Chapter 3). The 'Welsh Laws of Hywel Dda', probably preserving material going back to the tenth century, regard an ox that can work without its usual partner as particularly valuable.[12]

Oxen would work a relatively short day, possibly in two shifts, with time to chew the cud between (see Chapters 3 and 4). Though they are slow compared with horses, the amount they achieved in a lifetime would still repay the effort of training them. The zooarchaeological record shows that most Anglo-Saxon

---

[8] Figures from ethnographic studies of places (in Spain and Nepal) where cattle and women haul manure at the present day: Bogaard, 'Middening and manuring', 33.

[9] Irish sources specify that it is a trained ox that attracts a high value (Kelly, *Early Irish Farming*, 48), and this must have been important in England, too. See Grocock, ' "To eat, to wear, to work" ', 81–5, for training oxen at Bede's World.

[10] Kelly, *Early Irish Farming*, 48; Watts, *Working Oxen*, 3.

[11] Watts, *Working Oxen*, 17.

[12] Jenkins, *The Law of Hywel Dda*, 176–7.

cattle lived at least to skeletal maturity at about four years of age, and some till seven, eight, or even older.[13] In the case of oxen, this would suggest a working life of some four years. At James Street in London, 47 per cent of the mid-Anglo-Saxon cattle whose age could be determined were four years old or more, including three oxen over seven years old, clearly veterans of the field.[14] Even if beasts were killed younger, they could already have completed one or more seasons' ploughing, but it is doubtful whether such a short working life would justify their training.

Dairying

In Anglo-Saxon England, cows, goats, and ewes were all milked. Goats were the least important dairy animal, simply because they were much less numerous than the other two (see the previous chapter), so most of the following discussion is concerned with cows and ewes.

Of the three, the dairy cow has a much greater yield. This was recognized in medieval Ireland, where a season's milk from a cow was worth 18d, that of a goat 1⅓d, and a ewe's only a farthing or ⅓d.[15] If this was based solely on yield (more likely than nutritional value; see p. 111), an early Irish cow gave over thirteen times as much milk as a goat, and fifty-four to seventy-two times as much as a ewe. Goats are traditionally supposed to yield a quart a day, ewes a pint. Modern figures are hard to come by for 'unimproved' cattle breeds, which are now rarely milked, but approximately 600, 200, and 60 gallons per lactation may not be too far out for cow, goat, and sheep respectively, so a cow may yield ten times as much as ewe, a goat four times.[16]

The specialist workers listed in the *Rectitudines* include a *kuhyrde*, whose perquisites are in milk (or rather, colostrum, immediately after calving).[17] He and the ox-herd both keep their *metecu* ('food cow') with the lord's herd, and the *esne* (male slave) receives a *metecu* as part of his annual subsistence. Thurketil of Palgrave ensured in his will (?before 1038) that each of his 'men' should have a *metecu*, too.[18] These cows were probably destined eventually to become meat in the modern sense, but at the end of a productive life as a dairy animal, as suggested by the age-at-death figures cited above. Thus people quite low on the social scale had access to cow's milk. Naomi Sykes's survey of animal bones shows a higher proportion of females in later Anglo-Saxon cattle populations

---

[13] O'Connor, 'Animal husbandry', 368–9.

[14] Armitage, 'The animal bone', 30–1.

[15] Kelly, *Early Irish Farming*, 52.

[16] These figures, calculated from various publications and websites, none of verifiable reliability, and all working in different measurements, should be regarded as no more than very broad approximations.

[17] *Rectitudines* 13, in Liebermann (ed.), *Gesetze*, i, 450.

[18] S 1527; Whitelock (ed.), *Anglo-Saxon Wills*, 68 (no. 24).

than earlier in the period, suggesting increasing access to cows' milk.[19] Her figures also indicate a decline in the culling of young animals (six to twelve months, both cattle and sheep/goat) around the Conquest, suggesting a greater emphasis on dairying in the Anglo-Saxon period than later.[20]

There is a clear connection between cattle and dairying in the associations of the Old English feminine noun *dæge* (Latinized to *daia*). Etymologically, this means 'kneader' (*hlæfdige*, 'lady', is literally 'kneader of bread'), but in Domesday Book these women are associated with *bouarii* or *uaccarii*, who take care of cattle.[21] The word later gave rise to 'dairy', the work of a *dæge* or the building where she does it. Perhaps dairying was becoming more complex in the later Anglo-Saxon period, and thus the preserve of a relatively small number of skilled women, while bread-making became more generalized. Skilled dairy-workers may have been particularly associated with cow-dairying as it became more important in the eleventh century.

Cow's milk is much lower in solid matter, both protein and fat, than sheep's (goat's milk is even lower).[22] But the fat in cow's milk is in larger globules than either goat's or ewe's,[23] so that, when the milk is left to stand, the cream rises easily to the surface. In the other species, it remains mainly dispersed in the milk. This makes cow's milk the best to make butter from: butter is made first, and then cheese from the skimmed milk. Sheep's milk on the other hand makes better cheese, both because it is richer in milk solids, and because they remain suspended. More cheese can thus be made from a given quantity of milk: 1 kilo from 4 litres, compared with a kilo from 9 or 10 litres for cow or goat.[24]

Despite the advantages of cows as a milking animal, ewes were clearly important in Anglo-Saxon dairying. Ælfric's shepherd has to milk his charges twice a day, and make cheese and butter.[25] The *Rectitudines*' shepherd receives milk as part of his fairly meagre customary dues (like the cow- and goatherds),[26] but it is the description of the *cyswyrhte* and her work which makes it clear that cows were not the main dairy animal on this estate. The 'cheese-wright' is described as making cheese first, and then butter for her lord's table from the whey.[27] This would be the wrong way round for cow's milk.[28] However, where sheep's butter has been made traditionally, as in Greece, this is precisely the

---

[19] Sykes, *The Norman Conquest*, 52, Fig. 49. Only two sites (North Elmham and Southampton) are involved here, but in different parts of the country, and probably different types of settlement.

[20] Sykes, *The Norman Conquest*, 35, table 9, and 38.

[21] See Pelteret, *Slavery*, 268–9.

[22] Figures from Thear, *Home and Farm Dairying*, 24, based on modern animals.

[23] Mackenzie, *Goat Husbandry*, 70–1.

[24] Thear, *Smallholder's Manual*, 190.

[25] Garmonsway (ed.), *Ælfric's Colloquy*, 22.

[26] *Rectitudines* 14, in Liebermann (ed.), *Gesetze*, i, 451.

[27] *Rectitudines* 16, in Liebermann (ed.), *Gesetze*, i, 451.

[28] Whey butter is made from cows' milk where there is a market for whole-milk cheese: see de Moor, 'Farmhouse Gouda', 108 and note 6; also <http://www.denhay.co.uk/west-country-farmhouse-cheddar> (consulted 16 August 2012).

procedure.[29] More butterfat is left in the whey than in that of cows or goats, but most of it has already gone into the cheese, so much less butter is produced than from cow's milk. This would explain why the *Rectitudines* butter is for the lord's table, and not used in his kitchen, for instance, and also why the woman who makes it is called *cyswyrhte*, after what is no doubt her main product. The name may distinguish her from a *dæge*, by now associated with cows, and perhaps with a more sophisticated set of techniques.

Most Anglo-Saxon sheep lived to adulthood, if not to old age;[30] husbandry was not driven by the butchery trade. Urban and 'high-status' sites normally received sheep that had already provided a substantial clip of wool or yield of milk, while young animals are mainly found at rural 'producer' sites.[31] At Eynsham in the eleventh century, a substantial cohort of lambs were culled at or before the end of their first summer, suggesting a specialist milking flock,[32] and the female animals (both ewes and cows) left by the reeve Abba in 835 must also have been intended for milking.[33] Anglo-Saxon sites generally do not, however, show a cull of very young lambs, making it unlikely that specialist milking flocks were common.[34] Even allowing for the systematic under-representation of bones of the smallest animals, this confirms the impression that most Anglo-Saxon sheep farming was 'general-purpose', not aimed at one main product. Most ewe's milk came from flocks that produced wool and meat as well, but a large flock might still produce a considerable quantity of milk in high season (May and June).

Dairy sheep may have outnumbered cows by a considerable ratio, although this no doubt varied from place to place. Domesday figures show a considerably preponderance of sheep over cattle (see Chapter 4). Abba left five cows and fifty ewes to Lyminge, and ten cows and a hundred ewes (among other livestock) to Folkestone;[35] the ten-to-one ratio may relate to their milk yield (see p. 110). Thus more sheep than cows would not necessarily mean that more sheep products were consumed. More work would be needed to produce the same amount of milk from ewes than from cows, certainly in terms of the milking itself, and probably in feeding and care; ewes' milk was evidently as desirable as cows', probably for its cheesemaking qualities.

Goats were also a milking animal, if not a common one: the goatherd of the *Rectitudines* receives dairy products as his perquisites.[36] Goat's milk is not as high in fat as ewe's,[37] but its physical characteristics are similar (see p. 111), so it would probably be made mainly into cheese, too.

[29] Mills, *Practical Sheep Dairying*, 260.
[30] O'Connor, 'Animal husbandry', 369.
[31] Dobney, Jaques, Johnstone, Hall, la Ferla, and Haynes., 'The agricultural economy', 144.
[32] Ayres et al., 'Mammal, bird and fish remains', 398.
[33] S 1482; Harmer (ed.), *Historical Documents*, 3–5 (no. 2), at 3.
[34] O'Connor, 'Animal husbandry', 372.
[35] S 1482; Harmer (ed.), *Historical Documents*, 3–5 (no. 2), at 3.
[36] *Rectitudines* 15, in Liebermann (ed.), *Gesetze*, i, 451.
[37] Ryder, *Sheep & Man*, 721.

It is not clear how long Anglo-Saxon animals stayed in milk. In early medieval Ireland, some at least were expected to milk through the winter.[38] Milk yield declines naturally in cows from about three weeks after calving, and tends to peak in May and June, reaching a minimum in November, all other things being equal.[39] In the mid-twentieth century, Biffen expected low-yielding cows to go dry five months into pregnancy.[40] Anglo-Saxon dairy animals were low-yielding by modern standards, but might also cease milking in winter because of low feed quality (or even quantity, in a bad year). Thus some Anglo-Saxon cows were probably dry from November through to May. At the present day, dairy goats may 'milk through', and only need to produce a kid every other year, but this is a modern development.[41] Dairy sheep, which have not received so much attention from breeders, normally go dry in winter even now.

Meat

In contrast to subsequent periods, medieval animal husbandry did not focus primarily on meat production,[42] but this does not mean meat was not valued in Anglo-Saxon England—indeed, it was the mark of an affluent lifestyle. Naomi Sykes suggests that there was greater emphasis on meat in the early Anglo-Saxon period than later.[43] This would be the period of 'abatement' outlined in Chapter 6, when pastoral farming was most important; as population grew, 'secondary' products were a more economical use of resources, but people still wanted meat.

Cattle destined to be eaten (in food rents, for instance) are usually designated by the Old English term *hriðer*, normally translated 'bullock'.[44] No doubt many cattle raised for slaughter were in fact male animals not needed for traction or breeding, but in an economy where livestock for a holding might comprise twice as many oxen as cows, there would not necessarily be more surplus male than female animals.[45] Thus a *hriðer* would sometimes be a heifer.[46] These beasts are often described as *eald*, usually translated 'full-grown' or 'mature',

---

[38] Kelly, *Early Irish Farming*, 41.

[39] Biffen, *Elements*, 618 and 616, Figs 96 and 95, respectively.

[40] Biffen, *Elements*, 539.

[41] Mackenzie, *Goat Husbandry*, 177–8.

[42] Albarella, 'Size, power, wool and veal'.

[43] *The Norman Conquest*, 94.

[44] For example by Whitelock in the will of Wulfgeat (?1006) (S 1534), who left a total of fourteen such animals to various recipients: Whitelock (ed.) *Anglo-Saxon Wills*, 54–6 (no. 19), at 55 (translation) and 54 (bequest).

[45] The reeve Abba left four oxen and two cows to stock half a ploughland: S 1482; Harmer (ed.), *Historical Documents*, 3–5 (no. 2), at 3.

[46] Nor does the word necessarily denote a living animal; provision made *c.* AD 909 for a feast at Winchester included 'tu hrieðeru oþer sealt oþer ferse' ('two *hriðer*s, one salt the other fresh'), in Robertson (ed. and tr.), *Anglo-Saxon Charters*, 38–40 (no. 20), at 38 (S 385).

rather than 'old',[47] but they must have included animals at the end of a working life. Many Anglo-Saxon cattle had only a couple of years of productive life before they were slaughtered,[48] but others lived considerably longer (see pp. 109–10). Early-modern proponents of plough-oxen pointed out that they could be eaten when no longer fit for work as one of their major advantages.[49] Thus a *hriðer* might also be an elderly animal, of either sex.

These elderly *hriðer*s must have made tough eating. O'Connor points out the 'scarcity of young calves at Anglo-Saxon sites', showing that cattle husbandry was not aimed at veal production,[50] but Sykes has shown that early assemblages do contain a substantial proportion of animals under two years old, suggesting that tender beef was a priority at that time.[51] Perhaps Anglo-Saxon cattle husbandry can best be seen as a compromise between a taste for tender meat and the need for the products and services the animals offered while alive. More animals were kept on to a greater age in the middle and later phases of the period, possibly because more oxen were needed for traction as agriculture intensified.[52]

A cattle carcass would provide much more meat than a sheep, so there was good reason to prefer beef to mutton, both among those who raised or moved the animals, and those who consumed them.[53] The status of cattle no doubt reinforced this preference,[54] and their greater size means that their contribution to the Anglo-Saxon diet must have been considerably higher than suggested by raw bone counts.[55]

The preponderance of relatively young sheep in the bone assemblages, again, suggests that most were slaughtered after only a couple of clips of wool, while their meat was still tender. These would be the best fleeces the animal was likely to produce, so meat would not have priority over wool quality, only over total weight.[56] Ewes might also have produced a reasonable amount of milk, again their best. High numbers of first-year animals, found on some

[47] For instance, in grants by Ealhburg and Eadwald to Christ Church, and by Ealhburg to St Augustine's (both mid-ninth century): S 1195 and S 1198; Harmer (ed.), *Historical Documents*, 8–9 (no. 5), at 8, and 9–10 (no. 6), at 9, respectively. In Ealdorman Oswulf's grant to Christ Church, (?806), there is 'an hriðer dugunde', which might mean a mature animal, or possibly a healthy one: S 1188; Harmer (ed.), *Historical Documents*, 1–2 (no. 1), at 1.

[48] O'Connor, 'Animal husbandry', 370–1.

[49] See Creasey, *The Draught Ox*, 3.

[50] 'Animal husbandry', 368–9.

[51] *The Norman Conquest*, 35, table 9.

[52] Sykes, 'From *cu* and *sceap*', 57, 62.

[53] Sykes, 'From *cu* and *sceap*', 57, 63. Anglo-Saxon food rents typically include a single *hriðer* but several sheep, for instance Earl Oswulf's grant to Christ Church (?806), with four sheep, or the will of Abba (835), with six: S 1188 and S 1428; Harmer (ed.), *Historical Documents*, 1–2 (no. 1), at 1, and 3–5 (no. 2), at 4, respectively.

[54] As it did among the Continental Germans: see Hamerow, *Rural Settlements*, 129.

[55] At eleventh-century Eynsham, where sheep bones were more abundant than those of cattle, it was calculated that more than twice as much beef as mutton was consumed: Ayres et al., 'Mammal, bird and fish remains', 394, Figure 10.14.

[56] Ayres et al., 'Mammal, bird and fish remains', 371.

mid-Anglo-Saxon sites, suggest a cull for meat, while second-year animals would have produced one clip, but still made tender eating.[57] Some Anglo-Saxon sites show a minor 'young peak' in their sheep bone assemblages, while others have a much more even spread across the age range, suggesting a variety of husbandry strategies, including a cull for lamb at some places,[58] but not a major emphasis on meat as opposed to 'secondary products'.

Although sheep meat was not as highly valued as beef,[59] the large numbers of sheep produced must have meant that much of the meat eaten in Anglo-Saxon England was mutton, like it or not. Regional variations, such as the cattle-dominated bone assemblages at York, or high numbers of sheep bones at West Stow in the Suffolk Breckland,[60] even if not determined by preferences in meat consumption, would nevertheless mean variations in diet, too.

Goats are unlikely to have been widely eaten, simply because of their low numbers. Dyer shows that kid was much more popular for eating than adult goat in the later Middle Ages,[61] and this may have been true before the Conquest, too, although evidence for goat consumption at any age is pretty scarce. Kid, *ticcen*, is fairly common in place-names, but does not appear, for instance, in food rents. The *bucca* required for a Bury funeral feast may have been a male goat.[62]

Of all the Anglo-Saxon livestock, pigs are the one single-purpose animal.[63] As a meat animal, however, they are extremely versatile. Both the flesh and the fat of pigs are normally preserved by salting and smoking,[64] as they spoil more quickly than those of other animals.[65] Preserved meats would be extremely valuable for those who could not afford to slaughter an animal for a single meal, but they are also an ideal commercial product, hence the huge herds of pigs belonging to major landowners. Flitches (sides of bacon) are relatively common in food rents, clearly valued by the landholding classes,[66] and holes in archaeological pig scapulae are regarded as evidence for bacon processing.[67] Values cited in Old English sources confirm that preserved products were important: a flitch of bacon was worth one *ore* (either sixteen or twenty pence) in a fragmentary will from Bury St Edmunds.[68] Although prices for pigs on the hoof vary a good deal, they are consistently lower than for the ready-processed

---

[57] Ayres et al., 'Mammal, bird and fish remains', 372.

[58] O'Connor, 'Animal husbandry', 369.

[59] See Sykes, 'From *cu* and *sceap*'.

[60] O'Connor, 'Animal husbandry', 372.

[61] Dyer, 'Goats', 28–30.

[62] Robertson (ed. and tr.), *Anglo-Saxon Charters*, 252 (Appendix 2, no. 8).

[63] See Albarella, 'Pig husbandry', 72. Biffen lists four 'categories of produce' from pigs: fresh meat, cured meat, lard, and bristles: Biffen, *Elements*, 568.

[64] See Wiseman, *The Pig*, 60–4, for the relationship between body-fat and the various uses of pigs. Also Biffen, *Elements*, 634 and Fig. 101.

[65] Rixson, *The History of Meat Trading*, 12–13 and 98–9.

[66] In, for example, a grant of land to Christ Church, Canterbury, by Earl Oswulf in ?806: S 1188; Harmer (ed.), *Historical Documents*, 1–2 (no. 1), at 1.

[67] Kelly, *Early Irish Farming*, 86.

[68] Robertson (ed. and tr.), *Anglo-Saxon Charters*, 252 (Appendix 2, no. 8).

animal, which would be worth thirty-two or forty pence just for the two flitches, plus the value of other products.

Lard was another very valuable pig product, especially since fat, with its high calorie-count, could be essential to surviving the winter, and appears in food rents accordingly.[69] With imported olive oil restricted to liturgical and medical uses, and butter probably produced in small quantities (see p. 112), lard was essential for cooking, eating, and household uses.[70] Meat was also leaner than at the present day, so less fat would be available from that source.[71] Lard was so ubiquitous in the Middle Ages that it was allowed in monasteries even in Lent (not being the *flesh* of a four-footed creature).[72] Two fat pigs for lard were worth three *ore* or four shillings in a late Bury food rent.[73] Payment for mast in Ine's laws is taken at increasing numbers of 'three-finger', 'two-finger', and 'thumb' pigs, interpreted as referring to the thickness of the animals' fat.[74] As the riddle quoted in the previous chapter confirms, the fatter the pig, the better.

The *Rectitudines* requires ten 'old' (full-grown) and five young pigs (in their first year) to be rendered at the time of killing (*sticunge*),[75] suggesting that about twice as many Anglo-Saxon swine might live into their second year as were killed in their first. Age-at-death data confirm a fairly systematic cull at one and two years of age at some sites,[76] presumably for young pork and more mature meat for preserving. Some of these data come from urban sites in London and York, and may reflect an organized commercial strategy. Pigs are traditionally slaughtered in the depths of the winter (shown in the illustrations for January in later medieval calendars), when newly fattened,[77] but since pigs can breed at any season, the age-at-death data do not tell us at what time of year they died. Year-old pigs to be eaten fresh could have been killed at any time of season, but the larger two-year-olds for processing are likely to have been killed in winter. Other sites show a more even spread from young animals to those approaching skeletal maturity;[78] nothing is to be gained in keeping pigs, apart from breeding stock, after they reach full size.

The archetypal poor-man's meat is the chicken, killed to make soup for invalids even in households where no flesh food can usually be afforded.[79] New

---

[69] Lufu's grant to Christ Church, for instance, and those of Ealhburg and Eadwald to Christ Church and Ealhburg to St Augustine's: S 1197, S 1195, and S 1198; Harmer (ed.), *Historical Documents*, 7–8 (no. 4), at 7 (Lufu), 8–9 (no. 5), at 8 (Ealhburg), and 9–10 (no. 6), at 9 (Eadwald).

[70] See Rixson, *History of Meat Trading*, 14–17, for non-food uses.

[71] Albarella, 'Pig husbandry', 72.

[72] Knowles, *Monastic Order*, 458.

[73] Robertson (ed. and tr.), *Anglo-Saxon Charters*, 196 and 198 (no. 104).

[74] Ine 49, in Liebermann (ed.), *Gesetze*, i, 110.

[75] *Rectitudines* 7, 6 and 6.1, in Liebermann (ed.), *Gesetze*, i, 448–9.

[76] At Flixborough, for example, even though other species at this site showed no such peaks: Dobney, Jaques, Johnstone, Hall, la Ferla, and Haynes, 'The agricultural economy', 125.

[77] Albarella, 'Pig husbandry', 84.

[78] Data and interpretation in this paragraph largely from O'Connor, 'Animal husbandry', 369–70.

[79] Chicken soup is recommended for various conditions in Old English medical texts: see, for instance, *Bald's Leechbook* II.56 (1), in Cockayne (ed.), *Leechdoms*, ii, 276.

evidence suggests its role in Anglo-Saxon diet has been underestimated: isotope studies have revealed that people of low status had too high a protein intake for it to have come from the major domestic quadrupeds.[80] Poultry may have provided the only flesh such Anglo-Saxons consumed (pig being the other likely contributor), but it was not scorned by the upper classes: hens appear in food rents (see the previous chapter), and there is a little Anglo-Saxon evidence for caponization, showing a demand for large, tender chickens among the affluent.[81] Improved techniques for sexing chicken leg-bones should increase that evidence,[82] but the practice was not yet as common as after the Norman Conquest.[83] This is in line with age-at-death data, with growing numbers of immature birds showing that meat became increasingly important from the twelfth century onwards.[84]

Some food rents also require geese, which would provide more flesh and, probably more importantly, fat. At Eynsham, immature goose bones appear with greater frequency as the Anglo-Saxon period progresses, suggesting an increasing emphasis on meat production.[85] There is no evidence geese were deliberately crammed in Anglo-Saxon England, but they instinctively fatten up in the autumn, coinciding with the availability of shed grain from the harvest,[86] so there would be fat geese for feasting in autumn and winter.

Eggs

Eggs, rather than meat, were the chief reason for keeping poultry in the Middle Ages.[87] The large number of eggs in a clutch, as well as their size, was probably one of the reasons chickens were domesticated in the first place,[88] and, like ducks and geese, they will keep laying to replace eggs removed. Eggs are also an extremely efficient way of turning plant food into protein that humans can digest.[89] The high nitrogen levels of low-status Anglo-Saxons suggest that 'secondary products' like eggs (as well as poultry) were a significant factor in the diet; chicken bones are usually found to be mainly from hens in lay,[90] and eggshell is being identified on an increasing number of Anglo-Saxon sites.[91] Only an estimation of the size of the original egg, and therefore of the parent bird, is

---

[80] Hull and O'Connell, 'Diet: recent evidence', 677.
[81] Dobney, Jaques, Johnstone, Hall, la Ferla, and Haynes, 'The agricultural economy', 176–7.
[82] Serjeantson, *Birds*, 275–9.
[83] Serjeantson, 'Birds: food and a mark of status'.
[84] Serjeantson, *Birds*, 281.
[85] Ayres et al., 'Mammal, bird and fish bones', 355–6.
[86] Serjeantson, *Birds*, 297.
[87] Albarella, 'Size, power, wool and veal', 27.
[88] Serjeantson, *Birds*, 165.
[89] Serjeantson, *Birds*, 169.
[90] Sykes, *The Norman Conquest*, 28.
[91] For instance from a possible eleventh-century kitchen at Eynsham: Ayres et al., 'Mammal, bird and fish remains', 381.

usually possible:[92] at Flixborough, for instance, most eggshell was attributed to chickens on this basis, with some 'thick' fragments assigned to geese.[93] The high proportion of female poultry bones at this site also suggests an emphasis on egg production. The importance of eggs in Anglo-Saxon food production is underlined by their appearance in London trade regulations in the eleventh century.[94]

No poultry would have laid all the year round as hens do today. Under natural conditions, hens lay most eggs in March, April, and May in England, tailing off as the days grow shorter in October and November; they stop laying altogether in the depths of the winter.[95] It was no doubt in the spring that most eggs were available in Anglo-Saxon England (although there is no evidence they were associated with Easter). In an early Irish source, fifty was considered a normal annual lay for a hen, while later medieval sources from England suggest around a hundred.[96] Another Irish text suggests that eggs should measure four inches around the middle and five around the long axis, about the size of a bantam egg,[97] and this would fit with the small size of early medieval chickens. The amount of food in egg form per hen would thus be much lower than today. Goose eggs are larger (smaller in the early Middle Ages than today, but still bigger than hens' eggs), and at least in Ireland they were valued more highly than hens'.[98] Numbers of eggs from geese would have been no greater, however, as they would also cease laying in the winter.

Wool

Wool is by far the most common fibre in Anglo-Saxon textiles,[99] so sheep were clearly of great importance in the domestic economy (see Chapter 7). But there is also evidence as early as the reign of Offa of Mercia (757–96) for the export of woollen textiles (*sagae*, cloaks or blankets) to Frankish territories;[100] their importance thus went well beyond household manufacture, or even local trade (see Chapter 9). The significance of wool is emphasized by the regulation of its price, uniquely for an agricultural product, in later Anglo-Saxon law: 'the wey of wool shall go for half a pound [120 pence], and let no-one sell it dearer [or cheaper, according to some manuscripts].'[101] It is not clear what made Anglo-Saxon wool textiles so attractive, but the work of scholars such as M. L. Ryder and Penelope Walton Rogers does show what kind of wool

---

[92] Serjeantson, *Birds*, 169–76.
[93] Dobney, Jaques, Johnstone, Hall, la Ferla, and Haynes, 'The agricultural economy', 180–1.
[94] IV Æthelred 2.11, in Liebermann (ed.), *Gesetze*, i, 234.
[95] Biffen, *Elements*, 641, Fig. 105; Serjeantson, *Birds*, 282.
[96] Stone, 'The consumption and supply of birds', 154.
[97] Kelly, *Early Irish Farming*, 104.
[98] Kelly, *Early Irish Farming*, 105.
[99] Walton Rogers, *Cloth and Clothing*, 61.
[100] See Loyn, *Anglo-Saxon England*, 85.
[101] Eadgar III, 8.2, in Liebermann (ed.), *Gesetze*, i, 200–6, at 204.

Anglo-Saxon sheep produced. By the early Middle Ages, selection over many centuries had led to considerable differentiation of wool types. A range is found in Anglo-Saxon textiles: fine and medium wools as well as 'generalized' types (comparable with a modern Shetland fleece) and hairy (comparable with modern Scottish Blackface).[102] From 'Danish' areas (in fact, York) Ryder found hairier fleeces, although again a range of types.[103] Anglo-Saxon pictures of sheep, other than in the Old English Hexateuch, usually have some indication of wool (Figs 4.3 and 4.4, Plates 3 and 5), supporting the impression of a considerable degree of selection for finer, softer, or more abundant fleeces.

Given the importance of wool in the Anglo-Saxon economy, we hear relatively little from our sources about its processing. At Hurstbourne Priors, Hampshire, the *ceorlas* had to wash and shear in their own time the sheep they rendered to their landlord.[104] Shearing is one of the *Gerefa*'s summer tasks, and the *Rectitudines* shepherd receives—presumably at shearing time—one bell-fleece, usually interpreted as the fleece of the bellwether, which led the flock.[105] No one is required to do any shearing in the *Rectitudines*, however. The Hurstbourne peasants rendered their sheep at Easter; it is probably because they handed them over before normal shearing time that the document requires that they shear them themselves. The law-code of Ine of Wessex states that 'Sceap sceal gongan mid his fliese oð midne sumor, oððe gilde þæt flies mid twam pæningum' ('A sheep must go with its fleece till midsummer, or pay two pence for the fleece'), implying that midsummer, or even later, was the normal time for shearing.[106] May and June were the usual time in the early twentieth century, in keeping with the *Gerefa*'s 'maio 7 iunio 7 iulio'.[107] The calendar pictures (for May) show sheep looking relatively woolly, and certainly reveal no distinction between shorn adults and unshorn lambs (Fig. 4.3 and Plate 3).

The importance of textile production on a large estate is emphasized by the number of relevant tools (*towtola*) in the *Gerefa*'s lists, as well as *sceara*, although these are not explicitly linked with wool.[108] Shears are a relatively common find in archaeology: examples exist in a wide range of sizes, fulfilling all the functions of modern scissors.[109] Only the largest and most robust are likely to have been used to shear sheep.[110]

It may be that some Anglo-Saxon sheep were not shorn at all. Two of the oldest surviving British breeds, the Soay and the Shetland, shed their fleece

[102] Ryder, *Sheep & Man*, 188–9.
[103] Ryder, *Sheep & Man*, 191–2.
[104] S 359; Robertson (ed. and tr.), *Anglo-Saxon Charters*, 206 (no. 110). The editor dates this document to the eleventh century, but only by its resemblance to the *Rectitudines*.
[105] *Gerefa* 9 and *Rectitudines* 14, in Liebermann (ed.), *Gesetze*, i, 454 and 451.
[106] Ine 69, in Liebermann (ed.), *Gesetze*, i, 118.
[107] Biffen, *Elements*, 557.
[108] *Gerefa* 15–15.1, in Liebermann (ed.), *Gesetze*, i, 455.
[109] Walton Rogers, 'Textile production', 296–8.
[110] Walton Rogers, *Cloth and Clothing*, 40.

spontaneously, and people pluck, or 'roo', it from the animals' backs.[111] This wild trait has been bred out of all extant English breeds, but it could have survived in some Anglo-Saxon sheep. These resembled a modern Shetland (see the previous chapter), and Ryder and Walton Rogers have shown that some of them had a similar fleece, so they may also have shared its fleece-shedding characteristic.

During the ninth century, an intensification of sheep husbandry has been detected at Flixborough, north Lincolnshire, associated with the production of fine textiles:[112] this was when sheep made up the highest proportion of the bone assemblage there, and a different type of sheep may have been introduced. There was also an increase in the condition known as 'penning elbow', thought to be caused by keeping sheep in confined spaces.[113] Artefacts associated with textile production appear either in greater abundance or in different forms at the same stage, suggesting that spinning and weaving became more important, with new techniques and equipment being introduced;[114] at the same time, the settlement was changing other husbandry practices in response to commercial links and demands.[115] The changes did not persist into the tenth century, and are not apparent at sites with smaller assemblages, but are what we might expect as overseas trade in woollens developed.

For wool yields we have no Anglo-Saxon figures, but later medieval records suggest a range of 1 lb 4 oz to 1 lb 12 oz per fleece, with ewes at the lower end and males at the higher.[116] The washing mentioned at Hurstbourne would make the fleece cleaner and softer (and easier to cut, resulting in less waste), but would reduce its weight. Plucked fleeces would be much lighter than shorn ones. The figure of two pence for a fleece (see p. 119) is nearly half the value of the sheep itself, so a sheep would justify its existence if it had been shorn twice or three times, and this is also what the age-at-death data suggest: most animals lived to yield at least two clips of wool.[117]

Given that wool was an export commodity before the Conquest, we might expect measures to be taken to improve both quantity and quality, for instance by keeping large numbers of wethers in the flock rather than culling male lambs. Evidence for wethers is, however, sparse, and does not always relate to wool production: the fifty on an estate lent to King Edward the Elder by the Winchester Old Minster may have been a wool flock, but other written references come from food rents.[118] At mid-Anglo-Saxon Brandon, in

---

[111] Ryder, *Sheep & Man*, 16.
[112] Dobney, Jaques, Johnstone, Hall, la Ferla, and Haynes, 'The agricultural economy', 187.
[113] Dobney, Jaques, Johnstone, Hall, la Ferla, and Haynes, 'The agricultural economy', 185–6.
[114] Walton Rogers, 'Textile production'.
[115] Dobney, Jaques, Johnstone, Hall, la Ferla, and Haynes, 'The agricultural economy', 189.
[116] Stephenson, 'Wool yields', 373.
[117] O'Connor, 'Animal husbandry', 369.
[118] S 1444; Kemble, *Codex diplomaticus*, no. 1089 (Winchester Old Minster); further references: S 385 and 1506; Robertson (ed. and tr.), *Anglo-Saxon Charters*, 38 and 58 (nos 20 and 32).

Suffolk, a greater interest in wool production has been detected than at nearby, but earlier, West Stow: more sheep lived to be adults, and more of them were males, probably wethers.[119] At Coppergate in York, statistical analysis suggested a high proportion of the sheep were wethers.[120] At Flixborough, however, despite the evidence for wool production, even specialization, wethers could not be identified.

Minor products

The use of horn, bone, skins and sinew for craft production has already been mentioned, to which we might add hog bristles and beeswax.[121] Goose feathers provided the vast majority of the pens that wrote Anglo-Saxon manuscripts, and goose down may have been used to fill pillows as well.[122] Along with eggs, feathers were the main 'secondary product' of geese.[123] Chicken feathers might also be used for smaller pens and other uses. More geese reached maturity in the Anglo-Saxon period than later in the Middle Ages, showing that secondary products were more important than meat.[124] At Eynsham, most goose bones in the early phases were from wings;[125] as this was before the monastery was founded, flight feathers must have had other uses, such as brushes. Geese would probably have their wings clipped on one side to restrain their migratory instincts (largely bred out of them at the present day),[126] so special arrangements might be needed to preserve a usable harvest of flight feathers.

Honey should probably not be regarded as a minor product, although it was undoubtedly produced in smaller quantities than, say, milk or meat. It was much sought after in the Middle Ages, because the diet was otherwise poor in high-sugar (and thus high-energy) foods. Even more importantly, honey was the raw material for mead, the most prestigious alcoholic drink, until overtaken by wine, and (probably not coincidentally) the strongest, in the absence of distilled spirits.[127] Honey occurs frequently in food rents. In Cambridgeshire, this and malt are still named in the king's 'farm of one night' in Domesday Book,[128] showing what was important to those at the very top of eleventh-century society. Beeswax was also needed for liturgical candles and probably domestic ones at the upper end of the social scale, although the

---

[119] Crabtree, 'Animals as material culture', 164–7.
[120] O'Connor, 'Animal bones from Anglo-Scandinavian York'.
[121] See also Hinton, 'Raw materials', 431–3.
[122] Serjeantson, 'Goose husbandry'; Gameson, 'The archaeology of the Anglo-Saxon book', 805–7.
[123] Albarella, 'Size, power, wool and veal', 27, and Serjeantson, *Birds*, 198.
[124] Serjeantson, *Birds*, 298.
[125] Ayres et al., 'Mammal, bird and fish remains', 355–6.
[126] Serjeantson, *Birds*, 293.
[127] See Banham, *Food and Drink*, 42.
[128] See for instance Great Domesday, fo. 189v, in *Domesday Book: Cambridgeshire*, ed. Rumble, under Fordham, Isleham, Chevely, and Great Wilbraham, all royal holdings.

'average Anglo-Saxon' almost certainly used tallow dips.[129] Wax and candles occur frequently in charms and medical recipes, probably chiefly due to their liturgical associations, but social prestige, and indeed their practical properties, no doubt played a part.[130]

WHAT PEOPLE DID FOR ANIMALS

Their own requirements for the animal products and services discussed were a major influence on how Anglo-Saxons kept their animals, but the terrain and resources at their disposal were equally important. How those influences may have intersected in different places is a main theme of Part II. Here we look more generally at livestock management.

Housing, feeding, and care

The Anglo-Saxons did not bring with them to Britain the Germanic longhouse, with accommodation for both humans and livestock under one roof.[131] This has been taken to mean that animals did not have to be kept under cover in the relatively kind conditions of Britain. On the other hand, the Venerable Bede described the Irish climate as so mild that there was no need to house livestock or store winter feed, implying that both were necessary and normal in eighth-century Northumbria.[132] Ælfric's *Colloquy* shows that plough oxen might be housed overnight in later Anglo-Saxon England,[133] and the *Gerefa* lists a number of buildings for animals (although its encyclopaedic character means that some of them may not have been common). However, buildings on archaeological sites are rarely identified as byres or stables, and a recent survey of Anglo-Saxon timber buildings does not discuss animal housing.[134] How common was it for Anglo-Saxon livestock to be kept indoors? Ælfric's ox-herd in addition to keeping them under cover sometimes watches over his charges at night outdoors.[135] The difference may have been seasonal, with animals housed in winter, at least at night, but outside in the summer, or regional: what was

[129] Hinton, 'Raw materials', 433. The lost-wax method of metal casting must also have used beeswax: Leahy, 'Anglo-Saxon crafts', 454.

[130] For example, *Lacnunga* 31, a 'good bonesalve' (and a very elaborate one), in Pettit (ed.), *Anglo-Saxon Remedies*, i, 18–20.

[131] Hamerow, *Rural Settlements*, 47; at 21, she attributes its decline on the Continent to a change in emphasis from cattle-rearing to arable farming, but climate was also improving at this time.

[132] Bede, *Historia Ecclesiastica* I.1, in Plummer (ed.), *Bedae Opera historica*, 12. The description of Ireland includes a number of features presented as miraculous, if not implausible (e.g. the instant death of snakes arriving there), so perhaps no element of it should be taken too seriously.

[133] Garmonsway (ed.), *Ælfric's Colloquy*, 21.

[134] Hamerow, 'Anglo-Saxon timber buildings'. She mentions it only briefly in *Rural Settlements* at 17, 26, and 45.

[135] Garmonsway (ed.), *Ælfric's Colloquy*, 22.

normal in Bede's Northumbria might have been unnecessary in the south. Social differences almost certainly existed as well: livestock belonging to peasants
presumably had to tolerate less comfortable conditions than the prized beasts
of the aristocracy. As the period progressed, it would be easier to keep animals
outside in any given area as the climate improved.

One of the *Gerefa*'s winter tasks is to 'stall cattle' (*hryðeran styllan*)[136] and a
small number of documents mention a *faldhriðer* (in various spellings).[137] A
hriðer is a head of cattle destined to be eaten (see pp. 113–14), while the first
element is modern English 'fold'. Portable folds for sheep are, however, usually
called *loca* in Old English, so it is possible that something more substantial is
meant here, and A. J. Robertson's translation 'stalled ox' may be correct. A
hriðer might receive special treatment, as the repository of a household's wealth
and a storehouse of future feasting, or might be fattened under cover in the
final stages of its life.

Ælfric's shepherd had to move his flock's folds (Lat. *caules*, OE *loca*),
periodically, and under early Irish law, full compensation was not payable for
a sheep left outside at night.[138] The *Rectitudines*' peasants had to spend the
night at their lord's sheepfold, so it seems that early medieval sheep were normally folded at night, and Ælfric's 'shepherd' explains why: *ne lupi deuorent
eas* ('so that wolves don't eat them'), quite apart from the thieves envisaged
in Irish law.[139] Another reason for folding sheep on arable land would be to
exploit their manure, as discussed in Chapter 3. These *loca* were clearly made
of hurdles or some other temporary construction, but whether sheep were ever
kept in more permanent structures, perhaps even covered ones, is not clear. *Loc*
occurs in place names, as we shall see in Chapter 6, so some *loca* must have
been erected in regular locations.

Swyn stigian (putting, or keeping, pigs in sties) was another of the *Gerefa*'s
winter tasks, presumably when they got back from the woods (see pp. 129–30,
under 'Herding').[140] In recent centuries, pigs have been the cottage animal par
excellence, kept in sties and fed on effectively free household scraps.[141] This
would also enable the poor of Anglo-Saxon England to produce meat without
sacrificing food that they could have eaten themselves. The *æhteswan* in the
Rectitudines is, for instance, entitled to a *stifearh* ('sty-pig or piglet', *porcellus*,

---

[136] *Gerefa* 11, in Liebermann (ed.), *Gesetze*, i, 454.

[137] Including a list of Bishop Æthelwold's gifts to Peterborough and a fragmentary inventory from
Bury St Edmunds. Another Bury list has '.iiii. feldhryþera', which Robertson translates 'grazing bullocks'. These may be a contrasting pair, as she supposes, but they may merely be orthographic variants. See Robertson (ed. and tr.), *Anglo-Saxon Charters*, 72–4 (no. 39), at 74 (S 1448) (Peterborough); 248
(Appendix 2, no. 3) (first Bury list); and 192–200 (no. 104), at 196 (second Bury list).

[138] Garmonsway (ed.), *Ælfric's Colloquy*, 22; Kelly, *Early Irish Farming*, 68.

[139] *Rectitudines* 4.1a, in Liebermann (ed.), *Gesetze*, i, 441; Garmonsway (ed.), *Ælfric's Colloquy*, 22.

[140] *Gerefa* 11, in Liebermann (ed.), *Gesetze*, i, 454.

[141] Albarella, 'Pig husbandry', 79–80; see Randell, *Fenland Memories*, 44–6, among many volumes of
rural reminiscences.

in the Latin) as part of his very meagre reward.[142] Pigs were probably taken from the herd to be fattened in sties for individual use.

Poultry would also need to be shut up at night to prevent theft or predation. One of the structures the *Gerefa* was responsible for was a hen roost (*henna hrost*).[143] This may have been some kind of portable coop, as used in Ireland, inside a building or in a tree, out of the way of predators.[144] In contrast with such flimsy structures, two quite substantial Anglo-Saxon buildings have been associated with poultry, on analogy with the ninth-century ideal monastery plan from St Gall in Switzerland.[145] This shows two circular buildings for *alendis anseribus* ('raising geese') and *cura et...nutritio pullorum* ('care and feeding of chickens', or possibly goslings), with a rectangular house for the poultry-keepers between them. At Cheddar, a row of three small buildings in the opposite configuration (square, circular, square) were identified as being fowl houses,[146] and at Yarnton, in Oxfordshire, a large roundish building was interpreted as a poultry run.[147] It seems unlikely, however, that much attention would be paid to housing such little-regarded livestock as poultry, even at St Gall, let alone that a standard plan was observed across Europe. In fact, many poultry probably spent the night in people's houses, as in later centuries.

Bede's statement (p. 122) that in Ireland, due to its 'mild and healthy climate' there was 'no need to store hay in summer for winter use'[148] should mean that hay-making was standard practice in eighth-century Northumbria. The provision of hay seems to be taken for granted, and a normal part of the cycle of work, in our sources. Meadow, as well as arable, has to be protected from intrusive livestock in Ine of Wessex's law-code.[149] The calendars show hay being mown with scythes in the summer (see Fig. 5.2). At both Tidenham, Gloucestershire, and Hurstbourne Priors, Hampshire, peasants were required to mow as part of their services, and at Hurstbourne, to stack the hay.[150] Ælfric's ploughman fills the mangers with *feno* (*hig* in Old English) for his oxen.[151] Environmental evidence at Yarnton, Oxfordshire, suggested that a traditional hay meadow, Oxey Mead, had its origin in the middle Anglo-Saxon period,[152] and Anglo-Saxon meadows have been identified by similar means at West Cotton, Northamptonshire, Market Lavington, Wiltshire, and Dorney,

---

[142] *Rectitudines* 7, in Liebermann (ed.), *Gesetze*, i, 449.

[143] *Gerefa* 11, in Liebermann (ed.), *Gesetze*, i, 454. It is, however, an afterthought, unless this is a rhetorical device.

[144] Kelly, *Early Irish Farming*, 103–4.

[145] See Price, *Plan of St Gall*, 72.

[146] Rahtz, *Cheddar*, 129–32.

[147] Hey, *Yarnton*, 69.

[148] Bede, *Historia Ecclesiastica* I.1, in Plummer (ed.), *Bedae Opera historica*, 12.

[149] *Ine* 40–42.1, in Liebermann (ed.), *Gesetze*, i, 106–8.

[150] S 1555 and S 359; Robertson (ed. and tr.), *Anglo-Saxon Charters*, 206 (nos 109 and 110).

[151] Garmonsway (ed.), *Ælfric's Colloquy*, 21.

[152] Hey, *Yarnton*, 47.

Fig. 5.2. July: mowing, British Library, Cotton Julius A. vi, fo. 6r.

(© The British Library Board, Cotton Julius A. vi)

Buckinghamshire.[153] Many place-names include elements meaning meadow or hay, and meadow features frequently in Anglo-Saxon charters, as well as in Domesday Book. Its importance is explored further in Chapter 6.

But Bede is also held responsible for the idea of a large-scale autumn slaughter in Anglo-Saxon England,[154] implying that insufficient fodder was available to see most livestock through the winter. However, the zooarchaeological evidence does not show many animals being culled in their first autumn, so a shortage of winter fodder was probably unusual.[155] In any case, an autumn cull and winter feeding are not mutually exclusive. A core breeding stock at least must have been kept for the next season, all the more precious for their small number, and likely to be pampered as a result. A few beasts would be slaughtered for the midwinter feast, even if plenty of fodder was available.

There is no mention in our written sources of other kinds of winter fodder, but archaeobotanical evidence now shows that vetches (*Vicia sativa* subsp. *sativa*) were grown on at least one Anglo-Saxon site (the differentiation of legume seeds is notoriously difficult). Vetch seeds are toxic to humans, so this must have been a fodder crop. The few Anglo-Saxon records of lentils might also represent a fodder crop, fed green, as they would not have produced a reliable seed crop even in the improving late-Anglo-Saxon climate.[156] Crops grown primarily for seed could be used as fodder if they failed, and successful ones, when threshed, would provide straw. The piecemeal threshing of cereals and legumes through the winter would also provide straw for bedding and fodder. There is evidence from a wide range of periods and cultures for leaves and branches being collected as winter feed.[157] In Ireland, the

---

[153] Campbell, 'Preliminary results', 76; Williams and Newman, *Market Lavington*, 136; Hiller et al., 'Anglo-Saxon archaeology', 57.
[154] *De temporum ratione*, ch. 15, in Jones (ed.), *Opera didascalica*, ii, 332.
[155] O'Connor, 'Animal husbandry', 372–3.
[156] For both vetches and lentils, see Moffett, 'Food plants', 352.
[157] Ryder, *Sheep & Man*, 82–3.

leaves of evergreen trees were collected for winter fodder,[158] and the possibilities of 'tree-fodder' in England are discussed in Chapter 7.

The decision as to whether to leave animals out at pasture in winter might depend on grazing quality. In the early twentieth century, cows (apart from high-yielding breeds) were expected to produce milk on 'average' grass alone from April to September, although with declining yields.[159] Outside this period, they would need 'concentrates' (high-nutrient foods) to stay in milk. If any Anglo-Saxon farm animals were fed 'concentrates', dairy cows and plough-oxen are the most likely candidates, as well as beasts being fattened for slaughter. However, oxen would not need the 'high feeding' that working horses received in subsequent centuries, since they cannot work a long day, or move fast, and their digestion is adapted to deal with bulky plants. The hay supplied by Ælfric's ploughman, plus the grazing provided by the headlands of the fields where they worked, would be sufficient to keep them in working condition.[160]

Pigs will eat pretty well anything, and Terry O'Connor sees their main value in the Anglo-Saxon economy as converters of rubbish to meat.[161] However, in medieval Europe, large numbers were raised on wood-pasture (see pp. 129–30), where they thrive uniquely on beech-mast and even acorns, which are poisonous to many animals.[162] Isotopic studies of Anglo-Saxon pigs show that most had a mainly vegetable diet, consistent with their living on wood-pasture rather than on domestic waste.[163] The Exeter Book riddle quoted in the previous chapter associates beech-mast in particular with fattening pigs. At Tidenham, the tenants paid an extra levy, presumably in pigs, when there was mast, because more would be produced in a good mast year.[164]

From pre-Conquest England, we have no evidence for how sty-fed pigs were fattened, but Irish sources mention cereals or milk.[165] Some pre-Conquest urban pigs had a very varied diet, probably including household waste.[166] A study of tooth wear in pigs from tenth-century Coppergate in York suggested a soft diet,[167] perhaps especially in the final, fattening, stage of their lives. Urban swine might, however, have had a different lifestyle to the average Anglo-Saxon country pig: after spring farrowing, new growth and the waste from human consumption during the abundance of summer would support growing piglets as they began to forage for themselves (this would be a little later for medieval pigs than modern

[158] Kelly, *Early Irish Farming*, 46.
[159] Biffen, *Elements*, 539.
[160] Creasey, *The Draft Ox*, 3; Watts, *Working Oxen*, 12.
[161] 'Animal husbandry', 372.
[162] Forsyth, *British Poisonous Plants*, 81–3.
[163] Hull and O'Connell, 'Diet: recent evidence', 673.
[164] S 1555; Robertson (ed. and tr.), *Anglo-Saxon Charters*, 204–6 (no. 109). For more on this text, see Faith, 'Tidenham', as well as Chapter 8.
[165] Kelly, *Early Irish Farming*, 82–3.
[166] Albarella, 'Pig husbandry', 79.
[167] Wilkie et al., 'A dental microwear study of pig diet'.

ones, which begin to eat solid food in their third week and are weaned at eight or ten weeks).[168] At other times, pickings might be considerably slimmer.

Ælfric's oxherd had to hand his charges back to the ploughman not only well fed, but *adaquatos*, watered.[169] Water is necessary for all livestock, although sheep seem to survive with very little. Lactating animals have particularly high requirements. People rarely settle where water is not available, but subsequent changes in the size of flocks and herds, as well as in the control of territory, might mean that water supplies could be a limiting factor in stock-rearing. Ponds and watercourses are often cited in charter bounds, which may mean that they were shared resources. Some may also have been artificial: ditching (*dician*) is one of the *Gerefa*'s spring tasks.[170] This is in the context of planting and sowing, but shows that digging water-courses was a normal part of farming operations. Place-names such as Shipbrook could denote a stream in which sheep were washed before shearing,[171] or one which they regularly crossed, or indeed one from which they drank.

Good housing and feeding, and adequate water were all intended to keep livestock healthy. Animal health was a serious concern: 'mortalities' affecting livestock were national news, reported in the Anglo-Saxon Chronicle alongside battles and the fall of great men. These were presumably outbreaks over which there was no hope of human control, but there were attempts at intervention when individual animals fell ill. The eleventh-century medical collection, the *Lacnunga*, contains a number of remedies for sick livestock. Not surprisingly, horses feature in several, but there are also treatments for dying *hryðeran*, lung disease in cattle, 'broken down' sheep and those with pocks or scab, and sudden death in pigs.[172]

Herding and control

The *Rectitudines* mentions herdsmen in charge of oxen, cows, sheep, goats, and swine among its *personae*. When animals were not kept under cover, human supervision would be essential to prevent straying, theft, and predation, especially in the winter, when wild animals might be driven by hunger to move closer to human habitation, and at crucial points such as lambing (see pp. 133–4). In the Anglo-Saxon period, potential predators included large carnivores, such as wolf and possibly bear, and birds of prey such as white-tailed eagle, once closely associated with human settlement.[173] The Fonthill Letter recounts complex

[168] Thear, *Smallholder's Manual*, 181, and Seymour, *Self-Sufficiency*, 76.
[169] Garmonsway (ed.), *Ælfric's Colloquy*, 22.
[170] *Gerefa* 12, in Liebermann (ed.), *Gesetze*, i, 454.
[171] Ryder, *Sheep & Man*, 185–6.
[172] *Lacnunga* CXXXII to CXXXVI, in Pettit (ed.), *Anglo-Saxon Remedies*, i, 96–8.
[173] Pluskowski, 'The wolf', 70–1; bear probably became extinct in the early fifth to early sixth century: Hammon, 'The brown bear', 100; Serjeantson, 'Extinct birds', 153.

legal proceedings arising ultimately from oxen being left unsupervised (OE *unlæd*), showing that the repercussions could be extensive.[174] Close supervision would only be possible where the ratio of people to animals was reasonably high. Near the settlement, either their owners or members of the community entrusted with this task could watch over flocks and herds without too much disruption to their other work. In transhumant regimes, people might spend whole seasons with their animals on distant pastures (see Part II). Often these were children or adolescents, like the young St Cuthbert, who stayed up at night looking after his master's sheep *cum aliis pastoribus* ('with other shepherds') in the 'mountains' by the river Leader.[175] Where animals ranged freely across open pasture and were only rounded up periodically, they would have to fend for themselves much of the time.

Herding involves not only keeping watch over animals, but also moving them. Ælfric's ploughman returns his charges to the oxherd at the end of the day, and the oxherd in the *Rectitudines* runs his own cow and two or more oxen with his lord's herd.[176] These were docile creatures, easy to manage despite their size. Sheep will follow their shepherd, behaviour that depends on their flocking instinct, and even the 'primitive' Soay will follow a human associated with food.[177] The presence of humans does not necessarily mean that they decide the itinerary, however. A traditional sheep management method in many parts of the world uses a bellwether, an experienced animal that the others will follow, fitted with a bell so that humans can find the flock. A suggestion that this method was familiar in Anglo-Saxon England comes from the *Rectitudines*, where the shepherd's benefits include a *belflys*, literally a 'bell fleece', generally interpreted as that of a bellwether. 'Hefted' sheep at the present day can be left to find their own way around their accustomed territory for long periods of time.[178] In many cases, the herders no doubt followed the animals where they would be going anyway, as suggested in Chapter 6.

In Ælfric's *Colloquy*, the shepherd stands over his sheep *cum canibus* (*mid hundum* in Old English).[179] Dogs must have played an important part in the management of sheep, and possibly of other animals. In early Irish sources, we hear of dogs which guard their master's sheepfold, as well as his house, calf-byre, and oxen, and such animals were highly valued, as were herding dogs.[180] Herd dogs and guard dogs have had much of their ancestral hunting behaviour bred out of them; both need to be aggressive towards intruders, while showing

---

[174] See Hough, 'Cattle tracking in the Fonthill Letter'.
[175] Anonymous Life, c. 5, in Colgrave (ed.), *Two Lives*, 68.
[176] Garmonsway (ed.), *Ælfric's Colloquy*, 22; *Rectitudines* 12, in Liebermann (ed.), *Gesetze*, i, 450.
[177] Grocock, '"To eat, to wear, to work"', 88.
[178] Recent experience reveals that hefting does not take generations; sheep learn much faster than humans usually give them credit for: Morton and Avanzo, 'Executive decision-making'.
[179] Garmonsway (ed.), *Ælfric's Colloquy*, 22.
[180] Kelly, *Early Irish Farming*, 115–16, 119–20.

drastically reduced aggression towards their charges.[181] They are the product of extensive breeding work, already at an advanced stage by the Anglo-Saxon period.[182] At York, remains of dogs were found ranging from 35 cm at the shoulder to the size of a wolf, suggesting a good deal of specialization.[183]

The difficulty of confining goats is proverbial, and thus many are likely to have been kept on open range, rather than close to settlements where they could cause damage.[184] Goats, like sheep, follow a daily circuit around their home range if left to themselves, and this can if necessary include a stop at a suitable location for milking by humans.[185] They need some human attention to ensure they are not stolen or predated, but in a 'natural' herd the stronger and more aggressive members do a great deal to protect the more vulnerable animals. A good expanse of territory is required for this natural home range to develop, however; goats kept by the poor must have been tethered instead.

Some kind of physical boundaries were certainly needed to keep livestock off arable land, and indeed gardens and other human property, even if small numbers were tethered. The provisions of Ine of Wessex and the *Rectitudines* for keeping crops and livestock separate, discussed in Chapter 3, show that this was a concern throughout the Anglo-Saxon period. While it was mainly the arable that was enclosed, some animals were no doubt kept in enclosures, especially where large numbers were grazing near human habitation. At Yarnton, mid-Anglo-Saxon ditches were interpreted as forming pens, a paddock, and larger enclosures for animals.[186] The increasing visibility of boundaries in settlements of this period is interpreted as showing greater investment in livestock management close to home as pressure on pasture increased.[187] The need to enclose livestock would increase as their numbers grew, and unrestricted access to grazing led to over-use, partition, and potential conflict (see Chapter 7).

The movement of pigs to wood-pasture in the autumn was a significant feature of husbandry regimes in some parts of Anglo-Saxon England.[188] Some wood-pasture was close to the main settlement, but the denns of the Weald could be many miles away, and the swineherds would have to live away from home with their charges (see Chapter 8). The importance of this custom in Anglo-Saxon England is demonstrated by the detailed regulations for breaches in the laws of Ine of Wessex, and the *micel sprec ymb wuduleswe* ('great discourse about wood-pasture') held by King Beornwulf of Mercia in 825.[189]

---

[181] See Coppinger and Schneider, 'Evolution of working dogs', esp. 27–35.
[182] Clutton-Brock, 'Origins of the dog', 18.
[183] O'Connor, 'Animal bones from Anglo-Scandinavian York', 439.
[184] Mackenzie, *Goat Husbandry*, 99–118.
[185] Mackenzie, *Goat Husbandry*, 103–4.
[186] Hey, *Yarnton*, 45–6.
[187] Hamerow, *Rural Settlements*, 89.
[188] See now Hooke, '*Wealdbæra* and *swina mæst*', for Anglo-Saxon pig pannage.
[189] Ine 49, in Liebermann (ed.), *Gesetze*, i, 110; Robertson (ed. and tr.), *Anglo-Saxon Charters*, 8 (no. 5) (S 1437).

Other animals might be kept on wood-pasture, as discussed in Chapter 8, but it was unauthorized pigs that concerned Ine, and in the proceedings before Beornwulf it was the *swangerefan* ('swineherd-reeves') who wanted more than the traditional three hundred pigs' mast. In Domesday Book, woodland in the south-east of England and East Anglia is still measured by the number of swine it could support,[190] and in Ine's law-code a tree big enough to shelter thirty pigs is worth twice as much as smaller ones.[191]

The mast season runs from early autumn to early winter;[192] some animals might be kept in the woods all year round, but in the *Rectitudines*, the *gebur*s are required to provide the swineherd with bread when he drives the pigs to the woods,[193] so animals were clearly moved periodically. The *Rectitudines* envisages that a swineherd might either be a slave (*æhteswan, seruus porcarius* in the Latin) or free, paying rent or tribute (*gafolswan*). Even if he was a slave, a swineherd's skills were evidently valued: one is worth *healfan punde* (120 pence) in the Ely Farming Memoranda, where two other unfree individuals are put at 5 *ore* each (80 or 100 pence).[194] Such value did not, however, improve his social status: when ex-King Sigeberht of Wessex was stabbed to death by a swineherd in ?757, his assailant's occupation only served to emphasize the depths to which the former monarch had sunk.[195]

The free swineherd's *gafol* was ten old and five young pigs (see p. 113); the size of the herd, however, is not stated.[196] The approximate number of animals one man could look after may have been common knowledge, possibly as many as in the will of Ælfhelm, who asked that two hundred swine be fattened on an estate in Hertfordshire he left to Westminster.[197] An even larger number, *twa þusendu swina*, was left by Ealdorman Ælfred between 871 and 889, to go with seven estates in Kent and Surrey.[198] These huge numbers must have required several people to look after them. Alfred's large herds were presumably being kept in the famous 'denns' of the Weald, ideal pannage country (see Chapter 9). At Wicken Bonhunt in Essex, higher numbers of pig bones have been found than on any other Anglo-Saxon site, and the population structure suggested a breeding herd.[199] Conspicuous consumption of this high-status animal (see Chapter 4, p. 89) was no doubt facilitated by the wooded character of that

---

[190] Darby, *Domesday England*, 172–8.

[191] Ine 44, in Liebermann (ed.), *Gesetze*, i, 108.

[192] No precise dates are given in any Anglo-Saxon source.

[193] Liebermann (ed.), *Gesetze*, i, 447.

[194] Robertson (ed. and tr.), *Anglo-Saxon Charters*, 254 (Appendix 2, no. 9).

[195] ASC A etc., *s.a.* 755, in Bately (ed.), *MS A*. Cf. the murder of St Kenelm by a *subulco* in one version of his Life, in Love (ed.), *Vita et miracula*, 129 and p. civ.

[196] In Domesday Book, peasants pay one pig in seven or ten (probably) for pannage, but they are not specialist swineherds; see Darby, *Domesday England*, 175–8.

[197] This is the Ælfhelm who left the stud mentioned in Chapter 4 (p. 80): S 1487; Whitelock (ed.), *Anglo-Saxon Wills*, 30–5 (no. 13), at 30.

[198] S 1508; Harmer (ed.), *Historical Documents*, 13–15 (no. 10), at 15.

[199] Crabtree, 'Production and consumption'.

county, and contrasts with low numbers of pigs in the Yorkshire Wolds, a much more open landscape.[200] We might expect smaller numbers in less wooded areas, but Domesday herds often exceed the capacity of local woodland.[201]

The evidence of the *Rectitudines* suggests that the swine of more ordinary Anglo-Saxons were combined into communal herds. The *gebur*s give their six loaves to the *inswa[n]*, translated *porcarius curie*, 'manorial? swineherd' in the Latin version. He must be the *æhteswan*, who looked after the *inheord*, his lord's pigs,[202] so the *gafolswan* presumably looked after other people's. In Ireland it seems that joint herding was widespread.[203] Later English swineherds also looked after herds drawn from a number of owners.[204] The Domesday peasants who paid (in pigs) for pannage[205] almost certainly combined their swine into large herds, rather than all staying in the woods with their own pigs.

Identification   Where animals are kept in common herds, or on open pasture, knowing which livestock belonged to whom is of vital importance. The obsession of Anglo-Saxon legislation with the retrieval of lost and stolen cattle, as well as the evidence of charms and the Fonthill Letter, demonstrate clearly that this was true in early medieval England.[206] Both branding and ear-clipping were probably practised, as suggested by a clause in Æthelred's third law-code, which requires that 'no one may kill a "head of cattle" unless he has the witness of two trustworthy men, and he must keep the hide and head for three nights; and a sheep's likewise. And if he gets rid of the hide before that, he must pay 20 ore.'[207] Similar provisions remained in force in early modern Scotland, notorious at the time for cattle-reiving, which by then was being suppressed elsewhere in Britain. On Islay in 1725, it was made explicit that the two witnesses should be familiar with the brands of the supposed owner, and the hide had to be kept until the animal had been eaten.[208] The Anglo-Saxon witnesses must have had to know the ear-clips too, as the head as well as the hide had to be kept: sheep have traditionally been marked on their ears rather than, or as well as, on their bodies.[209] Although the marking of livestock is not mentioned in other Anglo-Saxon sources (unless the mysterious *sporwreclas* of the Fonthill letter are marks of some kind),[210] it must have been of vital importance in tracing lost or stolen animals throughout this period.

---

[200] O'Connor, 'Animal husbandry', 372.
[201] Albarella, 'Pig husbandry', 77.
[202] These compounds with *in-* seem to be analogous to *inland*; see Faith, *English Peasantry*, 15–55, esp. 16.
[203] Kelly, *Early Irish Farming*, 82.
[204] Albarella, 'Pig husbandry', 77.
[205] Darby, *Domesday England*, 175.
[206] See Hough, 'Cattle tracking in the Fonthill Letter', and Hollis, 'Cattle-theft charms'.
[207] Æthelred III, 9–9.1, in Liebermann (ed.), *Gesetze*, i, 230.
[208] Haldane, *The Drove Roads of Scotland*, 10.
[209] See Ryder, *Sheep & Man*, 668–9 *et passim*.
[210] See Hough, 'Cattle tracking in the Fonthill Letter', 881–3.

Breeding

Our sources do not tell us much about livestock breeding. If we relied on written evidence, we might have to assume that Anglo-Saxon cattle had achieved some kind of parthenogenesis. References to bulls are almost non-existent in Anglo-Saxon documents, and only one is mentioned in the Domesday returns.[211] Nor does the zooarchaeological record add a great deal, for most bone reports offer no evidence on the sex of *Bos* remains. A valuable exception is mid-Anglo-Saxon James Street in London, where cattle were sexed by their horn cores, identifying three cows, one bull, and three oxen.[212] The bull was over ten years old, evidently having had a long career at stud. Given the importance of ox traction (see pp. 108–10), the majority of bull calves must have been castrated, and the number of bulls on any farm, or farming community, would have been small. The Irish legal text *Críth Gablach* suggests one bull to seven cows, or two for twenty.[213] In spite of their rarity, given the value attached to cattle in general, it is surprising that neither the *Gerefa* nor *Rectitudines* mention bulls or any workers or operations associated with them.

Cows can breed at any time of year, but spring or early summer calving, when there is plenty of fresh grass to provide milk for the young, is best for healthy calves.[214] The gestation period is nine months, and thus mating can take place from high summer onwards. Cows might cease milking (see p. 113, under 'Dairying') during their pregnancy, or be dried off deliberately. Given the importance of cattle, especially oxen, it is unlikely that cows were allowed to give birth entirely without human intervention, but there is no Anglo-Saxon evidence for what that intervention consisted of, for instance extra feed (see p. 126), given that grass quality would be reduced during the winter, or housing, either during pregnancy or for calving. Calves would be left to 'run' with their mothers as long as they were suckling, and probably longer: no 'calfherd' is mentioned in the *Rectitudines* to go with those for cows and oxen.

We have no evidence for the careful selection of breeding animals, normal in later periods, but it is more likely in the case of cattle (and of course horses) than other, less valuable species. Evidence from London and Flixborough suggests that some selection was taking place, resulting in different sizes of horn and various skeletal elements,[215] but whether these were a by-product of breeding for higher milk yields, for instance, or better muscle conformation, or as an end in themselves, we cannot tell. Even where no deliberate selection was

---

[211] Darby, *Domesday England*, 164. There are none in the documents edited by Robertson (ed. and tr.), *Anglo-Saxon Charters*, otherwise an excellent repository of livestock references.

[212] Armitage, 'The animal bone', 30.

[213] Kelly, *Early Irish Farming*, 48.

[214] Wild cattle mate in late summer and autumn, and give birth early in the following summer, and the males only join the main herd during the mating season: Legge, 'Aurochs and domestic cattle', 26–7.

[215] Armitage, 'The animal bone', 30, and Dobney, Jaques, Johnstone, Hall, la Ferla, and Haynes, 'The agricultural economy', 187.

taking place at breeding, stock trading would bring new genetic material into herds, as farmers would presumably choose animals with desirable characteristics, such as size, colour, or yield.

Unlike cows, ewes cannot breed throughout the year, but only come into season in the autumn (November and December in wild sheep, but starting in September in most British breeds).[216] October is the traditional tupping month in lowland Britain, November in the hills.[217] With a gestation period of about five months,[218] March and April are the traditional months for lambing (as in early Irish sources), April and May in upland areas.[219] It is not clear how much, if at all, breeding was controlled in Anglo-Saxon flocks. On open range, the rams would probably only join the ewes in the mating season, as in wild sheep.[220] Sheep can always distinguish members of their own flock from other sheep, both by sight and by smell, and mixed flocks on common grazing will separate readily,[221] but rams are aggressive during the breeding season[222] and will compete to mate with each others' ewes. Feral rams rarely survive beyond four years, while ewes may live to ten or even older.[223] Thus a feral flock contains considerably more ewes than rams: Ryder envisages a hypothetical Iron Age flock with only one ram to about twenty ewes, while later medieval figures suggest one to thirty.[224] Competition, and the loss of valuable stock, could be minimized in domesticated flocks by castrating the majority of male lambs, and of course by eating them.[225] There is no evidence for devices to prevent unwanted mating in Anglo-Saxon England,[226] nor the (now) traditional method of monitoring it by raddling, marking the ram's chest with a dye (traditionally red, hence the name) which will rub off on the ewes as they are served,[227] so that, if a ram is not mating enthusiastically, or he is serving the ewes but they are not conceiving, he can be replaced. Both would, however, be within contemporary technical capability.

We also have no evidence for whether ewes kept on open pasture through the winter were brought in to a sheltered area at lambing time, though this would make supervision easier. Hurdles or other shelters might be erected to provide protection from the elements and predators,[228] especially useful since lambs are naturally born at night.[229] The ewes could also be kept on richer

---

[216] Biffen, *Elements*, 608; Ryder, *Sheep & Man*, 11, 12.
[217] Ryder, *Sheep & Man*, 681.
[218] Ryder, *Sheep & Man*, 11.
[219] Biffen, *Elements*, 550, Kelly, *Early Irish Farming*, 69.
[220] Ryder, *Sheep & Man*, 7.
[221] Ryder, *Sheep & Man*, 7–8.
[222] Ryder, *Sheep & Man*, 11–12.
[223] Ryder, *Sheep & Man*, 81.
[224] Ryder, *Sheep & Man*, 82; Campbell, *English Seigniorial Agriculture*, 155.
[225] Ryder, *Sheep & Man*, 30–1.
[226] Ryder, *Sheep & Man*, 681–2.
[227] Biffen, *Elements*, 553–4; Ryder, *Sheep & Man*, 681–2.
[228] Biffen, *Elements*, 555.
[229] Ryder, *Sheep & Man*, 13.

pasture than usual, or given extra hay, to make sure they produced plenty of milk.[230] Lambs on open range wean themselves in early autumn, and males then join the rams,[231] while ewe lambs remain with the mother until the following year.[232] The survival of Anglo-Saxon lambs may have been quite low by modern standards. In feral Soay sheep, first-year mortality exceeds 50 per cent.[233] While this would be very high for a flock receiving human care, later medieval lambing rates were only in the sixties to eighties per hundred ewes,[234] implying a mortality rate of 10–40 per cent. Multiple births are rare in 'unimproved' sheep.[235] Ryder's Iron Age flock would provide twenty or more surplus ram lambs each year from a flock of one hundred. Unless there was considerable pressure on grazing, Anglo-Saxon male lambs would probably be castrated rather than culled.

Pigs will breed throughout the year, and produce more than one litter. Gestation takes slightly under four months.[236] Thus sows impregnated while out on wood-pasture, where it would be impossible to control mating, would farrow somewhere between midwinter and Easter. Unsupervised mating in the woods might result in crossing with wild boar, still present in England in the Anglo-Saxon period,[237] as well as miscellaneous domestic and feral males, so any attempt at selection for desirable characteristics must have been fairly ineffective. Whether measures were taken to restrict the activities of boars (which are notoriously hard to handle) at any time of year, we have no evidence. In the later Middle Ages, fifteen piglets per year per sow was considered reasonable,[238] but even unimproved breeds will sometimes produce nine to twelve in a single litter,[239] and breed twice a year.[240] In early medieval Ireland, a litter of nine was considered plausible, with the runt often hand-reared.[241] This impressive fecundity would, however, be reduced by the tendency of sows to lie on and even eat their new-born young.[242] No doubt some piglets would in any case be too small or sickly to survive: such infant casualties would be invisible in the zooarchaeological record, especially if sows farrowed in the woods.[243] In the Anglo-Saxon period, productivity must also have depended on feed quality and

---

[230] Biffen, *Elements*, 556, describes the feeding of lactating ewes under more modern conditions.

[231] Ryder, *Sheep & Man*, 13.

[232] Ryder, *Sheep & Man*, 13.

[233] Ryder, *Sheep & Man*, 81.

[234] Stone, *Decision-Making*, 41; Campbell, *English Seigniorial Agriculture*, 155.

[235] See Stone, *Decision-Making*, 41.

[236] Thear, *Smallholder's Manual*, 179.

[237] Albarella, 'Wild boar', 63–4.

[238] Stone, *Decision-Making*, 115 and n. 57. This is consistent with Biffen's 1932 figure of fourteen in two litters: Biffen, *Elements*, 570.

[239] Albarella, 'Pig husbandry', 72 and 86.

[240] Albarella, Manconi, Vigne, and Rowley-Conwy, 'Ethnoarchaeology of pig husbandry', 305.

[241] Kelly, *Early Irish Farming*, 81.

[242] Thear, *Smallholder's Manual*, 179–80. Seymour, however, claims that sows allowed to farrow naturally have no such vices: *Self-Sufficiency*, 81–2.

[243] Sykes, *The Norman Conquest*, 34.

quantity, as for other species. A survey of age-at-death data for pigs from several Anglo-Saxon sites showed that a large number of animals lived into adulthood, possibly indicating a cull of sows once they had produced a good crop of piglets, or it was clear that they were not going to.[244] Wicken Bonhunt (Essex), the only site where pigs were the most common species in the bone assemblage, shows a different pattern from anywhere else, with a larger number of pigs living into their third year: this is thought to reflect the population structure of a large breeding herd, rather than animals selected for eating.[245]

Goats and poultry were probably left to their own devices as far as breeding was concerned. This would of course make selection for desirable characteristics impossible.

Beekeeping

As insects, bees require very different management to domestic mammals and birds. Eva Crane states that beekeeping, as opposed to the harvesting of wild honey, began in Britain 'before Roman times', and that the coiled straw skep was introduced by the Anglo-Saxons, but there is no real evidence for the latter statement.[246] In fact, we have no evidence for the materials or construction of Anglo-Saxon hives at all. The seventh-century poet Aldhelm described bees living in 'little huts elegantly constructed of osiers, or with bark stitched together', but this description is almost certainly drawn from literary sources, not from his own observation.[247] In Ireland, the hollow-log hive seems to have been replaced by wickerwork skeps from the eleventh century, but the straw skep was apparently unknown in the Middle Ages.[248] At James Street in London, the excavators suggested that the burnt material in which the bees were found resulted from either a house fire, or from burning rubbish after deposition, possibly for hygienic reasons.[249] If the former, they suggest that a skep was attached to the outside of the house, but it is also possible that a swarm had taken up residence without human assistance. The Old English charm to prevent bees swarming, cited in the previous chapter, shows that this was enough of a concern to require supernatural assistance. Another possibility is that the hive was destroyed by fire, either deliberately in order to extract the honey, or accidentally in the process of smoking the bees out, for the same purpose. We have no Anglo-Saxon evidence for how honey was extracted from hives, and whether the bees were killed in the process, but this was hard to avoid with traditional hives.[250]

---

[244] Dobney, Jaques, Johnstone, Hall, la Ferla, and Haynes, 'The agricultural economy', 146–7.
[245] Crabtree, 'Animal exploitation'.
[246] *World History of Beekeeping*, 251–2.
[247] *De uirginitate prosa*, vi, in Ehwald (ed.), *Aldhelmi opera*, 233. See Casiday, 'St Aldhelm's bees'.
[248] Kelly, *Early Irish Farming*, 110–11.
[249] Leary, 'Life and death', 11.
[250] Traditional methods are described by Crane, *World History of Beekeeping*, 341, 484–4.

At York, some of the bees were damaged, suggesting they had died in some kind of processing.[251]

The *Rectitudines* sees beekeepers and swineherds in similar terms. Both could be either a slave or a free *gafol*-payer, rendering a certain amount of his produce every year.[252] This may be the only connection between the two, or it may be that both honey and pig products were thought of as 'semi-wild', derived ultimately from 'free' resources.[253] Anglo-Saxon beekeepers may have moved their charges to the woods to feed, like the swineherds, although they would need to do so in the spring and summer, when trees and other plants were in flower, not in the autumn: there is some evidence from Ireland for hives being moved to take advantage of wild sources of nectar.[254] Some hives, and therefore beekeepers, may have remained permanently in the woods, and been identified with 'the wild', rather than with human habitation and farming.

CONCLUSION

With the industrious bee we conclude our discussion of Anglo-Saxon animal husbandry. A major theme to emerge from this chapter is 'non-specialization': evidence for flocks or herds raised for a single product or purpose, such as milk or meat, is rare. Even the 'normal' modern regime, where meat is the main aim and everything else is secondary, was a later development. 'Secondary' products often seem to have been more important, in fact, or equally so. The obvious, and probably major, exception to this generalist generalization is provided by the huge herds of swine occupying many woodland areas. Apart from a few bristles, and possibly pigskin, meat and fat were their only products. These pigs may well have been raised for the market, at least in the later part of the period, and commercialization was probably the stimulus for such specialization as did exist, sheep raised mainly for wool, for instance, or for milking. Given that wool is the agrarian product with the best-documented trade, however, there is surprisingly little evidence for a sheep-husbandry regime focused systematically on this one commodity, although some parts of the country were raising more sheep by the end of the period. We need to remember that, even though trade, including trade in farm products, was becoming increasingly important in the latter part of the Anglo-Saxon period, it was still insignificant by modern standards.

---

[251] Hall and Kenward, 'Setting people in their environment', 397.

[252] *Rectitudines* 4.5, in Liebermann (ed.), *Gesetze*, i, 448.

[253] Bees were not fed before the nineteenth century: Crane, *World History of Beekeeping*, 493.

[254] Kelly, *Early Irish Farming*, 111. Crane, *World History of Beekeeping*, 347–50, cites references to 'migration' of hives going back to 250 BC, but her first examples from the north or west of Europe are early modern.

The other thing we should bear in mind, although the evidence for it is slim, is the difference between the large-scale farming operations of landowners and the essentially subsistence regimes of most of the population. The latter may have been required to produce certain foodstuffs for their superiors (although we have no evidence for how obligations such as *feorm* were divided up among producers), but otherwise they ate what they could produce, and anything they were able to sell or exchange would simply be what they could spare from their own production. Although a degree of specialization may have been imposed by the environment, their security would be maximized by diversification, so that an outbreak of sheep pox, for instance, would not leave them without animal products for immediate and future consumption. And, even in good years, no species would be managed with only one product in mind; that would be to court similar disaster if anything went wrong. To cull all one's geese for meat, for instance, even if the price was high, would be to deprive the household of potential eggs for the future, when they might be a life-saver. And to slaughter an ox might leave a household unable to produce cereals for the following year.

This chapter completes our survey of Anglo-Saxon crops, livestock, and farming practices. In Part II, we explore how they might have been combined into functional farming operations on the ground.

PART II

'Thorgils holds Collaton from Judhael. In the time of King Edward Cola held it and (it) paid tax for half a hide. There is land for three ploughs. There is one plough there with three *villani* and one bordar. Half an acre of meadow there and two acres of pasture and six acres of wood-land. Three cattle eleven sheep. Formerly twenty shillings now it is worth five shillings.'

Domesday Book, Devon, ed. F. and C. Thorn

Fig. 6.1. Collaton, South Hams, Devon (line drawing).

(© Jane Peart)

6

Farms in their landscapes

Introduction to Part II

Not only does this book have two authors, Banham, who has written Part I, and Faith Part II, but we have approached the subject very differently. The preceding chapters have looked at the practicalities of farming; the following chapters look at how people managed land and livestock in a variety of regions. These regions are broadly the ones identified in Joan Thirsk's *The English Rural Landscape*: coastal and riverside marshlands, woodland, downland, moorland, and wolds; the chapters attempt to emulate Thirsk's alertness to regional differences.[1]

Farming in Anglo-Saxon England began in the aftermath of the collapse of a regime. One important aspect of the post-Roman period could well have been that once the pressure to produce grain for the army and for export was gone there was a period of 'abatement' in much of the countryside. 'Abatement' describes a situation in which, when a demand to produce a surplus, or a particular type of food, has stopped, people invest less energy than formerly in producing food.[2] In these regional chapters this is interpreted to mean that Anglo-Saxon farmers, at least early in our period, invested much less effort than had their Romano-British predecessors in growing cereals. People do not normally choose to work harder than they need! They often seem to have been content to use the fields which earlier generations had carefully enclosed and cultivated, but they may have used them much less intensively, perhaps as often as animal enclosures as cultivation plots. When reasonably fertile, easily-worked soil was readily available, many farmers seem not to have relied on animals to restore the fertility of the land they cultivated: they simply let it rest. Chapter 13 describes this 'laid-back' style of farming.

There is a strong environmental argument for envisioning early Anglo-Saxon farming as having a strong bias towards livestock husbandry and moving away from extensive or intensive crop production. There is one primary fact about how land and vegetation behave. The key shapers of the landscape are not

---

[1] Thirsk, *English Rural Landscape*.
[2] La Bianca, *Sedentarization and Nomadization*, 16–20.

people but livestock. The environmental writer F. W. M. Vera has made a strong case against envisaging the naturally occurring deciduous forests of northern Europe before the modern era as having reaching an unchecked 'forest climax' in which trees grew unchecked to a vast height and then died and decayed. Instead, he sees them as having been controlled by vast numbers of grazing animals, both wild and domesticated, who created areas of natural 'wood-pasture', 'a park-like landscape where the succession of trees is determined by large herbivorous mammals…' and wild boar, resulting in a mixture of standard trees, low-growing shrub and brush, and open grassland.[3] Many of Vera's examples come from continental Europe but there are English examples of all that he describes, and an Old English vocabulary for it. Chapter 7 on Woodland draws on his work. From an English perspective Oliver Rackham hammers home the same point: 'Almost all land by nature turns to woodland. Let a field be abandoned…and within a year it will be invaded by oaks springing up from acorns dropped by passing jays, or by birches from wind-blown seed. In ten years it will be difficult to reclaim, in thirty years it will have "tumbled down to woodland." The same happens to chalk downs, heaths, fens, and some moorland *whenever the grazing and burning cease that had held trees in check*' (my italics).[4] So it is a significant fact that, where measurements can be taken, there does not seem to have been a wholesale regeneration of woodland in post-Roman Britain.[5] This points to a much more pastoral economy in which there were enough animals to restrict the growth of new woodland. Of course unknown numbers of wild grazers would have outnumbered their domesticated counterparts.

A remark made earlier in this book that 'Anglo-Saxons valued animals more than plants' (p. 75) receives ample endorsement in the following chapters. The need of their grazing animals—cattle and sheep and goats—for pasture, the benefits their pigs could gain feeding on the autumn mast, can be seen to have had a vital influence on the ways that people thought about and defined 'their' territory and moved their livestock within it: the latter part of this chapter discusses the ramifications of this.

The emphasis we both place on the importance of livestock could turn some entrenched beliefs on their head. One concerns the location of early settlements. Conventional wisdom for a long time had it that incoming Angles and Saxons (for those who believe in incoming Angles and Saxons) looked primarily for land which was easy to cultivate—hence, for instance, the frequency of early settlement on the light river gravels, leading to the judgement that 'the

[3] Vera, *Grazing, Ecology and Forest History*, 110–12.
[4] Rackham, *History of the Countryside*, 67.
[5] The idea that post-Roman Britain reverted to dense woodland has long been rejected because of pollen evidence, which can distinguish between pollen from cultivated and wild plants: Dark, *Environment of Britain*.

whole Anglo-Saxon movement was essentially a river-valley settlement.'[6] But can we be sure that finding easily worked arable land was in fact their main concern? As the chapters which follow attempt to show, many different kinds of land, much of it what we would describe as 'marginal', could be, and was, cultivated in the past. If we take animal husbandry seriously, we can look at arable faming from a different perspective. Is it not just as likely that what primarily attracted settlers to river valleys were their stretches of riverside grassland where their cattle could graze and which could provide winter fodder? The Thames valley, for instance, supported ordinary farmers like those at Yarnton in the middle Anglo-Saxon period, described in Gill Hey's work, who carried on modest mixed farming between the lush riverside pastures. But earlier this had been the heartland of wealthy, prestigious, even royal, individuals—the kind of people for whom the 'palaces' at Drayton and Sutton Courtenay were built.[7] Their wealth, if it came from the land, and from trade in its products, is much more likely to have been on the hoof than growing in the small fields. As we have seen, wealth and cattle were virtually synonymous. So to see early medieval England from the point of view of livestock husbandry, as the following chapters attempt to do, is not only a good starting point in understanding its landscape—it might well be in tune with how Anglo-Saxons saw it.

A shift towards pastoralism, a term used here to indicate a rural economy in which animal husbandry was of greater importance than agriculture, need not have been a direct consequence of Germanic settlement. It could have represented a return to much earlier pre-Roman farming practice in Britain: the system which in our concluding chapter we describe as 'ancient farming'. Archaeological evidence of Bronze Age farming systems in the Fenland studied by Francis Pryor shows the knowledgeable management of animals and 'fairly intensive' stock farming with flocks of 2,000–3,000, similar in size to those of medieval landowners such as the Cistercian monks. The Iron Age has been called 'the age of sheep' and many areas of arable, like those on the downland, would have been unviable without them.[8] The return to, or conservation of, these earlier farming methods and field systems is a topic which Chapter 12 revisits in detail.

In order to understand the importance of pastoralism, the livestock as opposed to the arable side of the farming economy, we first need to broaden our idea of what 'pasture' was in Anglo-Saxon England. We are used to seeing cattle and sheep on land that has been carefully managed to produce the best quality

---

[6] Loyn, *Anglo-Saxon* England, 31. Gravel extraction has provided the opportunity for archaeological investigation of such soils, which may have disproportionately emphasized their importance as early settlement areas.

[7] For settlement evidence: Blair, *Anglo-Saxon Oxfordshire*, xx, 6–29; Booth et al., *The Thames through Time*, 83–99. For prestigious sites: Blair, *Anglo-Saxon Oxfordshire*, 29–34; Booth et al., *The Thames through Time*, 100–3. On Yarnton: Hey, *Yarnton*.

[8] Pryor, *Farmers in Prehistoric Britain*, 100–7; Lock, Gosden, and Daly, *Segsbury Camp*.

grass. This has been achieved by seeding a limited range of grasses chosen for their nutritional value and their capability to retain this when stored as hay or silage. Early and unimproved animals were nearer to their feral forebears than today's breeds and, like them, were much more omnivorous: they would eat holly, bushes, seaweed, salt-marsh plants, young bracken—whatever provided a bite. Plates 6–8 show animals used for conservation projects, brought in to keep down the regrowth of unwanted vegetation on a range of these pastures. Perhaps the most enduring and common practice—also the least familiar to the English today, although still familiar in Wales—is the use of woodland as pasture.[9] Even when common rights in woodland to take timber had been severely curtailed, it continued to be a source of free grazing: Gainsborough is just one of many eighteenth-century artists who naturally enlivened their woodland scenes with cows and sheep and their guardians. It is worth stressing that animals did not simply graze on the grass growing in woodland. Even today's cows, fed on protein-rich mixes and improved grassland, will enthusiastically eat leaves if given the chance, stripping them from growing trees and browsing hedges. Plate 8 shows cattle in Burnham Beeches, Buckinghamshire, relishing this kind of fodder. It seems likely that 'tree fodder' was sometimes regularly cut and supplied to pre-Conquest cattle by pollarding trees (cutting off the lower branches close to the trunk) and lopping ('shredding') the new growth on the trunk.[10] It is notable that when our earliest representations of grazing animals also show trees, these almost always have trunks bare to above grazing height, as if they had been systematically lopped or pollarded. Yorkshire farmers still feed lopped branches to their cattle.[11] The tender succulent growing points at the top of plant stems were what animals most enjoyed—Plate 3 shows a sheep nibbling what looks like the growing tip of a sapling—but grazing animals will also strip mature trees of their bark and leaves, and cows loved the alders which flourished in wet 'carrs'. However, a sharp distinction between areas of woodland and areas of settlement is inappropriate. In Anglo-Saxon England woodland was a valuable pasture resource, but it was also farmed and settled: Chapter 8 visits some of these woodland farms.

LIVESTOCK MANAGEMENT

Keeping animals involves moving them, and the following chapters are full of animals on the move. We do not know whether cattle on ordinary farms were

---

[9] Wales: Fleming, 'Working with wood-pasture'; Rackham, *History of the Countryside*, 119–21; Vera, *Grazing Ecology and Forest History, passim.*

[10] Rackham, *History of the Countryside*, gives a clear depiction of these practices at Fig. 5.1 on 66.

[11] 'Black Welsh sheep will gnaw the bark of Ash, Elm and Beech branches cut and laid down for them just as readily as deer will do…': Elwes, *Guide to the Primitive Breeds of Sheep*, 7. Yorkshire farmers: Jean Birrell, pers. comm.

Plate 1. January: ploughing, British Library, Cotton Tiberius B. v, fo. 3r.

(© The British Library Board, Cotton Tiberius B. v)

Plate 2. November: pigs at mast, British Library, Cotton Tiberius B. v, fo. 7r.
(© The British Library Board, Cotton Tiberius B. v)

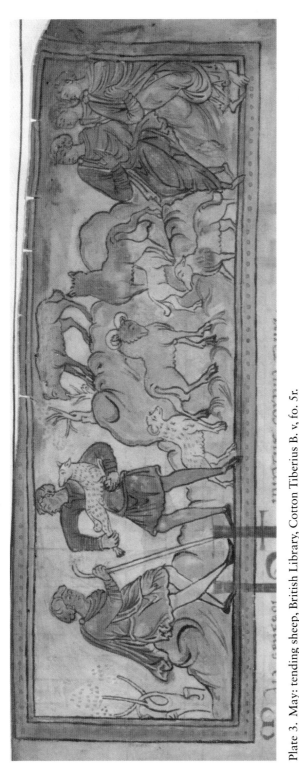

Plate 3. May: tending sheep, British Library, Cotton Tiberius B. v, fo. 5r.

(© The British Library Board, Cotton Tiberius B. v)

Plate 4. Hens 'like ours at home, red in colour', British Library, Cotton Tiberius B. v, fo. 79r.

(© The British Library Board, Cotton Tiberius B. v)

Plate 5. Sheep, British Library, Cotton Tiberius B. v, fo. 78v.

Plate 6a. Fenland: Highland cattle and Konik ponies graze the restored grasslands of Baker's Fen, part of Wicken Fen Nature Reserve, Cambridgeshire.

(Photograph © Steve Aylward, National Trust)

Plate 6b. Saltmarsh: Herdwick sheep on the saltmarsh of Morecambe Bay, Lancashire.

(Photograph © Holker Hall Estate)

Plate 7. Heathland: Exmoor ponies on Sutton Heath, Suffolk.

(© David Addy)

Plate 8. Wood pasture: Browsing at Burnham Beeches and Stoke Row Nature Reserve.
(Corporation of the City of London, photograph © Howard Cooper)

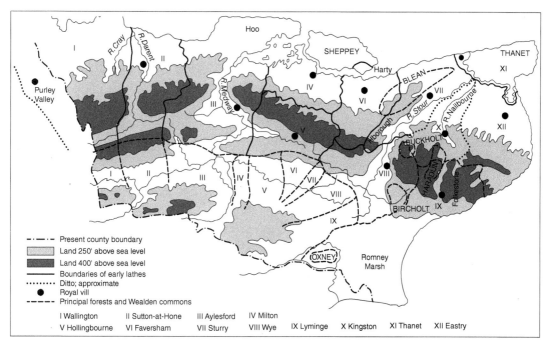

Fig. 6.2. Kentish droveways and lathes.
Witney's map of the Kentish lathes—territorial and administrative divisions akin to the hundred—shows them to be closely related to the pattern established by the links between communities and their pasture resources, notably the pig-pastures of the Weald.

(From Witney, *Jutish Forest* (Athlone Press, an imprint of Bloomsbury Publishing plc))

brought in at night as the working oxen seem to have been in Ælfric's *Colloquy*.[12] There is almost no archaeological evidence from ordinary rural sites of buildings specifically to house animals, nor of the longhouses known on the Continent in which cattle and people slept under one roof.[13] But even if they are simply kept penned near the farm in some way, as they seem increasingly to have been from the middle Anglo-Saxon period on, cattle, and to a lesser extent sheep, need to be moved from enclosure to enclosure to avoid sickening the grass and exposing themselves to infestation.[14] Grazing and browsing animals have to be moved off growing crops, including hay, from the time these begin to show in early spring. In many farm systems their manure is a valuable asset after a crop is carried in late summer, at which time they should to be moved back onto the cut field. In the winter they should be moved away from low-lying

---

[12] See p. 122.
[13] See p. 122; Hamerow, *Early Medieval Settlements*, 50–1.
[14] Hamerow, *Rural Settlements*, 73–5, 88–90, on middle Anglo-Saxon enclosures, some of which may have been used for animals, and on stock ways.

land which floods in the winter and off land where winter weather conditions are dangerously bad to what the knowledgeable reeve in the late Old English text *Gerefa* calls *winterdun*, 'winter-hill'. On low-lying land which floods easily they might need shifting at other times too. Most important of all, if their winter feed is grown in a particular place, they require a source of summer food elsewhere. Moving the animals to grazing away from the farm is known as transhumance. It was common in one form or another throughout medieval Europe and continued well after that in many upland regions.[15] In this chapter, and in the regional studies in Chapters 7 to 11, seasonal grazing is seen as a key to how Anglo-Saxon farmers perceived and organized their countryside.

ANIMALS ON THE MOVE

Long-distance trackways, such as those that criss-cross downland and moor-land, are still there for us to see, but as animals have been moving around the English landscape for millennia these are difficult if not impossible to date. This makes the Old English names for tracks and ways, when they can be dated to the pre-Conquest period, particularly useful. Della Hooke has mapped some Worcestershire drove ways which she is able to show from charter evidence to be pre-Conquest (at the latest) in origin. *Weg*, our modern 'way', which appears in pre-Conquest place-names and in the numerous 'hay ways' (from OE *hig* or *heg*) in charter boundaries and in place-names like Hailey and Hay-don, Hayford and Highway, show that it was often important to bring this important winter fodder over quite a distance. The 'hay way of the Buckland people' appears in a Devon charter of the eleventh century, and this broad road onto the moor is a main route today.[16] The hay that the Buckland people brought down from the moor was probably a mixture of coarse grasses mixed with bracken. Better quality purpose-grown hay is likely to have been culti-vated on damp meadowland. Filice Lane, from OE *fileðe*, 'hay', in nearby Hor-rabridge leads to the village's well-watered meadows along the river Walkham.[17]

If animals have to be moved any distance, as they would have been in the case of many of the grazing areas described in this chapter, they cannot be driven too fast or they will lose condition. So they need to feed on their slow travels by grazing the verges, as in the case of the 'sheep-way' at Shipway in Kent and the many 'swine-ways'. The hollies found along some ancient tracks

---

[15] Dixon, 'Hunting, summer grazing and settlement', for the Scottish uplands.

[16] Hooke, *Landscape*, Fig. 55, at 161; Hooke, *Pre-Conquest Charter Bounds of Devon and Corn-wall*, 195–9; Cole, '*Weg*: a waggoner's warning'. Taylor, *Roads and Tracks*, 163–8, discusses the later evidence for drove roads.

[17] Hooke, *Pre-Conquest Charter Bounds of Devon and Cornwall*, 198–9.

may be signs of prolonged use as drove ways, since young holly was much appreciated as fodder—and animals need a supply of fodder when they stop for the night.[18] Sheep require water primarily while lactating but cattle have to have water at least twice a day: they came down to drink at the 'milk burn', and jostled through the 'funnels' which led off the moor to the 'worthy' farms on the edge of Dartmoor.[19] Pigs might drink at the 'swine brook'. Although Anglo-Saxon pigs were hairier and thus better protected against sunlight than their modern counterparts, in order to cool down in hot weather they seem to have been as glad as modern breeds to wallow in muddy ponds, like the wallow (*sol*) from which Sole Farm on a muddy Berkshire hillside gets its name, and where pigs still luxuriate in wallows at farms nearby.

SHEPHERDS AND SHIELINGS

We need to remember that many early Anglo-Saxon farms and their fields were small patches of living space and cultivation amid wide stretches of open moor, fells, wolds, woodland, or downland, just as some farms still are today. It is also worth reiterating a point made earlier: what had kept them open were large numbers of animals, both wild and domesticated. It has been calculated that to keep the tree cover down on the 20,000 ha of Bodmin Moor, for instance, would require 5000 modern cattle or horses, 8000 young cattle or ponies, or 50,000 sheep to graze the area, and in the past even greater numbers of traditional types of animals, which were smaller, would have been needed.[20]

Place-names can be a clue as to how this kind of landscape and the animals ranging over it were managed. Cornwall retains many more British elements in its place-names than more eastern counties and among these are the pair *hendre* and *hafos*. *Hendre* denotes the 'home' or 'winter' settlement. From here the animals were taken for the summer up to the farm's summer settlement, the *havos*, on the 'rough ground' as moorland is called in Cornwall. Wales retained this pair of names and this kind of farming well into the modern period. In this system the sheep and cows were taken up by a group of guardians, perhaps the young women from the home farms. Herring has found traces of their summer settlements, which had up to ten huts with room for dairying and wool-working

---

[18] Atkin, 'Hollin names'; Spray, 'Holly as a fodder'. I am grateful to Ann Cole for advice here.

[19] Faith, 'Some Devon farms', 76–9. Fig. 10.4 shows the access of some Devon farms to Dartmoor.

[20] Herring, 'Shadows of ghosts', 94; Fox, *Dartmoor's Alluring Uplands*, 71 calculates that Dartmoor supported up to 10,000 head of cattle (his figures are only for cattle) in the later Middle Ages. This is many times the number of all animals combined today; hence the extensive regrowth of gorse on the moor, which would formerly have been checked by grazing, can now only be controlled by regular 'swaling' (burning) by the commoners: Richard Kitchen, pers. comm.

as well as for daily living, and small areas of attached arable land.[21] Naturally practices differed from place to place, but while it was universally important to keep animals off the growing crops and hay back at the farm, it was only where the home farm and its pastures were widely separated, with some kind of settlement on the latter, that we should expect to find the *havos–hendre* arrangement of Cornwall. (This pair of names does not seem to have had an Old English equivalent, although the various Somertons and the Scandinavian 'summer' place-names in Lincolnshire could well be the equivalent of *havos* and Wintertons of *hendre*.)[22]

Whether on 'rough ground', on mountainsides, on saltmarsh, on heaths, or in woodland glades, domestic animals were often far away from the farmstead, sometimes in remote and dangerous places. Sheep in particular were such vulnerable animals that they needed to be kept together and guarded at night: wolves were their most dangerous predator, but eagles and hawks, and feral dogs and cats, could take lambs. But unlike pigs, which will scatter, sheep have an instinct to flock. In open country they do not range very widely but become 'hefted'—a term which may come from the OE *hæftan*, 'to bind or confine'.[23] That is to say, the young stock, by following the experienced ewes, became habituated to a particular area where they always graze and to which they return at night. The most secure way to protect them overnight thus was to keep them in an enclosure, a fold, OE *fald, falod*, or in the probably less substantial construction known as a *loc*. A Middle and Modern English term for a shepherd was 'looker'. The 'lookers' who patrolled Romney Marsh well into the nineteenth century stayed with their flocks and they may well have folded them at night.[24] The term is generally derived from OE *locian*, 'to look, watch', but another possible origin could possibly be *loc*, the Old English word for the fold: a moveable fold made from hurdles lashed together is a *lochyrdl*. (Gainsborough's sketch of a hurdle can be seen in Fig. 7.9). The 'lookers' clearing', *lokeres leage*, at Fovant, Hampshire, was likely to have been a safe clearing related to a drove way of some kind onto the high chalk downs, remote from the valley settlement. The shepherds who used the *lokeres weg* on the wooded Berkshire Downs, recorded

[21] Herring, 'West Cornwall's rough ground', 39; Herring, 'Shadows of ghosts'; Herring, 'Early medieval transhumance', further discussed in Chapter 13. For this as a feature of British farming in Wales and the south-west: Silvester, 'Wales'; for Devon: Fox, *Dartmoor's Alluring Uplands*; for Ireland: Gardiner, 'Time regained'. Wrathmell, *Wharram Percy*, 105, suggests that some place-names on the Yorkshire Wolds such as Arram, Bootham, and Cottam 'may indicate buildings occupied in the summer months during seasonal grazing on the Wolds'. Bil, *The Shieling* is a thorough description of all aspects of transhumance in a Scottish context but has wider implications. Fox, *Seasonal Settlements* pioneered the study of this topic in an English context.

[22] This evidence is discussed more fully in Chapter 12. Lincolnshire 'summer' place-names are discussed in Chapter 11.

[23] Bosworth and Toller, *Anglo-Saxon Dictionary, s.v.* 'hæftan'; Hart, *Practice of Hefting*.

[24] Smith, *Place-Name Elements*, i, *s.v.* 'fald'. The folds that appear in charter boundaries as landmarks seem more likely to have been permanent structures for night shelter rather than the regularly shifted enclosures used for close-folding.

at Stanmore in Beedon, Berkshire, in a tenth-century charter, might have had to keep an eye out for the wolves of nearby 'wolf ridge', now Woolvers Hill and one of the jobs of the shepherd in Ælfric's *Colloquy* was to drive his flock in the evening to their folds, *hira locum* (translating the Latin *caulas eorum*), where they would be safe from wolves.[25] Young cattle too were penned away from the farm, as they must once have been somewhere near Challock, in Kent, 'the calves' *loca*'. Another term for the shepherd, whose job it was to move the fold and the sheep, was *faldere*, 'folder'. Several place-names appear to have this element: Fortherley, Northumberland, and possibly Faldingworth and Fallingworth in Lancashire and the West Riding of Yorkshire.

Seasonal pasturing, where the animals were out all summer, needed not just folds but gathering places. Pounds or corrals would have been essential at times of sorting and managing the sheep, collecting the ewes for milking, castrating the rams, and so on. Their guardians would have needed shelters nearby, sturdy enough for a season out on the fells, on the moors, or in the marshes.[26] A very important part of the shepherd's job was making cheese and butter. Chapter 5 has shown that these were much more likely to have been made from sheeps' milk than from cows'. Harold Fox has identified places, often on the edge of moorland, with the Old English elements *smeoru* and *butere* in their names as locations where the milk from animals pastured on the moor was made into cheese and butter. None of these sites appears in the written record before the Conquest, but Fox argues that they belonged to a period of 'personal transhumance' before the eleventh century when farmers turned their stock out in summer under the personal supervision of young women from the farm. (He drew a contrast with the rough male world of paid herdsmen or 'guardians' which succeeded it.) If sheep or cattle were milked where they were pastured, then a cool place for cheese-making and water for washing the equipment were needed. One of these dairying sites, Smeardon Ridge, near Godsworthy in Peter Tavy parish in west Devon, lies within one of its lobed enclosures: it is a patch of rocky pasture with a spring to provide the water needed for cooling the milk and keeping the dairying vessels clean (Fig. 6.3).[27]

It may be that the evidence is there, but we have not yet found a way of identifying the common characteristics that would make it possible to say that such-and-such a place was used as a seasonal settlement. The archaeology of uplands has produced some promising beginnings. The earliest form of settlement at Hound Tor on the eastern side of Dartmoor, superseded in the thirteenth century by a hamlet itself later deserted, consisted of three sunken-featured buildings, which perhaps had turf walls and bracken roofs. These

[25] *Ælfric's Colloquy*, 41; S 881; S 542, Kelly, *Charters of Abingdon Abbey*, no. 42.

[26] Pryor, *Farmers in Prehistoric Britain*, 100–5 and *passim*, has excellent explanations of the structures needed for managing and manipulating livestock, based on the author's knowledge both of prehistoric animal husbandry and of managing his own sheep.

[27] Fox, *Dartmoor's Alluring Uplands*, 148–50.

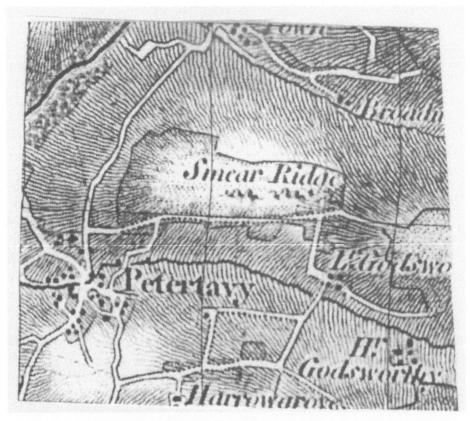

Fig. 6.3. Smear Ridge (now Smeardon Down), Peter Tavy, Devon.

(© Cassini Publishing Limited 2007)

were identified by the excavators as the shelters for herders staying up on the moor for the summer and sound very much like the shepherd's hut 'lightly built in the summer' where St Cuthbert and his horse miraculously found food—the horse snatched a bite from its thatch and uncovered the shepherd's carefully hidden supplies, still warm![28] Sunken-featured buildings are not any longer thought of as living-places, as they once were, but as the general-purpose kind of structure used in much of Britain, as useful as a garden shed and probably within the competence of the average Anglo-Saxon to put up.[29] Those at Hound Tor would not have housed a family, but they could well have provided shelter for a shepherd, or a couple of women sent up for the summer, perhaps growing a little barley to help them through. Nearby streams would be needed for storing butter and cheese. Fox adds examples from elsewhere in England—

[28] Smith, *Place-Name Elements*, ii, 103–4; Hound Tor is discussed by Fox, *Dartmoor's Alluring Uplands*, at 77–80, 140–8. Bede, *Life of St. Cuthbert*, ch. 5: Webb and Farmer, *Age of Bede*, 49.
[29] Hamerow, *Early Medieval Settlements*, 48–9.

Salmonby on the Lincolnshire Wolds may be one—and suggests other Dartmoor sites which could have been used both for hill sheep and dairy cows moving to wet pastures.[30] Features which Catherine Stoertz has identified from crop-marks at Butterwick and elsewhere on the Yorkshire Wolds are small clusters of sunken-featured buildings, little curvilinear 'settlement enclosures', and what look like small curving fields too.[31] Several of the curved enclosures appear to have had a gap in their wall of a size which could have been closed by a hurdle to provide a pen handy for managing small numbers of sheep. One has recently come to light at Wharram Percy, revealed in a new survey almost by chance.[32] Similar little groups of enclosures, which have come to be called 'Butterwick-type settlements', have been found elsewhere in Yorkshire (Fig. 6.4). Wrathmell describes them as 'much-revisited traditional' sites, 'seasonal rather than permanent' settlements, in effect interpreting them as shielings. If he is right, then there could hardly be a better name for the type than 'Butterwick'!

PASTORALISM AND ITS LANDSCAPES

The particularity and precision of the words that Anglo-Saxon people used to describe their environment shows how important they considered the differences between landscape features to have been.

Open land

Feld, open land, was used early on, particularly in forest areas, to mean a tract of land free of trees. 'Open country', 'unencumbered ground', in literary texts, it was contrasted both with hills and with woodland and was valued for its open (perhaps also its flat) character. Its early meaning had nothing to do with arable or fields, although in some cases it was applied to what became areas of predominantly arable land, such as the Warwickshire Feldon in the southern part of the county, as opposed to the Warwickshire Arden, the name for its

---

[30] Fox, *Dartmoor's Alluring Uplands*, 140–8. For Salmonby on the Lincolnshire Wolds, used first by Anglian herders and later by Scandinavian sheep-farmers, see Faith, 'Structure of the market for wool'.

[31] Stoertz, *Ancient Landscapes*, 51–5 and Figs. 7.7, 30, 59; Taylor, *Fields in the English Landscape*, Chapter 1; Wrathmell, *Wharram Percy*, 164–8.

[32] At Wharram itself the wealth of artefactual evidence assembled over the many years of investigation at the site of the deserted medieval village has made it possible, though not uncontroversial, to date the curvilinear enclosures and sunken-featured buildings there to the middle Anglo-Saxon period. The interpretation of the bone evidence does not look compatible with the site's having been a shieling throughout its period of use: it supposes an autumn slaughter, including of sheep, highly unlikely at a seasonal settlement. However, a great deal of other activity was going on at Wharram at the time, notably ironworking, and there is also as yet unexplained evidence of prestigious, perhaps ecclesiastical, contacts, so Wharram cannot be taken as typical.

Fig. 6.4. Crop-marks showing 'Butterwick-type enclosures' on the Yorkshire Wolds.

(From Stoertz, *Ancient Landscapes* © English Heritage)

woodland.[33] While a *feld* could simply be an open space (such as a battlefield), in the countryside an important use of the term was for unrestricted rough grazing.[34]

Rivers and meadows

Important as they were as a water source, streams and meadows were essential in another way. Riverside vegetation was a vital part of the winter fodder supply, whether or not it was deliberately cultivated as hay. In many peasant farming systems today it is the availability of sufficient winter feed that determines the number of working animals which can be kept. Winter feed was equally as vital to Anglo-Saxon farmers and it is a factor we will constantly meet throughout all the regional studies in this book. We need to remember that, before modern dredging and embanking restricted them to a single channel, rivers were much more 'braided', with several channels threading through well-watered meadows. Young stock benefited from the 'early bite' of new grass which winter-flooded river- and stream-side meadows provided when the waters went down, 'brookland' in the Sussex term.[35] If given time to recover after this early grazing, meadows then gave a supply of grass or other vegetation which could be dried and mown for winter feed. Because it governed the number of animals that could be kept through the winter, hay was an extremely valuable resource: in some places it was precious enough to be stored in the church along with the corn.[36] From the eighth century hay meadow was deliberately improved on the Thames flood-plain at Yarnton by seeding.[37] As it was essential to protect the pasture and the hay meadow along the river by keeping the stock off the growing grass it was important to rural communities also to have access to other sources of pasture nearby. In Kent the various kinds of *pays* had distinct characteristics and types of husbandry, yet they were linked in 'estates' which combined them into wider economic units, as Alan Everitt firmly established. His work and that of Harold Fox has shown the ties between settlements and different pasture areas, of which river meadow was a vital component.[38] Sue Oosthuizen has shown how important pasture was in the formation of Cambridgeshire territories. Long narrow bands of grazing land following the lie of the Bourn Valley, which survived as commons and headlands, are just one example of strings of loosely linked commons which she and Christopher

---

[33] Gelling, *Place-Names in the Landscape*, 235–45; Gelling and Cole, *Landscape of Place-Names*, 269–78.

[34] Bosworth and Toller, *Dictionary, s.vv.* 'feld-gangende', 'feld-hryther'; Gelling and Cole, *Landscape of Place-Names*, 274.

[35] Thorburn, *Mostly Rodmell*, 5.

[36] Bosworth and Toller, *Dictionary, s.v.* 'heg'.

[37] Colgrave and Mynors (eds), *Bede's Ecclesiastical History*, 18–19, 416–17; Hey, *Yarnton*, 47.

[38] Everitt, 'River and Wold'; Fox, 'People of the Wolds', 77–101.

Taylor have identified.[39] The 'Lambourn people's boundary', recognized in a charter of the eleventh century, circumscribed the land on both sides of the upper waters of the little river Lambourn in the Berkshire Downs. As well as the river meadows, this comprised the slopes of the chalk downland and their wooded crests, where forty of the priest's pigs were allowed to run *on wudu and on feolde*, 'in the woodland and on the open land'.[40] Terms we are used to using such as 'Thames Valley' beg the question of whether a river alone, important as it may have been as a route, could ever have shaped a rural economy. It was not solely the river but the integration into a larger economy of its meadowland, its arable land, and its woodland that supported early farming.

Woodland

An Old English text distinguishes between woodland, *wudulond, feldlond* or open land, and pasture land, *etelond*.[41] Today 'woodland' has come to mean exclusively an area where trees are the predominant vegetation, but in the past it had a much wider range of meanings which denoted how the land was used. Its primary importance was as wood-pasture. (Wood-pasture could also be indicated by the element *wald* in some regions such as Kent, where it 'always seems to indicate pasture'.)[42] The practice of wood-pasturing—turning animals out into woodland to graze and browse on leaves, bark, and growing bushes— was an essential element in peasant livestock husbandry, as it still is in parts of Europe. When a Kentish tanner bequeathed all his 'meddowes, pastures, feed-ingewoods, underwoods' late in the sixteenth century, he evidently thought of all of them as places where he could turn out his animals to feed.[43]

Woodlands played a central role in defining territories.[44] *Hwicce-wudu, Limenweara wold*, and *Weowara weald* were respectively the woodlands of the Hwicce of the West Midlands, the people of Lyminge, and the people of Wye in Kent. In her pioneering work Della Hooke has traced back the link between a territory and its woodland and showed how transhumance—seasonally moving stock to grazing—lay at the heart of the formation of early territories and their sense of identity. Their names preserve that link long after these territories fragmented. *Hwicce-wudu*, Wychwood, is many miles from the western border of the territory of the people whose wood it was, the Hwicce (and the link between them had probably already broken by the eighth century).[45] Place-

[39] Oosthuizen, 'Medieval greens and commons'.

[40] S 934; Robertson (ed. and tr.), *Anglo-Saxon Charters*, 240–1 (Appendix I.5).

[41] S 214, K 299 (*Upthrop*); Vera, *Grazing, Ecology and Forest History*, 110–12.

[42] Everitt, *Continuity and Colonization*, 143.

[43] I owe this quotation to Tina Bond. It is from the Kent History and Library Centre, Maidstone, reference PRC17/53/276.

[44] The practice of wood-pasture is the subject of Chapter 8, 'Woodland'. Hooke, *Trees*, 191–221 describes the species of trees typical of wood-pasture.

[45] Hooke, *Anglo-Saxon Landscapes of the West Midlands*, 48–55.

names which have the element *-ingas* are thought to have originated as a way of denoting territory associated with a group who shared a common identity derived from a particular individual (although whether that individual is likely to have been leader, lord, or ancestor is still disputed) or from a particular feature. Several such groups laid claim to woodlands. Smaller *-ingas* groups claimed the wood pastures of Bardingley, Kent, and the fen of Finningley, Northamptonshire.[46] Within great woodlands such as the Weald, areas belonged to a particular community whose farmsteads and arable could be twenty miles or more away, like the swine-pasture denns of Kent and East Sussex.[47] Some of these evolved into woodland settlements with their own churches dedicated to their own particular range of saints.[48]

Animals were likely to have been turned out in some of the many places whose names contain the element *lēah* (which only much later came to have the sense of 'lea', pasture or meadow.) As the multitude of place-names ending in -ley or -leigh show, this is the most common of all the place-name elements that indicate the nature of the local landscape and its vegetation.[49] Some *lēahs* could well have originated as clearings used by particular kinds of domestic animal, possibly with breeding purposes in mind, and several place-names suggest that these were enclosed in some way, as would be appropriate to this kind of function. There are several stud-*lēahs*, now Stoodley or Studley, and *lēahs* may have been reserved for young stock like the stirks (bullocks or heifers) of Stirchley, Shropshire, the calves of Calverley, Yorkshire West Riding, and Chawleigh, Devon, and the lambs of Lambley, Northumberland and Northamptonshire.

Wolds, downs, and hills

Valleys, being sheltered, provided the safest kind of grazing, and livestock and animal names are frequently found combined with the elements OE *cumb* and *denu* and ON *dalr*, all of which mean 'valley'. However, to judge from place-names, there seems not to have been any kind of hill where a few domesticated animals could not be grazed. One of the most common elements was *dun*, 'hill, upland expanse', used for a 'low hill with a fairly level and fairly extensive summit'.[50] Although livestock are also associated with other kinds of hill—the rounded hill or tumulus, *beorg*, the steep hill or *clif*, the ridge or *hrycg*—none seems to have been as highly valued as the *dun*. The attraction of a *dun* was that it provided excellent dry pasture—many of these are what we call 'downland' today. Because a *dun* was a low hill, not a mountain, it was suitable for animals that needed occasional or regular supervision: herds of horses at Stad-

[46] Smith, *Elements*, ii, 22, i, 302–3.
[47] Chatwin and Gardiner, 'Rethinking the early settlement of woodlands'.
[48] Everitt, *Continuity and Colonisation*, 121–6, 250–3.
[49] Hooke, 'Early medieval woodland'; Hooke, '*Wealdbæra* and *swina mæst*'.
[50] Gelling, *Place-Names in the Landscape*, 140–57; Gelling and Cole, *Landscape*, 164–73, at 164.

don, Devon, calves at Callerton, Northumberland, lambs at Endon, Stafford-shire, swine at Swindon, Wiltshire. Like woods and *feld*, hills were central to territories and peoples, like the wooded 'broad zone of common pasture' on the chalk downs of North Kent studied by Everitt. The parishes here have *wald* in their names, a term which having meant 'woodland' came to mean the uplands we call wolds. A later chapter (11) looks at the good use to which Scandinavian farmers put the poor soils of the Lincolnshire Wolds.[51]

RESOURCES, TERRITORY, AND IDENTITY

If their animals were as important to early farmers as good arable land, then laying claim to and securing adequate and safe grazing grounds must have been vital to the establishment and survival of a community of whatever size. The basic communications network of the countryside was deeply influenced by the movement of livestock across country between different resource areas. It sur-vives today in the patterns of roads and tracks, from the Kentish drove ways onto and crossing the North Downs, described and mapped by Alan Everitt, to the ancient and deeply worn tracks from the clay vale onto the Oxfordshire Chilterns, described by Frank Emery, with the pattern they laid down followed by parish and township boundaries.[52]

Later in the Middle Ages each village might have had a drove way leading to its own discrete upland pastures or common. In pre-Conquest England pastures can often be seen as belonging to larger communities. In some places in Kent a '*scir* way or common stock drove' led to the Downland, and there are many such drove ways serving large numbers of different farms which all belonged to a rec-ognized small polity, the *scir*.[53] The *scir* (pronounced 'sheer') was a small unit, not a modern county, and it long pre-dates administrative boundaries.[54] The name survives in the many 'shire moors' and 'shire woods', such as Sherwood, Notting-hamshire. (Common pastures underlie some feudal lordships too: around great areas of open commonable land are 'forests ringed by major lordships', in Charles Phythian-Adams' words about Cumbria.[55]) Similar common pastures often per-sist as the rationale for the divisions of later counties, such as the southern Devon hundreds which encircle and share the common pasture of Dartmoor, or their Kentish equivalents, the lathes, each with its own swine pasture in the Weald. John Blair's description of the origins of the Surrey hundreds as being derived from early *regiones* or tribal territories brings to the fore their administrative

---

[51] Everitt, *Continuity and Colonisation*, 147, 47–8.
[52] Everitt, *Continuity and Colonisation*, 141–72; Emery, *Oxfordshire Landscape*, 64–8. See Fig. 6.2.
[53] Everitt, *Continuity and Colonisation*, 35–9.
[54] Jolliffe, 'Northumbrian Institutions', 11–12.
[55] Phythian-Adams, *Land of the Cumbrians*. For other north-western examples the work of Mary Higham is particularly relevant: Higham, 'The *erg* names of Northern England'.

role, but he is in no doubt that their shape and alignment result 'essentially from the presence of the Weald…each includes enough woodland pasture to serve the settled non-Wealden areas.'[56]

Common grazing grounds remained constant elements in changing political contexts. In the formation of the polities that became the various kingdoms of Anglo-Saxon England it was acknowledged rights in territory that mattered, not political boundaries. True, 'it is groups and associations of peoples that form the raw material of early political development, not the carving up of territory'.[57] But one of the most important if not the most important, reason for groups to claim territory was to ensure access to grazing grounds for their flocks and herds. This was one of the factors which as well as being a source of conflict gave people a sense of common investment. Hooke showed how the link between settlements and their sometimes distant pastures were central to the formation of early territories and to their sense of identity, and Sue Oosthuizen has recently proposed that this could have been a factor in the formation of kingdoms themselves.[58]

In an era of very limited policing livestock needed guarding not only from natural but also from human predators. Phythian-Adams suggests that the British place-name element *caer* in Cumbria could have indicated places which were both defended centres of territories *and* places connected with transhumance, well placed to protect the herders and their flocks. His description nicely encapsulates their mixture of economic and social life: they were martial training centres as well as being 'defensible male camping sites for the summer', assembly points for war and for 'manly sports'.[59] Perhaps these included horse-races, like the Sheriff's Races still held at the yearly autumn round-up of the horses and cattle of the freemen of Oxford on the city's Port Meadow.

Not all common pasture was remote upland. The Sandlings area of south Suffolk has notably light, acid, and sandy topsoil, easily blown away by the wind and starved, like all East Anglia, of rain. Yet, as with the Breckland to the north of the county, it was a focus for affluent Romano-British and then for early Anglian settlers. By the early seventh century it provided the setting for the rich elite of the Sutton Hoo burials and the Anglian 'palace' at Rendlesham. One of the twin resources of their territory was the heaths, whose short grass and young birch and oak could support limitless numbers of sheep. It is ponies and sheep, reintroduced onto the Sandlings by a Grazing

---

[56] Witney, *Jutish Forest*, 31–55; Blair, *Early Medieval Surrey*, 22. The west Devon hundreds are discussed in Chapter 10.

[57] Davies and Vierck, 'The contexts of the Tribal Hidage'.

[58] Hooke, *Anglo-Saxon Landscapes*, 48–53; Oosthuizen, 'Archaeology, common rights'.

[59] Phythian-Adams, *Land of the Cumbrians*, 84–5, at 85. Perhaps the situation was often like that of the Borders in the time of the reivers, when each family group had its own group of huts, described in Roberts et al., *Drove Roads of Northumberland*.

Animals Project, that nowadays keep the grassy site of the Sutton Hoo burials beautifully trim (and it is intriguing to speculate whether even in the seventh century sheep kept down the vegetation around and on the barrows, and so preserved their dominance in the landscape).[60] Plate 7 shows Exmoor ponies thriving on Sutton Common today, keeping the regrowth of bracken and scrub at bay for the Suffolk Wildlife Trust. The second resource was the marshy river valleys, which even after modern drainage and water management still flood in winter and bring a flush of rich spring grass. Along the lower reach of the river Deben the remnants of the 'Shire fen' are still vast common meadows supporting many head of cattle. We do not know what made the elite of this area rich, but some of that wealth surely lay in its sheep and cattle.[61]

PASTORAL HUSBANDRY AND THE HUNDRED

Our modern way of thinking tends to draw a distinction between economic activity and social and spiritual life. This is a hindrance to trying to understand early England, when social and economic, even spiritual, concerns were intertwined. One of the most important aspects of running stock on open ground is the periodic need to round them up, for management purposes (such as counting heads, checking for damage and sickness, possibly branding or marking with some kind to indication of ownership, gelding, selecting for slaughter), but also for marketing and exchange. Then as now this needed the cooperation of all the owners, who would be out, perhaps on horseback, rounding up the animals, driving them into the established driftways, penning them, and sorting and claiming them: the annual 'drift' still brings the ponies down off Dartmoor today. The occasions when the animals were first turned out on the upland pastures and the round-up when they were gathered were communal affairs which brought together the dispersed farming community of a wide region, perhaps one of the few occasions on which they met (a suggestion I owe to Alex Woolf). Many traditional meeting places which seem to us today to be at 'remote' sites, like barrows and isolated trees on heath, down, and moor, may have been at places which were once not considered remote at all, but were well known to the local farmers and shepherds who frequented them. These gatherings may also have been among the occasions when farmers and authorities came into contact, presenting opportunities for authorities to tax this elusive group. 'Neatgeld' and 'Beltane-cow', paid to lords of shires for grazing rights, were payable at Beltane, the first of May, the traditional date for the beginning of

---

[60] Williamson, *Sandlands*, ch. 3, and Williamson, *Sutton Hoo and its Landscape*.
[61] Warner, *Origins of Suffolk*, 61, 64, 118.

summer pasturing.[62] This was also the time for traditional celebrations and bon-fires. Beltane fires were lit in Cumbria into the eighteenth century, and although payments and customs of this kind survived much longer in the north-west, there are traces of them elsewhere. Recent work by Aliki Pantos suggests that we ought to look at meetings and markets as different aspects of a single occasion.[63] An archaeological study of hillforts on the Oxfordshire Ridgeway bears this out. The authors have drawn on a modern study of sheep farming on the Scottish Borders that stresses the importance of the yearly ram auctions there. These occasions were genetically important for introducing new blood to a flock; they demonstrated the higher status of the most skilful farmers; they re-established social connections between a 'core group' of farming families; and they brought in others from a wider periphery. None of this would have been possible without the very close interdependence of the 'hefted' sheep, their owners, and the territory that sustained them. The archaeologists argue that the enormous amount of labour and skill that went into the building and upkeep of Segsbury Camp hill fort, their focus of study, helped create the community for which the Camp became a centre for yearly gatherings that combined 'market, fair, marriages and feasting'.[64]

In Anglo-Saxon England the nearest points of contact that most people had with government were within the territorial unit known as the hundred, and below it the township or tithing. By the time the Domesday commissioners came round collecting the information they needed for the great survey it was expected that it would be common knowledge in which hundred a township (*tūnescipe*) lay and how many people were (male) members of it. *Villani*, 'members of the vill', was the term they used for them, and *tūnesmanna*, 'township-men', was the Old English term which Maitland thought *villani* translated. (Tithings were their equivalent in some parts of England).[65] A great deal of tenth-century legislation dealt with the hundred, its business, and the business of its court.[66] While much modern scholarship stresses the fact that by then it had important administrative and military roles, there is also a long tradition in England of seeing the hundred, which first comes into the written record in the tenth century, as something much, much older, and rooted in the working life of the countryside. In Patrick Wormald's words, 'the 'old local court was

[62] Phythian-Adams, *Land of the Cumbrians*, 85; Jolliffe, 'Northumbrian Institutions'; Adams, *Agrarian Landscape Terms*, 32; Herring, 'Shadows of ghosts', 98.

[63] Pantos, 'Anglo-Saxon assembly-places', 169.

[64] Lock, Gosden, and Daly, *Segsbury Camp*, 147–50, at 148.

[65] For townships and tithings and the regional distribution of these equivalent institutions: Winchester, *Discovering Parish Boundaries*, 21–9; Maitland, *Domesday Book and Beyond*. O'Brien, 'Early medieval shires', uses the vill or township as the principal unit of analysis when describing the small Northumbrian shires of Yeavering, Breamish, and Bamburgh.

[66] Hlothhere and and Eadric 8: Attenborough (ed. and tr.), *Laws*, 20–1, Liebermann (ed.), *Gesetze*, i, 10. Alfred 22: Attenborough (ed. and tr.), *Laws*, 74–5, Liebermann (ed.), *Gesetze*, i, 62.

reorganised and renamed as the hundred'.[67] O. S. Anderson, a Swedish historian from a historical tradition which has never been as inhibited as the English about the notion of popular assemblies, thought that hundreds often derived from ancient districts and that it was the gatherings or *things* which took place at their meetings that gave them their importance: 'the *thing* was what mattered…a district centred on the moot rather than the manor.'[68] It is not hard to imagine that a lot of time at these meetings must have been taken up by livestock business, even marketing.

There are hundreds named from 'stud-folds' and one (Scipe, Wiltshire) from shippon, a cowshed. Swanborough Tump in Kent, where the men of Swanborough met, was 'the mound of the herdsmen's enclosure'. The Kentish equivalent of the hundred was the lathe. K.P. Witney built on J. E. A. Jolliffe's earlier work ('ungraciously received in Kent') in his study of the Weald of Kent. In Witney's maps of the Wealden drove ways and the Kentish lathes, each with its Wealden common, the 'grain' of the landscape appears very clearly, with its administrative structure corresponding to the lie of the land as Fig. 6.2 shows.

In Cornwall, drawing on landscape evidence, Peter Herring considers that the units through which pasturing business was organized were the huge and ancient Cornish hundreds. They have this in common with the much smaller hundreds of west Devon: each contains an area of moorland. The Cornish hundreds link uplands with lowlands and they 'divide Cornwall between them in a way which provides a sensible allotment of the upland grazing'. Three have a large pound into which the animals were driven. Oliver Padel suggests that Cornwall's main spinal route, which became part of the boundary between two of its ancient hundreds and which a section of the A30 road now follows, once had 'a series of recognised market-sites strung along it'.[69]

It is intriguing then that when we are able to see documentary evidence of the hundred at work it appears that much of its business is to do with managing and marketing livestock. When the hundred enters the written record in the law codes of the tenth century, it clearly has an important role in matters relating to *yrfe* or *feoh*, livestock. (Both these OE words meant 'property' as well as 'cattle', just as *peculium* did in Latin.) There is a good deal in the codes to suggest herds (and possibly also flocks) at large in open spaces. In fact VI Æthelstan 8.7 says that 'many heedless men do not care where their cattle wander' as they are so confident in the security system. This law assumes that stock would be under the care of herdsmen, *hyrdas*, who were employed by ordinary people of the township (*tunesmanna*) as well as by the king and the nobility. It is the local community which administers and polices this most

---

[67] Wormald, 'Courts', 127.

[68] Anderson, *Old English Hundred-Names*, 161, 213; Cam, *Liberties and Communities*, 88–9.

[69] Pearce, *South-West Britain*, 223–5 and Fig. 91; Herring, 'Shadows of ghosts'; Herring, 'Early medieval transhumance', 52; Padel, 'Ancient and medieval divisions of Cornwall', 213.

contentious area of rural life. The hundred and the tithing both have duties.[70] Closest to home was the tithing, the group of ten, under the tithingman, who must have settled the kind of dispute that arose between neighbours, particularly those involving livestock and their pastures. The 'Laws of Edward the Confessor', a post-Conquest legal text probably compiled by someone who knew a bit about the practice of Anglo-Saxon law although not its texts, tells us that the tithingman had to bring to court (we are not told what court this is, but it is probably that of the hundred) 'disputes between townships and neighbours…pastures and meadows, haymaking fights between neighbours and many other such which frequently arise'.[71] Stolen animals always caused problems and great stress was laid on the fact that neighbours, but not strangers, knew whose animals were whose (the fact that animals had a wide range of colours and markings must have helped in identifying them). They were called on to vouch for the ownership of new additions bought at market.[72] Strays must often have wandered off: trackers were used to follow them by their hoofprints. A charm gives a remedy which advises filling the hoofprint with wax: was this magic or an early instance of police procedure?[73] Boundaries mattered and were known to all. In the case of the tricky situation when the stock have crossed the boundary, 'if anyone follows a trail from one *scyre* (district) to another his neighbours must help until the *scyre gerefa*, the reeve, is informed.' The latter was to take the posse to the boundary where the reeve of the other *scyre* should take over. It is clear that the *scyre* is here considered to be much the same thing as the hundred: in a later version of the same law the men of one hundred should follow a track (presumably of livestock) into another hundred and it is the hundredman who then takes over the search.[74] Ideas of common responsibility come through strongly in this legislation, which suggests that stock-owning farmers, whatever their differences, were accustomed to acting as if they had common goals. Tithing and hundred are where livestock business 'and many other such which frequently arise' should be settled by neighbours. The purchase and sale of livestock, retrieval of strays, and the identification of stolen animals seem to have caused more trouble than any other aspect of rural life and did so doubtless throughout our period, but it was through the tithing and the hundred that these conflicts could be managed.

---

[70] While the tithing remained as a unit in local government until the nineteenth century, it seems to have ceased to function in some areas: Winchester, *Discovering Parish Boundaries*, 22–5.

[71] Liebermann (ed.), *Gesetze*, i, 627–72, at 651–2. For this text: Wormald, *Making of English Law*, 409–11.

[72] 'No-one is to have any strange cattle except with the witness of the men of the hundred or of the tithingman': I Edgar 4, known as 'Ordinance of the Hundred': Robertson (ed. and tr.), *Laws*, 16–19, 192–5; This clause is reinforced by IV Edgar 8–11: Robertson (ed. and tr.), *Laws*, 34–7; Liebermann (ed.), *Gesetze*, i, 210–12.

[73] Hough, 'Cattle tracking'; Hollis, 'Old English "cattle theft charms"'.

[74] VI Æthelstan 8.4: Attenborough (ed. and tr.), *Laws*, 156–69, at 164–5; 173–83; I Edgar 2–5: Robertson (ed. and tr.), *Laws*, 16–19; Liebermann (ed.), *Gesetze*, i, 192–5.

As we shall see in the following chapters, people managed their animals differently in different places, and over our period the early shift towards pastoralism was to be reversed. But knowledgeable husbandry, the movement of animals, sometimes over considerable distances, to their customary grazings, their careful supervision, and above all the intense association of a particular group—whether an entire 'people', a *scir*, a parish, township, or small settlement—with its grazing lands were to remain part of Anglo-Saxon farming, albeit in very differing circumstances. In the regional studies which follow, animals and the demands which they and their owners made on the landscape will play an important part.

7

Coasts and riversides

Fig. 7.1. Cattle grazing on Rainham Marshes.

(Photograph © RSPB)

Although the raids and migrations of the fifth and sixth centuries were new in scale, it was nothing new to undertake a journey across the German Ocean, as the North Sea was once called. Northern people knew those seaways well. The people of the eastern seaboard already had links with Norway and Sweden.[1] The Essex coast and the margins of the Thames Estuary have a marked resemblance to the European northern seaboard, and their people are likely to have shared some basic characteristics. They had access to sea routes and are likely to have been handy at boatbuilding and seamanship: boat burials may be one expression of this maritime mindset shared by the North Sea peoples.[2] Their lands of sands, marshes, and creeks are not 'marginal', except in the literal

[1] Hines, *Scandinavian Character of Anglian England*, 117–19.
[2] Carver, 'Pre-Viking traffic in the North Sea'.

sense. Quite the reverse: they can give good returns to farmers who know how to exploit their possibilities for animal husbandry and who have access to markets. Sheep can do well in these seemingly bleak conditions, feeding on a wide range of saltmarsh plants, even on seaweed, and given adequate drinking water cattle can do well too: the Essex marshes supported large numbers in the nineteenth century[3] (Fig. 7.1). The live resources— fish, eels, shellfish, and wildfowl—were freely available to all with a grasp of the technologies to trap them, and it is by traps, weirs, and nets that much coastal fishing was carried on. (Deep-sea fishing seems to have been a later development.)[4]

THAMES-SIDE

On the north bank of the Thames, at the mouth of the estuary, large-scale excavations in the 1960s and 1970s disclosed 250 buildings at a settlement site of over eighteen hectares on the gravel terrace near Mucking (Fig. 7.3). Helena Hamerow's reinterpretation of the finds on the site has made Mucking the source of much of current thinking about the nature of early English settlement and it gives us a glimpse into a farming community and its use of resources.[5] It was a favoured site: people had been living there, or thereabouts, since the Bronze Age, and under the Romans a villa farm had been built. From the early fifth century the nature of material culture there became markedly Germanic and this suggests that life at Mucking had become heavily influenced by incomers with new ways. The newcomers built substantial rectangular timber houses which differed both from the kind which had evolved on much of the Continent and from the sub-Roman houses they could have encountered in England. The nearest counterpart is a new type of dwelling which had been evolving at about that time in some areas of north-west Germany such as at Bremerhaven, perhaps a clue to the origin of the settlers. At Mucking the buildings were not longhouses with the livestock housed under the same roof as its owners, but purely dwellings: cooking and craftwork were carried out in small sheds, loosely clustered round the dwelling house. Houses and sheds shifted over time, perhaps as their timber uprights rotted, and were rebuilt on another site, so the settlement as a whole drifted up the hill. Not all the houses were occupied at once—the total population at any one time has been estimated at about ten households—and there does not seem to have been any desire to lay the dwellings out according to a regular plan.

Although the Mucking settlers lived in an apparently disorganized scatter of farmsteads—the site has even been interpreted as a kind of transit camp—there

---

[3] Cattle can cope with tidal rivers and creeks, drinking the fresh surface water which overlies the heavier salt water. I am grateful for this useful information to an anonymous informant in Cambridge in 2011.

[4] Barrett et al., 'Dark Age economics'.

[5] Hamerow, *Mucking*.

is absolutely no reason to think of them as impoverished transients. They continued to bury their dead in their two cemeteries over a period of two hundred years: a tangible sign of emotional and social commitment to a place. They were in touch with other peoples and were located near important trading routes: the Thames itself to London and a ferry crossing from Tilbury to the north Kent shore, which brought them into contact with the richest culture in southern England and one which was closely connected with the Continent. They were in the orbit of London, which by the eighth century was developing into an international commercial centre and just downstream from the minster established at Barking in the seventh, an exceptionally rich consumer of luxury goods and with its own toehold in the rural economy. They were using cash: some of the earliest East Saxon silver coins, three *sceattas* of the 680s, come from the site. Some had enviable portable wealth in the shape of jewellery, silver and bronze buckles, elaborate swords and shields, and luxury objects such as glass beakers. Several of these objects are of a kind associated with Kent and the Isle of Wight.

There are no signs that the people at Mucking were trying to fit in with, or adapt themselves to, the indigenous population, or to continue long-established field systems. The area is thickly sown with Anglo-Saxon place-names, one of which, nearby Waltons Farm, *weala-tūn* ('farmstead or village of the Britons'), may denote a group which remained in some way recognizably British, as *wealh* was used in Old English to indicate 'Briton' as well as 'slave'. The villa had fallen out of use; its ditches had silted up. The newcomers built over its fields, ignored most of its boundaries, and looted its ruined buildings for lead. They did not bury their dead alongside the Romano-British dead but established a new cemetery on a proud position on a slight promontory overlooking the estuary—a site not unlike that of the high-status early seventh century burial at Prittlewell, near Southend.[6]

Mucking gives the impression of a community where goods were coming in: it is hard to see in the archaeology what was being traded in exchange. Of the crafted goods found, there is no way of knowing what was bought and what was made on site. Many early farmers must have been able to fashion and repair their own iron tools, so the sickle and shears, pins and knives found there need not have been made by an expert. At least one inhabitant kept a horse, a fourteen-hand animal of the useful cob type favoured by countrymen today but large by Anglo-Saxon standards, and looked after it so well that it reached the good old age of twenty years.[7] Metal bridle fittings have been found, although the leathers have long gone. Tools of skilled metal workers have been found, and at least one brooch-maker was at work in the sixth century casting bronze brooches from a mould: a brooch found just up the coast at Paglesham is of the

---

[6] *Prittlewell Prince.*
[7] See Chapter 5.

Fig. 7.2. Old English settlement names on the north bank of the Thames.

(© Cassini Publishing Limited 2007)

type that it would have produced. People made pottery and fancy metal-bound wooden buckets used as containers. They tanned and worked leather. They grew grain, including barley. Any of these may have produced a tradable surplus, but the more likely foundation of their economy was animal products, particularly woollen textiles. There was an inherited skills base to draw on: many of the inhabitants of the coastal *Wurten*, the raised settlements of the Saxon homeland, specialized in wool production. Shears and loomweights suggest that the Mucking sheep were valued for their wool as well as for meat and milk. Spindle whorls, some made from scraps of Roman pottery, and pottery loomweights, carefully matched for weight so they would keep the vertical threads uniformly taut, have been found in large numbers on the floors of huts which were evidently used as weaving sheds—one advantage of their dugout

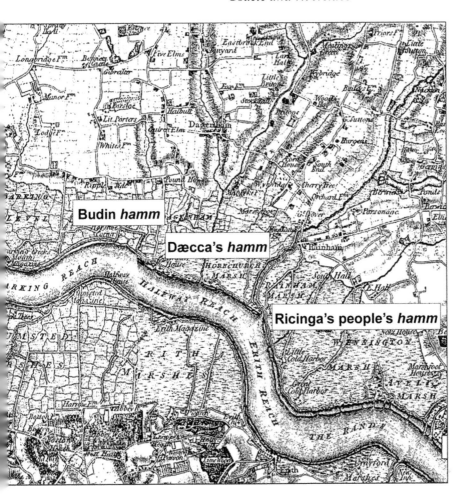

floors was that they provided enough height for an upright loom. Loomweights are not found on Romano-British sites, so these and the upright loom, on which the weights kept the warp threads taut, were an Anglo-Saxon innovation in England. The earliest arrivals brought the technique to Mucking, where they appear in fifth- and sixth-century contexts.[8] Fig. 7.3a shows an example.

Mucking may well have been just one of several small hamlets in the locality with a self-sufficient economy. People farming at nearby Stifford in the seventh century had much the same kind of site, two miles from the Thames bank and at the lowest crossing of the Mar Dyke, still tidal at that point. They too had plentiful meadow- and workable land on the lighter soils of the gravel terrace. From the seventh century on the inhabitants of an early Anglo-Saxon settlement

[8] Hamerow, *Mucking*, 132; loomweights: pers. comm. Zena Kamash.

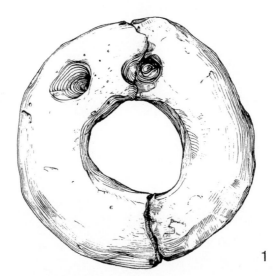

Fig. 7.3. Mucking, Essex: animal-related finds:
a: Clay loom-weight 'marked possibly to denote its place on the loom, or as a mark of ownership'.

(© Hamerow, *Excavations at Mucking*, ii)

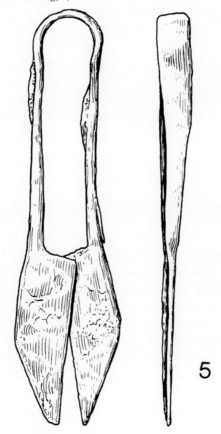

b: Iron shears.

(© Hamerow, *Excavations at Mucking*, ii)

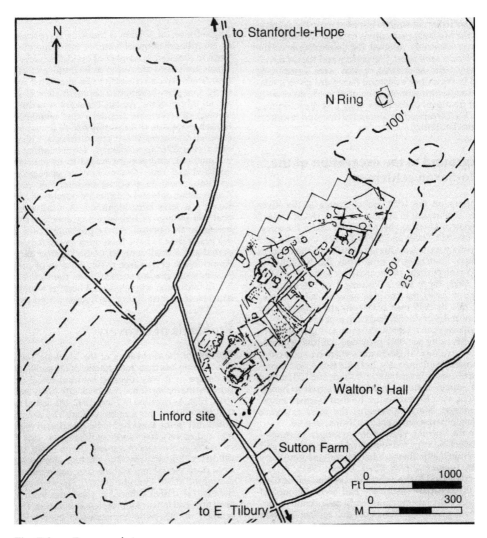

to Stanford-le-Hope

N Ring

100'

50'

25'

Walton's Hall

Linford site

Sutton Farm

to E Tilbury

Ft 0 1000
M 0 300

Fig. 7.3. c: Excavated site.

there buried their dead wrapped in good quality striped and plaid woollen blankets and lived in sizeable timber houses.[9]

Raising sheep for wool alone at such settlements ideally would have entailed concentrating on producing wethers, as their wool is better than that of ewes, and keeping them throughout their adult life to maximize returns, but there must also have been lactating sheep and their ewe lambs. The animal bones from the Mucking site are not very revealing as their survival is poor. Sheep, pig, and cattle are all represented, but not in informative numbers or proportions that would indicate at what age the Mucking sheep were butchered, which

[9] Wilkinson, *Archaeology and Environment*, 23, 54–7.

would tell us whether they were being raised primarily for wool. Much more revealing of the importance of livestock in the life of such communities is the way in which the people of Mucking and other coastal settlements like it defined, claimed, exploited, and organized their territories. Mucking was part of a larger territory typical of the early 'resource areas' referred to in the previous chapter that had some kind of socially recognized identity. Fig. 7.4 shows its varied pasture resources. These 'resource territories' are likely to be old. Some share the ancient common element *ge*, 'district'. Vange (*fenn-ge*, 'fen district') is one such area, now narrowed down to the small parish of Vange itself but at one time the whole north bank of the Thames as far as the fen of Fenchurch in the City of London may have been regarded as 'the fen region'—and fens remain at Orsett and Bulphan.[10] Fens make good wet pasture for cattle, as those in Plate 6a demonstrate. Upstream from Mucking were early riverside properties whose names illustrate the importance of pastoralism in the economy (Fig. 7.4). These are the string of *hamms* as shown in Fig. 7.2, stretches of riverside meadow, at *Ricingahamm* (Rainham), *Budinhamm* (later Barking), *Daeccahamm* (Dagenham), and *Angenlabeshamm*, all of which appear in a seventh-century charter to Barking Abbey. The personal names Dæcca, Angenlaf, and Rica are of a very early type, and dropped out of use as far as we know, so it is possible that these riverside holdings could have gained their association with these three men in the settlement period.[11] As important as their date is the kind of properties they were. The *hamms* were freshwater marsh and meadow five or six feet above sea level at high tide which would have provided extensive grazing for cattle as well as sheep. As Fig. 7.1 shows, Rainham Marshes are grazed today. The *hamms* were bounded by small streams draining into the Thames, like the *Writolaburn*, now the Beam, which still mark parish boundaries. As well as serving as boundaries, these little streams and creeks provided access through the marshes to the settlements which developed along the gravel terraces. They also provided a safe haven for pulling up boats, for it would have been unsafe to beach them on the muddy tidal banks of the Thames.[12]

The riverside *hamms* were the southern element of territories which stretched north across the gravel terraces and up into the wooded hills of the Essex forest. Despite the threat from wolves—the 'wolf-pit' is a landmark in a South Weald charter—this was evidently established and inhabited wood-pasture in the seventh century with scattered farms—another landmark is the *hem stede*, a homestead. Individual Anglo-Saxon men had already left their mark on the woodland place-names, just as others had done on the riverside meadows. They were owners of areas of cleared land, such as the open land at Widmund's *feld* (possibly Wyfields, north of Great Ilford) and 'Freobearne's slope'. These

---

[10] Gelling, 'Place-names of the Mucking area'.
[11] Hart, *Early Charters of Eastern England*, 127–35; Reaney, *Place-Names*, xxii.
[12] Gelling and Cole, *Landscape of Place-Names*, 46–55, for the nature of *hamms*.

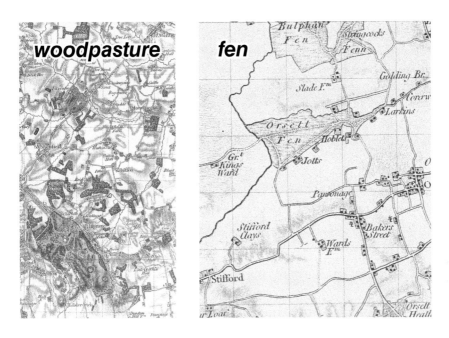

Fig. 7.4. Pasture resources in the Mucking area.

(© Cassini Publishing Limited 2007)

places had their names by, and perhaps well before, the late seventh century and alert us to something which proves to be a recurrent and important theme in early farming: private properties co-existing with common rights.

Another of Barking Abbey's endowments was 'ten hides called Celta', the land through which flowed the river *Celta*, a word possibly of Celtic origin which gave Childerditch its name, now the Mardyke, 'a relic of the early wanderings of the Thames'. It links the wooded hills of Horndon, the 'thorn hill', with the fenland at Orsett, cuts through the gravel terraces, and then flows into the Thames at Purfleet, 'Purta's creek'.[13] On its northern stretch, the southern edge of the Wooded Hills where there was wood-pasture and extensive areas of common and heath, were areas named from natural features: woodland clearing, river, and hill—Warley, Childerditch, and Horndon. Barking's property here also contained fenland, which was only gradually brought under cultivation and never settled but was an important pasture resource for cattle and ponies. Once much more extensive, the fen included Bulphan, the 'fen belonging to the *burh*', perhaps Tilbury. Bog iron was extracted at Orsett, 'at the ore pits', and may lie behind the name of Benfleet, 'tree-trunk creek', part of the sunken forest which stretched across the whole marsh at Dagenham and Rainham. Another fenny area where Camden spotted 'subterranean trees' in the sixteenth century was Thurrock, which may have taken its evocatively sludgy name from the term *thurruc*, the bilge of a ship.[14] Cattle and sheep must have been the basis of the local economy, possibly raised on such a scale as would provide a marketable surplus. Both were important. The fen, overlying alluvial deposits, provided grazing suitable for cattle, better watered than the wood-pasture on the higher ground and the fen herbage could have been cut for winter fodder. All the Thames-side parishes also had 'pasture for sheep' recorded in Domesday—the usual formula in Essex for detached marsh grazing.[15]

COMMON RIGHTS AND PARISH BOUNDARIES

It is always very difficult to determine when resources which had been used by the people of a wide region, such as the farmers and the greater and lesser landholders of the entire north bank of the Thames, began to be associated with a particular community such as a single settlement, a manor, or a parish. Even when manorial property boundaries became established, people retained rights derived from established farming practice in land now belonging to a neighbouring manor. A lucky survival in a Barking Abbey gospel book is a lease of a small property at Stifford in about 1090 to Gilbert, a dependant of the bishop of Bayeux. This reveals a little about the resources of the Mucking area. For

[13] Hart, *Early Charters of Eastern England*, 23, 145; Hunter, *Essex Landscape*, 21.
[14] Gelling, 'Place-names of the Mucking region'; Reaney, *Place-Names of Essex*, xxiv.
[15] Darby, *Domesday Geography of Eastern England*, 241–4.

twenty-four pence a year Gilbert was to have 'thirty acres north of the brook (Mardyke) and the meadow belonging thereto, twelve acres south of the brook, thirty acres at The Stone' (Stone Hall or Stone Ness). Two farms, one in Stifford and one in Aveley, were reckoned as having enough arable for half a plough-team between them, an arrangement which may suggest that each had a small-holding in a common arable field, perhaps something like the small field system which Stephen Rippon thinks was laid out at Mucking in around the eighth century, or perhaps each had a share in a single strip field.[16] This area was later divided between the parishes of Stifford, Greys Thurrock, and Aveley, but in the eleventh century their farmers evidently still 'intercommoned', sharing both grazing and arable. No woodland is recorded in 1086, and it looks as though by then Stifford's economy was based on arable and meadow and had lost what links it may originally have had to the woodland.[17]

When large territories broke into smaller privately owned landholdings these fragments sometimes retained elements of the old links. A small property in the Vange district which King Edgar gave land to his thegn Ingeram in 963 was a compact area with pasture (and by 1086 a mill and a fishery) bounded on one side by Vange creek, but it also had some detached woodland. Its boundaries show that this corner of Essex was then highly privatized: five other major landowners, some being aristocratic members of the royal court (*ministri*), then had land in the vicinity, probably estates of a very similar configuration. The asso-ciation between Ingeram's estate and its woodland suggests that private rights in wood-pasture were firmly linked to his property by the time of his charter.[18]

Common rights in pasture also underlie some major divisions of the landscape into parishes. Parish boundaries were not established until the very end of the Anglo-Saxon period (and some later than that).[19] By the time they were formal-ized it must have been widely accepted (probably not without conflict) that the people who farmed a certain area had the right to put their animals on a spe-cific area elsewhere, on occasion some distance away. Parishes reflect a much more crowded landscape than that of the early settlement period. But the shape of parishes can still tell us a good deal about how people claimed and viewed their landscape, and reveal how strongly this perception was marked by the needs of livestock. The parish boundaries of the Warleys, the Horndons, and Childerditch show strongly marked north–south axes, and the strikingly narrow and elongated morphology of these 'parallel parishes' or 'coaxial systems' has many counterparts (Fig. 7.5). The shaping forces seem to have been the move-ments of livestock up to the woodlands and down to the marshes. Valuable as the riverside marshland was, it was probably the wood-pasture of the forest that was the primary focus of the region. The northern parts of three hundreds

[16] Rippon, *Beyond the Medieval Village*, 258. For strip fields see Chapter 13.
[17] Hart, *Early Charters of Essex* 43–5; Hart, *Early Charters of Barking Abbey*, 35–6.
[18] S 717; Reaney, *Place-Names of Essex*, 174–5.
[19] Blair, *Church in Anglo-Saxon Society*, ch. 8.

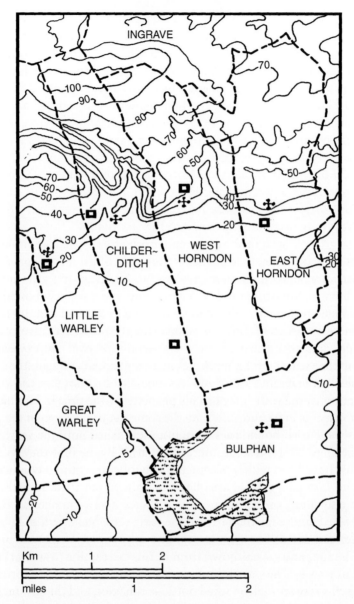

Fig. 7.5. The 'parallel parishes' on the north bank of the Thames.

(From Hunter, *Field Systems* © Richard Hunter).

of Barstable, Chafford, and Becontree are all forest land and the hundred court of Becontree hundred, possibly an ancient assembly-place of the users of the forest, was at Becontree Heath. So when Odilred gave to the nuns of Barking land stretching from the Thames up into the forest he was giving part of an area whose configuration had been shaped by its users: by farmers whose economy was based on the seasonal movement of livestock. In 1086 the manor of Mucking, by then also in the hands of the nuns, had pasture for 300 sheep, where they ran a flock of 250. This was marsh-pasture adjacent to the lands of the manor, and when the parish boundary was established, it ran down to the Thames to ensure this valuable resource was included. Woodland, cultivable land on the Thames terraces, fen, and marshland were the linked assets of these substantial estates. The minster would benefit from its varied resources, but it did not arrange the landscape in order to do so: its 'grain' had already been created by generations of farmers.[20]

COASTAL SALTMARSH

Downstream from Mucking, where the north bank of the Thames estuary merges into the coast off which lie the islands of Canvey, Wallasea, and Foulness, we come to a rather different use of the mixed resources of the land, and a different balance in the rural economy between arable and stock (Fig. 7.6).[21] From the sea this low-lying part of the Essex coast and the lower reaches of the Thames present few clues to safe landfalls. Even the great Beowulf and his troop of fighting men relied on a *saecg wisade lacucraftig man landgemyrcu*, 'an experienced seaman who guided them along the coast', so it is likely that early settlers here either already knew the coast or depended on the knowledge of the skippers of the boats that brought them, using known landmarks like the small headland at Havengore that marked the favourable opening to a creek leading to the river Roach. They would have come to a much more indented coast than today's, for the action of the tides has worn away several long headlands or 'nesses' (ON for 'nose') such as at Foulness, or, like The 'Naze' of Walton-on-the-Naze, has entirely destroyed them. What is now drained and cultivated clayland extending to the coast was then a complex of saltmarsh, small islands, and creeks, unwalled and subject to flooding at exceptional tides. Given the vulnerability of their own homelands to flooding, it is small wonder then that the migrants who settled on the Essex coast and along its rivers and estuaries had an eye for raised ground further inland which would provide a dry foundation, or at least a safe haven in times of exceptional tides, which continued to threaten. Hence the place-names with the Old English element *eg*, 'island', which seems to have meant by extension 'an area of dry land in wet country' at Canvey, Beckney, and Pudsey, or the little hills, *duns*, albeit no more than forty metres above sea level, at Canewdon and Ashingdon. Further inland were the wooded Rayleigh Hills, also an area of early Anglo-Saxon settlement. Iron Age and Romano-British coastal dwellers had been using areas of saltmarsh

[20] Hunter, 'Field systems in Essex', 31–5.
[21] *Overview of Coastal Sand Dunes*, 32–3.

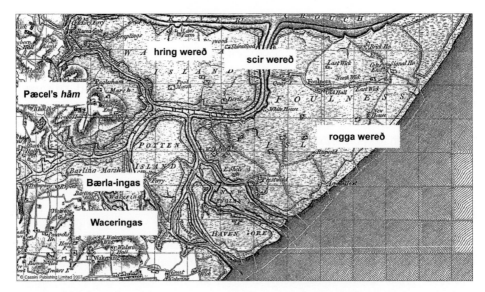

Fig. 7.6. Old English settlement names on Wallasea and Foulness Islands, Essex.

(© Cassini Publishing Limited 2007)

and foreshore which are now submerged except at low water. They had exploited its natural resources, boiling sea water for salt and running sheep flocks
for the wool which in this intensively Romanized part of the country could find
both a market and the transport networks to supply it. Both these industries
had been in decline by the end of the Roman period, possibly as a result of
rising sea-levels or more frequent high tides.[22]

The Saxons brought to this part of Essex a term *wered, werod, or werd*,
which seems to have been used both for a coast and a bank, and sometimes a
marsh. In their homeland it had meant 'an island in a river' and the Dutch cognate term means a banked enclosure.[23] A bank up to which the high tide reached
could well have been called by a word which meant both 'bank' and 'coast'.
Recent wide-ranging work by Stephen Rippon on a variety of marshlands
shows how what looks to us—though very likely not to the early settlers—such
unpromising land could have been brought into cultivation in the early Middle
Ages. Some of the strategies followed on the Somerset Levels studied by Rippon included building a sea-wall to keep out the tides, but this was probably

---

[22] *Hullbridge Survey*, 197–207.

[23] Reaney, *Place-Names of Essex*, 148–9. Reaney points out that this element also occurs in Devon
as *warthe* or *ward*. Rippon, *Transformation of Coastal Wetlands*, 204–7, considers place-names of this
type to be mostly thirteenth century or later, but the Old English personal name elements in some of
these place-names, none of which is at all typical of such a late period, argue against this. The presence
of rich burials at Prittlewell, and of a stylistic link between metalwork at Mucking and Paglesham,
could be taken as supporting the case for a sea-based colonization of the area. See further, *Prittlewell
Prince*; Reaney, *Place-Names*, xxiii–xxvi; and pp. 165–6 for metalwork at Mucking.

not done on the Essex marshes before the thirteenth century. A smaller-scale and more individualistic strategy was to build lobe-shaped enclosures protected by low ring-dikes which protected the land within from the highest tides and made it possible to take a crop off.[24] Possibly early cultivation was limited to the summer season: a term for these banks in the Netherlands is 'ring dikes' or 'summer dikes'. On these Essex marshlands islands of slightly raised ground, such as can be seen at Rugwood (where it raises the farmhouse just above flood level), may have provided natural platforms for settlement. Even in the floods of 1953 the farmhouse and farm buildings at Rugwood Farm remained dry.[25] Ringwood—ring *werod*—on Wallasea Island may have been enclosed and cultivated land inside a circular bank. OE *hop* was another word for an enclosed piece of marshland and in Essex as well as Stanford le Hope there is a lost *Deorwines hoppe* ('Deorwine's marshland enclosure').[26] Some of these enclosures seem at one time to have been privately owned, such as Priestwood (the priest's *werd*); the *werd* belonging to the *burh* (possibly Tilbury), now Burwood on Foulness (another farm on a raised platform); and *Til-* or *Tyles werd*, now Tillettsmarsh. Rippon found that on the reclaimed marshland of the Somerset Levels a recurrent pattern was for one or more farmsteads to occur on the edge, or just outside, the enclosure, which remained single holdings rather than developing into larger settlements. He suggests that they were part of a colonizing process created in an open landscape. Possibly similar colonization by family groups lies behind the places on Canvey, Wallasea, and Foulness which contain personal names that associate them with a group or an individual; 'Cana's people's hill' at Canewdon, Wacer's people' at (now Great and Little) Wakering, Pæccel's farm at Pagelsham, and Curra's farm at Corringham.

On the eve of the Conquest the marshland farmers were mostly 'free men', recorded as such and counted, but seldom named, in Domesday Book. Some evidently had quite substantial mixed farms, in which sheep played such a major part that we might well consider them to be as much specialists, although on a smaller scale, as the monastic sheep owners who were beginning to make their mark. There were three big farms at Sutton: on one two men farming jointly had pasture for 300 sheep on which they ran a flock of 200, and another had pasture for 100, fully stocked. Other coastal farms had land assessed at a hide or a fraction of a hide, and pasture for thirty to one hundred sheep. When their livestock is recorded, we can see that these were smaller enterprises, owned by farmers who had flocks of forty to one hundred sheep, kept a few pigs and very often a horse (perhaps one like the Mucking cob), and ran a single ploughteam or none. Their farms were scattered, perhaps sometimes forming part of a little hamlet on their 'island' of higher ground. At Pudsey, originally 'Pud's island' or

---

[24] Rippon, *Transformation of Coastal Wetlands*, 152–77, Fig. 51; Rippon, *Transformation of Coastal Wetlands*, 155, sections 1–4.

[25] Information kindly supplied by the present owner.

[26] Reaney, *Place-Names of Essex*.

'raised ground in the marsh', there were four farms. This is not very different from the settlement pattern today, with its five dispersed farms. At one, apart from the farmer's family, there was a little group of eight smallholders, perhaps working as farm labourers; there were three at another and two at a third. At the fourth there were two *villani*: these were anonymous 'men of the township' whose status we don't know. All four farmers kept a horse and ran between twenty-five and eighty sheep on the marsh. Three kept pigs for household use. Two had a ploughteam, one half a team—perhaps four oxen. The marshland can have provided very little grazing suitable for cattle: fresh water was in very short supply and no meadow for winter hay is recorded on any of the farms there.[27] This was a perennial problem for coastal farms: one of the shortcomings of the manor of Barling in 1222 was that 'there is no ox-pasture' on its 'little marsh'.[28] These farms were small-scale, individually owned enterprises with attached pasture rights; they possibly had the kind of enclosure which was given the name *wered*. But there may also have been joint enterprises: Domesday records that 'six free men in the hundred of Barstable with twelve hides have pasture for 300 sheep' without specifying where those twelve hides were.[29] These larger farmers were clearly rearing sheep for the market, albeit on a small scale, for their flocks were much bigger than would be needed for domestic use, and it is tempting to imagine they or their farm workers used horses for shepherding as well as for transporting people and goods. It is also likely that most marshland farmers were handy with a boat as the Crouch was on their doorstep (perhaps on occasion over it) and provided the obvious link to the inland road network or to the coastal route to the Thames. Domesday does not generally provide us with information about the grazing owned by the *villani* or the flocks they kept, but any constraints there may have been on the size of peasant flocks could not have included shortage of pasture.

There is virtually no archaeology of sheep husbandry for the pre-Conquest period in this area of Essex, but elsewhere on the Essex marshes there are traces of the small bridges and wattle hurdles which took the sheep over the winding creeks. We don't know if each flock had its shepherd or whether the shepherd had a dog: the fact that each farm had a horse evokes the picture of a farmer riding out to check on his sheep, as hill farmers occasionally still do today (although many more have enthusiastically taken to the quad bike.) There must have been lactating ewes on the marsh. If they were milked, as they certainly were later in the Middle Ages to produce the famous Essex sheep cheese, any structures like the 'wicks' used by the later cheese makers have left no trace, although the marshland was divided into 'wicks' at Tillingham by the early thirteenth century, and Shopland may have taken its name from the 'shops' or

---

[27] Pudsey: *Domesday Book: Essex* 24.32, 34, 36, 37; Benton, *Rochford Hundred*, 214.
[28] Hale, *Domesday of St Paul's*, 64.
[29] *Domesday Book: Essex*, 30.21.

storage sheds there. Perhaps a 'shelter built on the saltmarsh for occasional transient use' discovered beside the Blackwater estuary was one of these. Common sense would suggest that such a valuable source of nourishment and by-income would have had a continuous history linking its Roman to its medieval appearances. And the fact that the grazing was on islands suggests that flocks could be shipped across and left down on the marsh all summer, as they were in the later Middle Ages, with lactating ewes milked and cheese made there.[30] The archaeology of marshland shielings, which must have been made of fragile materials like reeds, has yet to be investigated. There is very little evidence of the practicalities of arable farming on the marshes. Foulness benefited from the alluvium deposited when the Thames and Medway rivers had flowed across the eastern part of the peninsula, and the marsh soils were later famous for their fertility.[31] In the nineteenth century manure was taken off Foulness to nourish the inland soils which were much poorer, so the name Sherwoods, *scearn-werd*, 'dung marsh', in Canewdon raises the possibility that valuable dung was already being collected and carted to the mainland well before that. The rye at Rugwood, 'rye *werd*', on Foulness, was a more salt-tolerant cereal than the barley or wheat grown in inland areas.[32]

Fowling and fishing, or rather fish-harvesting, also played a part in the local economy. The fish traps found along the Blackwater estuary may have had their counterpart in the creeks and along the Roach; by contrast, however, the Crouch was at this time edged with reed swamp, difficult to penetrate. Five landless men at Leigh in Rochford in 1066 could have been making a living from these occupations on the marsh. The weir at Warley, *wer-lēah*, which is well inland, could well have been a fish weir on land at the coast which belonged to the *lēah* at the inland location. The salt industry which had been so important in Roman Essex had left its mark in the 'Red Hills' of debris along the coast—useful dry perches for sheep at flood tides and possibly used as small dry islands by 'lookers' (shepherds) or marsh dwellers. Saltworking continued on the Blackwater and Colne estuaries and in Tendring Hundred, but apparently not in our area, at least not on a large enough scale to be recorded in Domesday. Perhaps salt was already easy to buy, and a new form of low-tech extraction, sieving salt mud, had replaced the more sophisticated Roman salt boiling.[33] But while these diverse uses were important, the evidence is that the marshland was used principally as summer grazing for sheep and it is primarily in the way that the coastal marshes of South Essex came to be divided that we can see the overwhelming importance of sheep in the local economy.

[30] Hunter, *Essex Landscape*, 17; *Hullbridge Survey*, 197–207.

[31] Lake et al., *Geology*.

[32] Benton, *Rochford Hundred*, 214. Thanks to Peter Burrows for an informative tour of Rugwood Farm, Foulness.

[33] Hinton, 'Raw materials', 430. Low-cost (in fact no-cost) ways of obtaining salt by sieving mud through sacks await their chronicler.

Marshland grazing rights owned by a community are a feature of this coast-
line and its islands and creeks. They may represent a stage referred to earlier
(p. 174–5) when large resource areas were being divided into those which
served the smaller communities that were to become villages and later parishes.
Some marshes were, and are today, physically part of a parish. But inland stock
owners also had rights in marsh pastures that were detached from the parishes
to which they belonged. Until the reorganization and 'tidying-up' of parishes
in the late nineteenth century these pasture grounds were preserved as the
detached outliers of inland or coastal parishes. J. H. Round, who knew Essex
well, recognized the importance of these outlying supplies of 'feed in the
marshes' and mapped them. Nine mainland parishes had outliers on Canvey
Island, six on Wallasea Island, and six, possibly seven, on Foulness (Fig. 7.7.).[34]
We can see from Domesday Book that in 1066 lords of manors and individual
farmers had rights in the marsh, and the parish outliers tell us that communities had rights there too. However, imagining how this situation came about
reminds us that the evolution of common and individual rights is not something
we yet properly understand. The situation is much like that of the Thames-side
parishes discussed earlier in this chapter. Physical divisions between each community's marsh were part of the articulation of parish boundaries, but there
may have been a time when, apart from what individual claims the *wered*
farms had managed to establish, access to the marsh was not regulated at all.
Perhaps the marsh once served the people of a broad territory with woodland
to the north and marshland to the south, as earlier suggested was the case
along the north bank of the Thames. Some parishes had more than one outlier,
and with some their portions were intermixed. These intermixed parochial outliers may have originated in an intermediate period, when the flocks of several
mainland communities grazed one or two established areas with each flock
'hefted' or habituated to its own particular area. In order to prevent gross over-
burdening of common pastures, in the later Middle Ages, grazing rights were
frequently expressed in 'stints', the number of animals each commoner was
allowed to put out. Stints have been a very common way of regulating and protecting a common resource and this may be one explanation for the way that
local people giving evidence to the Domesday commissioners in 1086 provided information about coastal grazing in terms of 'pasture for so many
sheep'. Possibly we should understand this as 'they are permitted to put out so
many sheep on a common pasture'. However, useful as such information from
Domesday Book has proved in establishing the importance of the marshes to
the economy, we cannot be sure that the figures for 'pasture for sheep' do not
apply only to the rights of the lord of the manor and not to those of the local
inhabitants.

---

[34] Round, 'Domesday Survey'; Benton, *Rochford Hundred*, 176; Darby, *Domesday Geography of Eastern England*, 241–4.

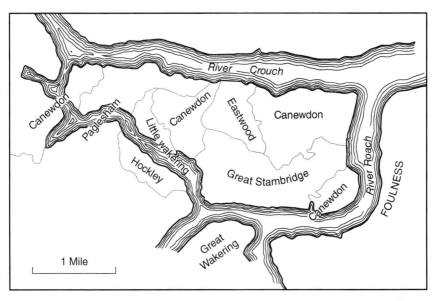

Fig. 7.7. Mainland parishes' grazing rights on Wallasea, represented by detached portions.
(From Round, *Domesday Survey*)

By 1066 a great range of people and communities had established rights in the marsh. A walker across the area in the summer of that year could have seen the flocks belonging to the manors of great monastic houses: those of Holy Trinity Canterbury at Milton and Southchurch, of Westminster Abbey at Paglesham, and of the canons of St Paul's at Barling. With pasture rights for 560 sheep, they collectively were actually grazing over 800. Many of the early coastal settlements had grown into substantial places with extensive pasture rights and several were now the sites of the home farms of substantial manors belonging to the family of Swein of Essex. Some owners used all their pasture rights and more, some kept fewer sheep than they had pasture for. Of the coastal manors at 'Cana's people's hill', which seems likely to have been an early individual settlement, there was now Swein's manor of Canewdon, with a population of twenty-five households and grazing for 600 sheep, but Swein had a flock of only 342. Great Wakering, also Swein's, had a substantial home farm with eighteen bordars at work and pasture for 300; Little Wakering, a much smaller place, the same: their pasture rights must have been established before the two gained separate identities. Each had a hundred sheep. Some of the family's manors further inland in the Rayleigh Hills also had large amounts of pasture: at Eastwood for 300, at Prittlewell for 200 sheep: both places were headquarter manors, had populations of over twenty households, and appear to have been highly oriented towards demesne production, with large numbers of bordars.[35]

---

[35] Round, 'Domesday Survey'; Benton, *Rochford Hundred*, 176; Darby, *Domesday Geography of Eastern England*, 241–4; *Domesday Book: Essex*, 24.24, 24.21, 24.29, 24.20, 24.22.

In spite of these large manorial flocks it is unlikely that the major landlords' sheep would have taken up all the marshland. At Heybridge, it was reckoned in 1222 that sixty acres of marsh could support 240 sheep. This is four sheep per acre, comparable with the four ewes and their lambs to the acre suggested by Francis Pryor for his Shetland sheep, the nearest counterpart to the probable early medieval type. (What was meant by an acre in 1222 is another matter.)[36] In spite of these large players, the marsh was far from crowded with sheep. The combined pasture rights of all the major religious houses on Wallasea and Foulness would only have amounted to 560 sheep. Swein's family had rights for 1200 more, but even if stocked to the full they would have taken up only a small share of the many thousands of acres of coastal marshes. Even the largest demesne flock, Swein's 342 head at Canewdon, was well below the size of those of the great sheepmasters of the thirteenth century, whose flocks were numbered in thousands. Nor did all the big estates use the whole of their quota for the demesne flock. Holy Trinity, Canterbury, or rather its lessees, kept well short of the numbers of sheep it had pasture for and this was also true of Barking Abbey. On the smaller coastal farms there is also a disparity between pasture rights and size of flocks: two of the four Pudsey farms put out only half as many sheep as they had pasture for, the other two more than twice as many.[37] It is likely that farmers and great landlords alike had been employing various strategies as regards keeping sheep. Some kept large flocks and were leasing or buying pasture rights, or simply overstocking. Some were prepared to rent or cede their entitlement. Behind all these decisions was a lively appreciation of the possibilities of the market.

These were the flocks of the coastal manors feeding on pasture close to the farm, but others too had a claim on the marsh. The inhabitants of the Rayleigh Hills, a few miles inland from Wallasea and Foulness, also had grazing rights there. Here were big players: Swein at Rayleigh and Eastwood; Wulfmer, another big Essex landowner, at Hawkwell; a king's thegn at Thundersley; Barking Abbey a manor at Hockley. But there are also anonymous free men with pasture rights, and the twenty-four *villani* at Hockley and others like them may also have put sheep out on the marsh.[38] There were also flocks which travelled a considerable distance, like those driven down from Warley and Dunton, two places in the Childerditch area discussed earlier, which for some reason looked east to the coastal marshes rather than south to the Thames as did their immediate neighbours.

The seasonal movements of flocks must have been formative both as a cultural influence as well as an agrarian activity. Marshland grazing continued while the marshes were turned over to arable, first walled in the thirteenth century and then ditched and drained through the seventeenth, eighteenth, and

---

[36] Hale, *Domesday of St Paul's*, 52–3; Pryor, *Farmers in Prehistoric Britain*, 106.
[37] *Domesday Book: Essex*, 24.32, 34, 36, 37.
[38] *Domesday Book: Essex*, 24.17–18, 20; 25.11; 24.16; 9.13.

nineteenth. The drove ways were physical features in the landscape and continued to be so, possibly shaping the pattern of roads and tracks extant today.
Flocks moving from the inland manors across to their grazing lands on Wallasea and Foulness would have had to cross the territory of several other communities, and the coastal farms too had to get their animals across their neighbours'
land. This may not have entailed crossing cultivated fields—the very small
numbers of ploughteams at work and the difficulties of feeding oxen on the
coast show that there was not likely to have been much arable there even in the
late Anglo-Saxon period—but it must surely have given rise to negotiation and
trouble.[39] A long, complex history of conflict and dispute settlement surely lay
behind the intermeshing of the pasture rights of so many different interests,
from the powerful lay and ecclesiastical landowners to the small communities
and individual farmers that we see in Domesday. It is cultural transmission, not
the written record, that creates rights. Some of these rights must have originated in the early days of settlement, some may even have been taken over from
British predecessors. They became formally articulated as the detached grazing
areas of communities and later became parts of parishes. As Anglo-Saxon
society developed, land became increasingly privatized and the church became
a major player in the economy. Grazing rights became an important resource
of manorial demesnes and the monastic houses in particular were to be the
large-scale flockmasters of the Middle Ages. But alongside these were farmers
like the Pudsey men, with the larger independent farms that we can see in
Domesday. They were just the upper layer of the free farmers, whose land was
separately assessed for geld and whose pasture rights are recorded. The sheep
of the anonymous *villani*, the 'men of the vill', who appear in Domesday simply
as numbers, are invisible to us, but cumulatively they may have been the most
common of all. In this small corner of the south-east at least, small-scale commodity production at the level of the family farm already had a large part to
play in this important sector of the early medieval economy.

FARMER-FISHERMEN BETWEEN THE WYE AND THE SEVERN

Between the lower reaches of the Wye and the Severn, land 'at Dydde's *hamm*',
now Tidenham, takes its name from its position on the *hamm*, the land between
the two rivers (Fig. 7.8). The area considered here extends from the Beachley
peninsula up the Severn and the Wye and inland to the south-western edge of
the Forest of Dean: some of the places discussed here were included in the
Forest by William I. There is an exceptional amount of pre-Conquest documentation relating specifically to Tidenham. This makes it possible to relate the

---

[39] One possibility is that stock were driven onto Foulness via the Broomway, which ran along the
coast: today it is linked to some of the sites of the *wered* farms by trackways. It is now under water
except at low tides, but this may be the result of coastal erosion.

Fig. 7.8. Severn shore with fish weirs.

(From Seebohm, *English Village Community*)

kinds of people whose status and obligations are described to the real circumstances of where they lived and how they made a living; above all it throws a light on what their skills were.

The two rivers have created a very diverse geography and landscape. The lower reaches of the Wye twist and turn in wide meanders between precipitous limestone cliffs to join the Severn below Chepstow. The meanders have rich alluvial land near the river, backed by steep tree-covered cliffs, from whose summits steeply incised wooded valleys run inland. Some of these woods were predominantly yew: a danger to livestock but a valuable timber, and falcons could be captured on the cliffs. By contrast, the Severn runs through a broad alluvial plain and is tidal as far as Tewkesbury. Its banks are nearly at sea level and in their natural state the Severn Estuary Levels on both sides of the river and the Estuary itself were vast expanses of saltmarsh which formed along the coast through the deposition of chiefly tidal mud. A vigorous Roman campaign of sea walling, ditching, embanking, and draining retrieved much land near the river for pasture and arable, but after the end of Roman rule rising sea levels and neglect resulted in the abandonment and flooding of these labour-intensive systems, allowing marshy conditions to return. Some recolonization took place in the late Anglo-Saxon period, notably on the Somerset side by go-ahead Glastonbury Abbey, and further down the estuary on the Gwent Levels, but there is no evidence of any similar enterprise in the Tidenham area.[40] Its landlord then was Bath Abbey whose main interest in the place was probably as a source of

---

[40] Rippon, *Transformation of Coastal Wetlands*, 54–7; Townley, *Fieldwork on the Forest Shore*, 83–5.

fish for the monks, rather than following Glastonbury into elaborate land-reclamation schemes. Between the high woodlands bordering the Wye and the Severn's banks is rolling cultivable land, indented by streams running into small tidal creeks, called 'pills', from OE *pyll*, 'creek'. The whole area was part of a large region exploited by Romans for the lead, iron, and timber in the Forest of Dean. Salt was then produced on an industrial scale at Lydney and centuries later was recorded at Awre in Domesday Book.[41] An important Roman road, still largely in use as the A48, ran from the *colonia* at Gloucester to the *civitas* capital at Caerleon. Land given to the church of Llandaff in the eighth century may be the successor to a substantial villa-estate; in the Roman period the area supported a prosperous managerial villa-owning class.[42]

The linear configuration of roughly parallel zones of resources—upland woodland, treed slopes, workable land, and salt marsh—presents a picture very like the Thames bank discussed earlier and raises many of the same questions. The bounds of property here given to Bath Abbey in the mid-tenth century delineate an area bound by the Wye-side woods to the north and the Severn in the south.[43] Its river borders make it look at first sight very like Barking's estate on the Thames and raise the possibility that this was originally an area of a similarly linked economy, in which access to wood-pasture supplemented arable farming on the lowlands. There may be similarities, but the very different nature of these rivers gave a strong local character to the rural economy. Grazing off the farm, on woodland, scrub, and marsh, must always have been important: people were still putting livestock out on the commons before these were enclosed in the eighteenth century and several of the villages continue to have their own small detached commons. Seasonal transhumance is a possibility. There are certainly many drove roads, some still used today, which lead to upland pastures and woodland. But Tidenham's farmers could draw on another resource: the rivers themselves.

FISHING

Strong tides and currents, hidden sandbanks, and occasional rocky outcrops make the Severn an exceptionally dangerous river, with no obvious inlets or landing places. The tidal rise and fall in the Severn, and up the tidal reach of the Wye, are the highest in Europe: it can be between fourteen metres at the spring tides and six at the neaps. Working the waters of a tidal estuary demanded a deep store of local knowledge of such matters as the times of high and low water, variations in the tidal flow according to the speed and direction of the

---

[41] Faith, 'Tidenham'.
[42] Finberg, *Gloucestershire*, 31; Davies, 'Roman settlements'; Davies, '*Liber Landavensis*'.
[43] S 610.

wind and the phase of the moon, and the differing range between high and low water between the spring and neap tides. Working on the river demanded attention to all these factors. Nevertheless, the Severn has a long history of use as a waterway. Several prehistoric crossings from the Somerset shore are known, and at the Gloucestershire end of one of these a stone pathway leading from a landing place marked by a standing stone testifies to serious, though undateable, use. Downstream there was a cross-Severn route from Sea Mills which bypassed Gloucester, forming a link in the Roman route from Ciren-cester to Caerleon. A ferry crossing to Aust was controlled by the lords of the manor in the Middle Ages and could have been in existence earlier. Knowledge of landing places and crossing points, shoals and shifting sands all were mat-ters for experienced boatmen. They added up to a formidable store of unwritten local knowledge. This brings us back to the question of Anglo-British relations in the period of settlement, which here perhaps occurred in the train of the western drive of the kings of Wessex in the late sixth century. The British preserved and drew on a native skills base which may have dated back to prehistoric times: the Welsh laws refer both to fishing from coracles and fixed nets in rivers. 'Welsh boatmen', the *scipwealas* mentioned in a late Anglo-Saxon survey, were among the skilled watermen of the area.[44] This kind of practical skill and knowledge could only be passed on from person to person, and this presup-poses a good deal of communication between British and Anglo-Saxons, per-fectly credible in view of the fact that Tidenham in the late Anglo-Saxon period had an Anglo-Welsh population. It may have been part of the area known as Archenfield, south-west of Hereford. The widest interpretation of this territory has it including the land bordered by the lower reaches of the Wye and the Severn up to Gloucester, which would thus include the Tidenham area. Links with Wales continued well into the period of Anglo-Saxon settlement. Land here given to the church at Llandaff remained in Llandaff's hands far into the ninth century. A church on the little Lancaut peninsula had a Welsh dedication to St Cewydd and the land there was still in Welsh hands in the twelfth century, its links with Wales emphasized by Offa's Dyke, which runs along the top of the Wye cliffs and cuts the area off from Mercia.[45] A tiny chapel with a Welsh dedication to St Tecla, Englished as 'St Treacle', is at the tip of the Beachley peninsula, also 'outside the Dyke', and may have served a Welsh community there: possibly a mainly maritime one. It was Welsh speakers who gave Stroat its name, formed from the *strata*, the Roman road on which it lay. Celtic dedi-cations, circular churchyards, *cymry* and *walh* place-names complete the impres-sion of an area of ethnic and cultural mix, as does the carving, locally presumed

---

[44] Hagen, *Anglo-Saxon Food and Drink*, 161–2; Robertson (ed. and tr.), *Anglo-Saxon Charters*, 204–7 (no. 109); McGrail, *Ancient Boats*, 266.
[45] Smith, *Place-Names of Gloucestershire*, 23, 43; Gelling, *West Midlands*, 114–18.

to be 'Celtic', fixed in Tidenham church tower. The overall impression is of a continuing Christian British population. While politically the West Saxon domination of the western counties was achieved through force, 'on the ground' we seem to see here indigenous British people 'becoming Anglo-Saxon' through their assimilation of Anglo-Saxon culture and language. Anglo-Saxons learning and adopting the river lore of the indigenous population could well have been the other side of this process of acculturation.[46]

Both the Severn and the Wye were intensively fished. The market value of fish pervades the documentation, and goes a long way to explaining the attraction of the area to major landlords. An enormous amount of unrecorded fishing, particularly eeling, must have gone on up and down both rivers, but the Tidenham peninsula had the kind of fishery which was a fixed structure and produced an income which could be estimated and recorded. Sixty-five fisheries on the Severn and forty on the Wye were recorded in a late pre-Conquest survey. What we see recorded in the survey and in Domesday Book is the income from fishing for the market. Domesday records sixty-five *piscariae* here, of which fifty-three were in the Severn and five-and-a-half in the Wye (it is not clear where the rest were). These were fisheries which were either in the lord's hand, or from which he could expect a profit from his tenants through leases or tolls: unrecorded private fisheries could have put the numbers up a good deal.[47] Fishing rights were included in land granted to the church of Llandaff early in the eighth century and according to the late Anglo-Saxon survey 'every valuable rare fish' belongs to the landlord, as does every alternate fish from each fish-trap on the estate, and 'no-one has the right of selling any fish for money when the lord is on the estate without informing him about it': he has rights of pre-emption or could simply commandeer it. Severn fish are notably salmon and elvers; the Wye is a famous salmon river. The 'valuable rare fish' are likely to have been porpoises and sturgeon come in from the sea. The 30,000 herrings (*haeringys*) and 6 porpoises owed as part of the rent for the Tidenham estate in the eleventh century are surprising, as we think of herring as a North Sea fish, so they may in fact have been pilchards brought in by northward currents from off the Iberian coast, although colder climatic conditions in the eighth and ninth century may have extended the southerly range of species like cod and herring. The fish, which would not have remained fresh during a long road journey and so one must assume were preserved, were probably brought across the Severn at an ebb tide and taken up the Bristol Avon on the flood, most likely by coracle.

---

[46] Faith, 'Tidenham', 40–2; Davies, *Wales in the Early Middle Ages*, 34.

[47] Robertson (ed. and tr.), *Anglo-Saxon Charters*, 204–7 (no. 109); Darby, *Domesday Geography of Midland England*, 37–8, where the figure should be 66.5.

The fish (and presumably eels, although they do not appear in the Tidenham documents) were caught in two kinds of trap: *haecweras* and *cytweras*, which took advantage of the tidal conditions of the Severn and lower Wye. Frederic Seebohm, who visited Tidenham when writing his *The English Village Community*, first published in 1883, watched the fishermen at work and sketched the fish traps. His description cannot be bettered and his illustration, which can be seen at the beginning of this section, matches in its essentials the Anglo-Saxon fish weirs that have been reconstructed or excavated since his time. Seebohm saw 'long tapering baskets arranged between upright stakes at regular distances. These baskets are called *putts* or *butts* or *kypes*, and are made of long rods wattled together by smaller ones, with a wide mouth, and gradually tapering almost to a point at the smaller or butt end. These *putts* are placed in groups of six or nine between each pair of stakes, with their mouths set against the outrunning stream; and each group of them between its two stakes is called a "puttcher."…If the baskets had been called "cyts" instead of "putts" the group would be a *cytweir*.' (The term survives in the name of Chitweir in the Wye). He interpreted *haecweras* ('hedge-weirs' in later English, from OE *haec*, 'hatch') as 'barriers or fences of wattle…to produce an eddy or entrap the fish'. They could be used as well to guide the fish into the puttchers, and he saw salmon fishers at work using them to create an eddy in which fish were caught from a boat in a stop-net stretched between two poles.[48] With the great advances in coastal archaeology since Seebohm's day knowledge of this kind of fishing technology has greatly advanced and borne out his observations: recently the upright timbers of late Anglo-Saxon fish weirs have been found across the river at Bridgewater Bay.[49] The 'ball of good net twine', *an cliwen godes nett gernes*, which the tenants had to provide to the landlord was very likely either for a fishing net that would be stretched between two coracles, as was the practice in sixth-century Wales and still is today, or for a fixed net which would trap the fish on an outgoing tide, as Seebohm described. Another technique, also requiring twine, but needing no fixed structure, was to take salmon in the Severn shallows on an ebb tide with a 'lave net'. Although we have no pre-Conquest evidence for this technique, the term seems to come from OE *lafian*, 'to pour water on or through', although a French derivation is possible. A lave net was essentially the same shape as a shrimping net, but much larger. The fisherman stood in the shallows and having spotted a salmon coming downstream, scooped it up in the net and landed it. Taking large fish this way the fisherman would have needed the Anglo-Saxon equivalent of 'the speed of a Rugby three-quarter, the eye of a county cricketer and…[he] must know every yard of the river-bed'![50]

---

[48] Seebohm, *English Village Community*, 151–4 (quotations on 152 and 153, cited from the 4th edn (1896); Bond, 'Fishing', Fig. 7.

[49] Townley, 'Fieldwork on the Forest Shore', 83–5.

[50] Waters, *Severn Tide*, 103.

CRAFTS AND SKILLS

Making fish weirs and 'hedges' depended on much the same range of skills and raw materials as making hurdles for use on dry land (Fig. 7.9).[51] The survey records solely what services the Tidenham tenants owed to their lord, but we can be sure that these were jobs which they well knew how to do because they did them on their own small farms. The services show how important and versatile were the skills of 'weaving' wood to make a moveable barrier or structure. Wattle fences made from 'rods' of willow or hazel woven between upright hardwood stakes of oak or ash must have been a material as useful as corrugated iron and wire, even electric fencing, are in our own day. For 'weir-building', *to werbolde*, for their lord, the *geburas* had to supply cut wood: forty stakes (*maera*) or a load (*fother*) of smaller rods (*gyrda*), or else build eight 'yokes' for the ebb tides, perhaps wattle-hedges of varying heights to match changes in the tide-level.[52] The same kinds of materials and much the same skills were required for their obligation to supply fifteen poles (a pole is a length of fifteen-and-a-half feet or thereabouts—there were regional variations) of *aecertyninge*, literally 'field-fencing'. The term *tynan* simply meant to fence or enclose, so it is not clear whether this meant constructing temporary barriers used to keep livestock off the crops or whether it was a quickset hedge of growing plants which they had to 'cut and lay', cutting the stem nearly through and bending it parallel with the ground. Cutting and laying hedges in this way became, with many regional variations, the principal method of creating permanent barriers in later England, but while 'hedges' frequently appear as landmarks in charter bounds, it is not clear whether or not they were 'plashed' (the old term for cut and laid) or simply left to grow freely.[53] Possibly more evolved forms of cutting and laying quickset (growing) plants were a post-Conquest phenomenon: the term 'plash' is French or Anglo-Norman.[54] However, 'heathering' is a word which hedgers still use today for finishing off the laid hedge with pliant withies woven between the stakes and if it comes from OE *hæthorian*, 'to control', this might indicate that the practice of cutting and laying originated before the Conquest.[55] The more likely kind of work that the Tidenham *geburas* had to do, and which they did on their own land, was making wattle fencing: driving stakes into the ground and interweaving them with hazel or willow rods. Peter Reynolds, who investigated the subject in great, hands-on, detail, notes that from the many illustrations in

[51] Berryman, *Use of the Woodlands*, 10–16; Rackham, *History of the Countryside*, 73, 87; Reynolds, 'The medieval fence'.

[52] Robertson (ed. and tr.), *Anglo-Saxon Charters*, 206–7 (no. 109); Seebohm, *English Village Community*, 155.

[53] Maclean, *Hedges and Hedgelaying*; Barnes and Williamson, *Hedgerow History*; Reynolds, 'The medieval fence'.

[54] Rackham, *History of the Countryside*, 181–6; Hooke, *Anglo-Saxon Landscape of the West Midlands*, 248–54.

[55] *Pace* Rackham, *History of the Countryside*, 187.

Fig. 7.9. Wood-weaving products. a: Rough fencing sketched by Thomas Gainsborough.

(From Hayes, *Drawings of Thomas Gainsborough* © 1970 A. Zwemmer Ltd)

medieval manuscripts the typical fence within the immediate environs of the farmstead was one of stakes interwoven with hazel. Cut wood was also needed for the work owed on the solider enclosure or palisade around the landlord's house, the *burhhege*, probably heightened by being planted on a bank. For this the *geburas* had to dig five poles and fence and dig one pole as an alternative to the field-fencing. The large upright stakes could have been used to make an effective barrier simply by filling the gaps between them with brushwood: See-bohm saw brushwood being used for this purpose, and gorse and thorn make a virtually impenetrable barrier.[56]

[56] Rackham, *History of the Countryside*, 65-6 and Fig. 5.1; Reynolds, 'The medieval fence'. Hey, *Yarnton*, 130–1 reports fence posts from the middle Anglo-Saxon period, which would have made semi-permanent, though not quickset, barriers if filled in with woven wattle.

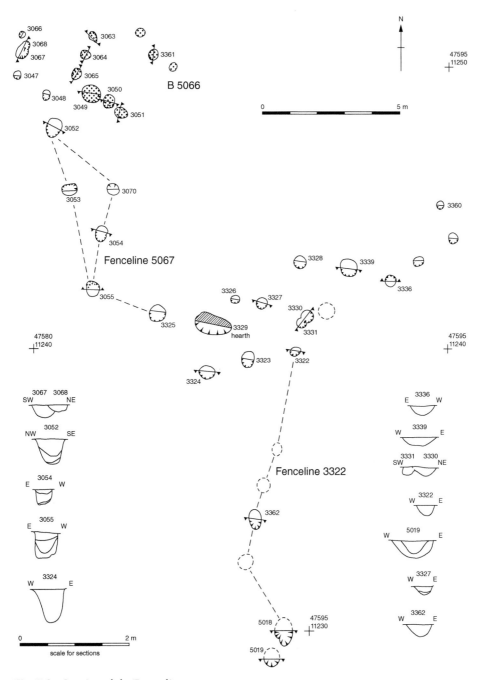

Fig. 7.9. Continued: b: Fence-lines.

(From Hey, *Yarnton* © Oxford Archaeology Unit)

Fig. 7.9. Continued: c: Hurdle.

(From Hayes, *Drawings of Thomas Gainsborough* © 1970 A. Zwemmer Ltd)

Although the term 'coppice' is much later, woodland managed by coppicing—cutting the young branches back to their base so that they can be harvested at regular intervals—is found on prehistoric sites and much coppicing was needed to produce all these uniformly sized stakes and rods of the right age, and thus the necessary flexibility, to weave between them. The sources for this wood cannot have been far away. Considerable stretches of deciduous woodland line the slopes and the *geburas* must have had access to this, so it was presumably in some way common and not a seigneurial monopoly. The extensive parish commons of the eighteenth century included Tidenham Chase.[57] Some of this woodland may have been 'coppice with standards', woodland managed to produce both the rods for wattle fencing as well as trees left to grow for timber for building. Woodland 'two leagues long and half a league broad', that is to say nearly three miles by over half a mile, was part of Tidenham manor in 1086. Woodland specifically measured in leagues which appears in some Domesday entries for this area, so naturally well-endowed with trees, was probably managed

[57] Herbert, 'Tidenham', 70.

for larger timber, which was brought down the Wye by boat or floated down bound in rafts: 'boats going into the forest', it is stated, had to pay toll at the new castle of Chepstow.[58]

INCOMES AND OBLIGATIONS

There was a good deal of cash in the local economy. The late Anglo-Saxon survey of the Tidenham estate describes it as consisting of 'thirty hides: nine inland and twenty-one *gesettes landes*'. This hidage is distributed between five different places: twelve hides at Stroat, five at *Middeltune*, five at the king's *tun*, Kingston, three at *Bispestune*, and three at Lancaut. At all except the last two there was land leased out for cash rent at twelve pence a yard-land. About half the estate's total area was leased in this way: fourteen-and-a-half hides. The people on the estate were of very varied status. Domesday records that 'thirty hides were reckoned there, ten of these were *in dominio*'.[59] These ten hides were *inland*, the home farm or farms of the estate, together with the holdings of its most dependent workers/tenants. On the Tidenham estate these were the *geburas*, the people whose work on the lord's fences has been described. Their later medieval equivalent, although with only half their land, came to be called villeins.[60] The survey's description of their obligations gives us an insight into the economy of these small farmers. The *geburas* had their own arable, probably a yardland, their own farm buildings, plough-teams and other livestock, including pigs, which were fed in part in the woods 'when there is mast'. There was common marsh pasture for cattle and possibly sheep on the Severn shore.[61] The *geburas* produced malt and honey, or could get them to pay their rent in these commodities, and so could brew beer and mead. A considerable amount of the income of the *villani* must have come from selling fish. In 1086 there were forty-two fisheries belonging to them in the Severn, two-and-a-half in the Wye (half a weir meant one that was either on the landward or the other side). As well as the fencing services described above, they did the demesne ploughing for, unusually, no team was kept on the Tidenham demesne. They ploughed the glebe arable as well. The ploughing arrangements strongly suggest that their arable was near to, possibly intermixed with, the landlord's and if that were the case, these arable areas may have been the nucleus of the common field systems which had developed by the thirteenth century. The houses, buildings,

[58] *Domesday Book: Gloucestershire*, S.1.
[59] Faith, 'Tidenham'; *Domesday Book: Gloucestershire*, 1.56.
[60] Herbert, 'Tidenham'.
[61] Herbert, 'Tidenham', 70: 'The Wharf' at Beachley Green, was originally a *waroth*, the area of dry ground in marshland which we have already encountered on the Essex marshes under a similar name.

and crofts of the *geburas* are likely to have been grouped in some way, and to have been near the fields.

The *geburas'* main obligation to the landlord was in the form of labour. The lord's enclosure, the *burh* that they had to hedge or fence, could have been at any one of the places on the estate, but the most prominent centre, in every sense, was probably at *Middeltune*. This has been identified with what is now Churchend, the west end of Tidenham village. This had traditionally been a significant place: there was a hillfort in Coombesbury Wood and the church was visible for miles and served as a landmark. If Bath Abbey or its representatives, Stigand or other lessees or their representatives kept a base on their Tidenham estate, it is likely to have been here. It was evidently the tax-collecting centre, and had given its name to the whole complex territory, in the sense that the abbey's estate, including most of the parts separately listed in the survey, is entered in Domesday under 'Tidenham'.[62]

Although by the late Anglo-Saxon period Churchend was likely to have been the most important centre, it seems there was a significant concentration of settlement at Milton and a tiny one at Lancaut, each surrounded by arable soon to be arranged into common-field systems. Both had some kind of seigneurial core, perhaps a church, a demesne farm, and dependent tenants with their own yardland farms and fisheries. But these must have been small islands of seigneurialized space—inlands—within a large area where there were also many independent farms. These were what the survey would have classed as *gesett land*: land which paid its own geld and was owned by the kind of people that G. B. Grundy described as 'ordinary inhabitants of the Anglo-Saxon community', not smallholder-tenants in the sense that the *geburas* were. Up the Severn at Stroat there were in 1086 two holdings of this kind and traces of others can be detected through their names: at the end of the peninsula are Bet(t)i's *lēah* at Beachley, Butta's *tūn* at Buttington, and, also on low land, Caegin's *hamm*, his river meadow at Keynsham. These place-names, though Old English in origin, are otherwise undateable, but Beachley and Buttington could have been part of the land described in the survey as 'land above the Dyke' and 'land outside the *hamme*' whose farmers could draw on some important sources of off-farm income: fishing, mining, and timber working. They were single farms, one of half a hide with a single farmer (*villanus*) with his own team and four-and-a-half fisheries, the other, of a yardland and a half, again with a single farmer with his own team and two fisheries. These were the properties of independent farmers, or rather fishermen/farmers, for it seems likely that their fisheries were as important as their land in terms of the value of their farms.[63]

[62] *Domesday Book: Gloucestershire*, 1.56.
[63] *Domesday Book: Gloucestershire*, 31.6, 39.11; Grundy, 'Saxon charters of Gloucestershire', 237–52, 245–51 at 246.

WOOD AND IRON

Farmers further upstream were much more involved in the economy of the Forest and its traditional trades and products. At Ælfwynn's *tun* on the Severn, now Alvington, where there was a demesne farm, the tenant farmers, who had arable for nine teams, were iron workers as well, paying their rent in honey and blooms of iron—both forest products. On the wooded hillsides, an area still marked by single farms and hamlets rather than villages, were Hygeweald's *feld*, now the hamlet of Hewelsfield with a manorial centre perhaps to be associated with Hygeweald's *tun*, which is how Domesday records the place (*Hiwoldestone*). William had made Hewelsfield part of the Forest of Dean, and Domesday gives us no further information about its agriculture. Madgetts, named from Modesgate, a break or gate in an Iron Age enclosure nearby, consisted of at least four big properties: one of two hides, one of a single hide, two of half a hide. They all had fisheries in the Wye below, assets valuable enough to have been snapped up by 1086 by the king, the abbot of Malmesbury, William de Eu, and Roger de Lacy.[64]

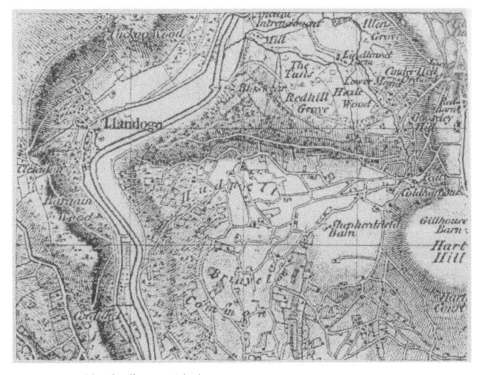

Fig. 7.10. Hudda's *healh*, near Tidenham.

(© Cassini Publishing Limited 2007)

[64] *Domesday Book, Gloucestershire*, E8, 32.12, 1.64, 39.10.

Another Anglo-Saxon farm on the uplands was Hud(d)a's *halh*s, his 'nooks' or 'hollows' (Fig. 7.10). If this comprised the area now covered by Hudnalls Farm and the wooded hillside called 'The Hudnalls', it was a considerable farm. The farmstead, and the fields where young stock were put out are likely to have been tucked away somewhere off the ridge and out of the keen winds that blow across the uplands here: such a siting would make them invisible from even a short distance away, as are their present-day counterparts, so the term 'nook' seems very appropriate. The steep, wooded hill of The Hudnalls runs down to the Wye and it is more than likely that whoever farmed here would have had their own fishery. It was still a considerable and distinctive area in the nineteenth century, as Fig. 7.10 shows.[65]

DROVING

These dispersed independent farmers may have been among the people mentioned in the late Anglo-Saxon survey who had obligations to the landlord but who were quite different from the *geburas* and the Domesday *villani* who were so closely involved with the economy of the manorial home farms. Some independent farmers are likely to have been among the people described in the *Rectitudines singularum personarum* as *geneatas*.[66] The *geneat* 'must work whether on or off the estate, whichever he is ordered to do, ride and provide animals for transport, lead loads and drive droves and do many other things'. We know from the duties of *geneatas* in other similar estate surveys that the 'many other things' might include escort duty and riding with messages. They are sometimes called 'riding men', and the fact that they had their own riding horses is a crucial part of their status. They were responsible independent farmers, sometimes with tenants of their own, and are found elsewhere in Gloucestershire and in several other parts of the country.[67] The survey is only interested in recording the duties of these people, not their economy, but it is clear that in addition to their own riding horses, they could provide packhorses and were experienced stockmen, able to 'lead loads and drive droves'. Farms detached from the main centres of the estate, like upland farms such as Madgett's, are a very probable setting for some of them. Like the two holdings at Stroat which were split off from the main manor after the Conquest, this was geld-paying land, *gesett land*. Early in the fourteenth century there were six major farmers there with their own tenants who owed services not on their landlord's land but on the Tidenham demesne. These services were very typical of the obligations of free people such as 'riding men'. They may possibly be the

---

[65] Gelling and Cole, *Landscape of Place-Names*, 123–33.
[66] Rect. 2, in Liebermann (ed.), *Gesetze*, i, 445; my translation.
[67] Faith, *English Peasantry*, 107–10, and for riding-men, 103–4; Faith, 'Tidenham', for *gesett land*.

much reduced counterparts of the pre-Conquest *geneatas*. In the thirteenth century drovers were employed on the Tidenham home farm.[68]

'Driving droves'—although it is a common phrase—raises an interesting possibility about the local economy. Roman Caerleon and Caerwent, on a good road out of south Wales to Gloucester and a Severn crossing to Bristol, must in their heyday have been customers for large numbers of cattle delivered as tribute or tax by the natives of the region, or as buyers in an open market. By the end of the thirteenth century great numbers of cattle, sheep, and horses were driven on the hoof from Wales into England.[69] The intervening period has yet to provide any evidence for this, and it may be significant that Bath Abbey expected its property at Tidenham to supply fish, not meat. Nevertheless it does seem as if cattle may have gone on being shifted between England and Wales in the late pre-Conquest period. A text of the tenth century known as *Dunsaete* sets out what the correct procedure is when disputes arise among the people called the Dunsaete, who include both Welsh living on one bank of a river— generally thought to be the Wye or one of its tributaries—and English on the other.[70] It does not specifically refer to trading, but it shows that both Welsh and English were evidently involved with livestock: compensation is set for horses, oxen, pigs, sheep, men (slaves), and goats. These rules bring to mind the preoccupation with cattle theft shown in the rules relating to the work of the hundred, discussed in Chapter 6. Cattle rustlers can be discovered by cattle-trackers. Crossing the river is supervised by some kind of official: it was evidently taken seriously as a boundary. None of this information amounts to evidence for long-distance droving, in fact crossing the Wye is evidently discouraged. But it does show that while crimes other than rustling are dealt with very sketchily, the problems of moving livestock in this border area were important enough to require careful rules.

The fishing and droving which played a big part in the late Anglo-Saxon economy around Tidenham could well have given it special characteristics. Both involved seasonal work which took people off the farm, sometimes for long periods. The salmon-fishing season was in the early spring (February to March), when the mature salmon were coming down the river after spawning. At high season fish weirs needed regular attention, but this is probably also true all year round when other fish were caught. The weirs were a good way from the farms and people had to be spared to tend them. This may have been work for women as well. In trades where the men were off the farm for long periods, women have frequently taken over traditionally male roles. We do not have any evidence for this until well after the Conquest, but in the thirteenth century several of the

---

[68] Fry, *Abstracts of Inquisitions*, 63–72; Herbert, 'Tidenham', 68–70.

[69] Britnell, *Commercialisation*, 113.

[70] Liebermann (ed.), *Gesetze*, i, 374–9; Noble, *Offa's Dyke Reviewed*; Gelling, *West Midlands*, 113–18.

Tidenham fisheries belonged to women.[71] If the cattle went off to distant markets as opposed to casual sales at the farm gate, this too would have taken those 'driving droves' away from the farm. Farmer-miners, like those at Alvington, also brought in an off-farm income from work which took them up into the Forest. There were clearly households which could draw on enough labour to cover these temporary absences, whether from an extended family or from a tied workforce of slaves or bordars. Fishing, cattle rearing, and mining were all part of the peasant economy in the land between the rivers. The rewards of supplying the market evidently made it worth investing labour in these off-farm activities and remind us that coast and riverside farm economics could all, to use a modern term, have been diversified.

[71] Fry, *Abstracts*, 68.

Fig. 8.1. Woodland and arable.
While today's fields are a great deal more extensive than the arable in the Anglo-Saxon period, areas such as the Chilterns, seen here, still display the earlier combination of woodland and cultivated land.

(© Jane Peart, from a photograph © Pam Brophy)

8

Woodland

'Woodland' in our period meant more than simply vegetation. Like Hardy's term 'Woodlanders', it implied something about the kind of people who lived there, the way they made a living, and the whole character of their environment. It was one word for what Oliver Rackham has christened the 'Ancient Countryside' of Lowland England: the land of small fields or small-scale common-field systems, ancient hedges, many woods, and heaths. He contrasted this with the 'Planned Countryside' of open-field agriculture and little woodland. Both these kinds of countryside were the product of long periods of change, but while parts of England moved first towards creating large common-field systems and later to enclosure, the 'Ancient Countryside', although much eroded and obscured by modern development, is still a recognizable and distinct landscape.[1]

The woodland economy was certainly ancient. It was well suited to the period of 'abatement' described earlier, when the pressure to produce grain and cattle for the Roman state had eased. In the area of Northamptonshire and Buckinghamshire which became Whittlewood Forest parts of the heavy claylands that had been worked by Romano-British farmers reverted to unbroken woodland but in others people continued farming, as the finds of pottery which can be dated to the period AD 400–850 show. Many of these scattered farms were viable enough to resist the attraction of shifting to lighter soils which influenced so many farmers in the middle Anglo-Saxon period.[2] Tom Williamson, from the perspective of a large area of south-east England, came to the conclusion about the deep roots of the wood-pasture economy there that 'many…farms and hamlets…incorporating Old English elements' were Anglo-Saxon or early post-Conquest.[3] These are important observations as there has been a tendency to see woodland farms solely as the result of a 'journey to the margin', a drive to extend the cultivated area under pressure from a growing population in the twelfth and thirteenth centuries.[4]

---

[1] Rackham, *History of the Countryside*, 4–5; Williamson, *Shaping Medieval Landscapes*, 1–8 and 91–122 for a well-illustrated survey.

[2] Jones and Page, *Medieval Villages*, 84–9; Parry, *Raunds*, 91–7.

[3] Williamson, *Shaping Medieval Landscapes*, 92.

[4] As for instance Roberts and Wrathmell, *Region and Place*, 169–70.

A variety of soils could support woodland and the underlying soils could differ over very short distances, patches of heathland on sandy acid soils with light tree cover, gorse and heather occurring near heavier and wetter soils, which enabled trees to grow to considerable height.[5] We cannot now walk through Anglo-Saxon woodland but we can see it through the eyes of the people who provided the information which went into the boundary clauses to charters that conveyed land there. In the southern part of the Berkshire Downs, between the open Downs and the Kennet Valley, the underlying chalk is capped with heavy clay-with-flint which supports a broad swathe of woodland: the whole area may have once been part of what the British had called *Cilterne*.[6] The boundary clause of a charter granting a small estate here at Chievely in the mid-tenth century shows just how diverse a woodland landscape, and its economy, could be.[7] It reveals a landscape much the same as we see in the region today, where cultivated land, woodland, and heath are in close proximity, as the scene that opens this chapter shows. Around Chieveley seems to have been an area where woodland was quite carefully managed. In about five miles of the boundary there were areas of what Rackham calls 'compartmented woodland' enclosed and protected for a particular purpose, most likely coppicing, by a *wyrtruma*—what we would today call a 'woodbank'. The king had an enclosure, a *haga*, here, part of whose outline can still be seen on the parish boundary. Elsewhere mature trees had been felled, leaving *stocs*, stumps. One possible interpretation of *stoc* is that it indicated coppiced woodland, where young branches had been cut back, leaving the 'stools' from which new ones would grow.[8] There was open though boggy land at 'the little heath *feld*', perhaps part of what is now Snelsmore Common, one of the many 'moor' names in the neighbourhood which indicate wet land, and there was pasture at 'sheep meadow'.[9] There were small patches of arable ('six acres') and quarrying for chalk, probably used as a dressing to break up the strong clay which made ploughing here such heavy going. The whole area was criss-crossed by 'ways' and paths, the 'roads many, not straight, often sunken' of Rackham's 'Ancient Countryside'. Some were wandering lanes, some were important route ways like the Roman road which appears as 'the street, *stræt*' or 'the stone way' or the 'army path' or the drove ways which brought the animals of the lowlands up into the woodland for pasture. This is the countryside where the

---

[5] For the overall distribution and nature of woodland in pre-Conquest England: Hooke, *Landscape of Anglo-Saxon England*, 139–69; Short, 'Forests and wood-pasture in lowland England'; Rackham, *Ancient Woodland*.

[6] Everitt, *Continuity and Colonization*, ch. 7 'The Downland economy', describes a very similar landscape of chalk hills capped by woodland, as does Williamson, *Origins of Hertfordshire*, 214 ff., describing the more northern part of the Chilterns.

[7] S 558; Kelly, *Charters of Abingdon Abbey*, i, 185–9 (no. 45). Hooke, *Anglo-Saxon Landscapes of the West Midlands*, 147–85, pioneered the use of charter bounds to investigate woodland.

[8] Rackham, *History of the Countryside*, 66, Fig. 5.1.

[9] Gelling and Cole, *Landscape*, 58–60.

'lookers' way' may have been named after the 'lookers' or shepherds who drove animals along it from the clay vale into the heathy woodland. Many more were the small winding 'ways' and frequent crossroads which made up a dense network of local communications. The Chievely boundary shows the great diversity of the woodland landscape. It is the fact that its soils and its vegetation could differ over quite a small area that accounts for many of the features of its economy.

What made the woodland economy, even on the smallest scale, viable, was the abundance of pasture. It would be hard to overestimate the importance of wood-pasture as an economic resource.[10] We have already seen how vital it was as a food supply for animals. It was abundant. Oliver Rackham has calculated that even the woodland recorded in Domesday Book could account for up to 24 per cent of the total area of a county.[11] The Domesday figures are notoriously difficult to interpret, but it is plain that recording woodland was thought important. Domesday Book records as a manorial asset woodland which belonged to a particular manor but was situated at some distance away—just as the Essex saltmarsh described in an earlier chapter was recorded under the headings of inland manors. Even so, as Sarah Wager's work on medieval Warwickshire shows, much could have been omitted: woods and groves are used as landmarks in charter boundaries for places where Domesday Book records none.[12] Woodland was evidently not only used as detached pasture by farms whose farmstead and arable land were elsewhere. On the contrary, farms embedded in woodland were evidently an important part of the rural economy. The following small studies show that they differed not only from region to region but even among themselves.

NORTH-WEST ESSEX

While woodland was a distinctive physical environment which encouraged particular ways of farming, we also have to take into account that the political and social environment mattered too. Anglo-Saxon farmers in the settlement period were living with very varied experiences of post-Roman Britain. It is not often that we can examine farms in this early period in any realistic and detailed way but several studies of its archaeology make this approach possible in north-west Essex. 'Barbarian' settlers gained land within the empire in a variety of ways, in which simple land-taking must have been important, but which also included various kinds of accommodation. An earlier chapter suggested

[10] Rackham, *History of the Countryside*, 4–5, 181. Everitt, *Continuity and Colonization*, has a good description of wood-pasture at 30.

[11] Rackham, *History of the Countryside*, 121. For the recording of woodland in Domesday Book see Darby, *Domesday England*, 171–207.

[12] Wager, *Woods, Wolds and Groves*, 143.

that post-Roman and early settlement Britain was an economy in 'abatement', in which livestock were as important as cereal cultivation to many farmers, or even more important, and Chapter 12 will illustrate some of the many places where farmers in the post-Roman period were content to work an 'inherited landscape' of fields and enclosures. Although, other things being equal, light, freely draining soils seem to have been the ones that were most attractive to them for growing cereals, Essex gives examples of how even in areas of heavy soils there could be continuity of occupation and cultivation past the end of Roman Britain. If, as has been suggested, the kingdom of the Trinovantes remained a 'sub-Roman enclave' into the sixth century, then it is a likely area for this to have been the case.[13] In places the descendants of, or successors to, the Romano-British owners of some prosperous and dominant villa estates or major farms may have maintained their economic position while their material culture was progressively Germanicized. Whether this was due to the acculturation of their owners, or their replacement by newcomers is an open question.[14]

When it comes to the ordinary peasant farm the settlers came into contact with a Romano-British rural population who became archaeologically virtually invisible but who could well have remained in the area while adopting Anglo-Saxon material culture. The *weala-denu*, 'Britons' valley' at (Saffron) Walden, marks a valley territory which was in some way recognizable to its neighbours as notably ethnically British. Regular rectangular field systems which remained visible into the nineteenth century at Littlebury, south of the Roman town of Chesterford, have been suggested as remnants of Roman land allotments and the town itself may have been the centre of a territory of which vestiges remained in the boundaries of neighbouring parishes.[15] Elsewhere an ethnic mix is inherently much more likely. On the more tractable Boulder Clay of the Essex Till the contours of the land, not simply the character of the soil, offered different possibilities to farmers: light soils on the valley sides, heavier on the interfluves. The pattern of Romano-British settlements traced by Tom Williamson through an extensive campaign of field-walking in north-west Essex shows intensive farming and settlement here, about 1.3 settlements every square kilometre. They followed the Iron Age distribution, the more prosperous concentrating on the margins of the lighter soils of the valley sides of the major watercourses while on the heavier level land between them settlements were fewer, poorer, and more evenly scattered. They were also less permanent. Williamson, an archaeologist (and smallholder) exceptionally alert to the realities of farming, suggests that Romano-British farmers in the area ran two different kinds of husbandry according to their land. Those with farms on

---

[13] Dark, *From Civitas to Kingdom*, 86–9; Kemble, *Prehistoric and Roman Essex*, 105–9.
[14] Kemble, *Prehistoric and Roman Essex*, 200; Hunter, *Essex Landscape*, 59–61.
[15] Bassett, 'In search of the origins', 25.

the valley sides kept their arable fields in good heart by close-folding their sheep on them during the fallow season, just as the West Stow people seem to have done. The farmers on the heavier soils of the upland plateaux spread muck from cattle byres and the domestic rubbish and sewage of the farmstead—hence the pottery scatters found on a permanently cultivated 'infield', while the 'outfield' was only cultivated sporadically and left to recover its fertility naturally. This kind of relaxed rotation was available to farms with plenty of available land, and we will encounter it again in the different environments described in Chapter 12. Many of these Essex farms subsequently fell out of use and are now under woodland, and others which may have continued are hard to trace archaeologically, although some outlines of their small squarish fields, and the minor roads which linked them to the main Roman ones can sometimes be traced. The farms on the lighter valley soils had a much better survival rate and, as we shall see, many laid down the foundations for later Anglo-Saxon and medieval settlement.[16]

When the movements of early Germanic settlers into Britain can be traced, rivers and their tributaries can be seen to have played an important part in the routes they took and the areas they settled. The very few place-names which passed from Brittonic into English are mostly the names of rivers, and a way of conceiving the landscape in which river systems and the resources associated with them were of prime importance could have been common to both cultures.[17] Many groups named themselves, or were named by their neighbours, in relation to the rivers along which they established their farms. The importance has already been stressed of looking at rivers as one part of a total 'package' of resources, in which the available land suitable for crops and the pasture on higher ground mattered as much as the river and its meadows. One of the most well-studied 'resource areas' in Essex is that of the Rodings: now a group of nine parishes on either side of the River Roding. The unit out of which the parishes came to be carved took its name not from the river but from Hrotha—in other words, the river and the surrounding area derived their name from a person: the original 'Rodingas' were 'the people of Hrotha'. The area was not an Anglo-Saxon creation. The river had previously had a British name, the Hyle, before it was renamed the Roding and the people who had been farming there when the Saxon immigrants came in very likely had much the same kind of territory that 'Hrotha's people' established.[18] Archaeologically they have left no trace of their presence. Like the Rodings, but on a smaller scale, little valleys associated with a group named from a single individual appear all over the region in Essex—as they do in much of southern England—such as 'Manna's people's valley' at Manuden and the *Pyttelingas* at Pitley (Farm), Finchingfield.

[16] Williamson, 'Development of settlement'; Williamson, 'Settlement, hierarchy and economy'; West Stow: see p. 270.

[17] Jackson, *Language and History*, 220, now supplemented and revised by Coates and Breeze, *Celtic Voices, English Places*.

[18] Bassett, 'Continuity and fission', 25–42.

The primary reason for settling along valleys is immediate and practical: people and their livestock need drinking water. There was no shortage of water in the part of Essex we will consider here, the 'Essex Till' of Boulder Clay, an area of well-wooded small hills, drained by the Roding and Chelmer flowing south and the Cam north, and by their tributaries. The more level areas between the rivers also have an accessible water table. Down on the coastal marshes sheep were the primary animal, and sheep are very small drinkers: only lactating ewes really need a regular water supply. Away from the coast, while sheep were also raised, a more wooded and better watered landscape meant that cattle and pigs were also important. The borders of the small rivers and streams provided land for winter fodder, both cut for hay and as grazing; much of this we would think of as too rough to be called meadow, although that is how Domesday Book describes it. Essex meadow was very unevenly distributed. Many of the north-west Essex rivers, especially in their upper reaches, are little more than streams. Before modern banking and dredging confined them to a single course they could well have been 'braided' multiple streams which were even smaller. They run through small valleys which cannot have provided much in the way of meadow land. Apart from hay, animals could have been fed over the winter on the by-products of arable hus-bandry—stubble grazing, straw, and beanstalks. Their principal other resource was the ample wood-pasture on the flanks of the small valleys through which these little rivers run.

This does not seem to have been an area where whole communities drove their animals to distant grazing: if this form of transhumance was practised, it co-existed with a typical woodland way of life in which settlements were surrounded by ample wood-pasture. The Old English place-names give the impression of lightly nucleated, scattered settlements in a well-wooded area: a pattern, notwithstanding the great diminution of woodland, not unlike that of today (Fig. 8.2). Place-names with the typically wood-pasture element *-lēah* are very common here and many come from ash, willow, and lime, from the woodland activity of coppicing (Yardley, from the OE *gierd, gyrd* for poles or 'yards'), or from woodland residents like Brock the badger, whose name is a rare Brittonic survival at Broxted. Even the major places—or what by the Conquest were major places—are mostly named from run-of-the-mill natural features, several with woodland associations: Thaxted is the 'reed place', for thatching; the Sampfords take their name from their sandy ford. 'Tye', from the Old English word *teag*, 'a small enclosure', is still used in Essex to mean common grazing or a green, but early tyes, valleys, and streams may have been privately owned, like 'Tila's tye' at Tilty. 'Plycca's valley' at Plegdon (Hall), pos-sibly 'Tippe's valley' at Debden, 'Manna's nook', *Ciccan eg*, 'Cicca's island', and *Ceawan rithig*, 'Ceawa's stream', at Chickney and Chaureth, all suggest individually owned farms with their natural resources close to hand. (It should

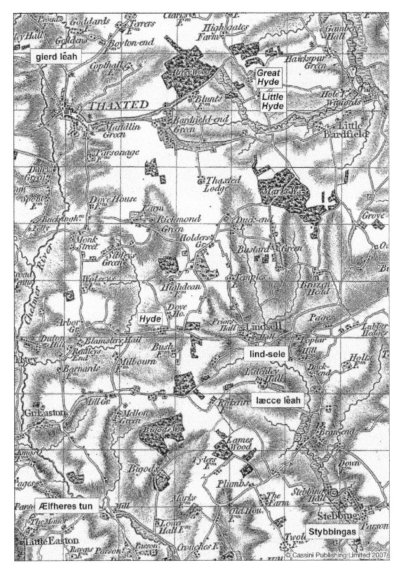

Fig. 8.2. Old English place-names in north-west Essex.

(© Cassini Publishing Limited 2007)

be noted that the asterisk means that the word following it has been interpreted as a hypothetical personal name: possibly some nickname, noun, or adjective unknown to us was meant instead. It is worth observing here that the hypothetical personal names assigned are always masculine.) Place-names like this give a hint of what could have been a body of Old English words, perhaps some of them in a local dialect, which were never written down and occur only as elements in place-names.[19] Some woodland may also have been in individual ownership. In Essex, as in some other counties, Domesday Book recorded woodland as if its prime use was as swine-pasture: under each manor the amount of woodland is reckoned as 'woodland for *x* pigs.' Most farms had readily available woodland and some were probably surrounded by it. For instance, Grim had 'woodland for 80 pigs' when he farmed at Lashley on the eve of the Conquest; very likely the small woodlands on the higher ground behind Lashley Hall are a relic of a once much larger wood.[20] This is the same way of measuring a resource as 'pasture for *x* sheep' on the coast, and raises the same problems: did he have the right to pasture eighty pigs, or did he own sufficient woodland for them? The second is not unlikely. One of the laws issued by king Ine of Wessex early in the eighth century indicates privately owned woods. It concerns swine trespassing on what appears to be private mast-pasture, for which the owner is to be compensated, the fines rising if the offence is repeated. There are rules about what was later called 'pannage', rent paid for permission to feed pigs in someone else's woodland. It is to be paid in pigs, 'every third pig when the bacon is three fingers thick, every fourth when the bacon is two fingers thick and every fifth when it is a thumb thick'.[21]

It is very unlikely that by 1066 pig-pasture was in fact the main pastoral use of Essex woodland. Domesday's recording of 'woodland: so many pigs' may be a relic of traditional rights which by 1086 were no longer a reflection of the situation on the ground. Although many people probably kept a pig, the use of woodland as swine-pasture may have been in decline by the eleventh century. By 1086 most demesne farms in our area had much more 'woodland for pigs' than they kept pigs to put there and the terms in which the Essex countrymen gave evidence about the extent of their woodland may be a relic of the earlier times of Ine's law, when a tree could be measured by the number of pigs it could shelter.[22] Sheep and cattle were the main users of open grassy spaces in woodlands and it is clear from the information in Essex Domesday that both single farms and larger settlements practised a mixed husbandry in which all kinds of livestock—including bees and goats—were very important.

The nature of the countryside itself is a strong argument for north-west Essex having had a deeply entrenched and long-lasting dispersed settlement pattern and for its scattered farms having been pastorally oriented. In 1086 the area supported more people and more plough teams per square mile than the south

---

[19] Reaney, *Place-Names of Essex*, 474, 471.

[20] *Domesday Book: Essex*, 90.51.

[21] Ine 49, in Liebermann (ed.), *Gesetze*, i, 110, and Attenborough (ed. and tr.), *Laws*, 52–3. Pigs and pig-keeping are fully described by Banham in Chapters 4 and 5.

[22] Ine 44, in Liebermann (ed.), *Gesetze*, i, 108, and Attenborough (ed. and tr.), *Laws*, 50–1; Darby, *Domesday Geography of Eastern England*, 256. On pig-pastures see O. Rackham, *History of the Countryside*, 75–6, 122. The large enclosures or 'swine-cotes' detected by Chatwin and Gardiner in the Sussex Weald and the woodland 'styes' in Wychwood are testimony to the continuing importance of woodland pig-pasture elsewhere in southern England: Chatwin and Gardiner, 'Early settlement of woodlands'.

of the county. On the face of it this would suggest that cumulatively farmers there had more land under the plough but the dissected and wooded nature of the terrain makes large stretches of arable unlikely. It also had a high proportion of *villani*, the men of a vill or township, with their own teams. Nicholas Higham has used these Domesday statistics in an ingenious way. He has interpreted ratios of this sort as an indicator of dispersed settlement. His argument runs like this: these farmers did not have undivided arable near enough to their neighbours' for a few shared teams to do the work, as farmers in a nucleated settlement working a truly common-field system would have had. Instead they each had a team, very likely smaller than the eight-ox team Domesday takes as the norm, or were partners in some kind of small-scale field system.[23]

The fact that north-west Essex had a dispersed settlement pattern with a great many farms which were either scattered or in small hamlets did not mean that all these farms were much the same or that it had an egalitarian social structure. Domesday Book shows a wide range of properties and social relationships between the powerful and their subordinates. Very similar places had different histories. Lindsell and Lashley both have names with elements which are a good guide to the nature of the local landscape of woodland clearings and streams. *Lind-sele*, 'cottages in the lime-wood', and *lӕcc-lēah*, 'cleared land by the stream flowing through boggy land', began as two settlements along the Stebbing Brook, which winds through wooded country until it joins the Chelmer two miles below Great Dunmow. When they first acquired these names they perhaps were an undifferentiated part of a valley territory which became known as the 'land of the Stybbingas' ('Stybba's people'), or possibly the 'people of the cleared land', centred on Stebbing. Part of Lashley (we do not know at what date) was known as 'Deorman's *lēah*'. Such a name marks private ownership and individual rights and Deorman's farm was a predecessor of the single farm there just before the Conquest whose owner, Grim, 'a free man', ran it with four farm workers and two slaves. He kept two plough-teams—up to sixteen working animals—had woodland enough for eighty pigs, and ten acres of meadow, five acres per team. This was a substantial independent farm which retains its character to the present day, now dignified as Lashley Hall.[24] Lindsell, the 'cottages in the limewood' further up the Stebbing Brook, which perhaps had originated in a small settlement of people whose economy was entirely woodland-based, had by 1066 developed in an entirely different way. There were now two main properties, one belonging to Horwulf, described as a 'free man', and one to Wulfmӕr (both dithematic names contain the element 'wolf': were they brothers? father and son?). Horwulf had two teams, four other cattle, forty pigs, twenty-eight sheep, and five hives (honey was a valuable woodland product); Wulfmӕr had a similarly sized outfit. Both had six acres of meadow.

---

[23] Higham, 'Settlement, land use and Domesday ploughlands'.
[24] *Domesday Book: Essex*, 90.51.

They were evidently men of some standing. Associated with each main farm was a group of *villani* with three teams: eight families at Horwulf's, nine at Wulfmær's. In spite of their similar properties—we might suspect a larger property had been split into two—they were already very different places which foreshadow the subsequent binary topography of the village. Wulfmær's property had a mill and a priest: two elements likely to have been the foundation for this small nucleation. (Its straggling street and possible second centre at Templars look like a secondary development.)[25]

Ciccan eg, 'Cicca's island', and *Ceawan riðig*, 'Ceawa's stream', now Chickney (Hall) and Chaureth (Hall Farm), are two small places whose names and positions reflect the importance of water-supply in determining settlement. There is no archaeological evidence at present that can tell us if the present-day farmsteads overlie earlier predecessors on the same sites but both command the same mix of territory which Williamson singled out as favoured by Roman farmers and which the Anglo-Saxon successors also valued. Each had access to a small stream, tributaries of the Chelmer, Chickney being perched on a little promontory between two streams, and the lighter soils of the valley slopes and wooded higher ground with heavier soils were likewise accessible to both. In spite of these similarities, by the eleventh century they had developed in very different ways. Chickney had become the property of Siward, a king's thegn, who may have built the church, fragments of which are still there: a priest had appeared between 1066 and 1086. With three plough-teams, supported by twenty acres of meadow, he had the greater part of the arable while the two *villani*, farmers of the township, had a team each. There were seven bordars, probably working on the demesne farm, some most likely as stockmen since Siward's demesne farm was livestock-oriented.[26] His livestock—two horses, three cows with calves, sixty sheep, twenty-four goats, and twenty pigs—almost certainly dominated the available pasture too, whether meadow or wood-pasture. When the Domesday text says that Siward held Chickney 'as a manor' we can envisage something familiar, for by then it had everything in place that we think of as 'manorial': the hall, the hall farm and its workers, the church and its priest. Quite distinct were the 'men of the township', albeit a very tiny township consisting of two *villani*, with their own farms. Chaureth in 1066 looked very different. It was much less organized around a demesne farm than its neighbour half a mile away. In fact, it consisted of two separate farms. Wulfric, 'a free man', had thirty acres (a quarter of a hide) and two unnamed 'free men' half a hide there: nominally sixty acres. These acreages probably express the geld obligation of the two farms rather than their actual size, but they were clearly on a much smaller scale than Siward's manor farm at Chickney.[27]

---

[25] *Domesday Book: Essex*, 14.2, 25.4.
[26] For bordars as demesne workers see Faith, *English Peasantry*, 70–5.
[27] *Domesday Book: Essex*, 34.9, 90.77–8.

Large farms like Chickney, some of which had a 'gentrified' future before them complete with moat and manor house and often with 'Hall' attached to their name, are clear enough in Domesday. They were separately entered and assessed for tax. They were independently viable mixed farms of a wide range of sizes and their owners are often members of a large class of unnamed free people who are a feature of Essex Domesday. Fifteen hundred and thirty-six freemen and sokemen are entered in this way. Most had land rated at under a hide—and Essex has a few 'Hyde' place- and farm names today (one is marked on Fig. 8.2)—but their holdings in actual size varied from an acre to over ten hides.[28] Though we have no archaeological record of their farmsteads, like Yardley these were often perhaps surrounded by their own land. If their owners did develop common-field farming, it was likely to have been on a small scale, involving a few neighbouring farms rather than incorporating all the arable of the parish.

John Hunter's detailed local study of the post-Conquest settlement pattern and social structure of the north-west Essex region after the Conquest shows a landscape in which the hamlet or the multi-focal village is much more common than villages of the 'Midland' type, and settlement is mainly dispersed, with greens, small woodlands, and isolated farms.[29] Nevertheless it was a landscape which had been shaped not only by peasant farmers but also by powerful lords. Hunter distinguished their 'primary' manors which appear in Domesday Book as valuable properties with large demesne labour forces. On these 'primary manors' the demesne is generally in a compact block rather than being distributed among tenant land in the common fields, and retained its separate identity, parts being often later made into parks. They have a manorial centre which may include a 'primary' green and which is markedly nucleated for the region. Typically the church lay next to the manor house and the territory of the manor became its parish. The owner's hall, domestic buildings (chamber block and kitchen), and farm buildings, possibly the whole complex fenced or walled with an entrance gate, may have given some of these prestigious centres the status of a *burh*.[30] 'Ælfhere's *tūn*' (now Bigod's Hall Farm) must always have profited from its valley-head site and its access to the Chelmer. This was a much bigger river than the little Stebbing Brook, and would have provided more water power for its mill than the Stebbing Brook would have done for those at Chickney and Chaureth. It had more woodland (for four hundred pigs) than they had, and more meadow (thirty-six acres). With more ploughs on its arable (three) than on the fields of its

---

[28] Boyden, 'Structure of landholding'; Faith, 'Hides and Hyde Farms'; Williamson, *Origins of Hertfordshire*, 141, for similar examples in that county.

[29] Hunter, *Essex Landscape*, 101–2, for this kind of development in Essex woodland.

[30] Hunter, *Essex Landscape*, 95–104. Essex has several major manors with names ending in -bury with no urban characteristics at all: Hallingbury and Quickbury are two in the region discussed here and Thaxted, which did become a town, has a large area quite apart from the town centre, marked on Ordnance Survey maps as 'The Borough', which includes the manorial site.

eleven *villani* families,[31] well before the Conquest Ælfhere's *tūn* was clearly a valuable and probably aristocratic property. Its name is of a form unusual for this part of Essex. In much of late Anglo-Saxon southern England it would have been obvious to all around as the property of an important man.

One possible explanation for its success is topographical. The 'primary' manorial sites may always have had a stronger hold on a major resource: meadow. Tom Williamson has connected the supply of meadow with some important differences in both social relationships and settlement. He links the character of meadow in an area very strongly with the character of lordship. He argues that where meadow was restricted to a limited area, highly nucleated 'manorialized' centres developed. Their demesnes depended on the livestock and labour of the local farmers, who also needed access to this limited resource and were thus more amenable to their farmsteads and their land being incorporated into manorialized nucleated settlements and common-field systems. Where meadows or other supplies of winter feed were widely available, albeit in scattered patches, dispersed farms with their own supplies could survive.[32] Wihtgar, a major late Anglo-Saxon landowner, ran a labour-hungry enterprise at Thaxted just before the Conquest. He had sixteen slaves at work, a pair to manage each of his eight plough-teams, so Thaxted evidently already had the strikingly arable character it has today, set among its huge cornfields. It may well be that Wihtgar's 120 acres of meadow were the key to the thriving of his Thaxted operation for they were the source of winter fodder for his eight teams, giving him, at fifteen acres of meadow per team, 'fuel' for traction well over the average: other farms in the vicinity had typically only between three and nine acres per team.[33] For a powerful man, owner of an area with a substantial concentration of meadow, there were opportunities for arable farming on a large scale. Wihtgar had his hands on two essentials of capitalist farming: land and fuel. The third was labour. Such an enterprise needed a considerable labour supply beyond the specialist work of the slave ploughmen. Wood-pasture farming may itself have produced just such a class of people. These were woodland cottagers on the edge of subsistence. One factor in the economy of the 'primary manors' may be the county's exceptionally large numbers of people entered in Domesday as *bordarii*. They were nearly 7,000 out of a total recorded population of 13,829 in 1066 and increased to half the recorded population by 1086.[34] After the Conquest we find bordars, a term that

---

[31] *Domesday Book: Essex*, 23.2.

[32] Williamson, *Shaping Medieval Landscapes*, 103–4. Williamson, *Origins of Hertfordshire* categorizes the Domesday information for Hertfordshire vills along similar lines at 157–66.

[33] In 1066 there were fifty-five *villani* families with thirty-four plough-teams, so the arable amounted to perhaps four thousand acres. Twenty years later their plough-teams had dropped to eighteen: it is just possible that this was a consequence of the arable of some of the dispersed farms of the neighbourhood having been incorporated into the common fields which were eventually to cover much of the parish: Hunter, *Essex Landscape*, 98–9; *Domesday Book: Essex*, 23.2.

[34] Darby, *Domesday Geography of Eastern England*, 225.

the Normans brought with them, closely associated with manorial demesnes. They were smallholders with heavy labour obligations who supplied the lord's *borde*, his table. But the people the Domesday clerks recorded as bordars may have been a wider group than that, although similarly badly provided with land and plough-teams. Large numbers are found in woodland areas, although not only there.[35] The economy of these small farmers, restricted by their poor provision of arable and winter feed, may have been increasingly insecure. Some may have opted for security over independence and accepted tenancies from the lords of 'primary manors' in return for labour on the home farm.

Alongside the great lords, the countryside of late Anglo-Saxon north-west Essex evidently offered some independent farmers the opportunity to thrive into yeomen and small gentry. For the owners of large and prestigious major manors with plenty of meadow it offered the opportunity to develop large arable-based demesnes and recruit the labour to work them. But for a smallholder, making a living there could be a risky business. When we look at other woodland areas we will be able to get a clearer idea of the economies of the small 'woodland' farm before the Conquest and to see how large and small enterprises related to each other in such a landscape.

THE WARWICKSHIRE ARDEN

Arden—the same name as Ardennes in France—and Feldon are the time-honoured names, respectively, for the 'woodland' part of northern Warwickshire and the southern part, which became an area of villages and fields. The change from *wudu* to *feld*, open land, is recorded on the signposts, and visible in the landscape seen while driving from the Feldon of Warwickshire to the Arden. The Feldon today is an area of valleys of the major rivers Avon and Stour, of large villages with church and manor house and extensive arable lands. There are still woods there, but broadly speaking woodland has been driven back to the margins of the parishes. By contrast, in the Forest of Arden, much of which is now covered by the outer suburbs of Birmingham, you can still see its sturdy oaks holding their own in pavements and on roundabouts, and feel the forest's presence in *lēah* place-names such as *scilf-lēah*, '*lēah* on a ridge', which with the addition of 'oak' gives the modern Selly Oak.[36] In the Feldon the main centre of habitation often has a name ending in -ton, while Arden abounds in place names ending -ley, -ly, or -leigh. We still do not have an adequate translation for this important term *lēah*, and it may well be that there is no one interpretation that will accurately represent the kind of place it would

[35] Faith, *English Peasantry*, 70–5. Harvey, 'Domesday England', 60–4 emphasizes the connection of bordars with woodland.

[36] But for a critique of this view of Feldon and Arden, see Wager, *Woods, Wolds and Groves*, 10–23, 166.

have conjured up for people in pre-Conquest England. *Lēah* has long been interpreted, following Margaret Gelling, as meaning 'wood' or 'clearing' and as having later shifted its meaning to 'pasture, meadow'. It continued to be used in place-name formation after the Conquest. Della Hooke has suggested a new interpretation: that *lēah* indicated grazing land of a particular type, 'stands of woodland interspersed with open glades and pastures set with scattered trees'—in short, wood-pasture, *wudu-læse* in Old English.[37] Unlike the element -*tūn*, which seems to have meant to contemporaries a specific man-made place and had to do with its habitation and particular function, -*lēah* was more general. Although many villages today derive the last element in their name from *lēah*, it originally signified an area, not a specific place in the way that the *tūn* did.[38] *Lēah's* continuing use to make names after the Conquest has meant that in accordance with Gelling's interpretation these later formations have been taken as indicators of post-Conquest assarting, the clearing of woodland in order to extend the area under cultivation.[39] This was clearly how some originated, but while post-Conquest assarting was undoubtedly very important, it cannot explain the *lēahs* with Old English personal names as their prefix, nor the many places in -*lēah* that are found in Domesday Book. These reveal something much older. Many *lēah* names are settlement names: they head a charter or are recorded, often for the first time in Domesday Book, to denote a place where people lived, not simply to describe a kind of landscape. Among these place-names, personal names of individuals form the largest category of prefix: an 'enormous category' of places had names which meant 'so-and-so's *lēah*'.[40] Their populations were enumerated in Domesday Book so evidently a *lēah* once associated with an individual, possibly thought to be owned by him and his family, was by then considered to be an area where a good many people lived, although not necessarily in close proximity, perhaps something more like a township.[41]

---

[37] Hooke, 'Early medieval woodland and the place-name *leāh*'; Kemble, *Codex*, vi, 214.22. Johanson, *Old English Place-Names* is a useful collection. The author assumes extensive woodland cover for early Anglo-Saxon England.

[38] Faith, '*Tūn* and *lēah*'. However, recent research by this author is beginning to suggest that some places with the element *lēah* in their names resembled the enclosed areas taken in from the woodland and surrounded by a boundary of some kind, further discussed in Chapter 12. The area enclosed was large enough eventually to include fully fledged common-field systems. They appear to be a larger entity than Gelling's enclosures but, like Hooke's, are a feature of wood-pasture landscapes.

[39] Gelling, 'Warwickshire place-names', 59–79; Gelling, *Landscape of Place-Names*, 237–42, 144–8. Gelling's interpretation is followed by the most widely read environmental historians, e.g. Rackham, *History of the Countryside*, 67; Rackham, *Ancient Woodland*, 127–30; Roberts and Wrathmell, *Region and Place*, 21.

[40] Hooke, *Anglo-Saxon Landscapes*, 156; for 'enormous category' see Gelling, Warwickshire place-names', 67.

[41] Gelling originally tentatively came to this conclusion, suggesting that in some of her Warwickshire examples '*lēah* was the equivalent of *tūn* and was used for a settlement which was the centre of a wood-land estate instead of one in open land'. She drew attention to the fact that many places called 'some-body's *lēah* had populations in 1086 which were enumerated for the Domesday survey': Gelling, 'Warwickshire place-names', 67.

In Arden good arable land is likely to have been not only in short supply, but in limited patches and hard to work. What was not clay was likely to be sandy heath. The Domesday clerks doggedly recorded that there was 'land for so many plough teams' at each place but the figures are strikingly low by comparison with the Feldon, so teams were thin on the ground. The rivers were small and the supply of meadow too was less than the topography would lead you to expect. People were thinly spread over a landscape which was still heavily wooded—every Domesday entry in Warwickshire records woodland measured in square leagues. Even this is considered to be an underestimate as the clerks perhaps recorded only woodland that would bring in revenue or was considered to be a manorial asset. Although most places had increased in value since the Conquest, nowhere round here was considered to be worth much in 1086.[42]

However, while the Arden woodland imposed limitations on some, it offered opportunities for others. Major landlords who had arable resources and head-quarters elsewhere valued its easily exploitable natural resources, not its very limited capacity to produce hard-won cereals. The normal aristocratic view of woodland was certainly as hunting ground, but also as a source of raw materials, particularly timber. Kemble drew attention to this in the mid-nineteenth century (although he thought that kings were 'inheritors of the heathen priest-hood in their power over the sacred woods and streams.'[43]) A royal or aristocratic manor with a highly capitalized centre could afford to use its woodland for specialized use such as hunting or fattening pigs on a large scale. Vagn, an important Scandinavian landowner on the eve of the Conquest, had a large demesne on the Alne at Wootton Wawen, where he built his church, parts of which are still there, and had his mills and slave teams.[44] This is where his major capital investment lay. Vagn's estate was created from what had once been a small territory known as 'the *regio*, the region, of the Stoppingas'. It comprised a stretch of the river Alne and its surrounding woodland. It was embedded among properties of a very different kind. On the edge of this little territory was 'Teodece's *lēah*', which covered a considerable area near Henley-in-Arden and whose bounds were recorded when the bishop of Worcester leased it out in the tenth century.[45] This *lēah* was an area of open woodland and the landmarks on its boundary were typical of the region: brooks and ponds and the 'eaves' of woods—this seems to have meant the edges of woods where the low branches attract browsing cattle—and there was a 'smooth meadow'.

[42] Darby and Territt, *Domesday Geography of Midland England*, 280–3, 290, 296; Wager, *Woods, Wolds and Groves*, 10–11.

[43] Kemble, *Codex*, i, pp. xl–xliii.

[44] *Domesday Book: Warwickshire*, 22.0.

[45] Bassett, 'In search of the origins', 18–19. It appears in Domesday Book as Ullenhall (the name of the modern parish): 'Ul(l)a's *halh*', his 'nook' or sheltered place, and his barrow at Oldberry was one of the landmarks about a mile away: S 1307; Hooke, *Warwickshire Anglo-Saxon Charter Bounds*, 78–83, with a map at p. 79. *Pace* Hooke, the 'shire way' and 'shire wood' on the Ullenhall boundary may refer to a small *scir* such as the Stoppingas' territory, rather than to the county.

Much but not all of its soils were heavy clay but in the same lease was lighter heathy land at the 'aspen *lēah*', now Apsley Heath. This is the same kind of resource territory as the Rodings in Essex, and on about the same scale. Domesday records land there for fifteen plough-teams but only six were at work for the twenty-three families.[46] While for these families the area had to provide them with a living, in Vagn's eyes Teodece's *lēah* was probably more use as hunting or timber land. Or perhaps swine-pasture, for some of the important estate centres, such as Stoneleigh, a vast estate which included a large arable demesne at Stoneleigh itself, the most profitable use of the woods was as pig-pasture for two thousand pigs.[47]

In this lightly-settled landscape there was room for expansion and by 1086 some *lēahs* were supporting up to fourteen families. A group in Warwickshire that appear in Domesday Book give us an insight into what their economy had become by the eleventh century and a few of their names, 'eagles' *lēah*', 'cranes' *lēah*', 'bent-grass *lēah*' (Arley, Ansley, Corley, and Bentley), give something of the flavour of the area. They lie along the Thame and Blyth rivers and their tiny tributaries work their way through Keuper Marl clay overlain by soils which could vary greatly in quality. This was an area of general poverty and lack of development which did not have sufficient decent arable to support demesne farms (perhaps also because it was poorly provided with the meadow for their teams) or much peasant ploughland. Yet people hung on in these woodlands. Gelling has suggested that some Arden farms may have been Romano-British in origin and only acquired their Old English names when that had become the predominant language. Without the archaeological evidence, hard to find in woodland, it could be argued that the individuals who put their names on this land, people like Teodece, Ul(l)a, Ælle, Cenhere, Bæddi, Fygela, Hucca could have been private appropriators of relatively uncontested land in any period after Old English had become common speech in the area. Some may have started as appropriations of considerable areas: Fillongley has the kind of name which had originally referred to a group and was large enough to have been split by 1086 between three different holdings.[48]

THE YEOMAN FARM

Among the people who made their living there, whether in Essex, the Chilterns, or Arden, two distinct groups with distinct ways of life seem to be especially

[46] *Domesday Book: Warwickshire*, 22.6.

[47] *Domesday Book: Warwickshire*, 1.4. Woodland was especially valuable 'when stocked', that is to say, when there was a good mast or acorn crop: Darby, *Domesday England*, 184. Wager interprets this differently, as 'when stocked with livestock' (and rented out): Wager, *Woods, Wolds and Groves*, 37–8.

[48] Gelling, 'Warwickshire place-names'; Darby and Territt, *Domesday Geography of Midland England*, Figs 105 and 307.

characteristic of woodland: yeoman farmers and cottagers. Neither of these groups was much involved in the economy of manorial lords, still less were they under manorial control. To start with the yeomen. Two descriptions of woodland peasants stress their comparative freedom and independence. For the fourteenth and fifteenth centuries R. H. Hilton contrasted the heavy labour rent demanded from tenants in the southern part of Warwickshire (which he believed to have been the earliest settled) with the freer conditions in the north. Alan Everitt speaks of the Midland forests in the early modern period as places where 'the instincts of the poor were anything but law-abiding and the authority of church and manor-house seemed remote.'[49] This was nothing new: many of the last generation of Old English landholders in Arden, just as in north-west Essex, had been 'free men'. There was something in the woodland which seems to have offered the possibility of thriving. Woodland districts could support substantial holdings which are not man-orial centres. Some of the *lēahs* in the Warwickshire section of Domesday Book give the impression of larger scale enterprises: demesne farms with enough arable for one or two teams managed by a slave or two set amid stretches of lightly settled land. Grim, farming at Lashley in Essex surrounded by his own privately owned woodland, and the owners of the eponymous Arden *lēahs* are the kind of people we would describe as yeoman farmers. Everitt described their early modern counterparts, who had sizeable holdings and common rights as 'surprisingly well-to-do'.[50] Because it was less manori-alized, much woodland countryside before the Conquest may already have had the comparatively undifferentiated social structure which Everitt sensed for a much later period. There are some practical reasons for this. Yeoman farms did not have the same need for a body of systematically exploited peasant labour, people who could be called out to work on the demesne, as happened on the big arable demesnes.[51] They may have been in much the same situation as the Hammonds describe in the period of enclosures, when 'It had been to the interests of the small farmer to have a number of *semi-labourers, semi-owners* [my italics] who could help at the harvest...'. Perhaps the woodland bordars, so plentiful in north-west Essex and accounting for a quarter of the rural population in rural Warwickshire, were their pre-Conquest equivalent.[52] Sally Harvey has drawn attention to the association between woodland in Domesday Book and people the clerks described as *bordarii*. Their numbers were highest in three of the forest and pasture counties: Hampshire, Worcestershire, and Cornwall.[53]

---

[49] Hilton, 'Social structure of rural Warwickshire'; Everitt, 'Farm labourers'.
[50] Everitt, 'Farm labourers', 423.
[51] Everitt, 'Farm labourers', 418; Hilton, 'Social structure' 134–8.
[52] J. L. and B. Hammond *The Village Labourer*, quoted in Crouch and Ward, *The Allotment*, 50. Warwickshire bordars: Darby and Territt, *Domesday Geography of Midland England*, 286–7.
[53] Harvey, 'Domesday England', 60–4.

COTTAGE ECONOMY

We have a rich literature from much later periods than that considered in this book about the lives of poor people in woodland areas. Although those with very small amounts of land appear in Domesday Book as 'bordars', 'cottagers' or 'men in the wood', or are entered as *villani* with very restricted resources, from earlier in our own period we have very little information to work with. These are the kind of people likely to have made the lightest impression on the archaeological record. But it is not too fanciful to draw parallels between how people may have managed a similar environment in similar ways over time. The growing literature on allotment-holders and smallholders is a promising new development.[54] The pioneer of such studies, George Sturt, thought that the Surrey cottagers he knew were the last survivors of England's peasantry into the early years of the twentieth century. All descriptions of cottage life stress its self-sufficiency and the ability of cottage people to turn their hand to any kind of craft. This is the economy of 'a bit of this and a bit of that' of which we see traces today in the small-scale enterprises that are set up in woodland areas, some to flourish, some to fail. In our period through to the nineteenth century a vital element in the 'cottage economy' was free access to common resources, and forest has been described as common land par excellence. We do not know much about the lives and economy of these very small farmers, but George Sturt and Flora Thompson both describe a way of life at the turn of the twentieth century which was able to survive as long as the commons remained.[55] Woodland's opportunities for off-farm occupations—the pottery, iron-working, and extractive industries that are not dealt with in this book—its open grazing and fodder resources, could support a virtually self-sufficient cottage economy based on a couple of cows, even a single cow or a few sheep for dairy products and a few chickens.[56] And, most probably, a pig. Then, as later, the pig was 'the cottage animal *par excellence*', kept in a sty and fed on what were effectively free household scraps. Woodland provided extra food from wild and hedgerow fruit and nuts and from wildfowl of all kinds: small birds were still part of the cottagers' diet into the early twentieth century.[57] Woodland provided fuel, building materials, the raw material for a wide range of essential crafts such as tool-making. It was because of this diversity that Thomas Tusser, who preferred 'enclosed land' to common fields, thought that

[54] Everitt 'Common land'; Cobbett, *Cottage Economy*; Thompson, 'Custom, law and common right'; Crouch and Ward, *The Allotment*; Ward, *Cotters and Squatters*.

[55] Sturt, *Change in the Village*; Thompson, *Lark Rise to Candleford*.

[56] Dyer shows the small median numbers of animals kept by the peasants in Feckenham Forest in Worcestershire in the thirteenth century: under ten sheep, three draught animals, five goats, and three pigs: Dyer 'Farming practice and techniques', 377. For later medieval woodland craftsmen see Birrell, 'Peasant craftsmen'.

[57] Samuel, '"Quarry roughs"', 207–8; Thompson, *Lark Rise to Candleford*; Astill and Grant, *Countryside of Medieval England*, 167–70.

'In woodland the poor man that have
scarse fully two akers of land
More merily live and do save
than t'other with twenty in hand.'

But that was because 'enclosed land' had

'mast, covert, close pasture and wood
And other things needful and good.'[58]

WOODLAND AGRICULTURE

It would be wrong to idealize the life of the woodlanders. Tusser may have been right to praise their self-sufficiency but such people were desperately poor. Everyone needed carbohydrate in some form and forest smallholdings were likely to have been short of vital cereals. The basic diet which supported most Anglo-Saxon people was heavily cereal-based, whether or not that cereal was brewed as beer, baked into bread, or stewed up as pottage.[59] C. C. Dyer has reconstructed the economy of a smallholder at Bishops Cleeve in Gloucestershire in the thirteenth century. He had three acres and a cow, and on that he could only provide for part of his family's mainly cereal diet. Dyer has also estimated that the 9000 calories needed daily for a couple and three children could be provided from land which produced six quarters and five bushels of grain (of which three quarters of barley would be brewed as ale), two flitches of bacon, milk and cheese from a cow, and garden produce.[60]

Much, perhaps nearly all, woodland contained patches, even large stretches, which could be used for arable and which nowadays may have developed into substantial fields. This, for instance, is the landscape of much of the modern Chilterns, where efficient farming has opened up very large areas for cultivation. But the arable of woodlanders is more likely to have been in small enclosures, like the six acres which occur on the Chieveley boundary discussed at the beginning of this chapter, or the early Anglo-Saxon farms of the Whittlewood claylands in Northamptonshire, which had about five acres of arable (2 ha) around the farmstead, intensively manured with household rubbish and the contents of latrines.[61] The woodland arable economy was thus likely to have been the home of the small-scale, low-technology agriculture which our studies describe and in particular of a range of low-technology solutions to creating a tilth—a cultivable soil. Small fields could be ploughed with less than a full team, dug over with a spade, or even ploughed by manpower alone. (Flora

[58] Tusser, *Five Hundred Points of Good Husbandry*, 135.
[59] Banham, *Food and Drink in Anglo-Saxon England*, 13–28.
[60] Dyer, *Standards of Living*, 117–18, 134–5.
[61] Jones and Page, *Medieval Villages*, 85–7.

Thompson remembered from her childhood in north Oxfordshire in the 1880s a man ploughing with a breast plough.)[62] Where the soil was not too heavy they are a likely case for ploughing with the ard or scratch plough. Small fields, often of awkward shapes, could be cultivated by the repeated passes in different directions that the ard needed to break up the land. Very probably, soil conditions and sheer conservatism could explain why many farmers may have continued with the ard. Lack of manpower could have been another important factor. People living in scattered woodland settlements would not have been able to bring together the resources in manpower and animals to put together large teams. Ample animal fuel, in the shape of hay-meadows, was likely to have been in short supply too, as Tom Williamson has emphasized.[63] When common-field systems did evolve in woodland, as in the Chilterns in the later Middle Ages, they typically involved a few neighbours, not an entire village.[64] In some woodland parts of England a single man ploughing with an ard could have remained a familiar sight for a long time. It was probably even harder work than the mouldboard plough, especially on heavy ground. This did not change: in one of the illustrations in a late Anglo-Saxon Psalter the ploughman has to sit on the plough-beam to keep the point in the ground. Eight centuries later in the woodlands sketched by Gainsborough, many of them in Kent where open-field farming made very little headway, a light plough is pulled by two horses but the ploughman is adding his own weight.

We are not yet sure of what exactly bordars were, but throughout England the people whom Domesday Book describes as bordars and cottagers, if they had arable at all, had very little, for when their plough-teams can be reliably counted they are miserably badly provided for, and the same is true for many of the people in woodland areas described as *villani*.[65] One contemporary description of the Domesday Survey contrasts 'those living in *tuguria* (shacks, cottages)' with 'those living in houses and owning fields', which suggests that cottagers were either landless or had small plots.[66] The Domesday plough-team figures from Arden quoted above show how deficient many of the woodland farmers there were in this respect. Alan Everitt's work on labourers in forest regions in the early modern period describes them as having only three acres or less, and this in an era of easily purchased flour.[67] If they had had enough land suitable for arable for a full team, their meagre provision of plough-teams shows cottagers and bordars could not spare animals to be used solely for traction. Moreover, the arable which could be carved out of woodland was often on

[62] Thompson, *Lark Rise to Candleford*.

[63] Williamson, *Shaping Medieval Landscapes*, 163–73.

[64] Roden, 'Field systems'.

[65] Lennard, 'The economic position of the bordars and cottars of Domesday Book'; Faith, *English Peasantry*, 70–5.

[66] Stevenson, 'A Contemporary Description of the Domesday Survey', 74; my translation.

[67] Harvey, 'Domesday England', 60–1; Everitt, 'Farm labourers', 418.

heavy land or in the case of heaths, acid soils. Later Arden field names were ruefully descriptive of its unrewarding soils, either sticky Keuper Marl or sandy heath: 'The Little Slangy Bit', 'Moss Field', 'Briery', 'Scrub', 'Benty Field'.[68]

If there was a big farm or manorial demesne nearby, forest smallholders might have been the kind of people who in very hard times would have traded poverty and independence for a meal in their bellies. The landlord 'outfitting' such a tenant in return for labour appears in Ine's law, in which a man who has accepted a smallholding from a landlord in return for rent and labour is free to give up his tenancy and leave, although he will forfeit the crops if he does. If he has been given a cottage as well, he is tied.[69] We seemed to see this kind of dependence at Thaxted in north-west Essex, where a labour-hungry demesne farm could benefit from the labour of the surrounding smallholders, people who lived by what Raphael Samuel has called 'proletarian landholding in the countryside' (see p. 212).[70] But Thaxted and other Essex centres like it were by 1086 islands of large fields and nucleated villages embedded in a predominantly woodland countryside of dispersed settlement. Most of the Chilterns and Arden were very different: both were large woodland districts quite distant from areas of fields and nucleation—the clay vales and the Feldon. This meant that they had few, if any, large demesne farms with high labour needs within daily reach.[71] As Margaret Gelling has conclusively shown, *tūn* and *lēah*, the terms with which this chapter began, are mutually exclusive.[72] Not simply differences in landscape and settlement, but in economy and social structure, or to put it in more human terms, way of life, divided the woodland from the world of arable farming.

[68] Gelling, *Place-Names of Warwickshire*, 339, 349, 851, 361. For the unsuitability of much of Midland England for large-scale arable farming see Williamson, *Shaping Medieval Landscapes*, 147.

[69] Charles-Edwards, 'The distinction between land and moveable wealth in Anglo-Saxon England'; Faith, *English Peasantry*, 76–80.

[70] Samuel, 'Quarry roughs'.

[71] Dyer, *Lords and Peasants*, 22–8.

[72] For a recent contribution to this subject see Faith, '*Tūn* and *lēah*'.

Fig. 9.1. Burderop Down, near Swindon, Wiltshire, where traces of field systems can be seen as low ridges.

(© Jane Peart, from a photograph © Brian Robert Marshall)

9

Chalk downland

The Berkshire, Hampshire, and Wiltshire Downs

The softly contoured chalk hills of Berkshire, Sussex, Hampshire, the Isle of Wight, Dorset, and Wiltshire have made a landscape on the grand scale, with open skies and distant views over miles of downland (Fig. 9.1). Kipling's phrase, 'the Naked Chalk', describes it well. The remote past is particularly visible here and this chapter takes the opportunity offered by an exceptionally wide-ranging body of archaeological work on Romano-British farming on the Hampshire and Wiltshire Downs to look at how, over a very long period of time, the Downland landscape demanded that farmers integrate livestock and arable husbandry in a particularly intensive way.

The chalk is new rock, a limestone composed of matter from the ocean floors. Some areas are capped with clay in which flints are imbedded; the latter can also be quarried from seams in the chalk itself. Flint, the prime material for tools for millennia, attracted concentrations of people in prehistory. Hillforts, barrows, beacons, and ridgeways, the work of early settlers and monument builders, are all visible to the traveller from miles away today and were part of the environment of people farming there in the Anglo-Saxon period, who reused some of these features as burial places and boundary markers. The chalklands are a landscape with such a strong character that we might well think they have always imposed a rather similar farming system on the people who lived there. For a great part of recent history they have been prime sheep country, and many of our best-known images of them are of an empty landscape, with just a shepherd and his hut as signs of human life. 'Chalk and Cheese' has become shorthand for the contrast between the distinctive settlement patterns and even divergent political cultures of the upland sheep walks and the heavy soils and lush grassland of the dairying vales. The author of the most extensive study of Downland archaeology sees this as essentially a 'grassland landscape' into which cereal cultivation has been forcibly intruded. 'Ultimately, widespread arable did not work....'[1] Yet with intensive inputs, it can be

---

[1] Fowler, *Landscape Plotted and Pieced*, 234.

made to work. The nineteenth-century writer Thomas Hughes fumed against the ploughing-up of his beloved Berkshire Downs in his time, and very large areas are cultivated today, significantly with large inputs of fertilizer. This is not just a modern phenomenon. The hillfort known as Uffington Castle on the Berkshire Downs is now surrounded by land under crop, but in the ninth century it was open grassland where the 'larks' barrow' was a landmark. Yet less than a mile away to the west, on just the same soil and elevation, large fields probably laid out by the late Anglo-Saxon period were still under the plough in the thirteenth century when arable was at a premium and land described as *super montem*, 'on the mountain', was cultivated on the steepest slopes of the scarp.[2] So when we come across signs that people were growing crops on the downs, we need to interpret this as the product of particular circumstances, and have an eye out for what might be have caused them to work seemingly against the grain of the landscape—and for how they were keeping the land in good heart.

The further our understanding of the archaeology of the chalklands advances, the busier they appear to have been throughout long stretches of their history (Fig. 9.2). Anglo-Saxon farmers here occupied a landscape which was already deeply incised with the traces of the ways their predecessors had managed the environment. These traces, mostly now appearing as low banks and shallow ditches often only visible from the air, reflect a farming strategy which had evidently proved successful enough to have continued from at least as far back as the Late Iron Age and into the Roman period. The largest survey so far of early chalkland farming was carried out by Peter Fowler and his team at Overton Down, Wiltshire.[3] Air photography reveals dense networks of fields covering large areas. Most of these fields are small—some but a single acre in extent— and they are regular, assembled in 'blocks' and with a common orientation, as if they had been deliberately laid out rather than simply accumulated. In size and shape they are more suited to cultivation by ard, even spade, rather than by mouldboard plough, and the faint traces of marks made by ards bear this out. They are often associated with longer linear features, some of which may be the tracks made by stock threading their way through cultivated fields on their way to grazing lands. The small paddocks close to the farmstead must always have been supplemented by areas of common grazing. Fowler sees traces of large-scale stock management at Overton Down in what he perceives as 'basically a British landscape'. The droveways he has revealed were for moving stock through cultivated fields to open pasture elsewhere. First and foremost there is the ridgeway itself, not then, perhaps never, a single track but a bundle of former track lines, a 'zone of movement' over long distances, perhaps

---

[2] Hooke, 'Anglo-Saxon estates'; Dean and Chapter of Winchester, Muniments, Custumal of the Church of Winchester, fo. 179.

[3] Fowler, *Landscape Plotted and Pieced*.

Fig. 9.2. Marlborough Downs showing archaeological features.

(© RCHM/English Heritage)

to stock markets as well as to the transhumant grazing he suggests. Such routes were ancient and remained respected, forming the basis of boundaries, and this suggests that the pastures to which they led were some kind of common resource.[4]

One possibility is that the fields themselves, although they were essentially used as arable as Fowler interprets them, may also have served periodically as stock enclosures, where sheep were folded at night to improve the soil.[5] In the absence of archaeological evidence either for or against this suggestion we can

[4] Fowler, *Landscape Plotted and Pieced*, 256–8.
[5] Lock, Gosden, and Daly, *Segsbury Camp*, Fig. 4.1 shows a very similar landscape south of Segsbury Camp on the Lambourn Downs. However, the authors incline to the view that sheep farming declined after the Late Iron Age in favour of cattle and arable (Gary Lock, pers. comm.).

only draw on practice from much later periods and bear in mind the constraints imposed by the environment itself. The chalkland topsoils are thin and once their turf was removed by ploughing erosion was a constant danger.[6] But these thin soils could grow barley and oats as well as grass if their fertility, now ensured by chemical inputs or huge amounts of treated sewage, was kept up. This demanded the concentrated application of fertilizer and the most obvious source of this was manure. Only sheep could do the job. Their manure was compactly packaged and dry, so it did not sicken the grass as cowpats did, and their sharp hooves—'little golden hooves' as they were known in the later Middle Ages—drove it into the soil. Moreover, as it is extremely difficult to eliminate weed and grass roots from plough soil even with modern equipment, the sheep played an essential role in nibbling the close turf down to a minimum so that weeds and longer grasses did not get a hold. On the wide expanse of the downs both these objectives could only achieved by careful stock management. One method was by confining the sheep to a small area until it was cropped virtually bare and their droppings were trodden in, then moving them on.[7] Another was close-folding in moveable enclosures, in all probability made of hurdles. This was widely practised on the Berkshire and Hampshire Downs into the twentieth century, when it was principally aimed at improving the grass. The suggestion made here is that the small cellular fields were themselves periodically used as enclosures to keep the arable land in heart by concentrated manuring. There are several ways in which this could have been done. One was to move the sheep from field to field and to plough up, on some kind of rotation, the field in which they had been confined. The other was to use one of the small fields permanently as what was known in Scotland as a 'tathing fold': a night enclosure in which the 'tathe', the sheep's dung and urine, was concentrated and from where it could be spread on neighbouring fields.[8] With either practice, this close integration of crops and animals would have needed careful management: driving animals past the fields to paddocks and more remote grazing to prevent them from straying onto crops. This meant carefully keeping up the walls or hedge banks and gave rise to the short lengths of droveway which thread between the fields. Feeding the livestock on the 'fog', the long grass growing on the abundant land outside the field systems, if left uncut into the early winter when it received a useful nitrogen boost, could have gone some way to cover winter fodder needs, as is the practice on some farms today.

The downs are an area where it is possible to get a glimpse of how the end of the Romanized economy might have played out in the countryside. While

---

[6] I am grateful to Dr Gill Swanton of North Farm, West Overton, in the heart of the Overton Down project area, for information about local conditions.

[7] Applebaum, 'Roman Britain', 19–55; Eagles, 'The archaeological evidence for settlement', 22; Welch, 'Rural settlement patterns', 14–25, on decline in fertility.

[8] Bil, *The Sheiling*, 122–3, demonstrates the importance of this 'tathing' to keeping marginal land in good heart.

that economy was still in full swing, proximity to a market of a day's journey there and back has been shown to be a crucial factor in whether a villa, in the sense of a fully Romanized building and by implication its land, was to develop. In northern Hampshire the downland had acted as an economic hinterland to Silchester, a town set in an area of poor sandy soils and woodland, unsuitable for cereal production on any scale. Probably the abandonment of such major towns removed a vital market which had made more commercialized arable farms based on villas viable. It may have had a more muted impact on small farmers outside the orbit of these towns, less stimulated by their economy, yet more able to weather their decline.[9] In a dry valley above Lambourn in the Berkshire Downs a farmhouse of the third and fourth centuries had a tessellated floor, mill, and corn-dryer, with associated farm buildings at some distance, perhaps in itself a mark of gentrification, and with fields on the adjoining valley sides. It presumably employed slaves. What there does not seem to have been in the area was a prestigious villa. Maddle Farm may have been just one of a string of similar farms along the Lambourn valley, where there is a scatter of Roman material.[10] Overton does not have a comparable villa site, but Fowler notes that the fourth-century intensive arable cultivation there was giving way to 'sensible farming', mainly shepherding in response to the demand for wool combined with 'intensive cultivation of the valley sides.'[11]

The combination of intensively manured fields and large expanses of grassland was probably what sustained a scatter of farms on the dip slope of the Hampshire Downs at Chalton, Hampshire, analysed by Barry Cunliffe. The farmers here were outside the range of influence of a major villa but nevertheless from the third and fourth centuries there are signs of indigenous growth: a larger area was brought under the plough and Cunliffe conjectures that as the arable was then comparable to, if not greater than, its seventeenth-century extent, the population may have been comparable too.[12]

Many Romano-British farms seem to have been discrete complexes centred on a single farmstead surrounded by its own fields and paddocks, and very probably with its own water source: a pattern very familiar to us today in Lowland England. Others centred on a group of dwellings, sometimes with some kind of perimeter boundary. One possibility is that the latter type of farm may have been home to a group (of kin?) practising some form of infield–outfield husbandry, in which the area close to home was permanently cultivated and manured and the outer area cultivated periodically and left as grazed fallow to recover its fertility. In either case, the group of people who could claim ownership or rights over the land would have been a very small one. If they related themselves to a territory which was larger than the farmhouse and its land, it

---

[9] Cunliffe, *Wessex to A.D. 1000*, 253–4.
[10] Fowler, *Landscape Plotted and Pieced*, 54–5; Gaffney and Tingle, *Maddle Farm*.
[11] Fowler, *Landscape Plotted and Pieced*, 229.
[12] Cunliffe, 'Saxon and medieval settlement pattern', 1–12; Cunliffe, 'Chalton, Hants', 173–90.

may have been an area marked out by the monuments of earlier generations. Fowler finds the long barrows of East and West Kennet, Lockeridge, and others above the Kennet Valley lay on boundaries between territories 'at the family group level.'[13] Life on these upland farms must surely have its own distinct character. They were mostly far from major Roman roads, and while some were within reach of important long-distance routes, many are more likely to have been linked by much the same network of informal upland tracks as their Iron Age predecessors. These continued to appear as ridgeways and other 'ways' in the boundary clauses of late Anglo-Saxon charters and some of them we still use today.[14]. They were part of a well-peopled landscape. Fowler judges that at Overton Down, Wiltshire, 'settlements may have occurred as frequently as every 400–800 m, set along droveways or tracks between the fields'. Nevertheless, they remained small and scattered enough to have left extensive areas of open downland. Like many early farms they seem to have been individualistic exercises which were nevertheless part of a rural economy that required some cooperation between communities in managing land and livestock.

While there is thus plentiful archaeological evidence for the downland being cultivated and settled in the Roman period, investigating whether, and where, this continued is an altogether more difficult matter. There were ample reasons why there might have been a retreat from the uplands. Although there were still considerable forests in the valleys—Melchet, Savernake, Selwood, Chute— which were important enough elements in the landscape to have kept their British names, the uplands were much more open, and finding enough winter fodder could have been a problem. There are other constraints on farming on the chalk. One is the water supply. While, as mentioned in the previous chapter, sheep can survive virtually without water except when lactating, cattle need ample supplies: this basic fact must have made a large impact on farming on the chalk. In the modern period when the water table has dropped due to extraction, there are many dry valleys, and some which produce streams only in winter. However, in the Anglo-Saxon period a higher spring line may have made settlement possible on many areas of the High Chalk which are now devoid of watercourses. The 'White Flood' which appears in a Hampshire charter was produced by a spring gushing down a chalky hillside which is now dry, as is the site of nearby White Flood Farm. Nevertheless drinking water for people and animals on the uplands was more often from the 'meres' or ponds rather than streams and so were important landmarks.[15]

The Anglo-Saxon settlers who from the later fifth century were moving south from the Thames Valley thus entered a landscape which had long been, in the phrase Fowler has borrowed from Gerard Manley Hopkins, 'plotted and

---

[13] Fowler, *Landscape Plotted and Pieced*, 221.
[14] Taylor, *Roads and Tracks of Britain*, 80–3, 88–90.
[15] S 693; Crawford, *Andover District*; Cole, 'Distribution and use of *mere*'.

pieced' and intensively worked. As we will see, the incomers picked up much of the specialist knowledge necessary to maintain the high standard of sheep-breeding that the Romans had introduced. This suggests that at the level of ordinary farmers there was a fair amount of peaceful contact and continuity, as well as the bloody conflicts that we know took place as the immigrant leaders gained political dominance and territories were carved up.[16] What the demographic balance was between Anglo-Saxon and Romano-British is much harder to determine. The transition to a Germanic material culture is traceable in the goods in burials but the ethnicity of their owners is impossible to ascertain and moreover the burial goods mostly come from cemeteries in river valleys, not on the downs.

Much the same kind of farming as had gone on before, but on a reduced scale, could have supported the inhabitants of a group of houses built in, or perhaps shortly before, the seventh century near Chalton, Hampshire (Fig. 9.3). These continued the Iron Age pattern of scattered farmsteads and small irregular fields, threaded through by trackways, like the ones investigated by Fowler at Overton. By the end of the seventh century there was a large nucleated settlement with substantial timber buildings on top of Church Down at Chalton. This may have been the *tūn* which gave Chalton, 'chalk *tūn*', its name. Similar High Chalk 'villages' had emerged at nearby Up Marden, Sussex, and Catherington, Hampshire. People at Chalton were buried with Germanic goods: either new settlers were now farming alongside the Romano-British population, or the local indigenous Britons were doing well, increasing in number, and adopting the new styles. Cunliffe sees the background to this as a 'gradual coalescence of the more dispersed population, or the imposition of a central authority over them, at one location from which all the traditionally farmed lands could be reached easily.'[17]

Just as large areas of woodland or marshland were once looked upon as common to the people of a particular area, so was open grassland in chalk country. Here too parish topography is revealing. Cunliffe suggested that the pattern of parishes which evolved along the edge of the Hampshire Downs reflected early notions of the spread of resources from lowland clays to upland chalk that belonged in some way to each community. Probably long before it was a 'shire' in the modern sense, a county, Hampshire had its own 'small shires', resource regions like 'the Cleres' and 'the Andovers', possibly also 'the land of the Basingas'. We can see them in the charters of the tenth century being broken up into what would become the parishes we know today, but before that they were much larger areas which contained river meadows, hill-side arable, and open downland. References to landmarks in charter bounds

---

[16] Yorke, *Wessex*, 43–51; Eagles, 'The Archaeological evidence for settlement'.

[17] Cunliffe, 'Chalton, Hants', 184; Cunliffe, 'Saxon and medieval settlement patterns', 1–12; Addyman, Leigh, and Hughes, 'Anglo-Saxon houses at Chalton, Hampshire'.

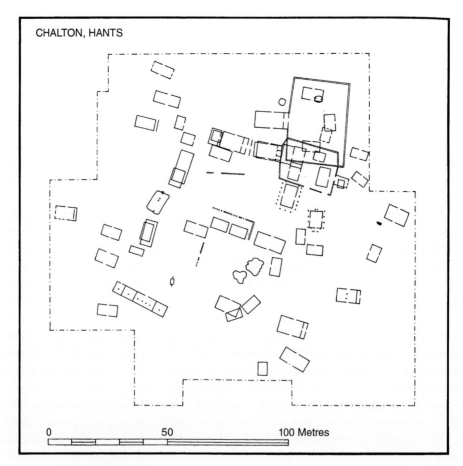

CHALTON, HANTS

0   50   100 Metres

Fig. 9.3. Chalton, Hampshire.

(From Cunliffe, *Wessex before AD* 1000)

necessarily come from a later date, most often the tenth century, but when they refer to common grazing it is probably to commons established well before the divisions into estates that the charters record.[18] Above Ecchinswell, a village that grew up on a little greensand island at the foot of the north Hampshire downs, there was a *gemaene hyll*, a 'common hill', shared with the neighbouring Sydmonton before the area was divided.[19] Such careful demarcation and division suggests that these precious resources were coming under pressure by the ninth century. On the downs through which the Itchen valley runs the bishop, the ealdorman, and the people of Worthy, of Crawley, and of Headbourn all had boundaries in place by the tenth century demarcating their grazing rights.[20]

[18] Costen, 'Settlement in Wessex', 102–3. Cleres, Basingas, and Andovers: Eagles, 'Small shires'.
[19] S 412; Crawford, *Andover District*. For these terms see S 1515.
[20] Roberts, 'Tichborne, Cheriton and Beaworth'; Roberts, 'Saxon Bounds of *Ticceburn*', 29–33.

This may be connected with the fact that from the ninth century or there-abouts there was a gradual shift away from upland farms of the Chalton type. Principally this was in favour of valley settlements which expanded and became increasingly nucleated. Some have been interpreted as the result of an orchestrated shift from the uplands in favour of the lowlands. At Overton villages developed between the foot of the downs and the riverlands and by the tenth century open fields were laid out on the valley sides, where sheep–corn husbandry could well have continued, but less intensively, by pasturing the sheep on the fallows.[21] The nucleated settlement described by Cunliffe at Church Down, Chalton, became deserted in the eighth to ninth century and new settlements were established on a lower contour, interpreted as 'a deliberate act of resettlement'. In the case of the village of Bishopstone, East Sussex, excavated by Gabor Thomas, a nucleated settlement near the church appears to have largely replaced the farms on the high downs.[22] The bishop of Chichester, whose land this was, must have been an important influence in this particular case but leaving on one side the question of agency there are several possible functional explanations for a general move off the chalk. Although the reasons must have been many and complex the most important may have been the simplest: the thin soils of the chalk, only kept fertile by dint of much labour and stock-intensive manuring, and where erosion was a constant problem, had simply given up the ghost and were no longer fertile enough to feed their inhabitants.

Another explanation may have been technological. The important innovation represented by the introduction of a mouldboard plough that could cope with heavier and more fertile soils, has been seen as crucial in the shift of cultivation onto the heavier soils found in many parts of England. While deep ploughing would have been of no benefit on the tops of the Downs as it only brought to the surface the chalk which was inches below the thin topsoils (as happens today), it could well have been one of the benefits of moving cultivation to the lower slopes and riversides, as is the case of the Overton area.[23] In contrast to the ard, which needed only a pair of oxen, even just a man or woman, to pull it, the heavier plough needed the traction power which a team of oxen provided. Land in the valleys was more suitable for cattle, with longer grass in meadows and the meadows themselves a source of winter fodder. The High Chalk, which had been intensively farmed, was now beginning to be used more as purely sheep pasture.

---

[21] Fowler, *Landscape Plotted and Pieced*, 234–6. With the 'Improved Husbandry' of the early modern period the Wiltshire Horn were bred expressly for the quantity of manure they produced and their ability to retain it until they returned to the fallows at night! I am grateful to Dr Virginia Bainbridge for information about them.

[22] Thomas, *Later Anglo-Saxon Settlement*.

[23] This shift is described in Chapter 12.

But not all the farmers left the downs. Large areas of chalkland on the Berkshire Downs were divided up in the ninth and tenth centuries to provide estates for the kings' associates. Hooke's analysis of the boundaries of these charters shows that even on the steep scarp slopes where still today the plough does not go there are 'furlongs' and 'furrows' as landmarks and in some places the arable continued right up past the ridgeway.[24] Some downland farms seem in fact seem to have been thriving in the ninth century and, while they must have had arable and a water supply of their own, one of their principal resources may well have been that they had control over considerable amounts of private grazing. Pressure on grazing may explain one of the rather surprising features of the late Anglo-Saxon downland: much of it appears to be 'privatized' and belonged not to communities but to individual farms. It seems odd today, when we expect much downland to be open country, to see that Anglo-Saxon charter bounds frequently record marker posts (*stapul*), gates and stiles, turnstiles and 'swing-gates', and thus by implication fences or enclosures of some kind. These have variously been interpreted as defences to keep livestock off ploughland and, more convincingly, as signs of enclosed common grazing land. Walking the downland section of the boundary of a large territory east of Alresford, Hampshire, in the tenth century for instance, you would have needed to look out for a stile, a gate, another stile, then four gates in succession, and then another stile, all used as landmarks.[25] In short this was not open downland in the sense of being entirely unenclosed, but pasture to which individual rights of access were carefully delineated. 'Ranscombe gate', for instance, was probably at the head of the Ranscombe valley, and may have been the farm 'gate' or access to the down for a farm in the valley, perhaps the forerunner of the modern Ranscombe Farm.

By the tenth century there were some sizeable dispersed farms on the downs: they appear in the charters of that period and may well be considerably earlier. While *tūn* and *ham* are by far the most common elements in Hampshire settlement names, there are also several places on the downs with the element *worðig* (pronounced 'worthy') in their names, some of the most easterly examples of place-names much commoner in the West Country. Although *worðig* could mean many kinds of enclosed space, often a very prestigious one, in this context it seems to have meant originally a single enclosed farm with a single owner. As well as leaving their mark on the place-names, these large farms can occasionally still be glimpsed in the landscape. The nucleated settlement of Cheriton, Hampshire, on the upper Itchen east of Winchester lies in a bowl of riverside land surrounded on all sides by downs rising at their highest to the

---

[24] Hooke, 'Regional variation', 127–36.
[25] S 242; Grundy, 'Saxon charters…Hampshire', 69–77, at 73 n. 3; Currie, 'Saxon charters', 115–17.

hill fort of Milbarrow Down, a focal point for the whole area. While the downs had large stretches of open grassland, which the charters record as *dun*, as at Gander Down, there were also extensive ranges of wood-pasture, marked by the *-lēahs* of Wheely (*weoleage*), Clinkley (*clincla leaga*), and so on, as well as a considerable tract of unbroken woodland at Hormer's Wood and smaller shaws and groves. There were in the Cheriton area outlying farms which the charter bounds of the tenth and eleventh centuries note as landmarks. 'Wulfred's *worðig*', was one, on the boundary between 'Cynehelm's *tun*' (Kilmeston) and the modern parish of Bramdean. The 'bee-*worðig*', now Beauworth, may have been another. It is likely that the landmarks in question were the worthys' boundaries.

About one farm we can say a little more. We can even hazard a guess at the name of one of its owners, though we cannot give him a date (Fig. 9.4). Two miles east of the village the boundary of Cheriton estate, now the parish boundary, makes an angular detour in order to take in the 'east combe' as far as the 'common *lēah*'. It does this quite specifically, running *thanon on oster-cumbe norðweardne*, 'northward up east combe to the common *lēah*' (*mænan leage*), *thanon on ostercumbe sutheweardne*, 'thence to east combe southward'. The boundary then returns to its normally smooth course, running 'along the way to Wine's headland', a point also marked in an adjacent charter. *Winnley*, a now lost name, may once have been 'Wine's *lēah*' in wood-pasture half a mile from the east combe.[26] This would be very fragile evidence for the existence of an Anglo-Saxon farm were it not for the fact that the area headed by east combe was later known as 'Hollow (or Holly) Hide', and this may well be 'the land which is called the Hyde', rented at seven shillings, which appears in the bishopric of Winchester accounts in 1301–2.[27] 'Hide farms' are common in many of the areas studied in this book, particularly at the edge of parishes and in areas of plentiful wood-pasture. They appear to have started life as substantial, independent family farms.[28] If Wine's farm had comprised a small valley, with a stream at its foot, its own woodland and arable, the whole reckoned at a hide, this would rank it among the large, self-sufficient holdings with immediate access to open pasture which will become increasingly familiar.

Dispersed farms like these, some large enough to comprise an entire little valley, and still known by the names of former owners, with their own ploughland and access to plentiful grazing, were a fixed enough part of the landscape to have made their mark on the charter boundaries of the ninth century. There is no credible way of linking them directly to production for the market. But it is interesting that prosperity was coming into Cheriton in the eighth and ninth

[26] Roberts, 'Tichborne, Cheriton and Beaworth'; Roberts, 'Saxon bounds'. I am grateful to Edward and Vandra Roberts for exploring this boundary with me.
[27] Page, *Pipe Rolls*, 311.
[28] Faith, 'Hides and Hyde Farms'.

Fig. 9.4. Wine's farm near Cheriton, Hampshire.

centuries. Someone there in the ninth century could afford a fancy strap end for a belt or possibly part of a horse's harness. If it was part of a horse's 'tack', this need not imply an aristocratic owner: David Hinton writes of a 'wider group of horse-owners' than the military aristocracy.[29] There is no possible way that we can link these chance finds to their erstwhile owners, but they are an indication that some people in this small place were in touch with the market. If wool production was profitable, Wine's worthy was just the kind of farm which could best have profited from it. Some of the coins found in Cheriton came from Southampton, the most thoroughly excavated market of the Anglo-Saxon period in southern England.

PEASANT PRODUCTION AND THE MARKET AT HAMWIC

On the west bank of the river Itchen where it joins Southampton Water, excavations have established the existence of a large production and trading site thought from the coin evidence to have been active between the late seventh century and the mid-ninth.[30] This was at one time called *Ham-wic*, the *wic* or trading place associated with the area known as Hamptonshire, whose *tūn* or centre was at *Ham-tūn*, now Southampton.[31] Coins probably minted at Hamwic itself or nearby from about AD 710 are evidence of a lively monetary economy in the *wic*. In the mid-eighth century there was a gap in the coinage generally in England, but the Hamwic *sceattas* may have been followed by a penny coinage continuing into the 840s.[32] The relationship of the economy of town and port to the economy of the countryside is an important and contested subject. Before the Conquest as well as after it there seem to have been producers at several different levels supplying this market. It was of interest to, and regulated by, the kings of Wessex. Ine was interested in maintaining the quality of the livestock standards, particularly with regard to sheep and wool, and ruled that sheep were not to be shorn until midsummer, much later than is generally done today, when sheep are reared for meat rather than wool. Before then, in Ine's law, a fleece is worth only two pence, presumably more after midsummer, when the sheep's sweat will have increased its lanolin content and thus its weight and quality. A ewe with her lamb was worth a shilling until a fortnight after Easter.[33]

Men who managed royal and ecclesiastical estates could well have been knowledgeable shepherds who sent sheep or wool to market. At the beginning

---

[29] Ulmschneider, *Markets, Minsters and Metal-Detectors*, nos 23, 24–6; Hinton, *Gold and Gilt, Pots and Pins*, 157.

[30] Andrews, *Excavations at Hamwic*; Hill and Cowie, *Wics*; Metcalf, 'Variations in the composition of the currency'.

[31] Eagles, forthcoming.

[32] Metcalf, 'Coins from the *wics*', 50–3.

[33] Ine 69.55, in Liebermann (ed.), *Gesetze*, i, 118, and Attenborough (ed. and tr.), *Laws*, 58–9.

of the tenth century a property at Beddington, Surrey, belonging to the Old Minster at Winchester had a wether flock of fifty, clearly singled out for wool production, which was under the care of the bailiff.[34] We would expect that he, or another estate official, would have supervised sending the wool to market and would very likely have dealt with a merchant known to the monks. Local farmers may have been supplying the market too. Some of the Hamwic sheep that can be identified by a shared genetic fault have been shown to have come from the nearby Itchen valley and do not seem to have been sent to any particular part of the town, as they would have been if they belonged to any one owner or trader.[35] Rather than it having been dominated by elites alone, this suggests that a variety of local producers were trading into this important market and that wool from minsters or royal estates could well have been sold alongside those from peasant flocks. Hamwic residents may also have been a market for woven cloth. The sheep slaughtered there were good quality animals. An improved white sheep type is thought to have been introduced into Britain in the Roman period, either from imported animals or by selective breeding, and the territory of the Atrebates, which included the Hampshire downland, was known for the high quality of its wool.[36] The Hamwic bones show that, at least on the farms which supplied it, improved late Roman standards were being maintained.[37] This has implications for how we interpret the economy of the region and the organization of production in the countryside. To maintain anything like a pure strain, or even to maintain the general quality of flocks, would have demanded knowledgeable animal husbandry that preserved the desired bloodlines and excluded others. Inspection, grading, and culling would have been important. It is possible that this is one of the ways in which in the hinterland of a major market like Hamwic the demands of the market were at work, influencing husbandry away from self-sufficiency and towards more specialization.[38] The quality of the cloth depended ultimately on the quality of the wool from which it was made and this in turn on the sheep that produced it and the care spent on them.

If local farmers were supplying Hamwic they were not necessarily taking their goods to town themselves: peasant production is generally mediated through a network of minor markets and wool in particular very likely reached the market indirectly via collectors of some kind, since there was a legal minimum amount in which it could be sold.[39] There are signs of this in the archaeological

---

[34] S 1444.

[35] Bourdillon, 'Countryside and town', 189.

[36] Bender-Jorgensen, *North European Textiles*, 149.

[37] Bourdillon, 'Countryside and town', 182–7; Bourdillon and Coy, 'The animal bones'.

[38] Crabtree, *West Stow*; Hamerow, *Early Medieval Settlements*, 149–52; Bender-Jorgensen, *North European Textiles*, 147.

[39] Masschaele, *Peasants, Merchants and Markets*; Faith, 'Structure of the market'.

record. Helena Hamerow's challenge to the widely held assumption that centres like Hamwic were solely for trading the produce of elite estates rests in part on the basis of the wide variety of imported, and therefore bought or bartered-for, goods found on ordinary rural sites.[40]

The distribution of coins minted in Hamwic in the countryside also illuminates up-country trade. In the Winchester/Hamwic area this shows that while some types of coinage were restricted to Hamwic itself, perhaps used there as part of a highly regulated marketing system, money was also changing hands at possibly informal or seasonal markets within a wider 'market area', undoubtedly stimulated by the presence of a major emporium with its mass of urban customers, yet not monopolized by it. A series of possible trading-places on good communication routes provided a network of minor staging posts at which the wealth generated in Hamwic trickled back into the countryside. Two villages up the Itchen, Otterbourne and Twyford, look, from their coin finds, to have been such places. Along the upper Itchen valley, coins and metalwork at Cheriton and Itchen Abbas may reflect some small prosperity brought by the trade in livestock, and one at least of the Cheriton coins was minted in Hamwic.[41] This stretch of the valley was served by the road known as the *herepath*, which led to an important river crossing at Alresford and to Neatham—'cattle vill'—which may have been a cattle-market just outside Alton. Traders may have been using the vestiges of a Roman marketing system based on the 'small towns' which flourished as the *civitas* capitals declined. Alton/Neatham may have been one of these: it had rights of toll recorded in Domesday Book, which has been suggested as a sign of continuity.[42]

Away from this busy corridor, where up-country farmers bought produce from itinerant chapmen, it is much harder to trace the effect of the market in the remote countryside. While there is plenty of evidence of the range of metal tools, or metal parts of tools, on Roman upland farms, as soon as we get into the much sparser archaeology of the early Anglo-Saxon period there is little material evidence to go on at the level of the peasant farm. There could well have been networks of internal trade of which only the most durable materials survive as evidence. Farmers up at Church Down, in Chalton in Hampshire, were able to get hold of bought or traded pottery, a piece of fancy bronze work, and glass beads, as well as poor-quality pottery. All this hints at a rural economy in southern Hampshire in the seventh to ninth century

---

[40] Hamerow, *Early Medieval Settlements*, 186; Hamerow, 'Agrarian production'. For a more 'statist' approach: Saunders, 'Early medieval emporia'.

[41] While coin finds are sparse, it is possible that pins may have been used as a small-denomination currency and they have an archaeological record which faintly shadows that of coins: Ulmschneider, *Markets, Minsters and Metal-detectors*, 23. An insufficient supply of coins, or of coins of small enough denomination to be used in each minor transaction, did not in itself preclude there having been a lively trading economy: transactions on credit were common in such situations. For this important argument see Graeber, *Debt*, 21–71. I am grateful to Dan MacIntyre for bringing this to my attention.

[42] Hinton, 'Towns of Hampshire', 149.

in which control of coinage and markets were of vital interest to rulers, one in which some minsters and royal estates were active but were not monopolistic producers. Petty and informal marketing may also have been important, and in this the cumulative output of smaller producers who were raising sheep on downland farms and producing woollens in urban households may have been considerable.

But the market itself was changing. Hamwic declined from the mid-ninth century and Winchester grew in the tenth with the foundation of the New Minster and its growing role as an administrative centre. Late Anglo-Saxon minsters were the nearest equivalent England had to royal palaces. The towns in which they were situated were becoming more like provincial capitals. Winchester's links with London drew in silver and by the end of our period it had its own mint. This may have been partly 'because it was creaming off trade profits which should have been Southampton's but a great many other factors must also have been involved.[43] One of these is the possibility that the rise of Winchester as a commercial centre was accompanied by the church's intensified exploitation of its lands. Both Old and New Minster now had vast estates. There was a major reorganization of the bishop's property at Bishopstoke in the tenth century to give better access to pasture. Alert landlords were increasingly able, and eager, to tap peasant resources of livestock and labour. Bishop and clergy, or rather their lessees, may well have been on the road to the quasi-capitalist stock farming which we see at work from the late twelfth century. In the year 900 a document was drawn up listing the obligations of the farmers, the *ceorls*, on one of the minster's properties in the Bourne Valley. One of these duties was shearing the demesne sheep, another was providing two sheep from their own flock and shearing them.[44] Winchester may have been beginning to resemble the wool-rich cities of the later Middle Ages with their urban bourgeoisie, its links with Flanders exploited by '*chenistes* ("knights") trading in wool and textiles gathered from the sheep of Wessex'.[45]

It is possible that some of the farmers of the 'worthys' lost out in this climate. The character of many of the farms of this type certainly changed considerably. Some were large enough to develop into major estates: *Æscesmere's worðig* into Ashmansworth, one of the bishopric's important manors, *Earmunde's worðig* into Armsworth House and Park. The cluster of worthys round Winchester, part of the church's earliest endowment there, show what an important part of the landscape these large discrete farms had once been and what prime land they had included.[46] Others may have remained the large independent

---

[43] Hinton, *Archaeology, Economy and Society*, 267.

[44] Neuk, 'Medieval Britain and Ireland', 233; Robertson (ed. and tr.), *Anglo-Saxon Charters*, 206–7 (no. 110). Deveson, 'Ceorls of Hurstbourne', has now established that these dues were owed at Stoke, the intensively exploited inland of the Hurstbourne valley estate, not from all the farmers of the surrounding countryside.

[45] Hinton, 'Towns of Hampshire', 159.

[46] I am grateful to Barbara Yorke for letting me see her unpublished paper on the Winchester worthys.

farms they formerly were, and may be represented by the smaller 'manors' in Domesday Book. Some became the home farms of larger estates. But some downland farms may ultimately have proved unviable and been divided into smaller holdings or incorporated into larger ones. They have left their mark on the landscape simply as place-names, or, like Wine's farm, as diversions in a parish boundary.

Fig. 10.1. Yadsworthy Farm, Devon.

Eadda's *worðig*, whose boundary's bank can be seen to pre-date the parish boundary, remains a family farm today. Faint plough-marks in the steeply sloping fields nearest to the farmstead could be produced by the light plough used in parts of the West Country in the early Middle Ages.

(Air photograph © RCHM/English Heritage)

10

Moorland

This chapter investigates the economy of farms with access to virtually unlimited open grazing for livestock in an area of well-watered moorland which, unlike the chalk downs, could have supported large numbers of cattle and horses as well as sheep (Fig. 10.1). Although the focus is on a particular kind of farm—the ring-fenced 'worthy'—farming on the margin of a large area of open land must have been a common experience in our period, particularly in the Highland Zone. A longer view is possible here than elsewhere in the book, for the area considered, Dartmoor and the settlements around its periphery, has a still visible archaeological record of farming practices which have been dated to the Bronze Age. To look so far back is to recognize the enduring challenges faced by people in this environment and to suggest some recurring responses. Visitors see the moor today as the domain of ponies, sheep, and cattle seemingly roaming at will and only periodically rounded up, a reflection of the fact that since the time of King John 'all the men of Devon' have enjoyed common rights on the moor.[1] If we think about such matters at all we probably think that it has always been used as pasture for large flocks and herds driven up there in long-distance transhumance systems.[2] But this is not the whole story. In the long history of humans on the moor there have been periods when people have brought parts of it into cultivation. For people farming on its fringes, the main subjects of this chapter, the moor was not distant but in easy reach. The contrast in the ways in which different kinds of farmer used the moor can tell us quite a lot about early medieval farming. It is worth taking a short excursus into prehistory to appreciate the strong influence which livestock, both in terms of their ownership and their management, have had on the landscape.

Dartmoor is essentially a dome of granite rising to 2,000 feet above sea level, capped by 'tors', piles of vast boulders which make dramatic climaxes on skylines visible across miles of open moorland and which still serve as landmarks. On the open moor the thin acid topsoil supports grass, gorse, heather, bracken, and occasional woodland: thorn does best against the strong winds but oak

---

[1] Hoskins, 'Dartmoor Commons'; Fogwill, 'Pastoralism on Dartmoor'.
[2] Fox, *Dartmoor's Alluring Uplands*.

and birch are also found. Rivers which rise on the high moor wind shallowly through their stony upper courses until they grow strong enough to cut deep valleys with steep, wooded banks as they come off the moor. Bleak though it is, Dartmoor was not always 'marginal land'. It is only comparatively recently that it has become widely peatified and in places boggy. The occupants of the hut circles of the Early Bronze Age may have been there only in the summer, managing flocks and herds rather than cultivating the soil, but they were succeeded by permanent residents who were both cultivators and stock-rearers.[3] In the later Bronze Age large-scale, highly organized delineations marked out the moor. These are the Dartmoor 'reaves', the defining elements of an extensive reorganization of the landscape revealed in a series of studies by Andrew Fleming (Fig. 10.2).[4] Their banks and walls, of which extensive traces remain, comprised long boundaries running 'terrain oblivious' along the flanks of the hills for miles, their ends marked by transverse walls. These 'contour reaves' separated the higher moorlands from the grazing land on the lower slopes, rather as the 'head dyke' does in many moorland areas today. Below them, and on a smaller scale, in 'parallel reave systems' close-set boundaries ran up to a terminal boundary, and between these ran smaller divisions, dividing each long block into a series of small fields or paddocks. Farmsteads and droveways were integrated into this pattern, the houses tending to cluster in 'neighbourhood groups', with small fields, probably laid out first, near to hand and larger ones further off. Fleming considers that it was these groups, of six to fifteen farmsteads, that were the creators of the field systems, but the reaves themselves, while there is no agreement about who created them, were evidently conceived and laid out with regard to some much wider conception of the landscape.[5] Similar large-scale territorial organization, sometimes called 'coaxial' because its main elements are roughly parallel, and small-scale farming are now accepted features of the pre-Roman landscape. The close association of small fields and farmsteads is very reminiscent of the Romano-British fields which Peter Fowler revealed on the Wiltshire Downs, and the importance of small groups, rather than single farms, has its parallels there too. These areas of enclosed land were one component in larger territories in which the rivers and the high moor were defining elements. Each group had access to the high moor and unenclosed grazing land situated along the watersheds between the many rivers which run off the moor.[6] Organization at the level of these larger units, or rather the social group that dominated them, may have been responsible for the land demarcations of the reaves, but within them it looks as though the neighbourhood group was the decision-maker, the boundary-builder, and so probably the

[3] Fleming, 'Prehistoric landscape of Dartmoor', 15.
[4] Fleming, *Dartmoor Reaves*.
[5] Fleming, 'Prehistoric Dartmoor in its context', 122.
[6] Fleming, *Dartmoor Reaves*, 41, Fig. 22; Fleming has provided an overview of the literature on 'coaxial' systems in the second edition of this work (Oxford 2008).

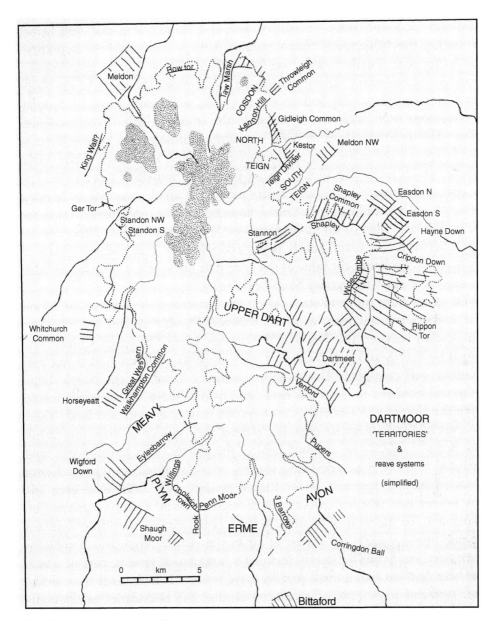

Fig. 10.2. Reave systems on Dartmoor.

(From Fleming, *Dartmoor Reaves* © Andrew Fleming)

unit within which the primary producers organized their lives.[7] The reaves were evidently laid out in an open landscape, where the growth of trees and shrubs had been kept down by grazing livestock (and we should envisage deer

---

[7] Herring, 'Commons, fields and communities' discusses the various levels of organization and community recognizable in such landscapes.

and boar in this landscape as well as cattle, goats, and sheep.) But while the high moor, in Fleming's view, acted as the common it is today for the groups that lived and farmed on its flanks very few droveways—a feature often associated with upland grazing and the passage of animals to it—have been identified which can be related to the reave system. The people who worked the field systems of the moorland and lived permanently among them seem to have been able to turn their stock, probably small flocks and herds, straight onto the adjacent moor, and very likely brought them in at night, perhaps close-folding them on their small fields to enhance their fertility. We see very much this kind of livestock husbandry and the small curvilinear enclosures associated with it in our own period.[8]

But the moor was also being used by a quite different sort of farmer and in a quite different way. Pastoralists were driving stock from some distance away up onto the moor for the summer season. Their droveways threaded their way through the fields and paddocks of the moorland farmers to the high moor. They built pounds big enough to corral flocks of animals for management and possibly protection at night.[9] This contrast and coexistence between long-distance, large-scale seasonal transhumance and short-distance, small-scale pasturing near the farmstead is one to which we will return. There is almost no archaeology of the Iron Age on the moor, although a small number of settlements on its eastern flank show that it was not entirely deserted.[10] But there are indications of power centres *off* the moor from which some kind of claim on parts of it could be asserted. Malcolm Todd calls them 'small fiefdoms'. There are good reasons for associating the power and authority of such centres with pastoralism. Only grazing would have kept the uplands open. Early medieval power was very commonly associated with livestock, whether as moveable wealth or tribute, and it is not too fanciful to imagine that among the assets of powerful men of the Iron Age, and no doubt through the Roman centuries too, there would have been flocks and herds. There was a fringe of hill forts around the south and eastern edges of the moor and some, like Cranbrook Castle near Chagford, are associated with reave-like boundaries on the moor. Some have associated linear earthworks which link valleys and areas of low ground: an arrangement of the landscape which we have come to recognize as a sure sign of transhumant pasturing.[11]

We do not need to imagine hill forts as the only centres of power. Charles, in Shirwell Hundred north of the moor, contains the element *lis* from the British word *lisso*, meaning a court, the power centre of an important person. From the time when the aristocracy of the West Country had become Christian and

---

[8] Chapter 6 outlines the archaeology and possible interpretations under 'Shepherds and shielings', pp. 147–51 and Fig. 6.4.

[9] Butler, *Dartmoor Atlas*, 67, 87–9, 90–101.

[10] Newman, *Field Archaeology*, 83, presents a much more modified picture of Iron Age 'desertion', in favour of 'more a case of individual desertions, over perhaps centuries'.

[11] Todd, *South-West*, 161.

literate, or had access to literacy and valued it, we have a new source of evidence which has recently been interpreted in new ways which illuminate their economic and social milieu. This is the corpus of inscribed stones with Latin inscriptions commemorating important British Christians. They are landmarks in open country, 'visible from a distance and effortlessly dominating their surroundings', like the stone of Prince (or chief, ruler) Iuriucus, son of Audetus, set up on Sourton Down. Work by Susan Pearce suggests that these were not simply demonstrations of prestige but were also waymarkers on droveways, part of a system linking together the components of large territories which comprised arable land off the moor and rights in the moorland, which 'provided a founding narrative which justified the exercise of rights'.[12] Such links were long lasting. On a less aristocratic scale the 'hay way of the people of Buckland' which linked Roborough Down with the moors above the Meavy and the right of the Buckland people to pass along it evidently survived even when later boundaries had intervened: the quotation comes from a charter of the eleventh century.[13]

The pattern of hundreds around Dartmoor also reflects links between moorland and lowland. Eight hundreds, their boundaries marked by the major rivers, include land on the moor, and they fan out around it, six stretching as far as the coast. Their meeting places are all off the moor, in areas which became those of heaviest settlement and centres of power. One explanation of this continuing pattern is that economic links continued between the largely arable-based economy of the lower lands and the extensive pastures of the moor.

THE UPPER PLYM AND MEAVY VALLEYS

What is now the parish of Meavy on the western edge of the moor is an area bounded on the west and south by the Plym and on the north by one of its tributaries, the Meavy. It has two significant areas of open land—Wigford Down to the south and Yennadon Down in the north—and abuts directly onto Ringmoor Down. This 'downland' had anciently been a favoured area for settlement and cultivation. The upper Plym and its tributaries have an exceptional record of prehistoric farms in the shape of hut circles and associated enclosures.[14] These can be found in small clusters near the source of the river on the moor and in larger groups going down the river: fifty at Legis Tor and sixty-five below Trowlesworthy Tor. One of the 'primary reaves' identified by Fleming,

---

[12] Pearce, *South-West Britain*, 58–62, at 58.

[13] Many of these stones have been moved from their original burial places to serve as waymarkers, and more recently several have been moved to churchyards. Pearce, 'Early medieval land-use', 15; Pearce, *South-West Britain*, 207, 56–62. For a discussion of their role in the West Country generally see Turner, *Making a Christian Landscape*, 140–3. For the quotation see S 963.

[14] Butler, *Atlas*, 77–92.

Eylesbarrow Reave, runs across Ringmoor and Wigford Downs, and on both there are several hut circles and traces of field systems. This is important from the point of view of our period, but not because we are suggesting continuity, quite the reverse. Wigford Down, like much of the lower moor, was cultivated in the Bronze Age, but by historic times it was open pasture, although two abandoned longhouses are a reminder of one of the much later occasional attempts to cultivate it, perhaps under the population pressure of the twelfth and thirteenth centuries.

This long perspective enables us to get some idea of what the challenges and appeals of different kinds of territory may have been to pre-modern farmers. Links to the river seem to have been important, both for the obvious practical reasons and as definers of space. The Bronze Age settlements on the moor associated with the reaves are well separated, either by the streams entering the Plym that form natural barriers between them or they are simply spaced along the bank, often about half a kilometre apart. Those along the upper Plym all have a river frontage, though some are set well back from the bank. Most sites show evidence of expansion, developing either into multi-lobed structures where additional enclosures have been added onto the outside, or perhaps where space allowed, with entirely separate pounds alongside.

If we follow the Plym and the Meavy down off the moor to where they are beginning to look less like streams and more like rivers, we come across a string of places whose names incorporate Anglo-Saxon personal names, very frequently with the Old English word *worðig* (see p. 232) used as a suffix (Fig. 10.3). Some are now single farms, others hamlets: Trowlesworthy, 'Cada's worthy' (Cadover), 'Goda's land on the Meavy' (Godameavy), 'Bella's worthy' (Belliver), 'Leofa's worthy' (Lowery), 'Eadswith's worthy' (Essworthy), and 'Beorhtwine's worthy' (Brisworthy).[15] 'Worthy' (which sometimes appears in the form of the suffixes 'ery' or 'over', occasionally 'ford') is a very common element in Devon place-names, both in major (parish) and minor (farm and hamlet) names. Although it appears as a generic linked to many Old English personal names, it continued in use, and many Devon worthys have post-Conquest personal or descriptive terms as their first element.[16] There are significant differences between the location of these Meavy worthys and the Bronze Age settlements on Wigford Down. People have moved off the moor. The farming population looks as if it has thinned out. The worthy farms are not clustered but widely spaced at a kilometre or more apart along the rivers or brooks. The

---

[15] Faith, 'Some Devon farms'. Fox, *Dartmoor's Alluring Uplands*, discusses place-names incorporating Anglo-Saxon personal names at 162–6. On the basis of names recorded in documentary sources he was of the opinion that Norman personal names replaced Anglo-Saxon ones in the period after 1100 and were beginning to do so before that.

[16] Gover, Mawer, and Stenton, *Place-Names of Devon*, s.v. 'worthy'; Padel, 'Place-names', 88–99. Svensson, 'Worthy-names', misleadingly bases his analysis and dating on post-Conquest examples. Costen, 'Huish and worth' remains authoritative on these elements.

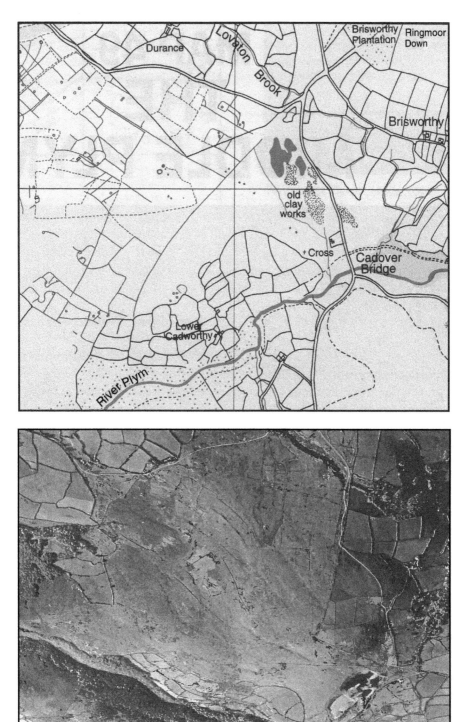

Fig. 10.3. Cada's *worðig*, now Lower Cadworthy on the edge of Wigford Down, Cadover Bridge, Devon. a: Traces of earlier land-use (Butler, *Atlas* ©). b: Air photograph (© West Air Photography) south at top.

interest in overall planning, whether stemming from communities or powerful individuals, which had laid out the reaves is no longer apparent. Each worthy is surrounded by its own fields enclosed by a long curving boundary, in some areas a massive stone wall, in others a turf bank. Whoever the people were who laid out the fields and farmsteads of Cada's worthy and the rest (and in spite of their solidly Anglo-Saxon names some farms may have been British in origin) were operating in a very different world both ecologically and socially, and very likely climatically, from their Bronze Age predecessors.

The term 'worthy' is still used in Devon to describe land taken in from the moor.[17] It seems always to have had connotations of 'enclosure'—King Ine of Wessex ruled that 'a *ceorl*'s worthy shall be fenced winter and summer'—and a strong boundary is a prominent feature of the farms we consider here, just as it seems to have been of the Hampshire worthys described in an earlier chapter.[18] None of the moor-edge worthys has become a significant place, in the sense of acquiring a church, or growing into a village. Even though the Anglo-Saxon element in their names strongly suggests that many were in existence by the Conquest, very few appear in Domesday Book under their own names, that is to say as 'manors'. Hoskins argued that many were rated for geld under the name of a nearby manor as the holdings of *villani*.[19] Yet they were evidently large enough, and their boundaries well enough established, to support over time not one farm but several, even a hamlet. Their names often commemorate an individual owner but very many now comprise at least two separate farms, or settlements: at Meavy, for instance, there are now Higher and Lower Belliver, Upper and Lower Lowery. By 1086 'Hnott's worthy' (Natworthy in Manaton) supported at least six families: those of Edward, who held the manor, two *villani*, two bordars, and a slave. An analysis of the manor of Rashleigh, in Wembworthy parish, shows that it was only a part of the parent 'worthy', and Rashleigh itself has developed over time from an oval enclosure, which later became the barton or demesne farm, while other farms have developed within its overall boundary.[20]

That these pioneers established their farms on the west, south, and eastern edges of the moor, but not on the steeper and colder north side, mirroring the distribution of prehistoric settlement, suggests that they had some choice of territory.[21] The present-day boundary of one farm's fields stops well short of the next. Bada's worthy has on one side an area called Merrifield, which may have been a boundary area of open land, *gemaere feld*, and the promontory

---

[17] Richard Kitchin of Withill Farm has been an invaluable source of information.

[18] Banham discusses this clause on p. 67.

[19] Hoskins, 'The highland zone in Domesday Book', 15–52.

[20] *Domesday Book: Devon*, 30.2; Hoskins, 'Devon', 45; Roberts and Wrathmell, *Region and Place*, 101–3. Perhaps *geburtun* would be better than Roberts and Wrathmell's translation of 'Bootown' at 103.

[21] Fox, *Dartmoor's Alluring Uplands*, 162–9, interprets these moor-edge farms as replacing earlier seasonal settlements.

prehistoric enclosure of Dewerston makes a formidable boundary between two of the Meavy valley worthys. Each worthy contains a stretch of river and it is the rivers that often served as boundaries: 'Bada's worthy' (Higher and Lower Badworthy) and 'Dudda's worthy' (Didworthy) face each other across the Avon at the beginning of its southward course off the moor. Most of the Dartmoor-edge worthys have curving outer boundaries which contain an area of between about thirty and seventy acres. The massive stone walls which mark many of the present-day boundaries between the land of the worthy and the open moor are, in form, 'corn ditches', with an outer ditch and an inner sloped bank. Designed to make it difficult for deer to leap from the moor onto farmed land, and easy to drive them out when they did so, these are sometimes considered to have originated in the period of forest law. It is uncertain when Dartmoor was declared to be royal forest—that is to say, an area where forest law applied, designed to protect the King's deer. Corn-ditches may have been part of the Conqueror's forest policy, but an earlier origin is possible. After Dartmoor was disforested in the thirteenth century they were no longer compulsory but continued to be maintained and new ones were built. They were essentially a common-sense response to local conditions: their massive walls not only acted as boundaries but also were an efficient way to dispose of stone cleared off land needed for cultivation; they kept the deer and other animals off crops and provided enclosed and more sheltered grazing near the farm for young stock before they were turned out on the moor, the equivalent of the 'in-by' land, the land near the farm or township, of the northern counties. They take a wavy route along contours and change their course to include some of the most massive boulders, which their builders have avoided the labour of moving. They have not been archaeologically dated: what we see today are those which have survived into the era of the Ordnance Survey and been mapped as field boundaries (often the moorside boundary has been taken into the boundary of the Dartmoor National Park). However, a considerable length of the present massive wall around the land of Yadsworthy overlies a much older and more modest earth bank, perhaps its original boundary, and it is possible that many of the worthy boundary walls that we see today also run along much earlier boundaries[22] (Fig. 10.1).

Many of the farms considered here have paired enclosures. Cadworthy (Cadover) has a large enclosure to the south-west and the north-east of the present farmstead, separated by a wide gully leading to the down situated above it. Other paired enclosures appear on many other worthys on the moor's edge like Afan's worthy, now Great and Little Ensworthy (and they also appear on farms in a similar position which have names of a different type). Martin Gillard's typology of farms on the edge of Exmoor, although he does not date

---

[22] Fieldwork by Andrew Fleming, Richard Kitchin, and the author in Spring 2008 revealed earth banks on farm boundaries at two locations which antedate the stone walls of their present boundaries: Faith, 'Some Devon farms'.

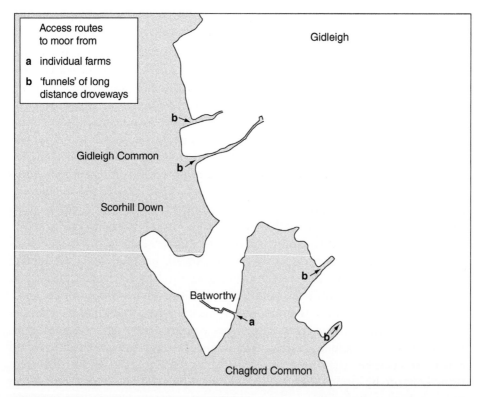

Fig. 10.4. Access to the moor from long-distance and short-distance droveways.

any specifically to the Anglo-Saxon period, shows many very similar features. He distinguishes 'small rural nucleations and isolated farmsteads' with 'long sinuous boundaries' enclosing regular field systems and suggests these boundaries were the frontiers of land units, possibly created as a single act, which contained several farmsteads. They all have immediate access to open downland or moorland, grazing ground which to this day is still open and unenclosed. Like Hoskins, Gillard considers that these land units were not the result of population pressure, but of conscious choice. They may have been under-exploited—he shows that some in the twenty years after the Norman conquest increased in value—but he queries the notion that this was 'marginal' land; indeed he goes so far as to say that Exmoor was more resilient than pasture land which was tied into large-scale arable systems supporting nucleated settlements.[23] They certainly show a remarkable capacity to survive; many worthy farms are going concerns to this day: Figs. 10.1 and 10.3b show examples.

The synergy of farmland with the open moor was an essential element in their viability. The Meavy worthys seem to cluster round the pasture of Wigford Down. Possibly the farmer of a worthy had some particular claim on, or associ-

[23] Gillard, 'Medieval settlement', 91, 112–13, 178.

ation with, not just the enclosed land surrounding them but also the adjacent down or moorland, several of which have tors bearing their name (although these names may have been given to them long after the worthys were named). Leofa's and Eadswith's each had an eponymous tor: Leather Tor on the hill above 'Leofa's worthy' (Lowery) and Eadswith's above 'Eadswith's worthy' (Essworthy), both farms now drowned under Burrator reservoir. The moor-edge worthys have a short lane leading from the farmstead, and it is important to note, *only* from that farm (or from its 'Upper' or 'Lower' offshoot) onto open land where such lanes widen into the funnels or 'strolls', walled or banked passageways down which animals could be herded off the moor and down which cattle made their way to water (and perhaps also for milking). These seem quite different from the long-distance droveway network by which 'all the men of Devon' brought livestock onto the moor: these bypass many farms and small places.[24] Fig. 10.4 maps examples of these types for part of the moor-edge.

If a typically Anglo-Saxon worthy on the edge of the moor was a large area of land within some kind of well-marked boundary, with its own stretch of water and private access to virtually unlimited pasture, this does not mean to say that the land within its boundaries would all have all been under cultivation, or indeed in use at all, when the farm was first laid out. In fact the way that so many were capable of supporting at least two hamlets in later times virtually establishes this. If these farms originated, as has been suggested, as clearings made by pioneers in an open landscape which seems not to have been under the plough since the Late Bronze Age, it would have been a sensible strategy to lay claim to a substantial area which would include river, woodland, perhaps on the steep valley sides, and moorland edge.

FARMING ON THE EDGE OF THE MOOR

There is a certain amount of evidence about how farming may have been organized within these large enclosures. This gives a strong impression that they involved the division of land for different uses. Medieval Devon and Cornwall both have traces of versions of 'infield–outfield' cultivation which involved long-lasting functional divisions of the land of an individual farm or settlement. In such systems, which are also widely found in the north and north-west of England, land in an area near the farmstead, the infield, was continuously and intensively cultivated, sometimes on some kind of shifting system which moved over blocks of land, while parts of the pastoral outfield were brought periodically into cultivation and then left to recover.[25] H. P. R. Finberg was able

[24] Fox, *Dartmoor's Alluring Uplands*.
[25] Infield–outfield systems are discussed in studies of individual regions in Baker and Butlin (eds), *Field Systems*.

to trace a version of this system in medieval Devon, in which the 'in-ground' of a farm was intensively cultivated; the 'middle ground' consisted of enclosed pasture; and the 'out-ground' was moor, furze, or downland which was attached to that particular farm. Parts of the outfield were taken into periodic cultivation and this episodic cultivation was still being practised into the seventeenth century. This could well have been the early medieval practice on the south and east sides of the moor, much more sheltered and with more possibilities for arable cultivation than the bleaker and windier western and north-western edges.[26] Periodic cultivation was also the strategy of some farms near to the waterlogged sites investigated by Ralph Fyfe and others on an area of the Culm Measures in mid-Devon.[27] They investigated pollen samples taken from moorland areas just beyond the margins of a ring of farms on the edge of high moorland at Rackenford Moor and Hares Down. Several of these farms have names which incorporate Anglo-Saxon personal names: 'Canna's worthy' at Canworthy, 'Bicca's ham' (Bickham), 'Bula's worthy' and possibly 'Eadswith's worthy' (Bulworthy and Essworthy). Where the boundaries of the earliest fields of these worthys can be traced, although not dated, they have much the same curved and lobe-like character of the other Devon worthys we have considered. Pollen cores were taken on the higher ground, beyond these field boundaries, so they cannot be considered to be evidence of what was going on within them, but they suggest intaking land beyond the farm and then leaving it fallow for a few years to recover its fertility. Fyfe believes this marks 'the emergence of the historic landscape', and that the farms and their outlying intakes were newly established together after AD 800. The authors interpret the increase in cereal production which it made possible to be a response to population pressure, and consider that it represented a significant change from a farming system which had remained virtually unchanged from the late Iron Age and through the Roman period.[28]

However, there was a rather different kind of husbandry which was also common to the West Country. This was 'convertible husbandry', in which small enclosed fields *within* the farmland were laid down as 'leys', land which was left fallow for long periods lasting up to seven years, possibly more, during which time the grass and weeds were allowed to grow back and were probably grazed. When these leys were brought into cultivation again, the accumulated vegetation gave them a 'nitrogen boost' through being ploughed back into the soil.[29] To outsiders used to a more intensive agriculture, it could have seemed a

---

[26] Finberg, *Tavistock Abbey*, 32–4. Hatcher, 'Farming techniques: south-west England', 387; Fox, 'Farming techniques: Devon and Cornwall', 303–15. Faith' 'Some Devon farms'; *Domesday Book: Devon*, 39.1; Fox, 'Farming techniques', 310; Darby and Finn, *Domesday Geography of South-West England*, 98–9 and Fig. 38.

[27] Fyfe et al., 'Characterising the late prehistoric'.

[28] Fyfe et al., 'Characterising the late prehistoric'; Fyfe, 'Paleoenvironmental perspectives', 18–20.

[29] Hatcher, 'Farming techniques: south-west England', 387; Fox, 'Farming practice', 303–15.

confusing system, and it would seem odd to us today, used to seeing the same field relentlessly cultivated year after year. It certainly seems to have struck the Domesday commissioners as eccentric or inefficient, to judge by the number of places where they recorded that, although there was land for so many plough-teams to work, fewer than this were actually there: they assumed that land suitable for arable would be subject to regular rotation or even permanently cultivated. At Willsworthy (*Wiflewurth* in Domesday Book), while there was considered to be land for four teams, there was only one there: this was on the home farm where four slaves did the work.[30] Convertible husbandry was 'deeply rooted in the routines and calendars of husbandmen in the south-west,' as Harold Fox remarked of these strategies.[31]

The sheer labour of constructing and maintaining boundary banks must surely have meant that farming close to the moor demanded the cooperation of a larger group than the single family. A worthy farm might have supported more than one family, observably so in Domesday Book, and many certainly did so in the later Middle Ages, when 'Higher' and 'Lower' holdings developed or were split off. Andrew Fleming and Nicholas Ralph investigated a series of enclosures on Holne Moor (Fig. 10.5). There the land was marked out in two principal 'lobes' or enclosures, with boundaries made by hedges and block walls which survive in part to the present day. The north 'lobe' was divided into four fields within which there were ploughing strips. These were long (up to 250 yards in one case) and may themselves have been divided for cropping.[32] The 'quillets', strips of arable, found at Rashleigh, are an example of something like this. Droveways allowed for the passage of stock onto the open moor beyond.[33] As the 'lobes' each enclosed both arable and closes for livestock, the excavators of the Holne Moor site suggest that they were units of ownership, not functional divisions. Their interpretation may relate to their supposition that 'a small early medieval hamlet' may have been the home of the group who were farming there.[34] But the presence of small stock enclosures might equally be evidence of a functional division, a sign that animals were being close-folded on intensively worked arable, as Fox suggested for the farms he studied. Examples from else-where in the West Country can be found where a pastoral enclosure is paired with one used for cultivation, and each contained smaller units. A farm at Zennor, Cornwall, had a kind of dartboard configuration. Within an outer curved boundary 'Four small fields near the house were manured and cultivated whilst five larger units further away were grazed and cultivated in turn.'[35]

---

[30] Faith, 'Some Devon farms'; *Domesday Book: Devon*, 39.1.

[31] Fox, 'Farming practice', 310.

[32] Fleming and Ralph, 'Medieval settlement', 101–37. Strip fields are discussed in the following chapter.

[33] Roberts and Wrathmell, *Region and Place*, 101–3.

[34] This is possibly represented in Domesday in the entry for Holne: *Domesday Book: Devon*, 20.11.

[35] Fowler, 'Arable fields'; Fowler, *Farming in the First Millennium*, 130–80.

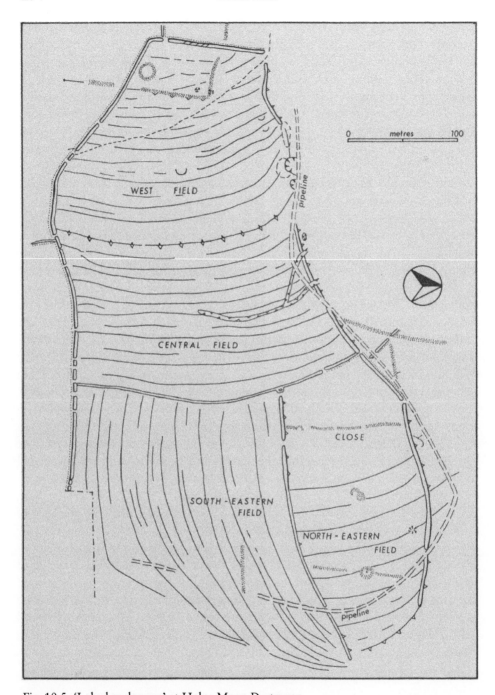

Fig. 10.5. 'Lobed enclosures' at Holne Moor, Dartmoor.

(From Fleming and Ralph, 'Medieval settlement' © Andrew Fleming)

These husbandry practices are those of the domestic economy of the small self-sufficient farm. Rather than moving their stock seasonally onto the high moor their owners may have kept their animals near at hand. Fox identified places on the edge of the moor with the Old English elements *smeoru* and *butere* in their names as places where the milk from animals pastured on the moor was made into cheese and butter. None of these dairying sites appears in the written record before the Conquest but Fox believed that they belonged to a period of 'personal transhumance' before the eleventh century when farmers turned their stock out in summer under the personal supervision of someone from the farm. One of these dairying sites is near a worthy farm, Smeardon Down near Godsworthy in Peter Tavy parish, and lies within one of its lobed enclosures: it is a patch of rocky pasture with a spring to provide the water needed for cooling the milk and keeping the dairying vessels clean: it is shown in Fig. 6.3.[36] Small-scale production of cheese and butter could have made a valued contribution to the economy of the worthy farms. But this is likely to have been on a very small scale, for even if the moor-edge farmers had unlimited grazing almost on their doorstep for their animals, they do not seem to have had many of them. We have no figures for their sheep and cattle on ordinary farms but a scrap of information from Domesday Book shows that even on the home farms of manorial lords they were not numerous: two tiny flocks (seven, twenty). Presumably one of these was at Meavy itself, although the King's manor at Walkhampton had fifty sheep. The numbers of plough-teams kept were often less than the commissioners thought adequate and we need to take into account that in the south-west the team was probably four or six oxen.[37] The fact that farmers so near the ample grassland of the moor were raising stock on such an unambitious scale leads us to look again at the contrast drawn earlier in the context of the Late Bronze Age. Then, it was suggested, the small mixed farms on the moorland, such as those on Wigston Down, were traversed by the coming and going of large flocks and herds from elsewhere. Large-scale transhumance was also important in the economy of the British chiefs with their waymarked transhumance routes. Domesday gives a very similar picture. Of the land which came under West Saxon control it was chiefly the large estates which seem to have continued this pattern of links between the moor and 'down-country' centres of power and production many miles away. It was not the places near the moor but by and large estates a good way off which had large flocks and herds on their demesnes. In 1086 the bishop of Exeter's 'down-country' manor of Paignton had 350 sheep and 20 cattle and there were 70 more sheep at its attached property at Ashburton on the edge of

---

[36] Fox, 'Butter place-names'.

[37] Darby, *Domesday Geography of South-West England*, 240–5; Lennard, 'Domesday plough-teams', 770–5. The 'reversed J' curves sometimes found in Devon and made by medieval ploughing might be confirmation of this: perhaps the smaller West Country plough teams could turn on a smaller headland than the Midland teams, which made a 'reversed S'.

the moor, significantly larger numbers than are recorded for other Devon man-ors.[38] They pastured on the moor in summer and the claims the bishop had there appear in the shape of the detached portions of his manors. Fox identified a large area, described in a charter of the early eleventh century as *Peadington*, with Paignton. Bounded on its eastern sides by the Dart and Webbern and reaching up to the moor, it was a detached part of the bishopric of Exeter's lands, possibly 'all the *parochia* pertaining to it in Saxon territory' mentioned in the ninth century as belonging to the minster. Paignton, near the coast, included Ashburton some 50 km away and its 'summer resource' may have been the area of moorland including the parish of Widecombe in the Moor and reaching right up to the tors, the highest points on the moor.[39] The bishop's animals would have made their way through an inhabited and worked land-scape. By 1086 many worthys had evolved into manors with recognizable demesnes, like Nottsworthy, or had split into two or more townships or else had grown into hamlets or villages. The inhabitants of all these places would have been using the same open moorland areas like Manaton, whose name contains OE *gemæne*, 'common', for their animals as the bishop did for his. Other large stock enterprises which may have moved the animals from the coast to the moor were on a royal manor at Cockington, with an outlier at Dewdon near Widdecombe, and a layman's manor at Kenton, linked with Chagford, both these outliers giving access to the moor. In Stanborough Hun-dred, it was the fertile lands of the South Hams which recorded the biggest flocks, and these were in King Edward's time in the hands of greater land-owners like Algar and Heca the Sheriff, who had large estates elsewhere.[40] Of the demesnes near the moor in Roborough Hundred for instance only Buck-land, Stoke, and Bickleigh had flocks of over a hundred sheep, and these were all were parts of a huge estate owned by Brictmer before the Conquest.[41] It seems as if it was not mostly the small farmers but the owners of large enter-prises who were driving their animals up onto the moor for the summer grazing. These were the people whose lowland lands could provide enough fodder to sustain sizeable numbers of animals through the winter, both through the hay and the grazing on the fallows which their larger arables provided.

Winter fodder was everywhere a vital element in controlling the amount of animals any kind of farm could sustain. The moor was valuable not only as summer pasture but as a source of winter fodder too, providing gorse and holly as well as hay. This winter fodder could well have been brought down using the waymarked access roads, such as the 'hay way of the Buckland people', which runs from Buckland Monachorum through Meavy to the moor via Sharpitor.

---

[38] Finn, 'Devonshire', 288.
[39] Fox, *Dartmoor's Alluring Uplands*, 120–3; Pearce, *South-West Britain*, 55–9.
[40] Faith, 'Cola's tun', 70–1.
[41] Darby, *Domesday Geography of South-West England*, Fig. 65; *Domesday Book: Devon*, 21.20, 28.15, 21.19.

Filham in Ermington on the edge of the moor is a *filith-ham*, 'hay-farm'. Filice Lane in Horrabridge could well have originated as its 'hay lane'.[42] The 'Buckland people's hay way' is a Devon example of the kind of ancient right of way which long-established communities were able to sustain through territory farmed by other people, like the droves to the marshes of the 'parallel parishes' and the Wealden ways discussed in earlier chapters. Does this mean that the communities which benefited from them were older than those whose lands they traversed, or simply more dominant? Pearce has suggested that estates, later to become parishes like Meavy and Walkhampton, were late formations inserted between the older territories and the moor. Cnut's charter of 1031 giving land at Meavy to one of his administrators, from which the hay-lane reference comes, would be an example of such a process.[43] We could look at this in another way: these estates were formed to incorporate, tax, and bring to church long-established communities of farmers who had brought the moorland edge under cultivation. Estates were not likely to have been carved out of virgin territory. Cnut's grant would hardly have been of simply a stretch of waste land: more likely it was an area which was already being exploited from a centre which was to become the village of Meavy. Its farms supported people who were potential payers of tax and rent, and who were later to provide a congregation for its church. It was the Cadas and Badas, their families and predecessors and successors whose labour had made them into viable farms and stitched the moorland edge into the fabric of the Devon farming economy.

[42] Hooke, *Charter-Bounds of Devon and Cornwall*, 199.
[43] Pearce, *South-West Britain*, 289; Pearce, 'Early medieval land-use', 15–17.

11

Wolds

WOLDS AS A *PAYS*

Old English *weald* or *wald* meant 'woodland' or 'forest', but in Modern English *wold* has come to stand for a wider kind of countryside, generally upland, much of which is no longer thickly covered with trees. In the Anglo-Saxon period many wolds still had scattered woods among cleared land 'which served as woodland for largely pastoral communities'.[1] Two classic studies have given us a vivid picture of the nature and economy of wolds in the Middle Ages. Both stress that they were part of a rural economy in which seasonal transhumance was important. Alan Everitt's 'River and Wold' introduced to English readers the idea of the individual character of particular *pays* or 'countrysides', landscapes as the people who lived and worked there experienced, described, and used them. It is the term that many French people use today to describe their place of origin (or that of its wine).[2] Everitt also stressed the essential linkages between different *pays*. He showed large-scale Kentish territories reaching from riversides up into the wood-pasture of the uplands, whose people used both as resources.[3] Harold Fox, looking principally at Leicestershire and Northamptonshire, found similar traces of links between valley and wold, both in the place-names that recall 'summer slopes' and 'summer shelters' for shepherds and cowherds, and in the strongly etched droveways that still determine the routes of lanes and parish boundaries.[4] This chapter will focus on Lincolnshire. The little groups of farms studied here had economies heavily dependent on the pasture of the Lincolnshire Wolds, the long belt of chalk upland running north-east to south-west down the county: the first group clinging to the edge, the second up on the heights. But while this close dependence on pasture has been a common theme throughout preceding chapters, these Lincolnshire

---

[1] Gelling and Cole, *Landscape of Place-Names*, 253–5, at 254.
[2] Everitt, *Continuity and Colonization*, 5–6.
[3] Everitt, 'River and Wold'.
[4] Fox,' People of the Wolds'.

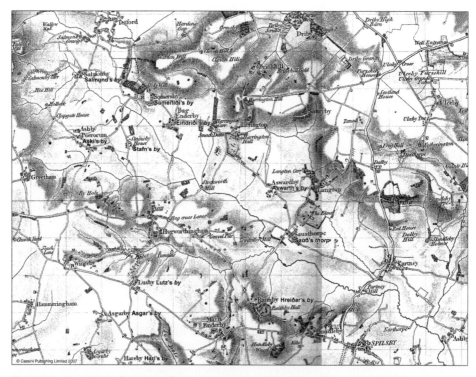

Fig. 11.1. Some Scandinavian place-names in the soke of Greetham, Lincolnshire.
(© Cassini Publishing Limited 2007)

farms are different in that we can put them in a particular cultural context: that of Scandinavian settlement.

WALESBY, OTBY, AND RISBY

Lincolnshire is an area with an unusually large number of Scandinavian names for places and people, and these are an important part of the evidence used in this chapter. Some are shown in Fig. 11.1. The kind of place-name term which is here used most frequently has the generic *-by* as its suffix with a Scandinavian personal name or a noun as a prefix, like the three discussed in this section: these are the *bys* of Val and Otti, and *hris*, 'brushwood'. *By* is a Scandinavian word which seems to mean 'farm' or 'farmstead'. The first of many problems in looking into Scandinavian settlement in England is whether the settlers used this term for something in their new surroundings that they had not hitherto encountered or whether they reproduced something that was familiar to them from their homeland. We have a small but crucial piece of evidence about this. It relates to settlement. Of two studies of settlements in Jutland during a period which includes that of the Danish invasions of England in the ninth century, one shows a trend towards greater regularity, while another stresses the coexistence of small, 'mobile' villages associated with dispersed single farmsteads.[5] So it is possible that the formation of new kinds of farm in England may have had its roots in what was beginning to happen in Denmark. However, the term *-by*, 'farm', had not been coupled with a personal name in Denmark in the way that it was in England: this usage is something new. Such names have given rise to an immense literature which has been very carefully assessed by Lesley Abrams and David Parsons. They tell us something important about their context: 'in general *-by* names are distinctively Scandinavian and were given in a purely Scandinavian, rather than an Anglo-Scandinavian context.'[6] In other words they date from *before* the time when there was a mixed population in England which had become over the years culturally 'Anglo-Scandinavian', from intermarriage and cultural choices. Rather, these names come from the period of invasion and settlement. If they date from the invasions of the mid-ninth century, or soon after, then it is possible that Otby and Risby, hanging onto the scarp edge of the north Lincolnshire wolds, were independent farms owned by Scandinavian farmers. They are within easy reach of a (very small) river crossing at Rasen (OE *ræsn*, 'plank, bridge'), which surely had some part in the local communications system, as well as a link to High Street, the Roman road from Caistor to Horncastle. Otby, 'Otti's *by*' or farm, is today a remote hill farm and Risby, 'the brushwood farm', a very small shrunken settlement. Walesby was different: it was a significant place which had formerly been part of a semi-industrial Roman iron smelting area that had supported a villa economy.[7] Walesby, established (or possibly renamed by) a Scandinavian Val, whose cross at Wal's Cross gave its name to a small hundred, Walshcroft, could well have been the centre of a small estate taken over by a Scandinavian lord. Domesday Book shows the range of resources even small places like this could call their own.[8] Otby and Risby are now part of Walesby parish but they were separately recorded in Domesday Book with substantial amounts of meadow: forty acres at Walesby and thirty-one acres at Risby. Each of the three townships today has its own large area of low-lying, and probably wet, 'moor'. All three had underwood, *silva minuta*, which was probably managed coppice.[9] The area suitable for arable must have been restricted to the thin soils over blown sand between both the scarp and the adjacent low moor and the lower slopes of the wolds.[10]

---

[5] Hamerow, *Early Medieval Settlements*, 53–8; Unwin, 'Anglo-Scandinavian rural settlement', 90.

[6] Abrams and Parsons, 'Place-names', 398.

[7] Jones, 'Romano-British settlements', 73.

[8] *Domesday Book: Lincolnshire*, 40.6; *Domesday Book: Lincolnshire*, 14.13, 16.11 (Otby), 4.20 (Risby), 40.6 (Walesby).

[9] Rackham, *History of the Countryside*, 121.

[10] Everson, 'Pre-Viking settlement', 91.

Not surprisingly this is a part of Lincolnshire where there is the lowest density of plough-teams recorded in Domesday Book.[11] Walesby supported twenty-seven families, yet only three-and-a-half teams were at work there, on land which probably included Otby. At Risby eighteen families had three teams at work on arable which is measured linearly, and may therefore have been laid out in some form of linear fields.[12]

However efficiently it was managed, the arable sector at both places seems inadequate to support such numbers of people, so this may have been an economy in which cattle played an important part. The watery riverside 'moors' and the wet woodlands could have provided plentiful summer grazing for cattle, which would have particularly relished the young alder shoots growing in the marshland of the 'carrs'. Lincolnshire in Domesday Book had about a sixth of the meadow of the whole of England and the uplands were particularly well supplied, enough to baffle Oliver Rackham, who says about this, 'I cannot explain why the men of Lincolnshire should have specialised in meadow or what they did with so much hay.'[13] If they had a lot of hay, perhaps they were feeding a lot of animals. The very generous amounts of meadow that Walesby, Risby, and Otby had in 1086 certainly suggests that enough hay could have been produced for livestock in fair numbers to have been fed there throughout the winter, and the modest numbers of plough-teams at work shows that rather few of these were working cattle. There could have been substantial herds on these manors, and if they were not being kept for work they were likely being raised for the market. This is one part of the Lincolnshire rural economy where peasant production for the market seems a distinct possibility.[14] Unfortunately Lincolnshire livestock are very elusive. Lincolnshire Domesday gives (almost) no livestock figures and when it does, it is those of the great landholder, not the run-of-the-mill farmer. As to how they were managed, we are also in the dark. The massive shift to arable farming in modern times has obscured most traces of what may once have been a considerable amount of transhumance, which at the best of times leaves a very faint archaeological imprint. But Fox has pointed us towards other kinds of information, of which the first is place-names. There are plenty of undatable and possibly quite modern names, Sheepwash, Cow Pasture, and so on, but we need pre-Conquest names, and those that appear in Domesday (or in pre-Conquest charters) are the only ones we can be sure are pre-Conquest. There are two places in Walshcroft Hundred called *Sumerlede* or *Summerlede* which cannot be identified, but from their place in the text are

---

[11] Darby, *Domesday Geography of Eastern England*, 48, Fig. 8.

[12] Darby, *Domesday Geography of Eastern England*, 60–2; *Domesday Book: Lincolnshire*, 14.13, 16.11, 40.6, 16.11, 4.20. Chapter 13 discusses other linear boundaries in Domesday Book.

[13] Darby, *Domesday Geography of Eastern England*, 62–4; Rackham, *History of the Country-side*, 335.

[14] For a fuller exposition of this suggestion, over a wider area, see Faith 'Structure of the market for wool'.

in the neighbourhood of Walesby, Risby, and Otby.[15] The name (it was also a surname in Lincolnshire) means 'summer slopes', where the stock were taken for summer grazing, and it is one of a handful of similar place-names in the county which have a 'summer' element. There are six other places with this kind of name in the county. Somerby in Yarborough Wapentake is on the edge of the Wolds, as is Horkstow, 'a shelter for lambs', further north, still along the scarp. In Scandinavian England the temporary shelters for the people in charge of the flocks and herds were called booths (ODan *boð*) and there are three Lincolnshire Boothbys. At one, Boothby Graffoe south of Lincoln, there is also a Somerton, on the Kesteven Cliff which is a smaller version of the scarp edge of the wolds. Another is south-west of Grantham, also with a Somerby nearby, in the hilly Kesteven Heath country. (It is an intriguing fact that there is a term which people who worked with sheep would have found very useful and which has a purely Scandinavian root, namely the word *kessen*, which is used to describe a sheep which has overturned, or in Lincolnshire English, 'cast', and is unable to right itself!)[16]

Fox's other source of evidence for transhumant pastoralism was the pattern of parallel droveways which took the stock from the settlements where they spent the winter up to the summer pastures and which can still be seen as the basis for modern tracks and roads and sometimes parish boundaries. These are not so clearly visible in the little area considered here as they have been in the 'parallel parishes' discussed for Essex or the many similar road patterns of Kent and Sussex. Several roads and footpaths which seem to be heading to or from the top of the Wolds end abruptly at the Roman road which runs along the top, as do modern field and parish boundaries. Where the present-day parish boundary of Walesby runs along the top of the wolds, it follows High Street. But these boundaries are a later layer in the palimpsest of the landscape, laid down when townships and manors and the church were evolved enough to need such demarcations. The wolds tops were once open common.[17]

THE UPPER LYMN VALLEY

The little river Lymn rises about a mile north east of Belchford, north-east of Horncastle, and, fed by becks, runs down small valleys between knobbly hills, and twists and turns its way south to run through the Fens to the Wash (by which point it has become the River Steeping). The upper Lymn valley has a long his-

---

[15] *Domesday Book: Lincolnshire*, 4.19, 28.22; Fellows Jensen, *Scandinavian Settlement-Names*, 70; Fox. 'People of the Wolds', 86. For *sumerliði* as a personal name meaning 'summer warrior' see Ekwall, *English Place-Names*, 430, *s.v.* 'Somerby'; Fellows Jensen, *Scandinavian Settlement-Names*, 26; Smith, *Elements*, ii, 167–8.

[16] Campion, *Lincolnshire Dialects*, 7.

[17] Winchester, *Discovering Parish Boundaries*, 57–8, for parishes bounded by Ermine Street.

tory of settlement.[18] The Roman 'small town' at Horncastle was a hub in a road system which connected the coastal ports and the salt works of the Wash to Lincoln and thence via High Street to Caistor and the Humber crossings. In the Roman period this had been an area of scattered hill farms with a strong pastoral element, serviced by a minor road system. The combination of Scandinavian place-names with Anglian archaeology shows that Scandinavian incomers took over some working farms or farm sites: Asgarby has a prestigious pre-seventh century burial in the parish; there is another Anglian burial at Aswardby and an Anglo-Saxon farmstead at Salmonby.[19] But in general settlers seem to have favoured new sites, and names of the hybrid 'Grimston' type, which gave a Scandinavian personal name like Grim to an existing place with the English suffix -*ton*, are rare here. The distribution of place-names suggests that the incomers avoided the valleys where there were large old-established settlements, detectable by their Old English names of an early type containing the element -*ingas*, such as Hagworthingham and Harrington. These big villages are about 2–3 kms apart on the prime sites on the more easily worked Spilsby sandstone, all but one south-facing. Greetham, now on Boulder Clay, had migrated from an earlier site, presumably on the river, to which *griot*, 'gravel', had given it its name. Greetham, which was the centre of the jurisdictional district known as a 'soke', is now a very small parish with no river access to speak of. Three Scandinavian *bys*, Salmonby, Ashby, and Stainsby, cut it off from the Lymn. Greetham may have originated as a large riverine estate, with a long frontage on the Lymn and its meadows and many square miles of upland pasture. Tom Williamson has made a strong case for places in Norfolk with names ending in *ham*, which can mean anything from village to farmstead, having been important, the 'core zones of estate arable or the estates themselves'.[20] They have the best land, access to the best water supply, and they became politically important as the centres of hundreds or royal estates (or both). In the Lymn valley Greetham seems to have had this role and it looks as if parts were later carved out of it to make the *bys* of Salmund, Eindriði, Aski, and Stafn.[21] Whether some of Greetham was conveyed to its new owners by sale or grant or taken by force—and it was by force that there were Danes in England at all—they remained attached to the parent settlement by the loosest of ties, that of the soke. Its people became sokemen of the soke of Greetham and their land was on its upland periphery[22] (Fig. 11.1).

---

[18] For a fuller treatment of this area see Faith, 'Structure of the market'.

[19] Fox, 'People of the Wolds', 92–4; Asgarby: White, 'Anglo-Saxon finds'; Salmonby: Everson, 'An excavated Anglo-Saxon sunken-featured building'.

[20] Wiliamson, *Origins of Norfolk*, 85–8, at 85.

[21] A feature of the southern Wolds is the dissected boundary and 'panhandles' between parishes, as at Greetham, Winceby, and Ashby. Angus Winchester has shown that these are the kind of odd shapes that result when a larger land unit has been broken up, in order to preserve access to pasture: Winchester, *Discovering Parish Boundaries*, 65–6. Much the same configuration is found on the Yorkshire Wolds: Wrathmell, *Wharram Percy*, 99–106, for a similar argument.

[22] For the social and economic position of sokemen in Lincolnshire see Faith 'Structure of the market for wool'.

It is on the low hills surrounding the Lymn valley and its tributaries that we find the *bys* of Salmund at Salmonby, Eidriði at Enderby, Sumerliði at Somersby, Aski and Stafn at Ashby and Stainsby, Asset and Lutz at Aswardby and Lusby, Raði and Hari at Raithby and Hareby, and the *thorp* of Saud at Sausthorpe. The river Lymn and its tributary becks are very often a major part of boundaries in the valley, and this is as true for the later Scandinavian intrusions into the landscape as it is for the 'primary' Anglian vills. Salmund's, Assert's and Eindriði's *bys* at Salmonby, Enderby, and Aswardby have their river frontages on the Lymn just as Harrington and Hagworthingham do. The tops and upper slopes of the Wolds are exactly the kind of land which modern agronomists classify as 'poor with thin soils overlying the chalk'. But while the upland areas that Scandinavians took over were inferior for raising crops they were very suitable for raising sheep—and the poorer the land and to some extent the worse the climate, the better quality their wool. (Hence the long wools of breeds native to many very extreme conditions: the Shetlands and Iceland at the most extreme. Even in temperate southern England it is the uplands—the South Downs, Lincolnshire, and the Cotswolds—that emerged as the prime wool-producing areas.) This may also go some way to explain the evidence for settlement in Roman Lincolnshire. As far as the limited archaeological evidence shows, this had been an area of scattered hill farms with a strong pastoral element, serviced by a minor road system which connected the area to the town at Horncastle and the main road (and water) network. In the area where Assert established his farm, Aswardby, there had been a considerable village. Roman and Scandinavian settlement are in much the same relationship at Enderby. There had been three Romano-British farms in the territory where later there were the *bys* of Aski and Stafn.[23] It is possible that many Roman sites went out of use precisely because they were not the kind that the Anglian settlers favoured. Scandinavian immigrants thus often came into a territory in which the land favoured by Romano-British farmers was lying empty. If this was the case, it was not so much a matter of newcomers having to take what land they could as of Roman hill farmers and Scandinavian incomers having a similar eye for land and its possibilities for raising sheep.

The Domesday figures for plough-teams at work on the upland *bys* show that in the eyes of the Commissioners the wold farmers were making very poor use of the area available for arable cultivation. Only small numbers of working plough-teams are recorded for the amount of land thought to be suitable for ploughing. This is the fine detail of the general picture of a generally underploughed area: Lincolnshire was a county with a very low ratio of teams to area and had an average of 2.2 oxen per person.[24] It was not a poor county, but its wealth did not come from arable farming, which was evidently in many

---

[23] Jones, 'Romano-British settlements', 69–72.
[24] Darby, *Domesday England*, 133.

places on a very small scale. While parts reached higher figures, the number of plough-teams per square mile over most of the Wolds was between one and two-and-a-half. Many people evidently made a living on very small amounts of land, or rather, on very small amounts of arable as indicated by the numbers of plough-teams they had. Three examples allow us to look a little closer.

WORLABY AND OXCOMBE

Worlaby and Oxcombe, Wulfric's *by* and the 'ox combe', are in a little range of high wolds cut by steep, stubby combes whose streams run into a small river. One of the striking things about the economy of this little region is the large number of people who were living there twenty years after the Conquest. Excluding the archbishop of York's tenant on the small demesne at Worlaby, there were thirty-five families living in the area, all but two of them headed by sokemen. We need to remind ourselves that this was two hundred years after some of these places, the *bys*, had been taken over by, or founded by, eponymous Danish settlers and their families and followers. So it is likely that they had evolved a form of husbandry compatible with the nature of the land, which by 1086 was evidently capable of supporting quite large numbers of people, probably considerably more than it had originally. If we are to get a little nearer to understanding how the economy of the people of the Wolds worked, we need to look not to their plough-teams but to their access to pasture. In other words, we should approach this landscape not as the Anglian settlers appear to have done, with an eye to riverside meadows and workable arable, but instead look to the hills. Some of the sokemen of Worlaby and Oxcombe if they were not making a living primarily from arable must have been making one from livestock. This looks like an area of classic hill-farming, where settlement is always likely to have been dispersed. There are no villages on this little stretch of the Wolds, and the small combes or dales (ON *dalr*), each with its stream, look like possible sites for the farmsteads that collectively might form little more than hamlets. This was just the kind of site that had been favoured by Romano-British farmers (or their British predecessors): the head of a little valley. The position of these farms, as well as their layout of paddocks and small fields, suggests that their owners worked their land with a strong emphasis on livestock, very much as the downland farmers discussed in Chapter 9 had done. Domesday shows that in 1086 the two settlements of Worlaby and Oxcombe had altogether between them 140 acres of meadow to support the forty-eight ploughing oxen and their supplier herds.[25] How this was economically possible can be explained by another Lincolnshire settlement in the wolds: Skammhal's *by*, Scamblesby. This is situated in steeply contoured country, but cultivation terraces a little to

---

[25] *Domesday Book: Lincolnshire*, 2.28; 3.54.

the north-west show that similarly steep slopes could be brought under the plough and the sides of the combes and the land on the 'tops' could provide a large area of open grazing for both sheep and cattle. Significantly, Oxcombe and Worlaby are now part of Maidenwell parish, which includes on the northern side of the river a large stretch of open moorland, precisely the sort of terrain that could have provided grazing land.

SOMERSBY, KETSBY, AND ENDERBY

Not all the Wolds farms were as stock oriented. The nineteenth-century boundaries of six parishes north of the Lymn meet, or nearly meet, on a stretch of the Wolds running roughly parallel with the river south-west of Tetford. This is a configuration very typical when common grazing has come to be divided up among separate communities.[26] The parishes do not all have a separate Domesday entry, but from the information given about the three that do, we can get an idea of the kind of farms they might have contained before the Conquest. Here too, on much the same kind of territory as Worlaby and Oxcombe, we find the identical phenomenon: populations which seem very large in relation to the numbers of plough-teams. The Domesday plough-team figures, although they are invaluable in giving a rough idea of the importance of arable in a given area, were intended to provide information about a manorial asset, the teams available to the population of the township, not about the individual farms, and it is clear that dividing teams to give fractions of an ox make nonsense of any attempt to allot plough animals equally between families:[27] Somersby's eleven families had two-and-a-half teams between them, Ketsby's eighteen families with the same number would have averaged less than a single ox for each family. At Ormsby, where there was one tiny holding and two larger ones, one with nineteen, averaging out the teams would have given each family eight-tenths of an ox! (It is true that Lincolnshire Domesday does have examples of people ploughing with but one ox, but this is singled out for particular notice and is likely to refer to ploughing with some kind of ard.) Instead of counting teams, we need to look for other indications of little local economies. It looks as though there were some families, such as the eight at Enderby with five-and-a-half teams, who were living in hamlets in which arable farming with some kind of field system that involved sharing plough oxen between neighbours was important. It was this part of Enderby that had a mill. The eleven families with two-and-a-half teams at Somersby, where there was also a mill, may also have been arable farmers, though in a very small way.[28] Perhaps there were a good many families whose living came not

---

[26] Winchester, *Discovering Parish Boundaries*, 61–2.
[27] *Domesday Book: Lincolnshire*, 28.36–7.
[28] *Domesday Book: Lincolnshire*, 28.3.

from their arable but from their livestock, or from working on a neighbour's farm. This may explain the fact that the upland farms and hamlets were able by 1086 to sustain many more people than traditional mixed farming with a substantial arable component would have been able to do. Extreme poverty, of the kind that comes from having too little land on which to make a living, was a feature of this part of England in the later Middle Ages.[29] Whatever the explanation, as least as far as Domesday Book records it, the southern part of the Wolds was one of the most highly populated parts of England.[30]

MARKETS

If farmers on the Wolds had surplus cattle, milk, cheese, hides, wool, or home-spun to sell, the more successful of them would not have had much difficulty in getting their products to market.[31] Remote though it may seem, this area was well served by the communications network laid down by the Romans, which remained in use—and continues to do so in many places to the present day.[32] Animals on the hoof could have been driven along the Roman road to Horncastle or Louth, crossing the river to the north at Farforth, 'the crossing point or passage for pigs or sheep', or the Lymn to the south at Tetford. Buskhow Street, now Bluestone Heath Road (another Roman road), is a south-east to north-west ridgeway bringing an important junction—possibly a market place—at Ulceby Cross within easy reach. Domesday records a 'new market' at Bolingbroke and a market at Partney on the old Roman routes to the Wash. After the Conquest peasant farmers were vitally important because cumulatively they were the most important producers of wool for the market. Evidence is simply not available to enable us to say whether this was already the case in our period, but the indirect evidence of a strongly pastoral economy on the Lincolnshire Wolds and the fact that so many families could make a living there, although apparently not from arable farming, suggests that its later fame as one of the premier wool areas of England had roots in its Anglo-Scandinavian, perhaps even in its Roman, past.[33]

---

[29] Hallam, 'Rural England and Wales', 966; 'The life of the people', 824.
[30] Darby, *Domesday England*, 94.
[31] Faith, 'Structure of the market', for the very high liquidity of pre-Conquest Lincolnshire.
[32] Owen, 'Romans and roads'.
[33] Faith, 'Structure of the market'.

12

Continuities and changes in arable husbandry

Many of the farming practices and much of the skill and knowledge described in the first five chapters of this book would continue to sustain people in the countryside for centuries to come. Although there may well always have been regional variations in tools and techniques, the exigencies of working by hand with natural materials imposed some longstanding continuities. Even when new equipment made new ways possible, as the introduction of the fixed mouldboard plough did, not all farmers adopted it. Several, probably the majority, of the farming systems described in this chapter bear this out: their small-scale arables are likely to have been worked by ards or some kind of early plough. Farmers may also have continued to cultivate traditional grains in some circumstances, and among these circumstances could well have been those where they were farming the same fields that their predecessors had. This too was the case in several parts of the country that will be described in this chapter. However, change did come, and the middle Anglo-Saxon period seems to have been a crucial time for it. Whether the 'cerealization' which is described in Chapter 2 was the result of population growth or some other cause, arable husbandry certainly changed, and the present chapter looks at some evidence for this in different parts of England over the whole of our period. The approach throughout is to attempt to construct a narrative, a sequence of one practice following another, with no claim to present an exact, or even in many cases a very rough, chronology. Broadly speaking, there was a move towards *making the land work harder*. Part of this was by reorganizing arable production. In some areas open-field farming would be the culmination of this strategy, and much attention has been paid in the past to its origins. While the following studies provide examples of places where this would certainly be the case after our period, none can show firm evidence for it before the Conquest. However, there does seem to have been a general shift away from cultivating small enclosed fields surrounding the farmstead and towards the laying out of distinctively linear fields, here referred to as 'strip fields'. There seems also to have been a tendency to rely less on infield–outfield farming, in which part of the land was under continuous cultivation and the rest was cultivated only episodically, and move instead towards cultivating the same piece of land, albeit in rotations of very varying length. Beyond suggesting that this was the broad 'direction of travel', generalization becomes hazardous, as the following small but varied examples show.

CONTINUITIES: ROMANO-BRITISH FARMING

All farmers in the past must have been skilled at making use of what was to hand. To begin with the soil. In many parts of England discussed in this chapter land would recover its fertility naturally if left uncultivated and would provide a 'nitrogen boost' when brought back into cultivation. We will see that many farmers tended to run versions of 'infield–outfield' husbandry to encourage this; it was an approach well suited to sparsely populated areas and periods of low population pressure. But in some places the land was so 'hungry' that this was not an option: if crops were to grow at all, the regular application of manure or some other nutrient was essential. West Stow in Suffolk, one of England's best-known Anglo-Saxon sites, is an example.[1] The incomers who settled at West Stow in the fifth century on the poor acid soil of the Lark Valley terraces in the Breckland of north-west Suffolk had a difficult set of circumstances to deal with. The regular distribution of early Anglo-Saxon sites in the locality along the Lark and Blackbourne rivers, some quite rich in material goods, would be hard to explain by the local soil quality, which was universally poor. This is an area where the evidence for the early Anglo-Saxon period shows signs of continuity, rather than change, in the period of immigration. 'After Rome', as probably 'before Rome' and 'under Rome', the same basic constraints would still have applied on these 'hungry' soils where 'successful cereal farming...would have had to be closely linked with stock-rearing' and 'must have included folding and the collection of manure from stalled animals'. In short, if it were not for the very different kind of houses they built and the different kind of pots that they used, we might well think that the people were farming at West Stow in much the same way as had the Romanized people of the region. They were also probably farming in a way not radically different from their eleventh-century successors. Later medieval Breckland farmers and their lords practised an intensified form of close folding, where the sheep were gathered together and folded on part of the fallow each night. In fact, manure became such a precious commodity that lords claimed rights over the output of their tenants' sheep. Local people then believed that the system had existed 'from time immemorial' and they were right, for in some form or other it probably had.

---

[1] West, *West Stow, the Anglo-Saxon Village*. For soil conditions in the area: Warner, *Origins of Suffolk*, 1–12; Bailey, *A Marginal Economy?*; Murphy, 'Iron Age to late Saxon land-use'.

Even so, the land remained low in fertility.[2] Where the soils demanded it, this extremely close integration of livestock and arable essential to keep up soil fertility may have been quite common. Farmers were well aware of its benefits.

What was also to hand for some early Anglo-Saxon farmers was a landscape deeply engrained with the practices of earlier users. Roman fields laid out on a large scale, in strips ten by thirty metres at St Ives, Huntingdonshire, or in the newly emerging rich siltland in the Wash may have left an infrastructure that was recognized and used by their Anglo-Saxon successors, farming in very similar conditions. Like their predecessors, they probably worked an infield–outfield system with an intensively cultivated core of land which was under crops year after year.[3] This 'extensive farming', as we will see, was practised in many different regions in the early to middle Anglo-Saxon period. But there are some places where it is clear that incomers made a decisive break with the past. Mucking, on the north bank of the Thames, whose settlement period site was described in Chapter 7, is one. There a new settlement and cultivation area were placed on top of what had once been a Roman field system.[4]

Elsewhere there is strong evidence that field boundaries remained in view, even if the fields within them were used in new ways.[5] As Fig. 9.2 shows, these are particularly distinct on the Wessex chalkland as mere mounds in the turf, where banks had eroded and eroded over time but they are still visible today. In our world of change, this is unexpected. It is more readily understood if we bear in mind that the downs in our period were unlikely to have been subjected to the deep ploughing, which would simply have brought masses of chalk and flint to the surface, such as can be seen today. When the mouldboard plough became generally used in these areas, as it was later, it was on the lower slopes and valley sides. If regular shallow cultivation ceased, the fields would very quickly revert to weeds and grass, and would provide useful rough grazing. In fact, it may well have been as much animals as people that ensured that very large numbers of Romano-British field boundaries remain visible.[6] Their determined nibbling would have kept at bay the regrowth of thorns, trees, and brambles which would otherwise have covered the land in dense scrub, as has happened on a great deal of the downland that we see today. Michael Costen suggests that small Romano-British fields in Somerset, laid out along long co-axial axes which themselves reflect prehistoric stock-routes, could perfectly

---

[2] Bailey, *A Marginal Economy*. West, *West Stow, the Anglo-Saxon Village*, 9–60, 108.

[3] Crowson et al., *Anglo-Saxon Settlement*; Hall and Coles, *Fenland Survey*; Taylor, *Fields*, 52–8, 67–9; Fowler, *Farming in the First Millennium*, 127–60.

[4] Hamerow, *Rural Settlements*, 15.

[5] For detailed studies of continuities in boundaries and field systems with Roman and Anglo-Saxon arrangements in East Anglia and Essex: Rippon, *Beyond the Medieval Village*, in particular 149–64.

[6] The Fields of Britannia Project, currently in progress at Exeter University under the supervision of Professor Stephen Rippon, will do much to expand this corpus. His *Beyond the Medieval Village* reviews the evidence of both coaxial and Romano-British fields in East Anglia at 149–64. There is a short survey of surviving field boundaries in Oosthuizen, 'Anglo-Saxon fields', at 381.

well have been used for livestock when the demand for grain slumped after the end of the Roman period.[7] Such continuities, although of fields of a rather different kind, were identified by Christopher Taylor in Dorset, another county where a Romanized but largely British population continued to farm under West Saxon rule much as they had always done, and the land went on being worked 'in a basically Celtic way'.[8] What can be shown to be a prehistoric tradition in Cornwall, and one which continued through the Romano-British period and after, was of enclosed stone-built hamlets surrounded by small enclosed fields (Fig. 12.1).[9] They seem suited to the kind of farming that Part I has described as a viable option for many farmers: cultivation on a small scale, using tools of the simplest kind and drawing on human labour as much as on animal traction: these are fields of a size which would have very likely been spade-dug or cross-ploughed with an ard. In fact, since spade cultivation was common in Cornwall and Devon in the medieval period and later, this would be the more likely interpretation.[10]

Unfortunately, archaeologists have traditionally been more concerned to investigate the morphology of fields than to provide us with much information about how they were used, so much is still speculative. Christopher Taylor and John Hunter have been more robust. They both suggest that small fields could have been used for arable, as units in some kind of infield–outfield system in which a field was periodically cultivated or left fallow. Some may have been used as vegetable plots, perhaps intensively manured. Shifting muck to the fields by the basketload or cartload and spreading it by hand is one of the small-scale strategies Banham suggests in Part I might have been quite common; it is still done in many parts of the world today. But muck-spreading was not the only way of preserving fertility. Taylor and Hunter both give an impression of a strikingly relaxed and unintegrated way of farming. Three factors made this possible. First, there was such a plentiful supply of pasture that the stock did not need feeding on the fallows after harvest. Second, there was such a plentiful supply of potentially arable land that it could be periodically cultivated and then left to recover its fertility naturally. And third, conversely, there was such a small supply of people that their carbohydrate needs could be satisfied from small and shifting areas of arable.[11] It is worth bearing these factors in mind when we look at other examples of early fields and farming.

Extreme examples of sparse populations in vast open landscapes are the people who in the fifth and sixth centuries were living near, or on, large areas of open moorland. Bodmin Moor is a good place to approach them, as Oliver Padel and Peter Herring have brought place-names studies together with

---

[7] Costen, *Anglo-Saxon Somerset*, 98–100.
[8] Taylor, *Dorset*, 41–8, at 77.
[9] Herring, 'West Cornwall's rough ground', 32–8; Rippon, *Beyond the Medieval Village*, 122–4.
[10] Gawne, 'Field patterns'; Herring, 'Medieval fields', 90–3.
[11] Taylor, *Fields*, 26; Hunter, 'Field systems', 5–7.

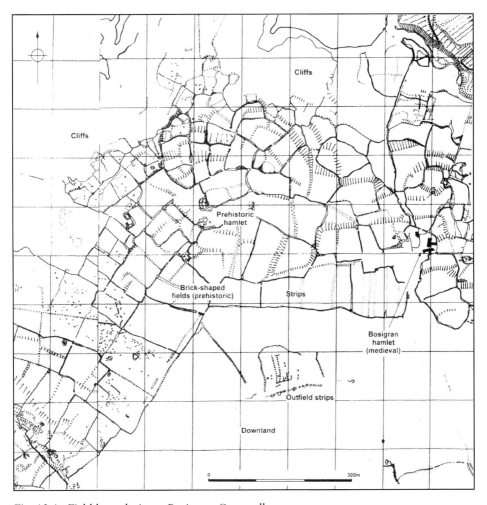

Fig. 12.1. Field boundaries at Bosigran, Cornwall.

(From Herring, 'Prehistory', in Dudley, *Goon, Hal, Cliff & Croft* © Historic Environment, Cornwall Council)

archaeology there in a very illuminating way. It might seem perverse to begin a survey of changes in farming in Anglo-Saxon England over the Anglo-Saxon period in the extreme west, which was at the beginning of our period—and in many ways remained—completely outwith Anglo-Saxon cultural and political influence. But to begin in the west has the advantage of showing how some of the changes in the farm economy came from within, arising out of the relationship of farmers to their environment rather than from any extraneous 'Germanic' influence. Moreover, the farming strategy adopted by people on Bodmin Moor turns out to have been very similar to what many farmers elsewhere were doing at much the same time. In its essentials this consisted of claiming and enclosing enough land to ensure that a small community, a 'township', had

a bounded space within which there was both room to grow its crops and protected pasture for those of its farm animals which needed to be kept close to
the farmstead. The balance between these two elements differed according to
the environment and no doubt changed over time. In some places the arable
would eventually reach the township boundary. In some areas, while the extent
of the township's land was known, a substantial physical boundary was not
found to be necessary. In some, farms eventually clustered to become hamlets
or villages, in some they remained scattered. The middle Anglo-Saxon period,
broadly conceived, seems to have been a time when this way of managing the
environment was coming into being.

CHANGES: STRIP FIELDS

Moorland

Earlier in this book it was suggested that the economy of early post-Roman and
early settlement period England was one of 'abatement', in which, while people
grew enough corn to provide essential carbohydrates, animal husbandry was
seen as providing better returns for less work. That people continued to work
the small Cornish field systems just described, with their long-established boundaries, seems a strategy particularly appropriate to this kind of rural economy, in
which little social and physical effort was invested in reorganizing the arable. If
it is right to assume that the fields were exploited on a relaxed 'infield–outfield'
system, given ample time to recover fertility between crops, this too speaks of
a similar lack of investment appropriate to small farms which could call on
almost limitless pasture for their animals. In the fields and farming systems
which succeeded them we can detect an altogether different attitude.

From the sixth or seventh century, Cornish rural life had been undergoing
some considerable changes. At the level of the homestead there was a change
from the small enclosed groups of dwellings or 'rounds' to a new kind of dispersed unenclosed farmstead, of the kind which we see today and which often
have the prefix *tre-*.[12] Another was in the way that stock was managed on the
'rough ground', as the moors were called. Herring and others have been able to
find traces of the kind of settlement which one would expect to have left the
frailest of traces in the archaeological record: the shieling or summer settlement
for the people looking after the livestock summering there. These turn out to
have had quite a well-rooted and visible presence as small settlements for the
family members, very likely single women, who were in charge of the animals
summering on the moor while dairying and spinning and weaving the wool
from a summer shearing or plucking. These shielings were common enough to

---

[12] Turner, *Making a Christian Landscape*, 29, 75–9; Rippon, *Beyond the Medieval Village*, 127–37.

appear as an element, *havos*, in Cornish place-names, paired with the *hendre* or down-country home farm.[13] The shielings on Bodmin Moor do not seem to have been kept up after the seventh century, and, although the moorland continued to be grazed, the animals were now more likely to have been kept near the farmstead. Changes in managing stock on moorland, particularly in the direction of keeping them near to the farmstead could well have made possible some important changes in arable farming, which involved a closer integration of the livestock, now nearer to hand, with the arable.

On Bodmin Moor, on the western flank of Brown Willy hill, a new kind of field was laid out (Fig. 12.2). Herring's description of this has produced one of the most archaeologically based studies of changes in farming practice that we have from anywhere in Britain.[14] Although dating evidence from the site itself is elusive, in his most recent interpretation Herring places its establishment 'at the latest in the tenth or eleventh centuries'.[15] What he presents would have represented a considerable break with the kind of farming which had simply continued to use the small fields of earlier generations. It certainly looks like the result of deliberate planning. A long perimeter boundary in the shape of a massive stone bank was laid out to produce a 'primary enclosure' or field. This was carefully subdivided into a series of regular strips which were laid off from the boundary at an angle of 65 degrees. Another 'field' was similarly laid out at the southern end of the first. The strips, effectively discrete fields, were much wider than the strips of open-field farming. They were all 108 feet (36 yards, 33 metres) in width and were separated by low stone banks, made by clearing the stone off the land.[16] They were measured out with extreme care, each measuring exactly six 'Cornish rods' of 18 feet across. They were cultivated in narrow ridges 4 to 6 feet broad, and they were laid out using the Cornish stave of 9 feet. Getting the strips of equal width seems to have been much more important than getting the lengths equal, so the areas may have differed a little (the area of each ranges from just under to just over a 'customary acre'), but it is clear that the aim was to make them all of equal value. This way of thinking about arable in terms of the width, not the area, of strips is reminiscent of the vocabulary of land measurement elsewhere in England, with its yardlands, rods, poles, and perches. It makes sense if we remember that the strips were laid out across land which varied in its quality in terms of slope and soil depth so that each strip had its share of good and poor land.[17] The new linear fields would have provided several advantages for their cultivators. The various kinds of plough with a mouldboard, which turned the earth over, described

---

[13] Herring, 'Shadows of ghosts', 89–92; Fox, 'Butter place-names'.

[14] Herring, 'Medieval fields'.

[15] Herring, 'Cornish strip fields', 73; Herring, 'Commons, fields and communities'.

[16] Herring, 'Medieval fields', 90–3, 96–9.

[17] Herring, 'Medieval fields', 81. The principle of sharing out land of different quality has frequently been invoked in discussions of the rationale of 'classical' open-field farming: e.g. Orwin, *Open Fields*, 61.

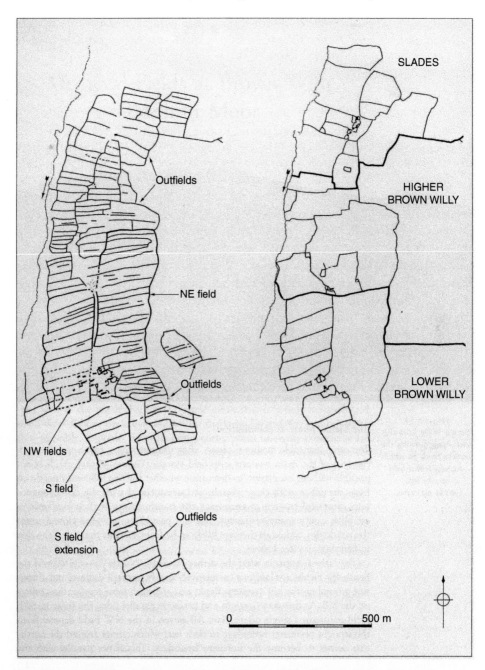

Fig. 12.2. Strip fields within an enclosure on Brown Willy, Bodmin Moor, Cornwall.

(From Herring, 'Medieval fields at Brown Willy, Bodmin Moor' © Peter Herring)

in Chapter 3 had very likely offered many advantages in cultivating fields of this shape, very different from the small squarish Romano-British fields for which intensive ard ploughing would have been appropriate. However, recent Cornish studies are not inclined to attribute the change to any specific new ploughing technology. Herring considers that these new fields were more likely to have been spade-dug than ploughed, creating 'lazy-beds', and he cites many examples of this technique on similarly stony ground in later Devon and Cornwall. It was highly labour-intensive but produced a deep and workable tilth in a way which no ard could do. (Gardeners who have created raised beds for growing vegetables will appreciate this.)[18]

In Herring's view, the fields appear to have been laid out and the land allotted for the benefit of four farmsteads, each with its own private range of small farm buildings (some were reused curved prehistoric enclosures) but 'arranged around a central area or town-place that was presumably communal.'[19] Over time, smaller fields were added, with less attention being paid to keeping the strips of equal size—fairly equal or proportionate would now do. Forming 'outfields' which supplemented the primary strip fields, these were a vital source of good hay—in short supply up on the moor—and could be temporarily brought into cultivation. Beyond the field boundaries, a long boundary was built so as to include the settlement and its fields, its water-supply, and a certain amount of rough grazing. This was stock-proof and in some places ditched, like the 'corn-ditches' on Dartmoor: we have always to remember on open ground like Bodmin Moor that it is as important to keep unwanted animals out as it is to keep the farm livestock in. Not just the domesticated sheep and cattle grazing the moor, but also deer and wild boar could devastate a growing crop. These boundaries divide the open moor, not unlike the way boundaries of what became 'manorial commons' and later parish commons do. They relate to grazing land to which a group had rights, but a group much larger than the little community on Brown Willy.

These Cornish strip fields, as far as can be deduced from later evidence, were managed very differently from the regimes of short rotations we associate with the most intensive forms of open-field farming that came to be adopted elsewhere in England. Instead, they were designed to incorporate convertible husbandry regimes which included long fallowing periods or 'leys'. But there was more to this than increasing productivity. Herring takes very seriously the strong sense of equity which underlay this decisive intervention in the landscape. He considers that the land was divided so scrupulously because creating equal shares was of prime importance and long strips of equal width were the best way to secure this. In his view the strip fields in their earliest form were the result of 'the lordly imposition of land division', the product of manorial lords'

---

[18] Herring, 'Medieval fields', 90–9.
[19] Herring, 'Medieval fields', 85.

requirement of regular tenancies in newly established 'bond hamlets'. However, as further examples in this chapter will show, the principal of equity between shareholders began to prevail even when a landlord's interest was not involved.[20] There may have been a variety of reasons, and a variety of agencies, lying behind the adoption of strip fields elsewhere in England. This is all the more likely in view of the fact that very similar developments were taking place on the Continent. Strip fields were beginning to replace small irregular 'Celtic' fields in north-west Germany in the seventh century. Hamerow has found that the form of farmsteads—the dwelling and its associated buildings—was beginning at this time to express a more individualistic sense of property and privacy. She considers that there was being established (literally) on the ground a 'direct link between the individual household and the land it cultivated'. This in turn chimes with the fact that while strip fields were laid out in ways that surely must have depended on cooperation among the members of a group, they were not necessarily cultivated in the communal way that later open fields were.[21]

East of Bodmin Moor, Dartmoor reveals extensive strip fields and more evidence for spade cultivation, although here too dating is problematic. The two 'lobe-like' enclosures on Holne Moor on its eastern side, described in Chapter 10 in the context of farming on the edge of Dartmoor, were each internally divided into four fields, which themselves were divided into ploughing strips, and were surrounded by a main boundary. The excavators, Fleming and Ralph, dated this bank to the period ending in the reign of King John when Dartmoor was royal forest, but such banks were common, and essential, before that.[22] Elizabeth Gawne, who in the 1970s mapped the field systems of the parish of Widecombe from documentary sources, and Phil Newman, who has recently assembled data from archaeological reports, both show that, as Newman says, the Dartmoor landscape 'appears to have been largely remade in the medieval period'.[23] Long narrow strip fields had been laid out, some along contours, some up and down slopes, and within them cultivation produced ridges which could have been the result of ploughing or spade cultivation. They are not the same everywhere—in some parishes the strip fields have boundary banks, in some not (and some were later walled). They are no more datable than the Brown Willy fields. In several cases they are associated with deserted settlements which were

---

[20] Herring, 'Cornish strip fields', 52–8. Herring also cites the regular obligations of 'conventionary' tenancies that can be seen in late medieval records for Cornwall. However, Cornish tenures were notably free and of the Duchy manors John Hatcher says, 'it is questionable whether they can be called manorialised at all'. Conventionary tenure 'resembled ordinary leasehold tenure' rather than the strict conditions of customary tenures elsewhere: Hatcher, *Rural Economy and Society*, 52–79, at 52. Herring and Turner both cite the spread of Christianity also as an agent of change. Turner in *Making a Christian Landscape*, 71–106, ascribes to it a transformation in the settlement pattern; Herring, 'Cornish strip fields', 73, sees it as promoting an ideology of equity.

[21] Hamerow, *Early Medieval Settlements*, 141; Dodgshon, *From Chieftains to Landlords* emphasizes the dogged individualism of runrig farmers in Scotland.

[22] Fleming and Ralph, 'Holne Moor', 101–37.

[23] Gawne, 'Field patterns'; Newman, *Field Archaeology of Dartmoor*, 88–123, quotation at 113.

established in the twelfth and thirteenth centuries, so some may have been fields set out by doomed attempts to established farms on the high moor. What they do seem to represent is extremely strong notions of equity and of the association of particular fields with particular farms. They look like the result of a determined campaign to allot hard-won arable between all those who had an interest in it. Hard-won and hard-worked: Gawne thought that the Widecombe strip fields were worked as the permanently cultivated part of an infield–outfield system.

Strip fields, however the actual cultivation was done, were evidently common in the West Country. Rippon emphasizes their differences from 'classical' open fields. While these involved all the arable of a township, the West Country strip fields were on a much smaller scale, typically taking up only 10 to 20 per cent of the cultivated ground of a parish. They lacked many of the key elements of the 'Midland' system such as common pasturing after cropping, and there was a multiplicity of fields in each township.[24] It could be that these differences are a matter only of degree, both the degree to which livestock and arable husbandry were integrated, and the degree to which the farming community was subject to commonly agreed rotations and practices. This could well have something to do with the environment and also with the size and nature of the community such field systems could support. In fully fledged open- and common-field systems livestock management needed to be closely integrated with arable farming: manuring the fallows was essential to maintain their fertility because the land was cropped so frequently. Furthermore, the fallows made a valuable contribution to winter feed. While smaller-scale field systems may have been less manure-hungry, in the rest of this chapter both environment and livestock management will be seen as continually relevant to the way that arable farming evolved in our period.

Woodland: Vale of York, Northamptonshire, Essex

Strip fields within an enclosure can be found in many parts of England. While their dating is seldom securely established—even Herring's dating of the Brown Willy example has changed over the years—the earliest datable examples, thought to be Romano-British, are at Roystone Grange in the Peak District.[25] But strip fields *look* early. They seem to have been a strategy particularly appropriate to a small group practising mixed husbandry on an unambitious scale. That they are often one element in a large enclosure points to something else as well: they were laid out by people laying claim to land.

---

[24] Rippon, *Beyond the Medieval Village*, 128–30. The fields illustrated there in Fig. 4.11 on 129, interpreted by Rippon as showing 'the fossilization of open field strips' do not have the furlong divisions of open field and look equally like a conglomeration of discrete strips, as Herring interprets the same fields in 'Cornish strip fields', 63.

[25] Roberts and Wrathmell, *Region and Place*, 99–100 and Fig. 4.12 on 100.

The study of British field systems has in the past paid very little attention to our period, but an exception was the work of June Sheppard.[26] She showed from the evidence of field names that farming in the south part of the Vale of York in the East Riding of Yorkshire after the Conquest had indeed involved individual tree clearances in the twelfth century. However, cultivation had begun before that. The farmers at what became the township of Wheldrake had built turf dykes (i.e. banks) to protect their crops from the boar and deer that abounded in woodland (Fig. 12.3). Although they were dealing with a very different environment, this was a strategy strongly reminiscent of the enclosed fields and settlements with their substantial banks that were set out on Devonshire moorlands. Within the area enclosed by the bank, cultivated land was laid out in furlongs on the easily worked sandy loams, comprising a single field of the kind that came to be called 'Old Field' or 'Town Field' in many places. Sheppard did not have any archaeological evidence for this land being held in strips, but she used the field names to support this interpretation. One of the furlongs, between the village street and the old boundary bank, was known later as 'Toft Acres', the same word as *tofteagre*, the term used in Denmark for 'strips held in severalty and continuous with the tofts to which they belonged'. Whether we should envisage this kind of arrangement as having been part of the original laying out and enclosing of the arable, or whether it is more likely to have been part of a later reorganization and reallotment of land, is another matter.[27] This infield was probably in continuous cultivation, with the cattle kept near the farms in winter to manure it and out in the wood-pasture during the rest of the year. There could also have been outfield to support the arable, and there was room within the dyke for this, so the relaxed convertible husbandry seen in Cornwall is a possibility. If we make allowances for the differences in environment, Sheppard's portrays Wheldrake as 'a hamlet with an associated small arable field set in an extensive woodland tract', a small community enclosing and intensively working just the amount of arable needed to support it and dividing the land equitably among its members, while turning its animals out in almost limitless pasture all around. This is very like the enclosed township lands and small settlements in the West Country described earlier. Sheppard found that the combination of Old Field and Town Field names in areas which have also have field-name evidence of woodland clearing was quite

---

[26] Sheppard's work, as with most of the work on field systems done at this period (Baker and Butlin's *Studies of Field Systems in the British Isles* was published in 1976), had almost no archaeological evidence to support it. While not necessarily interpreting it as evidence of an 'infield', recent work by Richard Jones shows many examples of intensive manuring near farmsteads long preceding the use of manure on open fields: Jones, 'Signatures in the soil', and Jones and Page, *Medieval Villages*, 92; so, too, Williamson, 'Development of settlement'.

[27] The field name 'Wandales', which denotes measured strips, is similarly Scandinavian, and could only have been used after Scandinavian usages had been well established in this part of Yorkshire: Sheppard, 'Field systems', 185.

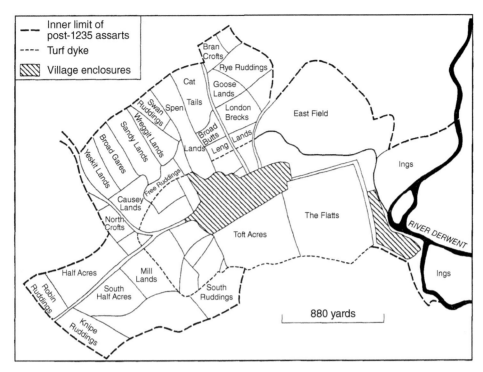

Fig. 12.3. Early enclosure at Wheldrake, Yorkshire ER.

(From Sheppard, 'Field systems of Yorkshire' © Cambridge University Press)

common in the West Riding of Yorkshire too.[28] Morphologically, and very likely in the way that they were managed, many places like Wheldrake, well bounded by its turf bank, would have been a larger scale version of the enclosed 'worthy' farms of the Hampshire Downs and the Dartmoor fringe which have been described in previous chapters: they had both pasture and arable well protected within their boundary.

The North-West

Strip fields are found in such a wide range of environments that we cannot explain them simply by the constraints that any particular environment imposed. Nicholas Higham's work on the north-west illuminates another area, albeit one with great internal differences, where open pasture was also plentiful, and easily worked land in short supply. By the time of Domesday Book this was an area of 'dispersed settlements...isolated farms and small hamlets separated one from another by fields, pasture woodland and considerable areas of inter-commoned "waste"'. The Dee valley in Cheshire was better suited to arable husbandry

---

[28] Sheppard, 'Field systems', Fig. 4.7 on 179.

than the uplands or the 'mosses', the peat moss areas of the lowland plain. While there is evidence on the ground of ridge and furrow, and evidence in maps and enclosure awards of open fields, establishing when open field husbandry was adopted here is very difficult: Higham considers the early fields were 'comparatively small groups of strips interspersed with other types of land' around the little hamlets, field systems which he describes as 'small scale and unsystematized'.[29] The farming regime was not one of regular rotations but of a single infield perennially cultivated. This was the core of what later expanded to be full open fields. Angus Winchester's mapping of township boundaries in this area shows that where land suitable for arable was in short supply pasture resources, even if those were many miles away, were vital. In the lowlands each township had its share of peat moss and moor (the local term for wetland); in the uplands each had its share of fell.[30] In the woodland areas, where people were living and farming as early as the eleventh century, massive banks occasionally make it possible to spot what may have been 'primary enclosures'. These are sometimes in pairs, enclosing farms with Old English names such as *tūn-lēah*, 'farmstead in wood-pasture', now Tunley. Set in their fields and home paddocks these farms were part of a landscape much like the small settlements in the Arden woodlands discussed in Chapter 8.[31] Higham's term 'small scale' would be a good description of many areas like this, where suitable arable land was in short supply but pasture was plentiful and there was no need to put the stock on the fallows. His word 'unsystematized' is more problematic: strip field farming may have been small-scale but that does not mean that the little groups which practised it had no ideas of order and this is a topic to which the next chapter will return.

Towards open fields

Constructing a banked enclosure, or even a solid brushwood barrier, within which an area of arable was divided into strips and intensively cultivated, was evidently seen as a good solution by many small communities. It was particularly appropriate to conditions in which native grazers flourished and where it was vitally important to keep deer and grazing domesticated livestock off the crops. An enclosure bank continued to be a feature in the north-west over the succeeding centuries, where 'its function was to protect growing crops from the trespass of stray stock but in areas that were frequently subjected to raids it also served as the first line of defence against marauders': a salutary reminder that the weather was not the only hazard that farmers had to take into account.[32]

---

[29] Higham, *Frontier Landscape*, 69; Bevan, 'Irregularity of fields'.
[30] Winchester, *North West*, 28–33.
[31] Higham, *Frontier Landscape*, 64–107.
[32] Elliott, 'Field systems of north-west England', 48.

However, there are parts of England where protection does not seem to have been seen as a priority, probably because a long tradition of clearing and cultivation had created a considerably more open and fully exploited landscape. Much more powerful people than small farmers had shaped these landscapes, in fact to move from the small enclosures to Sue Oosthuizen's study of the Bourn Valley in Cambridgeshire is not unlike moving from a peasant economy to capitalist farming. She has revealed very large-scale landscape planning from well before our period.[33] Detectable under the open fields which succeeded them, long boundaries traversed the valley. Like coaxial systems, they joined different resource areas, meadow, arable, and grazing, but Oosthuizen thinks they are in fact much more like the great linear elements on Salisbury Plain. They do not seem to have been related to transhumance—Oosthuizen uses the nice phrase 'back door grazing' to describe what was the more probable local practice—but they do seem to have been laid out in a landscape which was very sheep-oriented, possibly grazed by large flocks owned by people who had no connection with the valley-dwellers. Running across what would later become parish boundaries, these features do not seem to connect pastures with small communities in the way that, for instance, the Thames-side parishes link a spread of resources to a particular settlement.[34] A more likely shaper of this landscape could well have been the owners of a large estate at Haslingfield who controlled the area from the middle Anglo-Saxon period, profiting from a landscape that had been laid out on a large scale, perhaps by some central authority. The land was worked much harder and manured more intensively than in the small-enclosure farming systems just described. In a foretaste of the sheep–corn husbandry which became 'best practice' in a much later era, the sheep were grazed on the fallows and on the long pasture strips. What made this large-scale reordering of the landscape possible was that the land was mostly open. Where there was little woodland, there were few wild grazers, so farmed land needed no animal-proof enclosures as it did on moors and in forests.

OPEN-FIELD FARMING

The distinction between 'open-field England' and the rest of the country has been a dominant factor in much English landscape history. It is heavily influenced by the evidence for the open-field system at its fullest extent, evidence which very often is based on eighteenth or nineteenth century enclosure awards. We would get a very different picture if we were to map areas where *some form* of cooperative arable and livestock husbandry had come into being in our period. The strip fields described earlier are examples—very widespread

[33] Oosthuizen, *Landscape Decoded*.
[34] See Fig. 7.4.

examples—of exactly such farming. If we were to include the strip fields laid out in middle Anglo-Saxon period England, much more of the Highland Zone, for instance, which is taken to include Devon and Cornwall, would need to be included. So too would areas, perhaps a great many, where several distinct farming systems coexisted. Some might have been on a very small scale. Roberts and Wrathmell's wide-ranging survey concludes that, before the emergence of 'classical' open-field agriculture, the small hamlet with a block of shares in arable land was the most typical kind of settlement, and that 'similar shares in arable land were found all over England, and for that matter Scotland and Wales, in circumscribed patches of variable size'. In another wide survey Rippon agrees: 'Sub-divided fields, and cooperative practices such as communal ploughing and crop rotation, can occur at any scale...'.[35] There could well have been many places where a few neighbouring farmers thought it worthwhile embarking on common-field husbandry on a small scale, combining their patches of arable into fields and dividing it into strips. Unfortunately we cannot yet draw such a map, for our knowledge of middle Anglo-Saxon period farming is still very patchy, and there are many changes, such as those described here, which are almost impossible to date. More illuminating than a map might be a signpost, for what we seem to see is a general direction of travel, a broad highway along which many farmers were traveling at different times and at different paces. For some, the road ended in open-field farming, for others strip fields did the job and were preserved. But the highway took them all from a variety of forms of extensive agriculture towards an intensification of arable production which depended on a closer integration of livestock and arable husbandry.[36]

The dramatic reconfiguration of the landscape which open-field farming seems to represent becomes much more comprehensible if we take proper account of the fact that the small-scale strip-field systems just described could sometimes have been a preliminary stage in its development. To briefly recapitulate its major elements: the enclosure would have contained the township's land for crops and its protected pasture, perhaps an area where young stock were safe. Strip fields, while they have seldom been revealed as clearly as those on Brown Willy, are a likely form of cultivation at this stage. Of these elements, by far the most important was the boundary, for it is by establishing a boundary—even if it is as much a symbolic as a physically effective barrier—that a claim to land is expressed.

---

[35] Roberts and Wrathmell, *Region and Place*, 143; Rippon, *Beyond the Medieval Village*, 19.

[36] Thirsk, 'Origins of the common fields'. Putting the animals on the fallows was thought to be one of the chief benefits of open-field farming; in fact it has been singled out as its defining characteristic. Grazing the fallows has been attributed to a lack of other pasture, but was practised even where this was readily available: West Stow is an example (see pp. 270–1). See also Lewis, Mitchell-Fox, and Dyer, *Village, Hamlet and Field*, 147–8.

TOWNSHIP BOUNDARIES

The evidence already cited—and this is a topic which has only recently begun to be investigated—suggests that in many areas, long before they needed to take all the land within them into cultivation, people thought it important to construct boundaries. These were particularly likely to have been seen as essential in woodland or moorland, where it was necessary to guard against depredations by wild grazers. The small-scale farming systems just described did not initially bring all the land within their boundary under the plough: there was room to expand the arable area within it. This happened at Brown Willy, where common fields were established in the late Middle Ages.[37] Some studies have emphasized the fact—and it is a fact—that later evidence shows that in much of pre-enclosure England open fields reached to the township boundary. They have drawn the conclusion that this implies that the arable reached the boundary from the start. The Yorkshire Wolds provide a dramatic example. In the later Middle Ages the small enclosures of the little township of Butterwick, which itself had eclipsed the small shielings of centuries before, were swallowed up and overlaid by what were some of the largest scale open fields ever recorded in England. The central Yorkshire Wolds became an 'occupied and bounded landscape' of open fields with nucleated villages embedded in them, whose arable, laid out in immensely long strips, reached the township boundary. Several studies of the origins of open fields have argued that Domesday Book can be used as evidence for their existence by 1086. Mary Harvey, who has used Domesday Book and other documentary material to analyse the open field landscape of the Wolds, proposed that the 'fiscal holdings' in Domesday Book—the carucates and bovates on which tax was assessed—reflected the actual division of the open fields between members of the township.[38] Mary Hesse has used the linear measurements given in the Domesday Book entries for some Suffolk manors in a similar way. These linear measurements, which are unusual in Domesday Book, appear to record the length of the township boundary. In this part of Suffolk all the land of many townships is known from later evidence to have been in open fields. Hesse concluded that by 1086 the arable already stretched to what would later be its full extent and that the most likely explanation is that open fields were already in place when these measurements were made.[39] David Hall's account of the development of open-field farming in Northamptonshire also uses Domesday Book as evidence and, in his view, too, plough-teams and ploughlands express real strips in real open fields. It was the apparent consistency of these holdings over time, in some cases right down to the eighteenth century, where they can be seen almost unaltered in the

---

[37] See note 43.
[38] Harvey, 'Planned field systems', 103.
[39] Hesse, 'Domesday land measures in Suffolk'.

field books and estate maps, that led Hall to the view that the whole system of fields, furlongs, and tenancies had been laid out at a stroke.[40] So it is important to ask: 'What exactly *does* Domesday tell us about fields?'

Arable was certainly considered important in 1086: the plough is king in Domesday Book. William wanted to know the real wealth of the country he had taken, and the old system of reckoning land in terms of hides was beginning to creak at the seams. Counting plough-teams and ploughlands may have been part of a more realistic approach, and in some counties may in fact have achieved this.[41] If we approach this knotty question—and explanations involving Domesday Book are unfortunately bound to be knotty—with a longer historical perspective, we can see it rather differently. As well as plough-teams and plough-lands, Domesday sometimes recorded what have come to be known as 'fiscal tenements'. These were the fractions of a hide called yardlands (also known as virgates), of which there were four to a hide. Their Danelaw equivalents were carucates and their fractions bovates, of which there were eight to a carucate. The words 'virgate' and 'yardland', 'bovate' and 'carucate' all refer to ways of measuring ploughed land, the first pair in terms of arable measured by the rod, the second in terms of the capacity of a plough-team. In later documentation the hide was commonly reckoned at 120 acres, but we have no evidence that in 1086 the term referred to arable alone, although common sense suggests that local people would have known roughly how much arable a hide contained in their part of the world. The hide was originally not only a unit used to measure land but to assess obligations and so too were its divisions, as they long continued to be. The Domesday commissioners recorded these because they were the units on which obligation to tax (geld) was assessed. Geld was levied at so many pence to the hide. When the manor owed geld for three hides each town-shipman owed his proportionate fraction of three hides' worth. The land for which he owed his tax, and on which it was calculated, was often known as the 'assessed land' or the 'assized land' because it had been assessed, or reckoned, to establish its due share of the obligation.[42] It is in the nature of rural life that what is assigned to an individual is assigned to his land. Cola of Collaton in Devon knew by 1086 what tax Collaton had to pay, just as the nameless inhabitants of England's other townships knew that if they had a yardland, they owed a yardland's tax. (His farm is Fig. 6.1.) So when the Domesday enquiry got under

[40] Hall, *Medieval Fields*, gives a very clear account of his position.

[41] Plough-teams and ploughlands and their recording are explained by Darby, *Domesday England*, 95–134, and discussed fully by Roffe, *Decoding Domesday*, 203–9. Roffe considers them an attempt to estimate agrarian realities as opposed to the purely fiscal meaning of hides and carucates. Darby, *Domesday England*, 120, n. 2, quotes Sally Harvey to the effect that the ploughland represents 'a new fiscal assessment which took the best basis it could, given the regional character of agriculture and of local administration'. For hides and their divisions as units for the assessment of obligations see Faith, 'Hides'.

[42] The term appears in the documents of the post-Conquest manor as *terra assisa*, 'assized land'. It was known in Old English as *gesett land* as mentioned earlier (p. 193). The subject is discussed in Faith, *English Peasantry*, 103–4, 217–18, and, with reference to many mapped examples, in Roberts and Wrathmell, *Region and Place*, 182–3.

way the commissioners were able to collect this information about townships, townshipmen, and their assets from what had been common knowledge for almost a century. Only archaeology will securely tell us *when* the common fields of Northamptonshire, or anywhere else, were laid out. But, with the tax system in mind, let us suppose that, broadly speaking, *how* they were laid out worked something like this. When this important development did come about, with the entire arable of the township combined into fields divided into strips and the strips assigned, an important principle had already been embedded in rural life, that of shareholding. Farmers had long become accustomed to paying their geld according to how much land they had measured in yardlands or bovates, or fractions of yardlands or bovates. These were now the basis of each one's claim to his due share of strips—so many yardlands' or bovates' worth.

It is occasionally possible to detect traces of earlier arrangements under later open fields. The work done by Edward Martin and Max Satchell on the field systems of East Anglia has brought together a very useful body of information based on much later documents and maps and on the present-day landscape.[43] Among the large-scale open-field systems familiar from a later date, Martin has also found some places where the farmland of a settlement was laid out in very small-scale arrangements: 'subdivided closes rather than true common fields'. These tended to be clustered near the farms rather than evenly distributed across all the fields. When it came to recording these units, officialdom was not sure what they were: were they furlongs? fields? closes? What they *seem* to resemble are the small strip fields described earlier, attached to a small settlement or even a single farm. They look early and were not to last: this was a kind of farming which had largely gone by the sixteenth century, while 'true' common fields in this part of the world lasted until Parliamentary enclosure in the eighteenth.[44]

Another example comes from Wharram Percy, not only the most thoroughly investigated single place on the Yorkshire Wolds, but one of the most thoroughly investigated places in the whole of England (Fig. 12.4). Recent earthwork surveying there has brought to light the archaeology of a possible early stage in organizing the arable. Al Oswald has identified what looks like a deliberate and organized restructuring, in which the curvilinear banks and enclosures of the middle Anglo-Saxon era, very like those at Butterwick, were erased by 'unusually broad ridge and furrow ploughing' reaching to an arable boundary (it is not clear whether this means an actual boundary, or simply the extent of the later arable). This was a deliberate and wholesale reshaping of the landscape: 'an episode of ploughing, which was perhaps brief but sufficiently intense to erase enclosure banks and ditches across a wide expanse of the plateau, between the eighth

---

[43] Martin and Satchell, *Wheare Most Inclosures Be*. Herring describes the small common-field system which had replaced Brown Willy's strip fields by the thirteenth century in 'Medieval fields'.

[44] Martin, 'Not so common fields', 21.

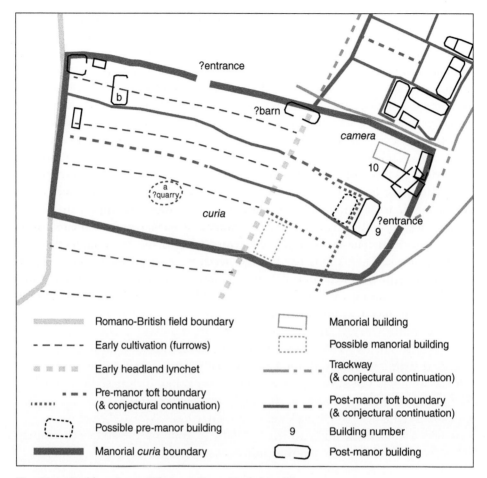

Fig. 12.4. Arable strips at Wharram Percy, Yorkshire ER.

(From Oswald, 'A new earthwork survey' © Alistair Oswald (English Heritage))

century or early ninth, and the final quarter of the twelfth century—but probably in the earlier part of that broad time-frame'. By then, the middle Anglo-Saxon curvilinear enclosures had been abandoned and a new kind of rural economy, one which was much more geared to crop production, was under way. Later Wharram, like much of the Yorkshire Wolds, became an open-field arable landscape. Perhaps this 'episode of ploughing' was its forerunner?[45]

MOVING THE FARM

Most of the changes in farming regimes described so far in this chapter did not entail moving the cultivated area: just extending it or managing it differently.

---

[45] Oswald, 'A new earthwork survey', quotation at 41.

This was not the case everywhere. In some regions, people changed not only where they lived, but where they grew their crops. A few downland farms continued late into the tenth century: Chapter 9, on Downland, gave an example of one of these: Wine's 'worthy' near Cheriton in Hampshire.[46] But by the end of our period most people had given up trying to cultivate the thin and eroded soils on the top of the chalk uplands (where centuries of ploughing by ard could well have contributed to the erosion that is still a problem today). They began to plough the heavier soils of the lower slopes and put their cattle onto the lush river meadows in the valleys. Their farmsteads moved too: we see today their strings of linear villages along the foot of the Downs. Farms established here were prime candidates for the entire 'package' of a heavier plough, open fields, and the much more organized form of pasturing on the fallows which open fields allowed. These places were among those where the renowned 'sheep–corn husbandry' would be developed, in which the animals spending the day on the downland (and for those in reach of it, Salisbury Plain) reserved their manure in order to deposit it on the fallows when they were brought in at night.[47] This was part of a widespread move in this direction which was beginning in our period and was to come to full fruition after the Conquest.

DISPERSED FARMS

The closer association of livestock and arable husbandry and a concomitant tendency to 'make the land work harder' were described earlier as the general 'direction of travel' which took many people in our period into the process of reorganizing their land in the various forms of, mostly linear, field systems that have been described in this chapter. It bears re-emphasizing that we know very little—much less than is generally assumed—about the extent to which these changes had proceeded by the end of our period. Some change looks as if it had been in the interests of powerful individuals: the lords of Haslingfield in Oosthuizen's description of the Bourn Valley in Cambridgeshire, for instance.[48] Much change, however, can be seen to have been the work of, and in the interests of, a particular group of people, the group of farmers who were becoming recognized as the 'township'. But Anglo-Saxon England was also dotted with farms which do not look like this at all. Some of them are still working farms today. They are physically different, standing alone, not in a village or hamlet, and the farmstead is generally embedded in the land of the farm, not grouped

[46] See p. 230 for the rearrangement of territory which accompanied these changes.

[47] See Chapter 9, n.21; Bettey, 'Downlands'; Fowler, *Landscape Plotted and Pieced*, 234–6; Taylor, *Dorset*.

[48] For Herring's suggestion that the Brown Willy strip fields were laid out at the behest of the estate owner see his 'Cornish strip fields', at 52. Rippon, *Beyond the Medieval Village*, makes a good case for the lessees of the powerful abbots of Glastonbury, rather than the abbots themselves, as being the agents of change which led to the creation of open fields in late Anglo-Saxon Somerset, and Faith in *English Peasantry* makes the case for lesser landlords also playing this role somewhat later.

with that of others. It is the distribution of these dispersed farms, rather than their economy, which has been the main concern of landscape studies. There is a good reason for this: for the pre-Conquest period these farmsteads are virtually invisible in the archaeological record. Very often this may be because the same site has been built on over and over again. In a few cases it is possible to see that a single farm with an Old English name has taken the place of a single Romano-British farm in the same place and with the same range of resources to deal with.[49] But the farms themselves are not quite invisible. The surviving boundaries of a few have appeared in the preceding chapters: Wine's worthy on the Hampshire Downs (Fig. 9.4) is skirted by the parish boundary; Eadda's boundary on the edge of southern Dartmoor (Fig. 10.1) survives as a low gorse-covered bank. Some *wereds*, raised dry ground on the Essex marshes (Fig. 7.6), appear in Domesday Book as substantial single farms with the livestock appropriate to a successful independent enterprise in good sheep country. Some of the small places in north-west Essex, thrived to become little 'manors' and hamlets, but others remained single farms. Many are there today, like Grim's farm with its 'woodland for 80 pigs' at Lashley on the eve of the Conquest and now gentrified as Lashley Hall (p. 209). The point about farms like these—and it cannot be stated too often how few we know anything about—is that they are not exclusively found in a particular *region* of England. They are not a regional phenomenon: they are a particular type of small economic enterprise, and can be found in a wide variety of regions. Their first salient characteristic is that the farmstead was almost certainly set within its own land (though we may not be able to locate it today). In a working day the farmer might have seen no one who did not belong to his own household: his family members and perhaps a farm worker. But a farmer in a township would have gone to work on land which was closely bordered by the land of his neighbours and he would have seen them at work not far off. The second characteristic of the dispersed farm is that its land was readily identifiable: it was hedged, banked, or bounded in some way. These two characteristics may well have influenced both their establishment and their survival. To take first their establishment. As to where to put a boundary, common sense and know-how must have been important, but so too was a knowledge of the soils. That is true of all farms, of course, but not all farms have boundaries. The boundary banks of the Dartmoor worthy farms, discussed in their Moorland setting in Chapter 9, run at precisely the line where the bracken, whose roots need comparatively deep soil, meets the gorse, which thrives in shallow soils. The Essex marshland farms of Chapter 7 are just about at the high-water mark, although their grazing grounds are liable to flood. These farms often look as if they had been laid out on chosen sites in uncontested, or not effectively contested, land. In other words, their boundaries look as if they record a confident 'marking out' of territory

[49] Gardiner, 'Late Saxon settlements'.

which was in some way *available*. If there had been settlement on the Essex marshes since the Romans gave up using them for salt and sheep, we have no record of it, and the single farms there have unambiguously Old English names. The Scandinavian sheep farmers, who established their remote farms on the Lincolnshire Wolds described in Chapter 11, were moving into spaces which the Anglian settlers of the river valleys seem to have ignored, to judge from the place-names. As far as archaeology can reveal, no one seems to have been farming on the edge of Dartmoor between the Late Bronze Age and the time, perhaps in the middle Anglo-Saxon centuries, when the 'worthy' farms were established.[50]

As to the reasons why some dispersed pre-Conquest farms have survived, we could approach this through looking at *where* they have survived, not from a regional point of view, however, but from an environmental one. In our own time technology and chemical inputs have made it possible to turn virtually any kind of land into arable. In some parts of England, land can either be grazed or put under the plough and that was also true to a certain extent in the Middle Ages, long before the vast chemical inputs of our own time. Williamson has shown how stiff, heavy land could be cultivated 'against the grain' of its natural characteristics. He has argued that the heavy soils in parts of the 'Central Region' put under the plough by open-field farming at its most developed were in fact much more suited to the predominantly livestock farming to which they later reverted. Light and thin soils could be productive if enough effort and muck were put into improving the soil structure and maintaining their fertility. He shows how skilled folding could achieve this in eastern England.[51] The Yorkshire Wolds around Wharram Percy, notable sheep walks in our period, were arable in the later Middle Ages. Today not a sheep can be seen on the farms on the Lincolnshire Wolds described in Chapter 11, which once supplied the market with wool. However, in many parts of Anglo-Saxon England, topography rather than soils would always have worked against the opportunities for putting much more land under crop, still less for embarking on a serious reorganization of the arable. The small valley farms of the South Hams region of Devon are an example. Here a multitude of places with the suffix -ton, from OE *tūn*, and prefixes derived from Old English personal names are still today single farms, not villages, although some have become small hamlets. Cola was the last farmer of Collaton before the Conquest, when, probably with a living-in farmhand, he worked it with a single team and kept a small flock, and the place has retained his name.[52] As can be seen from Fig. 6.1 it is still a small

[50] Newman, *Field Archaeology of Dartmoor*, 83 ff., has recently modified this view and suggests 'individual desertions, perhaps over centuries'. The dating referred to here is that favoured by Fyfe, 'Palaeoenvironmental perspectives', as marking a break with Romano-British practice.

[51] Williamson, *Shaping Medieval Landscapes*, 132–7.

[52] Faith, 'Cola's tun'. My thanks to the owner, Mr Eyre, for describing changes in farming at Collaton to me.

valley farm, with its grazing for cattle in the wet meadows and woods along the river, and with corn and sheep on the dry hilltop. While more of the hillside land could be brought under the plough (as in World War II, when it was ploughed by horses) there can never have been much prospect of Collaton becoming anything but a small mixed farm. This may have been true of a great number of the more isolated farms mentioned in previous chapters— the remote places in the windy uplands above the river Wye, for instance, and the Essex marshland farms. Places like these were not over-dependent on arable production in our period and so were to a great extent insulated against the shift towards reorganizing the arable fields and their management. They could even be said to have survived precisely because they were immune to the forces which were beginning to change farming. In the Somerset parishes studied by Costen, the ring-fenced 'worthy' farms at the woodland and upland borders of parishes remained much the same kind of place, while at the centre of the parish, where there were much greater possibilities for expanding arable farming, settlement became nucleated and open fields were laid out.[53] The substantial Hyde (hide) Farms which survive on the edges of parishes or in woodland are mostly undated, but their name reminds us that they had once been reckoned in the way that prevailed as a land measurement (or assessment) long before the Conquest.[54] These substantial farms are all likely to have continued to practise mixed farming, as many of them still do today.

A case can be made for seeing all the changes which have been described in this chapter as practical solutions to practical problems and that approach has produced a large body of expert scholarly literature. But a case can also be made for a change in the way that people thought about land, ownership, and community. That will be part of the subject of the final chapter.

[53] Costen 'Huish and worth'; Rippon, *Beyond the Medieval Village*, Figs. 1.4 and 1.5 at 24–5 show the contrast between the nucleated settlement of Stogursey, in western Somerset, and the dispersed farms at the edge of the parish.

[54] Costen, 'Huish and worth'; Faith, 'Hides and Hyde Farms'.

13

Conclusions

In many ways, the picture we have revealed of Anglo-Saxon farming looks very familiar: the same animals were kept (apart from the duck), and many of the same crops were grown. The land had to be cultivated in order to grow them, just as it does now, and livestock grazed on pasture, and ate hay in the winter, just as most of their successors do today. But there were also many differences. One of our reasons for writing this book was to get away from the idea that pre-industrial farming was 'static'. No period in English farming has been static. Modern readers, even young ones, will be aware of the many changes that have taken place in their lifetime, probably the most evident being the extent to which agriculture has become subject to governmental and European intervention and subsidy. The eighteenth and nineteenth centuries had been times of technical innovation and upheaval in the countryside and the early modern and medieval periods had seen change in all aspects of rural life. And we hope that we have shown that if farming in 1066 was not the same as it was in the thirteenth century, let alone in the centuries that followed, it was not even the same as it had been in the fifth.

FROM ANCIENT TO MEDIEVAL FARMING

During the period covered by this book, the landscape and food production of lowland Britain was in large measure transformed. In the early centuries following settlement, the countryside would look in many ways prehistoric to modern, or even Roman, eyes (and just as alien to later medieval ones). By the time of Domesday Book, one might have seen something recognizable as the beginnings of 'traditional English farming'.

In immediately post-Roman Britain, it is likely that farming, now freed from the demands of imperial armies, elites, and towns, with large-scale cereal production thus no longer being required, reverted to something resembling the *status quo ante*, and farmers probably went back to growing the crops that they themselves needed plus enough to support non-productive members of the population. Their own needs seem to have been supplied by the hulled cereals, emmer, einkorn, and barley, that had been grown since farming began in Britain. Meanwhile, there were evidently a sufficient number of grazing animals to prevent the landscape reverting to wilderness on a large scale. Given the thinly scattered human population at this time, livestock farming took on a renewed importance in the rural economy; using much less labour-intensive methods than either arable farming or the animal husbandry of later centuries, a small number of people could supervise fairly large numbers of livestock on extensive areas of land.

This 'abatement' was the physical context in which Anglo-Saxon settlement took place in the fourth and fifth centuries. There is no evidence that 'our Germanic ancestors' brought new farming methods with them when they arrived in Britain. This is not to say that Anglo-Saxons did not bring new ideas, seeds, even animals, only that there was no major change in the overall picture. Large-scale transformation only began later, probably gradually and at a different pace in different areas.

Signs of change become visible around the middle of the Anglo-Saxon period: free-threshing cereals, especially bread wheat, were grown more widely as hulled cereals declined in importance, and arable farming as a whole began to expand in comparison to livestock husbandry; indeed, the two must have become more and more inextricably linked as increasing numbers of livestock were kept close to human settlements. As human population expanded, the areas available for open grazing had to contract. Huge empty spaces would still be apparent to modern eyes, but these were significant reductions compared with the post-Roman period. More of England was probably ploughed, too, instead of being worked with hand tools, and this may have been the time when the heavy mouldboard plough started to make an impact. Both of these developments would mean that more oxen were needed for traction, and these animals would be kept near the arable fields where they worked, allowing those fields to be fertilized with their dung. Growing human populations would also increase the demand for animal food products, and more milking animals might be kept close to settlements to facilitate dairy production. These milking animals included sheep, as well as cows, and larger numbers of sheep must also have been kept as the wool trade expanded. It is also in the middle Anglo-Saxon period that we start to see pig pannage, with huge herds kept on wood pasture in some parts of England.

Some of these changes, such as the transition to free-threshing cereals, can be observed beginning in the middle of the Anglo-Saxon period, or even before. Others, like the increasing importance of the mouldboard plough, can only really be detected at the latter end of the period, but probably have earlier origins. The pace and geographical spread of change remains something of a conundrum. Often we have only very patchy evidence for what seems to be a new phenomenon, and it is hard to tell whether that is because it was actually a rare phenomenon, or because there is a problem with the survival of evidence. Similarly, is what appears new really new, or is it just rising above the horizon of visibility for the first time? And once a new practice was established, did it rapidly become widespread, or remain of limited importance and geographically restricted? In many cases, we can only say that what was the case at the beginning of our period had changed by the end.

Nevertheless, all these changes, if often hard to pin down, added up to a revolution in farming, not perhaps as all-encompassing as the Neolithic one, but comparable to those of the eighteenth or twentieth centuries. They had profound and long-lasting effects on the farming of England (and thus on many other aspects of economy, society, and culture) in succeeding centuries. If open-field farming, as seen in English local records from the thirteenth century onwards, was not yet in operation, the elements were available—the crops, the tools, the techniques—which allowed its development after the Conquest. Similarly, the large-scale sheep husbandry which became such a feature of late medieval English farming, and the trade which sustained it, had its beginnings in our period. While the major players in the market for wool are not our concern, we find peasant farmers whose flocks were large enough to contribute surplus to the network of markets which were such an important part of England's wool trade. The influence of Anglo-Saxon farming extended even beyond the Middle Ages: the 'suite' of crops and livestock that we take for granted today was established at this time, even though we no longer raise them in the same ways. The association between the plough and cereal crops in England also goes back to the later Anglo-Saxon period.

It is not only for its impact on later English farming that Anglo-Saxon agriculture is worth looking at, however. The sheep has lost its importance as a dairy animal, and is now losing it as a source of textile fibre, but its role in pre-Conquest England was highly significant. The horse, the object of so much sentiment as it was displaced by the tractor, had yet to enter agriculture in the early Middle Ages. The chicken and goose, and their eggs, underestimated as they have been in the archaeological literature and probably as underestimated in Anglo-Saxon England, were vital sources of protein. But the duck was not merely overlooked: it really was absent from Anglo-Saxon farmyards.

One thing that emerges very strongly from our investigations is the importance of cattle, stretching back to the pre-Christian origins of Anglo-Saxon society, when they almost certainly had ritual functions, and very possibly totemic significance, too. Even when these were lost, as Christian beliefs and practices became more widespread, cattle retained their importance, no doubt enhanced by the memory of these former roles, as a major repository of moveable wealth and a marker of status. As the largest animals raised for slaughter, their contribution to Anglo-Saxon diet must have been considerably greater than archaeological bone-counts suggest. With the growing importance, and intensification, of arable farming, the role of the oxen that pulled the plough became more and more vital, especially where the heavy mouldboard plough was in use, with its full team of eight oxen in Domesday Book.

COOPERATION

Our period can be seen as one in which people built up a fund of 'social capital' through the practice of everyday life. Anglo-Saxon farmers must have cooperated on many agricultural tasks, and shared many resources. Because this was also a feature of later open-field farming, but not of commercial post-enclosure agriculture, there has been a tendency to associate any evidence for cooperation with open fields. But it was probably an extremely common phenomenon, limited only by the availability of neighbours, especially in areas where settlement was dispersed. Cooperation has certainly not been limited to arable farming at any period: just as Ine of Wessex envisaged that *ceorls* might have 'grass *or* crops' in common, so, as late as the 1960s, haymaking was an occasion when neighbouring households, down to eleven-year-olds, could be called upon to help. Tasks that, like haymaking, require a concentrated burst of activity, are always most likely to have been carried out in cooperation.

It is unlikely there were written bylaws in Anglo-Saxon England, as in the later Middle Ages, to ensure that no one felt unfairly exploited and all could rely on each other. The Anglo-Saxon written sources that do deal with the business of making sure that agricultural tasks got done, the *Rectitudines* and *Gerefa*, unfortunately focus on vertical relationships, between landlords, and their representatives, and the people who did the work, and have little to say about the equally vital horizontal ones, between the people who needed to get on with each other in order to complete the work in time, and indeed to live alongside each other all year. After Ine's time, written royal law also ceased to intervene in rural affairs. Local custom must have been passed down by word of mouth, but people must also have had a strong 'instinctive' feeling of mutual obligation, of 'what was right', based on shared experience, to guide them in such matters. If the whole community turned out to help a certain farmer to plough or make hay, everyone involved would have a clear idea of what sort of reciprocation should be expected, but that idea is unfortunately lost to us for ever.

ORGANIZATION

It was this sense of mutual obligation, the 'moral economy' of the peasantry, that made possible the considerable degree of organization seen in the Anglo-Saxon countryside. The formidable tariffs which the lawcodes record of compensation for personal injury, even if somewhat formulaic, show that country life was not all cooperation and contentment. But they also show that there were thought to be appropriate ways of settling quarrels which might otherwise lead to violence. The Hundred Ordinance of Edgar's reign has an impressive set of procedures for dealing with that most fundamental of rural crimes, cattle theft, which may simply codify long-established practice.

An important element in this organization by the end of our period was the township—Latin *villa*, OE *tunscipe*—the basic social entity in the countryside, with communal responsibilities and some kind of administrative capability. This seems to be irrespective of settlement layout and distribution: the township is a group of neighbouring farms, whether clustered or dispersed. In the enquiries from which Domesday Book was compiled, the township has a vital role in supplying information. It had a fiscal role too: however small his share of land, every free landholder, as a member of the township, owed his share of geld. By the time of Domesday, it was known to all, and often marked out on the ground, what exactly the township's land, the 'townland', included (and it was on some townlands that the change to open field farming would take place).

SCALE

If by the end of our period the township was an important part of how life was organized in the countryside, that may be because over the whole of the period Anglo-Saxon farmers were living in a world that was, in perceptual terms, shrinking. Their prehistoric predecessors managed it on a grand scale, only divided it on a large scale, and envisaged it on a large scale too. Prehistoric 'coaxial' boundary systems can be read as recording long-distance movements of animals to and from pastures, but these large-scale demarcations of the landscape were not just of practical significance at the time they were laid out. Moving animals through the land was of course as familiar to Anglo-Saxon farmers as to their prehistoric predecessors, and putting animals out on common land which was never used for cultivation continued to be the mainstay of many farms for centuries to come. But it looks as if the scale on which this was done, both in terms of the numbers of animals moved and the distances that they were moved, was becoming much smaller in our period. Common pastures seem to be envisaged less as belonging to whole territories, like the 'shire fen', and seen increasingly from the point of view of individual settlements. It would not be true to say that long-distance pasturing disappeared: particularly in the Highland Zone distant pastures continued to be used, as they are in some regions today. But, within huge areas of grazing used by many communities, there were beginning to be areas reserved to, and policed by, particular townships, perhaps the forerunners of parish or manorial 'commons'. By the end of our period, the township, its townland, and its commons expressed the boundaries of many people's working world.

REORGANIZATION

The essential factors for a change to open-field farming were in place, or coming into place, in our period. But the necessity and the evidence for such a change have proved very elusive. There were many factors at work which brought about the changes that we do find towards more intensive farming: a growing population, increased pressure from landlords, and the growth of the market. Farmers were evidently quite capable of making both individual and collective decisions about what they grew and how they grew it, how and when they ploughed, how they managed their livestock. As members of tithings and townships they had responsibilities towards other townships and to the larger hundred and shire. Already we see that important group in later English rural history, independent farmers with a voice in local government. But these farmers do not seem to have felt the need to undertake the major reorganization of the landscape represented by open-field farming. It may be that in this, as in other aspects of rural life, it was the steep population growth of the twelfth and early thirteenth centuries that brought about profound change. That more people were being fed implies that there had been an increase in arable capacity. The small arable systems we have found in many areas of England would certainly have allowed for their expansion within the township boundary.

That is not to say that no reorganization took place, however. We have seen the appearance of 'strip-fields' in different parts of the country, and the subdivision of previously wide-open pasture. The increasing integration of arable and pastoral operations must have led to changes in the layout of farmland, as well as greater use of physical boundaries. Settlement nucleation, too, where it took place, will have changed the appearance of the landscape. It is very likely that reorganization took place even where we can now see no trace of it. In fact, the familiar rural landscape features of the present day, not only the fields and hedges of enclosure, but medieval ridge and furrow too, must have obliterated the evidence for most Anglo-Saxon organization of farmland, just as they are themselves being destroyed by agrarian change and urbanization in the twenty-first century.

GEOGRAPHICAL VARIATION

England encompasses a wide variety of terrain, in terms of soil, underlying geology, and even climate. The studies in Part II of this book show that these differences led to very various strategies being adopted by Anglo-Saxon farmers in different places. Some of their choices may not have been forced upon them by their environment, of course: every decision was the result of a calculation that took into account what the farmer wanted to do, as well as what circumstances allowed. A good deal of variation would no doubt be observable at a very small scale, if we were able to go back to Anglo-Saxon England and look at it, as well as more obvious large-scale regional differences. Even though most Anglo-Saxon farmers were, as we saw in Chapter 5, 'generalists', the balance between different elements on individual farms might vary hugely. Some of this would certainly be due to cultural tradition, 'the way we've always done things round here', or even 'in our family', as well as the social emulation that probably made bread wheat such an important crop, or the demands of landlords, or of markets. A very important result of this would be that changes might proceed very slowly, and at different rates in different places, due not only to whether a farmer was able to adopt new practices, but also whether he wanted to. Not everybody would want to copy their neighbours, or it might take several generations before the advantages of unfamiliar ways of doing things became apparent. Although every Anglo-Saxon farmer was facing essentially the same set of challenges—how to feed a household, as well as having to render to various power figures the payments they felt entitled to, with only very meagre resources to call upon—the ways in which these challenges were overcome must have been infinite in their variety.

A SUSTAINABLE AGRICULTURAL SYSTEM

Anglo-Saxon farming was sustainable because it had to be: there was no other means of livelihood to fall back on. Although the exploitation of the land in our period would be classed as 'low-input' and 'low-impact' by modern analysis, Anglo-Saxon farmers were using their resources as economically as they knew how, and would let nothing go to waste. A versatile animal like the sheep was enormously useful in this respect: subsisting on pasture that might not support cattle, during its lifetime it produced high-calorie food that could, in the form of cheese, be preserved for winter, as well as providing wool to keep people warm, and at the end of its life it yielded more food, along with skin, horn, and bone. Pigs and poultry, too, using up free food that would otherwise go to waste, were major contributors to sustainability. Diversification would mean that a disaster affecting one crop, or species of livestock, would not leave people completely destitute, even if life became more of a struggle than usual.

We have argued that our period was one of intensification: as population grew, more food had to be extracted from the same natural resources. The land was never anywhere near its 'carrying capacity', indeed there must have been huge areas of open country by modern standards, but there may well have been a *perceived* shortage of land in some places, and for some purposes, leading farmers to adopt new methods. 'Cerealization' allowed more calories to be produced from the same acreage than by livestock farming. More animals also had to be kept on more restricted areas of land, and probably more fodder crops raised to feed them. Resources that had once been freely available to all were increasingly parcelled out among owners and holders of rights. Cerealization itself probably led to an intensification of livestock husbandry, as more oxen were needed to intensify arable operations.

But intensification does not seem to have led to fundamental problems. The famines reported in the Anglo-Saxon Chronicle show that such events were exceptional (even if they seemed to come thick and fast in some periods). Most of the time, most people could expect to have enough to eat. Not a great deal, by modern standards, in most cases, but enough to preserve life. Although changes must have been traumatic for some people, and no doubt caused real suffering, on a larger scale Anglo-Saxon farming adapted to new circumstances and supported a growing population, including a prosperous ruling class and an increasing number of towns. Anglo-Saxon farming was thus not only innovative, but successful. This was the basis of the prosperity that made England worth conquering, twice, in the eleventh century.

Whether Anglo-Saxon farming has lessons for the twenty-first century is another matter: the Anglo-Saxon population was tiny by modern standards, and largely rural, and most of it was producing its own food. Transport issues were limited to carting food rents and tithes over distances of a few miles, and storage was a matter for individual households, even if some of those were huge aristocratic or ecclesiastical ones. It would be impossible to return to Anglo-Saxon conditions, to provide every household in modern England with a hide of land to grow their own food on, or even the yardland (quarter hide) of later peasants, and few modern English households would know what to do with it if they were given one. The Anglo-Saxons' low-input, low-impact methods could not be replicated in modern conditions, but they do show how peasant farming, which has served the human race well over most of history and across the world, has worked in lowland Britain. At a time when looming environmental disaster can be attributed at least partly to intensive farming methods, and food prices are going up, not just because foodstuffs themselves are more expensive, but because most of the cost goes on oil for transport, there is surely an argument for growing more food nearer to where it is needed, and relying less on manufactured chemicals and machinery (which in turn depend on oil), and for exploiting more of the by-products of farming, rather than having to dispose of them at great expense, again largely on fuel. Anglo-Saxon farming offers examples of thrifty and workable agricultural methods and strategies that may look increasingly attractive as the twenty-first century progresses.

Glossary

aftermath regrowth after a meadow has been mown or, by extension, after a crop has been harvested

bellwether a wether (q.v.) which leads the flock, and can be located by the sound of its bell

bullock a young ox

cotsetla (OE) a cottager

coulter an iron 'knife' at the front of a plough, that cuts into the soil vertically to guide the ploughshare

fallow (adjective, of arable land) not currently growing crops

fallow (verb, of arable land) to keep temporarily free of crops

feorm literally 'hospitality', a render of agricultural produce, originally to kings, by extension to lords and religious communities

fold (noun) an enclosure for livestock, to confine and protect them; may be temporary, made of hurdles, or permanent

fold (verb) to place or keep livestock in a fold, especially, of sheep, on arable land, in order to for them to deposit their dung

free-threshing (of cereals) with no inner chaff adhering to the grain, so that they are ready for milling after threshing; not hulled

gafol tribute or rent

gebur (OE) a peasant of low status, generally holding land on the inland (q.v.) of an estate

geneat (OE) a peasant whose duties towards a lord were less demeaning than those of lower status

gore (derived from OE *gar*, 'a spear(head)') a triangular field or section of a field

headland a strip, usually uncultivated, along the edge of a field, on which the plough and team turn

hulled (of cereals) with inner chaff adhering to the grain, so that they need extra processing after threshing before they can be ground into flour

inland the portion of an estate devoted to providing produce for the owner and containing the housing and smallholdings of the inland workers

mast woodland forage, usually for pigs, usually acorns and beechnuts

mouldboard the part of a plough (originally wooden) which turns the soil over, located behind the share *open fields* unfenced arable fields in which members of a community have shares

ox the castrated male offspring of a cow, usually employed in traction

pannage feeding pigs in wood-pasture, especially fattening them on mast in the autumn

secondary products foods etc. provided by livestock during their lifetime, for example, milk, eggs

share the main cutting part of a plough, usually made of iron, which slices into the soil horizontally

stint (restriction on) number of animals someone is entitled to keep on common pasture

tathe the urine and manure deposited by sheep kept within an enclosure, used to enrich and warm the soil

thegn (OE) an Anglo-Saxon above the level of the peasantry, but without high office or territorial responsibility; lowest level of the aristocracy

transhumance seasonal movement of livestock away from the settlement to which they belong

wether a castrated male sheep

Bibliography

Place of publication is London except where stated.

Abrams, L., and D. N. Parsons, 'Place-names and the history of Scandinavian settlement', in J. Hines, A. Lane, and M. Redknap (eds), *Land, Sea and Home: Settlement in the Viking Period*, Society of Medieval Archaeology Monograph, 20 (Leeds, 2004), 379–431.

Adams, I. H., *Agrarian Landscape Terms: A Glossary for Historical Geography*, Institute of British Geographers Special Publication, 9 (1976).

Addyman, P., D. Leigh, and M. J. Hughes, 'Anglo-Saxon houses at Chalton, Hampshire', *Medieval Archaeology*, 17 (1973), 1–25.

Albarella, U., 'Pig husbandry and pork consumption in medieval England', in Woolgar, Serjeantson, and Waldron (eds), *Food in Medieval England*, 72–87.

Albarella, U., 'The wild boar', in O'Connor and Sykes (eds), *Extinctions and Invasions*, 59–67.

Albarella, U., 'Size, power, wool and veal: zooarchaeological evidence for late medieval innovations', in G. de Boe and F. Verhaeghe (eds), *Environment and Subsistence in Medieval Europe*, Papers of the Medieval Europe Brugge 1997 Conference, 9 (Zellik, 1997), 19–30.

Albarella, U., 'Tawyers, tanners, horn trade, and the mystery of the missing goat', in P. Murphy and P. E. J. Wiltshire (eds), *The Environmental Archaeology of Industry*, Symposia of the Association of Environmental Archaeology, 20 (Oxford, 2003), 71–83.

Albarella, U., 'Alternate fortunes? The role of domestic ducks and geese from Roman to medieval times in Britain', in G. Grupe and J. Peters (eds), *Feathers, Grit and Symbolism: Birds and Humans in the Ancient Old and New Worlds*, Documenta archaeobiologiae, 3 (Rahden, 2005), 249–58.

Albarella, U., K. Dobney, A. Ervynck, and P. Rowley-Conwy (eds), *Pigs and Humans: 10,000 years of Interaction* (Oxford, 2007).

Albarella, U., F. Manconi, J.-D. Vigne, and P. Rowley-Conwy, 'Ethnoarchaeology of pig husbandry in Sardinia and Corsica', in Alabarella, Dobney, Ervynck, and Rowley-Conwy (eds), *Pigs and Humans*, 285–307.

Alderson, L., *A Chance to Survive: Rare Breeds in a Changing World* (London and Newton Abbot, 1978).

Anderson, L., 'The molecular basis for phenotypic changes during pig domestication', in Albarella, Dobney, Ervynck, and Rowley-Conwy (eds), *Pigs and Humans*, 42–54.

Anderson, O. S., *The Old English Hundred-Names* (Lund, 1934).

Andrews, P. (ed.), *Excavations at Hamwic*, ii: *Excavations at Six Dials*, CBA Research Report, 109 (1997).

anon., 'Archaeologists find "cow-woman" in Anglo-Saxon dig', Manchester Metropolitan University News, <http://www.mmu.ac.uk/news/news-items/1594/> (accessed 8 August 2012).

anon., *Overview of Coastal Sand Dunes, Saltmarsh and Vegetated Shingle by Natural Area*, English Nature Reserve Research Reports, 317 (Peterborough, 1999).

Applebaum, S., 'Roman Britain', in Finberg (ed.), *Agrarian History*, i.2: 3–277.

Armitage, P., 'The animal bone', in Leary et al., *Tatberht's Lundenwic*, 28–35.

Armitage, P. L., and J. A. Goodall, 'Medieval horned and polled sheep: the archaeological and iconographic evidence', *Antiquaries Journal*, 57 (1977), 73–89.

Ash, H. B. (ed. and tr.), *Columella*, i: *De re rustica I–IV* (Cambridge, MA, 1941).

Astill, G., 'Fields', in Astill and Grant (eds), *The Countryside of Medieval England*, 62–85.

Astill, G., 'An archaeological approach to the development of agricultural technologies in medieval England', in Astill and Langdon (eds), *Medieval Farming and Technology*, 193–223.

Astill, G., and A. Grant (eds), *The Countryside of Medieval England* (Oxford, 1988).

Astill, G., and J. Langdon (eds), *Medieval Farming and Technology: The Impact of Agricultural Change in Northwest Europe* (Leiden, 1997).

Aston, M., and C. Lewis (eds), *The Medieval Landscape of Wessex* (Oxford, 1994).

Atkin, M., 'Hollin names in north-west England', *Nomina*, 12 (1988–9), 77–88.

Attenborough, F. L. (ed. and tr.), *The Laws of the Earliest English Kings* (Cambridge, 1922).

Ayres, K., C. Ingrem, J. Light, A. Locker, J. Mulville, and D. Serjeantson, 'Mammal, bird and fish remains, and oysters', in Hardy, Dodd, and Keevill, *Ælfric's Abbey*, 341–432.

Backhouse, J., *Medieval Rural Life in the Luttrell Psalter* (2000).

Bailey, M., *A Marginal Economy: East Anglian Breckland in the Later Middle Ages* (Cambridge, 1989).

Baker, A. R. H., and R. A. Butlin (eds), *Studies of Field Systems in the British Isles* (Cambridge, 1973).

Baker, P. S., and M. Lapidge (eds), *Byrhtferth's Enchiridion*, EETS ss, 15 (Oxford, 1995).

Ballantyne, R., 'Charred and mineralised biota', in G.Thomas, *The Later Anglo-Saxon Settlement at Bishopstone*, 164–76.

Banham, D., '"In the sweat of thy brow shalt thou eat bread": cereals and cereal production in the Anglo-Saxon landscape', in Higham and Ryan (eds), *The Landscape Archaeology of Anglo-Saxon England*, 175–92.

Banham, D., *Food and Drink in Anglo-Saxon England* (Stroud, 2004).

Banham, D., 'Race and tillage: Scandinavian influence on Anglo-Saxon agriculture?', in M. Kilpiö, L. Kahlas-Tarkka, J. Roberts, and O. Timofeeva (eds), *Anglo-Saxons and the North: Essays Reflecting the Theme of the Tenth Meeting of the International Society of Anglo-Saxonists in Helsinki, August 2001* (Tempe, AZ, 2009), 165–92.

Banham, D., 'The staff of life: cross and blessings in Anglo-Saxon cereal production', in S. L. Keefer, K. L. Jolly, and C. E. Karkov (eds), *Cross and Cruciform in the Anglo-Saxon World: Studies to Honor the Memory of Timothy Reuter*, Sancta Crux/Halig Rod, 3 (Morgantown, WV, 2010), 279–318.

Banham, D., '*Orceard* and *lectun*: a preliminary survey of the evidence for horticulture in Anglo-Saxon England', in G. Owen-Crocker (ed.), *The Anglo-Saxons: The World Through Their Eyes* (Oxford, 2014).

Banham, D. A. R., 'The Knowledge and Uses of Food Plants in Anglo-Saxon England' (unpublished PhD dissertation, University of Cambridge, 1990).

Barber, L., and G. Priestly-Bell, *Medieval Adaptation, Settlement and Economy of a Coastal Wetland: The Evidence from around Lydd, Romney Marsh, Kent* (Oxford and Oakville, CT, 2008).

Barnes, G., and T. Williamson, *Hedgerow History: Ecology, History and Landscape Character* (Macclesfield, 2006).

Barrett, J., A. M. Locker, and C. M. Roberts, '"Dark Age Economics" revisited: the English fishbone evidence, AD 600–1600', *Antiquity*, 78 (2004), 618–36.

Bassett, S., 'In search of the origins of Anglo-Saxon kingdoms', in S. Bassett (ed.), *The Origins of Anglo-Saxon Kingdoms* (Leicester, 1989), 1–27.

Bassett, S., 'Continuity and fission in the Anglo-Saxon landscape: the origins of the Rodings (Essex)', *Landscape History*, 19 (1997), 25–42.

Bately, J. (ed.), *The Old English Orosius*, EETS ss, 6 (Oxford, 1980).

Bately, J. (ed.), *The Anglo-Saxon Chronicle: MS A*, The Anglo-Saxon Chronicle: A Collaborative Edition, 3 (Cambridge, 1986).

Baxter, I., 'A donkey (*Equus asinus* L.) partial skeleton from a mid–late Anglo-Saxon alluvial layer at Deans Yard, Westminster, London SW1', *Environmental Archaeology*, 7 (2002), 89–94.

Beckett, J. V., *A History of Laxton: England's Last Open Field Village* (Oxford, 1989).

Bender-Jorgensen, L., *North European Textiles until AD 1000* (Aarhus, 1992).

Bendrey, R., 'The horse', in O'Connor and Sykes (eds), *Extinctions and Invasions*, 10–16.

Benton, P., *The History of Rochford Hundred*, 2 vols (Rochford, 1867).

Berryman, R. D., *Use of the Woodlands in the Late Anglo-Saxon Period*, BAR, British Series, 271 (Oxford, 1988).

Bettey, J., 'Downlands', in Thirsk (ed.), *The English Rural Landscape*, 27–49.

Biffen, R. H. (ed.), *Elements of Agriculture…by…W. Fream* (12th edn, London, 1932).

Bil, A., *The Sheiling: The Case of the Central Scottish Highlands* (Edinburgh, 1990).

Birch, W. de Gray (ed.), *Cartularium Saxonicum: A Collection of Charters relating to Anglo-Saxon History*, 3 vols and index (1885–99).

Birrell, J. 'Peasant craftsmen in the medieval forest', *Agricultural History Review*, 17 (1969), 91–107.

Blair, J., *Early Medieval Surrey: Landholding, Church and Settlement* (Stroud, 1991).

Blair, J., *Anglo-Saxon Oxfordshire* (Stroud, 1994).

Blair, J., *The Anglo-Saxon Age: A Very Short Introduction* (Oxford, 2000).

Blair, J., *The Church in Anglo-Saxon Society* (Oxford, 2005).

Bogaard, A., 'Middening and manuring in Neolithic Europe: issues of plausibility, intensity and archaeological method', in R. Jones (ed.), *Manure Matters*, 25–39.

Bökönyi, S., 'Horse', in I. L. Mason (ed.), *Evolution of Domesticated Animals*, 162–73.

Bökönyi, S., 'The development of stockbreeding and herding in medieval Europe', in D. Sweeney (ed.), *Agriculture in the Middle Ages: Technology, Practice and Representation* (Philadelphia, 1995), 62–75.

Bond, C. J., 'Fishing', in Lapidge, Blair, Keynes, and Scragg (eds), *The Wiley Blackwell Encyclopedia of Anglo-Saxon England*, 190–1.

Bond, D. A., 'Faba bean', in Smartt and Simmonds (eds), *Evolution of Crop Plants*, 312–16.

Bond, J. M., 'Burnt offerings: animal bone in Anglo-Saxon cremations', *World Archaeology*, 28 (1996), 76–88.

Booth, P., A. Dodd, M. Robinson, and A. Smith, *The Thames Through Time: The Archaeology of the Gravel Terraces of the Upper and Middle Thames*, i: *Early Historical Period, AD 1–1000*, Oxford Archaeology Thames Valley Landscapes Monograph, 27 (Oxford, 2007).

Bosworth, J., and T. N. Toller, *An Anglo-Saxon Dictionary* (Oxford, 1890), *Supplement* by T. N. Toller (Oxford, 1921), and *Enlarged Addenda and Corrigenda* by A. Campbell (Oxford, 1972).

Bottema, S., T. C. van Hoorne, H. Woldring, and W. H. E. Gremmen, 'An agricultural experiment in an unprotected salt marsh, part 2', *Palaeohistoria*, 18 (1980), 127–40.

Bourdillon, J., 'Countryside and town: the animal resources of Saxon Southampton', in Hooke (ed.), *Anglo-Saxon Settlements*, 177–95.

Bourdillon, J., and J. Coy, 'The animal bones', in P. Holdsworth, *Excavations at Melbourne Street, Southampton 1971–76* (1980), 79–121.

Bowie, G., 'Corn drying kilns, meal milling and flour in Ireland', *Folk Life*, 17 (1979), 5–13.

Boyden, P. 'A study in the structure of landholding and administration in Essex in the late Anglo-Saxon period' (unpublished PhD thesis, University of London, 1986).

Brady, N., 'Food production in medieval Ireland: aspects of arable husbandry', in Klápště and Sommer (eds), *Processing, Storage, Distribution*, 137–43.

Brady, N., 'Labor and agriculture in early medieval Ireland: evidence from the sources', in A. J. Frantzen and D. Moffat (eds), *The Work of Work: Servitude, Slavery and Labour in Medieval England* (Glasgow, 1994), 125–45.

Britnell, R., *The Commercialisation of English Society, 1000–1500* (Manchester, 1996).

Bruce-Mitford, R., *The Sutton Hoo Ship Burial: A Handbook* (1979).

Burroughs, W. J., *Climate Change: A Multidisciplinary Approach* (2nd edn, Cambridge, 2007).

Butler, J., *Dartmoor Atlas of Antiquities*, v: *The Second Millennium* BC (Tiverton, 1997).

Cam, H., *Liberties and Communities in Medieval England: Collected Studies in Local Administration and Topography* (1963).

Cameron, E., and Q. Mould, 'Devil's crafts and dragon's skins? Sheaths, shoes and other leatherwork', in Hyer and Owen-Crocker (eds), *The Material Culture of Daily Living*, 93–115.

Campbell, B. M. S., *English Seigniorial Agriculture, 1250–1450* (Cambridge, 2000).

Campbell, G., 'The preliminary archaeobotanical results from Anglo-Saxon West Cotton and Raunds', in J. Rackham (ed.), *Environment and Economy in Anglo-Saxon England*, 65–82.

Campbell, J., E. John, and P. Wormald, *The Anglo-Saxons* (Oxford, 1982).

Campion, E., *Lincolnshire Dialects* (Boston, 1976).

Carver, M., 'Contemporary artefacts illustrated in late Saxon manuscripts', *Archaeologia*, 108 (1987), 117–45.

Carver, M., 'Pre-Viking traffic in the North Sea', in S. McGrail (ed.), *Maritime Celts, Frisian and Saxons: Papers presented to a Conference at Oxford in November 1988*, CBA Research Report, 71 (1990), 117–25.

Carver, M., *Sutton Hoo: A Seventh-Century Princely Burial Ground and its Context* (2005).

Carver, M., *The Birth of a Borough: An Archaeological Study of Anglo-Saxon Stafford* (Woodbridge, 2010).

Casiday, A., 'St Aldhelm's bees (*De uirginitate prosa*, cc. iv–vi)', *ASE*, 33 (2004), 1–22.

Castell, M., 'Sweetness for salt', *Country Smallholder* (March 2005), 18–19.

Chadwick, A. (ed.), *Recent Approaches to the Archaeology of Land Allotment*, BAR, International Series, 1875 (Oxford, 2008).

Charles-Edwards, T., 'The distinction between land and moveable wealth in Anglo-Saxon England', in P. H. Sawyer (ed.), *English Medieval Settlement* (1979), 97–104.

Chatwin, D., and M. Gardiner, 'Rethinking the early settlement of woodlands', *Landscape History*, 27 (2005), 31–49.

Christie, N., and P. Stamper (eds), *Medieval Rural Settlement: Britain and Ireland, AD 800–1600* (Oxford, 2012).

Clapham, A. R., T. G. Tutin, and D. M. Moore, *Flora of the British Isles* (3rd edn, Cambridge, 1987).

Clayton, G. A., 'Common duck', in I. L. Mason (ed.), *Evolution of Domesticated Animals*, 334–9.

Clutton-Brock, J., 'Origins of the dog: domestication and early history', in Serpell (ed.), *The Domestic Dog*, 7–20.

Clutton-Brock, J., *Horse Power: A History of the Horse and Donkey in Human Societies* (1992).

Clutton-Brock, J., *A Natural History of Domesticated Animals* (Cambridge, 1999).

Coates, R., and A. Breeze, *Celtic Voices, English Places: Studies of the Celtic Impact on Place-Names in England* (Stamford, 2000).

Cobbett, W., *Cottage Economy* (Bath, 1975).

Cockayne, T. O, (ed.), *Leechdoms, Wortcunning and Starcraft of Early England*, 3 vols, Rolls Series, 35 (1864–6).

Cole, A., 'The distribution and use of *mere* as a generic in place-names', *English Place-Name Society Journal*, 25 (1992–3), 38–50.

Cole, A., '*Weg*: a waggoner's warning', in Padel and Parsons (eds), *A Commodity of Good Names*, 345–9.

Colgrave, B. (ed. and tr.), *Two Lives of St Cuthbert* (Cambridge, 1940).

Colgrave, B., and R. A. B. Mynors (eds and trs), *Bede's Ecclesiastical History of the English People* (Oxford, 1969).

Comet, G., 'Technology and agricultural expansion in the middle ages: the example of France north of the Loire', in Astill and Langdon (eds), *Medieval Farming and Technology*, 11–39.

Cooke, N., F. Brown, and C. Phillpotts, *From Hunter-Gatherers to Huntsmen: A History of the Stansted Landscape*, Framework Archaeology Monograph, 2 (Oxford and Salisbury, 2008).

Cool, H. E. M., *Eating and Drinking in Roman Britain* (Cambridge, 2006).

Coppinger, R., and R. Schnieder, 'Evolution of working dogs', in Serpell (ed.), *The Domestic Dog*, 21–47.

Corbet, G. C., and J. Clutton-Brock, 'Appendix: Taxonomy and nomenclature', in I. L. Mason (ed.), *Evolution of Domesticated Animals*, 434–8.

Costen, M., 'Settlement in Wessex in the tenth century: the charter evidence', in Aston and Lewis (eds), *The Medieval Landscape of Wessex*, 97–113.

Costen, M., 'Huish and worth: Old English survivals in a later landscape', *Anglo-Saxon Studies in Archaeology and History*, 5 (1992), 65–83.

Costen, M., *Anglo-Saxon Somerset* (Oxford and Oakville, CT, 2011).

Crabtree, P. J., 'Animal exploitation in East Anglian villages', in J. Rackham (ed.), *Environment and Economy in Anglo-Saxon England*, 23–9.

Crabtree, P., 'Production and consumption in an early complex society: animal use in middle Saxon East Anglia', *World Archaeology*, 28 (1996), 58–75.

Crabtree, P., 'Animals as material culture in Middle Saxon England: the zooarchaeological evidence for wool production at Brandon', in A. Pluskowski (ed.), *Breaking and Shaping Beastly Bodies: Animals as Material Culture in the Middle Ages* (Oxford, 2007), 161–9.

Crabtree, P. J., *West Stow, Suffolk: Early Anglo-Saxon Animal Husbandry*, East Anglian Archaeology, 47 (Ipswich, 1989).

Crane, E., *The Archaeology of Beekeeping* (1983).

Crane, E., *The World History of Beekeeping and Honey Hunting* (1999).

Crawford, O. G. S., *The Andover District: An Account of Sheet 283 of the One-Inch Ordnance Map* (Oxford, 1922).

Crawford, R. D., 'Domestic fowl', in I. L. Mason (ed.), *Evolution of Domesticated Animals*, 298–311.

Crawford, R. D., 'Goose', in I. L. Mason (ed.), *Evolution of Domesticated Animals*, 345–9.

Creasey, J. S., *The Draught Ox* (Reading, 1974).

Crouch, D., and C. Ward, *The Allotment: Its Landscape and Culture* (1988).

Crowson, A., T. Lane, K. Penn, and D. Trimble, *Anglo-Saxon Settlement on the Siltland of Eastern England*, Lincolnshire Archaeology and Heritage Reports, 7 (Exeter, 2005).

Cunliffe, B., 'Saxon and medieval settlement pattern in the region of Chalton, Hampshire', *Medieval Archaeology*, 16 (1972), 1–12.

Cunliffe, B., 'Chalton, Hants.: the evolution of a landscape', *Antiquaries Journal*, 53 (1973), 173–90.

Cunliffe, B., *Wessex to AD 1000* (1993).

Currie, C., 'Saxon charters and landscape evolution in the south-central Hampshire basin', *Proceedings of the Hampshire Field Club and Archaeological Society*, 49 (1994), 103–25.

Curwen, E. C., 'More about querns', *Antiquity* 15 (1941), 15–32.

Darby, H. C., *The Domesday Geography of Eastern England* (Cambridge, 1952).

Darby, H. C., *Domesday England* (Cambridge, [1977], pbk repr., 1989).

Darby, H. C., and I. B. Territt, *Domesday Geography of Midland England* (Cambridge, 1954).

Darby, H. C., and E. M. J. Campbell, *The Domesday Geography of South-East England* (Cambridge, 1962).

Darby, H. C., and R. W. Finn, *The Domesday Geography of South-west England* (Cambridge, 1967).

Dark, K., *From Civitas to Kingdom: British Political Continuity 300–800* (Leicester, 1994).

Dark, P., *The Environment of Britain in the First Millennium* (2000).

Darlington, R. R., and P. McGurk (eds), *The Chronicle of John of Worcester* (Oxford, 1995).

Davies, D. R., 'Peas', in Smartt and Simmonds (eds), *Evolution of Crop Plants*, 294–6.

Davies, W., '*Liber Landavensis*: construction and credibility', *EHR*, 88 (1979), 335–51.

Davies, W., 'Roman settlements and post-Roman estates in south-east Wales', in P. J. Casey (ed.), *The End of Roman Britain*, BAR, British Series, 71 (Oxford, 1979).

Davies, W., *Wales in the Early Middle Ages* (Leicester, 1982).

Davies, W., *Water Mills and Cattle Standards: Probing the Economic Comparison between Ireland and Spain in the Early Middle Ages*, Chadwick Lecture, 21 (Cambridge, 2011).

Davies, W., and H. Vierck, 'The contexts of the Tribal Hidage', *Frühmittelalterliche Studien*, 8 (1974), 223–93.

de la Cruz Cabanillas, I., 'Shift of meaning in the animal field: some cases of narrowing and widening', in I. Moskowich-Spiegel and B. Crespo-Garcia (eds), *Bells Chiming from the Past: Cultural and Linguistic Studies on Early English*, Costerus, NS, 174 (Amsterdam and New York, 2007), 139–50.

de Moor, Janny, 'Farmhouse Gouda: a Dutch family business', in Harlan Walker (ed.), *Milk: Beyond the Dairy. Proceedings of the Oxford Symposium on Food and Cookery 1999* (Totnes, 2000), 106–16.

Deveson, A., 'The ceorls of Hurstbourne revisited', *Proceedings of the Hampshire Field Club and Archaeological Society*, 64 (2009), 105–15.

DiNapoli, R., *An Index of Theme and Image to the Homilies of the Anglo-Saxon Church* (Hockwold-cum-Wilton, 1995).

Dixon, P., 'Hunting, summer grazing and settlement: competing land use in the uplands of Scotland', in Klápště and Pesez (eds), *Medieval Rural Settlement in Marginal Landscapes*, 27–46.

Dixon, P., 'Of bannocks and ale: cereal processing in Scotland, c. 1100–1750', in Klápště and Sommer (eds), *Processing, Storage, Distribution*, 155–72.

Dobbie, E. van K., *The Anglo-Saxon Minor Poems*, Anglo-Saxon Poetic Records, 6 (1942).

Dobney, K., A. Ervynck, U. Albarella, and P. Rowley-Conwy, 'The transition from wild boar to domestic pig in Eurasia, illustrated by a tooth developmental defect and biometric data', in Albarella, Dobney, Ervynck, and Rowley-Conwy (eds), *Pigs and Humans*, 57–82.

Dobney, K., D. Jaques, C. Johnstone, A. Hall, B. la Ferla, and S. Haynes, 'The agricultural economy', in Dobney, Jaques, Barrett, and Johnstone, *Farmers, Monks and Aristocrats*, 116–89.

Dobney, K, D. Jaques, J. Barrett, and C. Johnstone, 'Evidence for trade and contact', in Dobney, Jaques, Barrett, and Johnstone, *Farmers, Monks and Aristocrats*, 214.

Dobney, K., D. Jaques, and C. Johnstone, 'Pastoral strategies: animal husbandry', in Loveluck (ed.), *Rural Settlement, Lifestyles and Social Change*, 87–90.

Dobney, K., D. Jaques, J. Barrett, C. Johnstone, J. Carrott, and A. Hall, 'Patterns of disposal and processing', in Dobney, Jaques, Barrett, and Johnstone, *Farmers, Monks and Aristocrats*, 70–115.

Dobney, K., D. Jaques, J. Barrett, and C. Johnstone, 'Zooarchaeological evidence for the nature and character of the settlement', in Dobney, Jaques, Barrett, and Johnstone, *Farmers, Monks and Aristocrats*, 217–45.

Dobney, K., D. Jaques, J. Barrett, and C. Johnstone, *Farmers, Monks and Aristocrats: The Environmental Archaeology of Anglo-Saxon Flixborough*, Excavations at Flixborough, 3 (Oxford, 2007).

Dodgshon, R. A., *The Origins of British Field Systems: An Interpretation* (1980).

Dodgshon, R. A., *From Chiefs to Landlords: Social and Economic Change in the Western Highlands c. 1493–1820* (Edinburgh, 1998).

Domesday Book: Cambridgeshire, ed. A. Rumble (Chichester, 1981).

Domesday Book: Devon, ed. C. and F. Thorn (Chichester, 1985).

Domesday Book: Essex, ed. P. Morgan and C. Thorn (Chichester, 1986).

Domesday Book: Gloucestershire, ed. J. S. Moore (Chichester, 1982).

Domesday Book: Lincolnshire, ed. A. Rumble (Chichester, 1983).

Domesday Book: Warwickshire, ed. J. Plaister (Chichester, 1976).

Dudley, P. (ed.), *Goon, Hal, Cliff & Croft: The Archaeology and History of West Cornwall's Rough Ground* (Truro, 2011).

Dyer, C., 'Farming practice and techniques: the West Midlands', in Miller (ed.), *The Agrarian History of England and Wales*, iii, 222–38.

Dyer, C., *Lords and Peasants in a Changing Society: The Estates of the Bishopric of Worcester, 680–1540* (Cambridge, 1980).

Dyer, C., *Standards of Living in the Later Middle Ages: Social Change in England c. 1200–1520* (Cambridge, 1989).

Dyer, C., 'Alternative agriculture: goats in medieval England', in R. W. Hoyle (ed.), *People, Landscape and Alternative Agriculture: Essays for Joan Thirsk*, Agricultural History Review Supplement, 3 (2004), 20–38.

Dyer, C., and P. Everson, 'The development of the study of medieval settlements, 1880–2010', in Christie and Stamper (eds), *Medieval Rural Settlement*, 11–30.

Eagles, B., 'The archaeological evidence for settlement in the fifth to seventh centuries AD', in Aston and Lewis (eds), *The Medieval Landscape of Wessex*, 13–32.

Eagles, B., with contributions by R. Faith, '"Small shires" and *regiones* in Hampshire and the formation of the shires of eastern Wessex', *Anglo-Saxon Studies in Archaeology and History* (forthcoming).

Ehwald, R. (ed.), *Aldhelmi opera*, MGH, Auctores antiquissimi, 15 (Berlin, 1919).

Ekwall, E., *The Concise Oxford Dictionary of English Place-Names* (4th edn, Oxford, 1960).

Elliot, G., 'The field systems of north-west England', in Baker and Butlin (eds), *Studies of Field Systems*, 41–92.

Ellis, Frank, *Peasant Economics: Farm Households and Agrarian Development* (Cambridge, 1988).

Elwes, H. J., *Guide to the Primitive Breeds of Sheep and their Crosses* (Trowbridge, 1983).

Emery, F., *The Oxfordshire Landscape* (1974).

Epstein, H., 'Ass, mule and onager', in I. L. Mason (ed.), *Evolution of Domesticated Animals*, 174–84.

Epstein, H., and M. Bichard, 'Pig', in I. L. Mason (ed.), *Evolution of Domesticated Animals*, 145–62.

Ervynck, A., A. Lentacker, G. Müldner, M. Richards, and K. Dobney, 'An investigation into the transition from forest dwelling pigs to farm animals in medieval Flanders, Belgium', in Albarella, Dobney, Ervynck, and Rowley-Conwy (eds), *Pigs and Humans*, 171–93.

Essex County Council Planning Department, Archaeology Section, *Archaeology of the Essex Coast: The Hullbridge Basin Survey, Interim Reports 1982–7* (Chelmsford, n.d.).

Evans, D. H., and C. Loveluck (eds), *Life and Economy at Early Medieval Flixborough c. AD 600–1000: The Artefact Evidence*, Excavations at Flixborough, 2 (Oxford, 2009).

Evans, G. E., *Ask the Fellows who cut the Hay* (1956).

Evans, G. M., 'Rye', in Smartt and Simmonds (eds), *Evolution of Crop Plants*, 166–70.

Everitt, A., 'Common land', in Thirsk (ed.), *The English Rural Landscape*, 210–35.

Everitt, A., 'River and wold: reflections on the historical origins of region and *pays*', *Journal of Historical Geography*, 3 (1977), 1–19.

Everitt, A., *Continuity and Colonization: The Evolution of Kentish Settlement* (Leicester, 1986).

Everitt, A., 'Farm labourers', in J. Thirsk (ed.), *The Agrarian History of England and Wales*, v: *1500–1640* (Cambridge, 1996), 396–65.

Everson, P. L., 'An excavated sunken-featured building and settlement site at Salmonby, Lincs., 1972', *Lincolnshire History and Archaeology*, 8 (1998), 61–70.

Faith, R., 'Hides and Hyde Farms in central and southern England: a preliminary report', *Medieval Settlement Research Group Report*, 13 (1998), 33–8.

Faith, R., 'Tidenham, Gloucestershire, and the history of the manor in England', *Landscape History*, 16 (1994), 39–51.

Faith, R., *The English Peasantry and the Growth of Lordship* (1997).

Faith, R., 'Cola's tun: rural social structure in late Anglo-Saxon Devon', in R. Evans (ed.), *Lordship and Learning: Studies in Memory of Trevor Aston* (Woodbridge, 2004), 63–78.

Faith, R., 'Forces and relations of production in early medieval England', *Journal of Agrarian Change*, 9.1 (2009), 23–41.

Faith, R., 'The structure of the market for wool in early medieval Lincolnshire', *Economic History Review*, 65 (2011), 674–700.

Faith, R., 'Some Devon farms before the Norman Conquest', in Turner and Sylvester (eds), *Life in Medieval Landscapes*, 73–88.

Faith, R., '*Tūn* and *lēah* in the rural economy', in R. Jones and S. Semple (eds), *A Sense of Place in Anglo-Saxon England* (Donington, 2012), 238–42.

Feldman, M., F. G. H. Lupton, and T. E. Miller, 'Wheats', in Smartt and Simmonds (eds), *Evolution of Crop Plants*, 184–92.

Fellows-Jensen, G., *Scandinavian Settlement Names in the East Midlands* (Copenhagen, 1978).

Fenton, A., *Scottish Country Life* (Edinburgh, 1976).

Fenton, A., *The Northern Isles* (Edinburgh, 1978).

Fern, C., 'The archaeological evidence for equestrianism in early Anglo-Saxon England, *c.* 450–700', in A. Pluskowski (ed.), *Just Skin and Bones? New Perspectives on Human–Animal Relations in the Historical Past*, BAR, International Series, 1410 (Oxford, 2005), 43–71.

Fern, C., 'Early Anglo-Saxon horse burial of the fifth to seventh centuries AD', *Anglo-Saxon Studies in Archaeology and History*, 14 (2007), 92–109.

Finberg, H. P. R., *Gloucestershire* (1955).

Finberg, H. P. R., *Tavistock Abbey: A Study in the Social and Economic History of Devon* (Newton Abbot, 1969).

Finberg, H. P. R., 'Anglo-Saxon England to 1042', in Finberg (ed.), *The Agrarian History of England and Wales*, i.2, 383–525.

Finberg, H. P. R. (ed.), *The Agrarian History of England and Wales*, i.2: *AD 43–1042* (Cambridge, 1972).

Finn, R. W., 'Devonshire', in Darby (ed.), *The Domesday Geography of South-West England*, 223–95.

Flechner, R., 'The making of the Canons of Theodore', *Peritia* 17–18 (2003–4), 121–43.

Fleming, A., 'Working with wood-pasture', in Turner and Sylvester (eds), *Life in Medieval Landscapes*, 15–31.

Fleming, A., 'Prehistoric Dartmoor in its context', *Proceedings Devon Archaeological Society*, 37 (1979), 115–31.

Fleming, A., 'The prehistoric landscape of Dartmoor: wider implications', *Landscape History*, 6 (1984), 5–19.

Fleming, A., *The Dartmoor Reaves: Investigating Prehistoric Land Divisions* (1988; 2nd edn, Oxford, 2008).

Fleming, A., and Ralph, N., 'Medieval settlement and land use on Holne Moor, Dartmoor: the landscape evidence', *Medieval Archaeology*, 25 (1988), 101–37.

Fleming, R., *Britain after Rome: The Fall and Rise, 400–1070* (2nd edn, 2011).

Fogwill, E. G., 'Pastoralism on Dartmoor', *Transactions of the Devonshire Association*, 86 (1954), 89–114.

Forsyth, A. A., *British Poisonous Plants* (2nd edn, 1968).

Fowler, P., 'Farming in the Anglo-Saxon landscape: an archaeologist's review', *ASE*, 9 (1980), 263–80.

Fowler, P., *Landscape Plotted and Pieced: Landscape History and Local Archaeology in Fyfield and Overton, Wiltshire* (2000).

Fowler, P., *Farming in the First Millennium AD: British Agriculture between Julius Caesar and William the Conqueror* (Cambridge, 2002).

Fowler, P. J., *The Farming of Prehistoric Britain* (Cambridge, 1983).

Fox, H., 'Approaches to the adoption of the Midland system', in Rowley (ed.), *The Origins of Open-Field Agriculture*, 64–111.

Fox, H., 'Butter place-names and transhumance', in Padel and Parsons (eds), *A Commodity of Good Names*, 352–64.

Fox, H., 'The alleged transformation from two-field to three-field systems in medieval England', *Economic History Review*, 2nd ser., 39 (1986), 526–48.

Fox, H., *Dartmoor's Alluring Uplands: Transhumance and Pastoral Management on Dartmoor, 950–1550* (Exeter, 2012).

Fox, H. S. A., 'Farming practice and techniques: Devon and Cornwall', in Miller (ed.), *The Agrarian History of England and Wales*, iii, 303–23.

Fox, H. S. A., 'The people of the Wolds in English settlement history', in M. Aston and C. Dyer (eds), *The Rural Settlements of Medieval England: Studies dedicated to Maurice Beresford and John Hurst* (Oxford, 1988), 77–101.

Fox, H. S. A. (ed.), *Seasonal Settlement: Papers Presented to the December Meeting of the Medieval Settlement Research Group 1993* (Leicester, 1996).

Francis, S., *British Field Crops* (2nd edn, West Stow, 2009).

Fry, E. A. (ed.), *Abstracts of Inquisitiones Post Mortem for Gloucestershire: Returned into the Court of Chancery in the Plantagenet Period*, pt. 5: *30 Edward I to 32 Edward III, 1302–1358* (1910).

Fyfe, R. M., 'Paleoenvironmental perspectives on medieval landscape development', in S. Turner (ed.), *Medieval Devon and Cornwall: Shaping an Ancient Countryside* (Macclesfield, 2006), 10–23.

Fyfe, R. M., A. G. Brown, and S. J. Rippon, 'Characterising the late prehistoric, "Romano-British" and medieval landscape, and dating the emergence of a regionally distinct agricultural system in South West Britain', *Journal of Archaeological Science*, 31 (2004), 1699–714.

Gaffney, V., and M. Tingle, *The Maddle Farm Project: An Integrated Survey of Prehistoric and Roman Landscapes on the Berkshire Downs*, BAR, British Series, 200 (Oxford, 1989).

Gailey, A., and A. Fenton (eds), *The Spade in Northern and Atlantic Europe* (Belfast, 1970).

Gameson, R., 'The archaeology of the Anglo-Saxon book', in Hamerow, Hinton, and Crawford (eds), *The Oxford Handbook of Anglo-Saxon Archaeology*, 797–823.

Gardiner, M., 'Time regained: booley huts and seasonal settlement in the Mourne Mountains, County Down, Ireland', in Turner and Sylvester (eds), *Life in Medieval Landscapes*, 106–24.

Gardiner, M., 'Late Saxon settlements', in Hamerow, Hinton, and Crawford (eds), *The Oxford Handbook of Anglo-Saxon Archaeology*, 198–217.

Garmonsway, G. N. (ed.), *Ælfric's Colloquy* (revised edn, Exeter, 1991).

Gautier, A., 'How do I count you, let me count the ways? Problems of archaeozoological quantification', in C. Grigson and J. Clutton-Brock (eds), *Animals and Archaeology*, iv: *Husbandry in Europe*, BAR, International Series, 227 (Oxford, 1984), 237–51.

Gautier, A., 'Cooking and cuisine in late Anglo-Saxon England', *ASE*, 41 (2013), 373–406.

Gawne, E., 'Field patterns in Widecombe parish and the Forest of Dartmoor', *Proceedings of the Devonshire Archaeological Society*, 52 (1963), 101–18.

Gelling, M., 'Some notes on Warwickshire place-names', *Transactions of the Birmingham and Warwickshire Archaeological Society*, 86 (1974), 59–79.

Gelling, M., 'The place-names of the Mucking area', *Panorama: Journal of the Thurrock Local History Society*, 19 (1975), 7–20.

Gelling, M., *Place-Names in the Landscape: The Geographical Roots of Britain's Place-Names* (1984).

Gelling, M., *The West Midlands in the Early Middle Ages* (Leicester, 1992).

Gelling, M., and A. Cole, *The Landscape of Place-Names* (Stamford, 2000).

Gillard, M., 'The Medieval Settlement of the Exmoor Region: Enclosure and Settlement in an Upland Region' (unpublished PhD thesis, Exeter University, 2002).

Gover, J. E. B., A. Mawer, and F. M. Stenton, *The Place-Names of Devon*, 2 vols, English Place-Name Society, 8–9 (Cambridge, 1931–2).

Graeber, D., *Debt: The First 5000 Years* (New York, 2002).

Grant, A., 'Animal resources', in Astill and Grant (eds), *The Countryside of Medieval England*, 149–87.

Greig, J., R. Pelling, M. Robinson, and C. Stevens, 'Environmental evidence', in Hey (ed.), *Yarnton*, 351–409.

Grigson, C., 'Culture, ecology, and pigs from the 5th to the 3rd millennium BC around the Fertile Crescent', in Albarella, Dobney, Ervynck, and Rowley-Conwy (eds), *Pigs and Humans*, 83–108.

Grocock, Christopher, '"To eat, to wear, to work": the place of sheep and cattle in the economy', in Hyer and Owen-Crocker (eds), *The Material Culture of Daily Living*, 73–92.

Groenewoudt, B. J., 'The visibility of storage', in Klápště and Sommer (eds), *Processing, Storage, Distribution*, 187–97.

Groves, C., 'Current views on taxonomy and zoogeography of the genus *Sus*', in Albarella, Dobney, Ervynck, and Rowley-Conwy (eds), *Pigs and Humans*, 15–41.

Grundy, G. B., 'The Saxon land charters of Hampshire, with notes on place and field names', *Archaeological Journal*, 87 (1921), 69–77.

Grundy, G. B., *Saxon Charters and Field Names of Gloucestershire*, 2 parts ([Bristol], 1935–6).

Gwara, S., and D. W. Porter (eds), *Anglo-Saxon Conversations: The Colloquies of Ælfric Bata* (Woodbridge, 1997).

Haddan, A. W., and W. Stubbs (eds), *Councils and Ecclesiastical Documents relating to Great Britain and Ireland*, 3 vols (Oxford, 1869–78).

Hagen, A., *A Second Handbook of Anglo-Saxon Food and Drink: Production and Distribution* (Hockwold-cum-Wilton, 1995).

Haldane, A. R. B., *The Drove Roads of Scotland* (Newton Abbot, 1973).

Hale, W. H. (ed.), *The Domesday of St Pauls of the Year MCCXXII or Registrum de visitatione maneriorum per Robertum decanum*, Camden Society, 69 (1858).

Hall, A., and H. Kenward, 'Setting people in their environment: plant and animal remains from Anglo-Scandinavian York', in R. A. Hall (ed.), *Aspects of Anglo-Scandinavian York*, 372–426.

Hall, A. R., and J. P. Huntley, *A Review of the Evidence for Macrofossil Plant Remains from Archaeological Deposits in Northern England*, [English Heritage] Research Department Report Series, 87–2007 (2007).

Hall, D., 'Field systems and landholdings in the Wharram parishes', in Wrathmell (ed.), *A History of Wharram Percy*, 278–90.

Hall, D., *Medieval Fields* (Princes Risborough, 1982).

Hall, D., and J. Coles, *Fenland Survey: An Essay in Landscape and Persistence*, English Heritage Archaeological Report, 1 (1994).

Hall, R. A., *Aspects of Anglo-Scandinavian York*, The Archaeology of York, 8.4 (York, 2004).

Hallam, H. E., 'England before the Conquest', in Hallam (ed.), *The Agrarian History of England and Wales*, ii, 1–44.

Hallam, H. E., 'The life of the people', in Hallam (ed.), *The Agrarian History of England and Wales*, ii, 816–53.

Hallam, H. E., 'Rural England and Wales, 1042–1350', in Hallam (ed.), *The Agrarian History of England and Wales*, ii, 966–1008.

Hallam, H. E. (ed.), *The Agrarian History of England and Wales*, ii: *AD 1042–1350* (Cambridge, 1988).

Hamerow, H., 'Anglo-Saxon timber buildings and their social context', in Hamerow, Hinton, and Crawford (eds), *Oxford Handbook of Anglo-Saxon Archaeology*, 128–55.

Hamerow, H., 'Overview: rural settlement', in Hamerow, Hinton, and Crawford (eds), *Oxford Handbook of Anglo-Saxon Archaeology*, 119–27.

Hamerow, H., *Mucking*, ii: *The Anglo-Saxon Settlement* (1993).

Hamerow, H., *Early Medieval Settlements: An Archaeology of Rural Communities in North-West Europe 400–900* (Oxford, 2002).

Hamerow, H., 'Special deposits in Anglo-Saxon settlements', *Medieval Archaeology*, 50 (2006), 1–30.

Hamerow, H., 'Agrarian production and the *emporia* of mid-Saxon England, c. 650–850', in J. Henning (ed.), *Post-Roman Towns: Trade and Settlement in Europe and Byzantium*, i: *The Heirs of the Roman West* (Berlin and New York, 2008), 219–32.

Hamerow, H., *Rural Settlements and Society in Anglo-Saxon England* (Oxford, 2012).

Hamerow, H., D. A. Hinton, and S. Crawford (eds), *The Oxford Handbook of Anglo-Saxon Archaeology* (Oxford, 2011).

Hammon, A., 'The brown bear', in O'Connor and Sykes (eds), *Extinctions and Invasions*, 95–103.

Hams, F., *Old Poultry Breeds* (3rd edn, Princes Risborough, 1999).

Hardy, A., A. Dodd, and G. D. Keevil, *Ælfric's Abbey: Excavations at Eynsham Abbey, Oxfordshire, 1989–92* (Oxford, 2003).

Harlan, J. R., 'Barley', in Smartt and Simmonds (eds), *Evolution of Crop Plants*, 140–7.

Harlan, J. R., The Living Fields: Our Agricultural Heritage (Cambridge, 1995).

Harmer, F. E. (ed.), *Anglo-Saxon Writs* (2nd edn, Stamford, 1989).

Harmer, F. E. (ed.), *Select English Historical Documents of the Ninth and Tenth Centuries* (Cambridge, 1914).

Harper, J., 'The tardy domestication of the duck', *Agricultural History*, 46 (1972), 385–9.

Hart, C. R., *The Early Charters of Barking Abbey* (Colchester, 1953).

Hart, C. R., *The Early Charters of Eastern England*, Studies in Early English History, 5 (Leicester, 1966).

Hart, C. R., *The Early Charters of Essex*, University of Leicester, Dept. of English Local History, Occasional Papers, 1st ser., 10 (2nd edn., Leicester, 1971).

Hart, E., *The Practice of Hefting* (Ludlow, n.d.).

Harvey, M., 'Planned field systems in East Yorkshire: some thoughts on their origin', *Agricultural History Review*, 31 (1983), 91–103.

Harvey, P. D. A., '*Rectitudines singularum personarum* and *Gerefa*', EHR, 108 (1993), 1–22.

Harvey, S. P. J., 'Domesday England', in Hallam (ed.), *The Agrarian History of England and Wales*, ii, 1–136.

Hatcher, J., 'Farming techniques: south-west England', in Hallam (ed.), *The Agrarian History of England and Wales*, ii, 383–98.

Hatcher, J., *Rural Settlement and Society in the Duchy of Cornwall* (Cambridge, 1970).

Herbert, N. M., 'Tidenham, including Lancaut', in C. R. Elrington et al. (eds), *The Victoria History of the County of Gloucestershire*, x (1972), 50–62.

Herring, P., 'Commons, fields and communities in medieval Cornwall', in Chadwick (ed.), *Recent Approaches to the Archaeology of Land Allotment*, 70–95.

Herring, P., 'Cornish strip fields', in Turner (ed.), *Medieval Devon and Cornwall*, 44–77.

Herring, P., 'Early medieval transhumance in Cornwall, Great Britain', in Klápště and Pesez (eds), *Medieval Rural Settlement in Marginal Landscapes*, 47–56.

Herring, P., 'Medieval fields at Brown Willy, Bodmin Moor', in Turner (ed.), *Medieval Devon and Cornwall*, 78–103.

Herring, P., 'Shadows of ghosts: early medieval transhumance in Cornwall', in Turner and Sylvester (eds), *Life in Medieval Landscapes*, 88–105.

Herring, P., 'Transhumance in medieval Cornwall', in H. S. A. Fox (ed.), *Seasonal Settlement*, 35–44.

Herring, P., 'West Cornwall's rough ground: a history', in Dudley (ed.), *Goon, Hal, Cliff & Croft*, 26–59.

Hesse, M., 'Domesday land measures in Suffolk', *Landscape History*, 22 (2000), 21–36.

Hey, G., *Yarnton: Saxon and Medieval Settlement and Landscape*, Oxford Archaeology Thames Valley Landscapes Monograph, 20 (Oxford, 2004).

Higgs, E. S., and M. Jarman, 'Yeavering: faunal report', in Hope-Taylor, *Yeavering*, 327–32.

Higham, M., 'Pre-conquest settlement in the Forest of Bowland', in J. R. Baldwin and I. Whyte (eds), *Scandinavians in Cumbria* (Edinburgh, 1985), 161–7.

Higham, M., 'The *-erg* names of Northern England', '*Aergi* names as indicators of transhumance: problems of the evidence', and 'Shay names: a need for reappraisal?' in A. G. Crosby (ed.), *Of Names and Places: Selected Writings of Mary Higham* (n.p., 2007), 1–10.

Higham, N., 'Settlement, land use and Domesday ploughlands', *Landscape History*, 12 (1990), 33–44.

Higham, N., *A Frontier Landscape: The North West in the Middle Ages* (Macclesfield, 2004).

Higham, N. J., and M. J. Ryan (eds), *The Landscape Archaeology of Anglo-Saxon England* (Woodbridge, 2010).

Hill, D., 'Prelude: agriculture through the year', in Hyer and Owen-Crocker (eds), *The Material Culture of Daily Living*, 9–22.

Hill, D., '*Sulh*: the Anglo-Saxon plough *c.* 1000 AD', *Landscape History*, 22 (2000), 5–19.

Hill, D., and R. Cowie (eds), *Wics: The Early Mediaeval Trading Centres of Northern Europe* (Sheffield, 2001).

Hill, P., *Dry Grain Farming Families: Hausaland (Nigeria) and Karnataka (India) Compared* (Cambridge, 1982).

Hiller, J., D. Petts, and T. Allen, 'Discussion of the Anglo-Saxon archaeology', in S. Foreman, J. Hiller, and D. Petts (eds), *Gathering the People, Settling the Land: The Archaeology of a Middle Thames Landscape* (Oxford, 2002), 57–72.

Hillman, G. C., 'Interpretation of archaeological plant remains: the application of ethnographic models from Turkey', in van Zeist and Casparie, *Plants and Ancient Man* (eds), 1–41.

Hilton, R. H., 'The social structure of rural Warwickshire in the Middle Ages', in R. H. Hilton, *The English Peasantry in the Later Middle Ages* (Oxford, 1975), 113–38.

Hines, J., *The Scandinavian Character of Anglian England in the Pre-Viking Period*, BAR, British Series, 124 (Oxford, 1984).

Hinton, D., 'Raw materials: sources and demand', in Hamerow, Hinton, and Crawford (eds), *Oxford Handbook of Anglo-Saxon Archaeology*, 423–39.

Hinton, D., 'The towns of Hampshire', in J. Haslam (ed.), *Anglo-Saxon Towns in Southern England* (Chichester, 1984), 149–65.

Hinton, D., *Gold and Gilt, Pots and Pins: Possessions and People in Medieval Britain* (Oxford, 2005).

Hinton, D. A., *Archaeology, Economy and Society: England from the Fifth to the Fifteenth Century* (1990).

Hoff, A., *Lov og landskab: landskabslovenes bidrag til forståelsen af landbrugs- og landskabsudviklingen i Danmark ca. 900–1250* (Aarhus, 1997).

Hollis, S., 'Old English "cattle theft charms": manuscript contexts and social uses', *Anglia*, 115 (1997), 139–64.

Hooke, D., *Anglo-Saxon Landscapes of the West Midlands: The Charter Evidence*, BAR, British Series, 95 (Oxford, 1981).

Hooke, D., 'Early medieval woodland and the place-name term *lēah*', in Padel and Parsons (eds), *A Commodity of Good Names*, 365–76.

Hooke, D., 'Regional variation in southern and central England and its relationship to land units and settlement', in Hooke (ed.), *Anglo-Saxon Settlements*, 123–51.

Hooke, D., '*Wealdbæra* and *swina mæst*: woodpasture in early medieval England', in Turner and Sylvester (eds), *Life in Medieval Landscapes*, 32–49.

Hooke, D. (ed.), *Anglo-Saxon Settlements* (Oxford, 1988).

Hooke, D., 'Anglo-Saxon estates in the Vale of the White Horse', *Oxoniensia*, 52 (1987), 129–43.

Hooke, D., *Pre-Conquest Charter-Bounds of Devon and Cornwall* (Woodbridge, 1994).

Hooke, D., *The Landscape of Anglo-Saxon England* (1998).

Hooke, D., *Warwickshire Anglo-Saxon Charter Bounds* (Woodbridge, 1999).

Hooke, D., *Trees in Anglo-Saxon England* (Woodbridge, 2010).

Hope-Taylor, B., *Yeavering: An Anglo-British Centre of Early Northumbria* (1977).

Horn, W., and E. Born, *The Plan of St Gall* (Berkeley, 1979).

Hoskins, W. G., *Devon* (1954).

Hoskins, W. G., 'The Dartmoor Commons', in L. Dudley Stamp and W. G. Hoskins, *The Common Lands of England and Wales* (1963), 185–90.

Hoskins, W. G., *Provincial England: Essays in Social and Economic History* (1963).

Hough, C., 'Cattle-tracking in the Fonthill Letter', *EHR*, 115 (2000), 864–92.

Hull, B. D., and T. C. O'Connell, 'Diet: recent evidence from analytical chemical techniques', in Hamerow, Hinton, and Crawford (eds), *Oxford Handbook of Anglo-Saxon Archaeology*, 667–87.

Hunter, J., *The Essex Landscape* (Chelmsford, 1999).

Hunter, J., *Field Systems in Essex*, Essex Society for Archaeology and History Occasional Papers, NS, 1 (Colchester, 2003).

Huntley, J. P., 'Saxon–Norse economy in northern Britain: food for thought', *Durham Archaeological Journal*, 14–15 (1999), 77–81.

Hurst, R. D., *American Farm Tools from Hand-Power to Steam-Power* (Manhattan, KA, 1982).

Hyer, M. C., and G. R. Owen-Crocker (eds), *The Material Culture of Daily Living in the Anglo-Saxon World* (Exeter, 2011).

Irvine, S. (ed.), *The Anglo-Saxon Chronicle: MS E*, The Anglo-Saxon Chronicle: A Collaborative Edition, 7 (Cambridge, 2004).

Isaakidou, V., 'Ploughing with cows: Knossos and the "secondary products revolution"', in D. Serjeantson and D. Field (eds), *Animals in the Neolithic of Britain and Europe* (Oxford, 2006), 95–112.

Jackson, K., *Language and History in Early Britain* (Edinburgh, 1953).

Jaques, D., K. Dobney, J. Barrett, C. Johnstone, J. Carrott, and A. Hall, 'The nature of the bioarchaeological assemblages', in Dobney, Jaques, Barrett, and Johnstone, *Farmers, Monks and Aristocrats*, 36–58.

Jenkins, D., *The Law of Hywel Dda* (Llandysul, 1986).

Johansson, C., *Old English Place-Names and Field-Names containing* lēah (Stockholm, 1975).

Johnstone, C., 'Donkeys and mules', in O'Connor and Sykes (eds), *Extinctions and Invasions*, 17–25.

Jolliffe, J., 'Northumbrian institutions', *EHR*, 41 (1926), 1–42.

Jones, C. W. (ed.), *Bedae Venerabilis opera didascalica*, 3 vols, Corpus christianorum series latina, 123 (Turnhout, 1975–80).

Jones, D., 'Romano-British settlements on the Lincolnshire Wolds', in R. H. Bewley (ed.), *Lincolnshire's Archaeology from the Air*, Occasional Papers in Lincolnshire History and Archaeology, 11 (Lincoln, 1998), 69–80.

Jones, G. E. M., 'Interpretation of archaeological plant remains: ethnographic models from Greece', in van Zeist and Casparie (eds), *Plants and Ancient Man*, 43–61.

Jones, R., 'Understanding medieval manure', in R. Jones (ed.), *Manure Matters*, 145–58.

Jones, R., 'Signatures in the soil: the use of ceramic manure scatters in the identification of medieval arable farming regimes', *Archaeological Journal*, 161 (2004), 159–88.

Jones, R., 'Manure and the medieval social order', in M. J. Allen, N. Sharples, and T. O'Connor (eds), *Land and People: Essays in Memory of John G. Evans* (Oxford, 2009), 217–25.

Jones, R. (ed.), *Manure Matters: Historical, Archaeological and Ethnographic Perspectives* (Farnham, 2012).

Jones, R., and M. K. Page, *Medieval Villages in an English Landscape: Beginnings and Ends* (Macclesfield, 2006).

Keefer, S. L., 'Hwær cwom mearh? The horse in Anglo-Saxon England', *Journal of Medieval History*, 2.2 (1996), 115–34.

Kelekna, P., *The Horse in Human History* (Cambridge, 2009).

Kelly, F., *Early Irish Farming: A Study based mainly on the Law-Texts of the 7th and 8th Centuries AD*, Early Irish Law Series, 4 (Dublin, 1997).

Kelly, S. (ed.), *The Charters of Abingdon Abbey*, 2 vols (Oxford, 2000).

Kemble, J., *Prehistoric and Roman Essex* (Stroud, 2001).

Kemble, J. M., *Codex diplomaticus ævi saxonici*, 6 vols (1839–48).

Kenward, H., and A. Hall, 'Dung and stable manure on waterlogged archaeological occupation sites: some ruminations on the evidence from plant and invertebrate remains', in R. Jones (ed.), *Manure Matters*, 79–95.

Kenward, H., and N. Whitehouse, 'Insects', in O'Connor and Sykes (eds), *Extinctions and Invasions*, 181–9.

Ker, N. R., *Catalogue of Manuscripts containing Anglo-Saxon* (Oxford, 1957).

Kibble, J., *Wychwood Forest and its Border Places* (2nd edn, Charlbury, 1999).

Kitchener, A. C., and T. O'Connor, 'Wildcats, domestic and feral cats', in O'Connor and Sykes (eds), *Extinctions and Invasions*, 83–94.

Klaeber, F., *Beowulf and the Fight at Finnsburg* (3rd edn, Boston, 1950).

Klápště, J., and J.-M. Pesez (eds), *Medieval Rural Settlement in Marginal Landscapes: Ruralia VII, 8th–14th September 2007, Cardiff, Wales, UK*, Ruralia, 7 (Turnhout, 2009).

Klápště, J., and P. Sommer (eds), *Processing, Storage, Distribution of Food: Food in the Medieval Rural Environment*, Ruralia, 8 (Turnhout, 2011).

Knowles, D., *The Monastic Order in England: A History of its Development from the Time of St Dunstan to the Fourth Lateran Council, 940–1216* (2nd edn, Cambridge, 1963).

Krapp, G. P., and E. van K. Dobbie (eds), *The Exeter Book*, Anglo-Saxon Poetic Records, 3 (New York, 1936).

LaBianca, Ø. S., *Sedentarization and Nomadization: Food System Cycles at Hesban and Vicinity in Transjordan*, Hesban, 1 (Berrien Springs, MI, 1990.

Lake, R. D., et al., *Geology of the Country around Southend and Foulness*, British Geological Survey (London, 1986).

Langdon, J., *Horses, Oxen and Technological Innovation* (Cambridge, 1986).

Langdon, J., G. Astill, and J. Myrdal, 'Introduction', in Astill and Langdon (eds), *Medieval Farming and Technology*, 1–9.

Langer, R. H. M., and G. D. Hill, *Agricultural Plants* (2nd edn, Cambridge, 1991).

Lapidge, M., J. Blair, S. Keynes, and D. Scragg (eds), *The Wiley Blackwell Encyclopedia of Anglo-Saxon England* (2nd edn, Chichester, 2014).

Larson, G., U. Albarella, K. Dobney, and P. Rowley-Conwy, 'Current views on *Sus* phylogeography and pig domestication as seen through modern mtDNA studies', in Albarella, Dobney, Ervynck, and Rowley-Conwy (eds), *Pigs and Humans*, 30–41.

Lavergne, L. de, *The Rural Economy of England, Scotland and Ireland* (Edinburgh and London, 1855).

Leahy, K., 'Anglo-Saxon crafts', in Hamerow, Hinton, and Crawford (eds), *Oxford Handbook of Anglo-Saxon Archaeology*, 440–59.

Leahy, K., *Anglo-Saxon Crafts* (Stroud, 2003).

Leary, J., 'Life and death in the heart of the settlement: excavations at 28–31 James Street', in Leary et al., *Tatberht's Lundenwic*, 6–39.

Leary, J., with G. Brown et al., *Tatberht's Lundenwic: Archaeological Excavations in Middle Saxon London*, Pre-Construct Archaeology Monograph, 2 (2004).

Lebecq, S., *Marchands et navigateurs frisons du haut moyen âge* (Lille, 1983).

Legge, A. J., 'The aurochs and domestic cattle', in O'Connor and Sykes (eds), *Extinctions and Invasions*, 26–35.

Lennard, R. V., 'The economic position of the bordars and cottars of Domesday Book', *Economic Journal*, 61 (1951), 342–71.

Lennard, R. V., 'Domesday plough-teams: the south-west evidence', *EHR*, 81(1966), 770–5.

Letts, J. B., *Smoke Blackened Thatch: A Unique Source of Late Medieval Plant Remains from Southern England* (1999).

Lewis, C., P. Mitchell-Fox, and C. Dyer, *Village, Hamlet and Field: Changing Medieval Settlements in Central England* (Macclesfield, 2001).

Lewis, H. A., 'The Characterisation and Interpretation of Ancient Tillage Practices through Soil Micromorphology: A Methodological Study' (unpublished PhD dissertation, University of Cambridge, 1999).

Liebermann, F. (ed.), *Die Gesetze der Angelsachsen*, 3 vols (Halle, 1898–1916).

Lock, G., C. Gosden, and P. Daly, *Segsbury Camp: Excavations in 1996 and 1997 at an Iron Age Hillfort on the Oxfordshire Ridgeway*, Oxford School of Archaeology Monograph, 61 (Oxford, 2005).

Love, R. C., *Three Eleventh-Century Anglo-Latin Saints' Lives: Vita S. Birini, Vita et miracula S. Kenelmi and Vita S. Rumwoldi* (Oxford, 1996).

Loveluck, C. (ed.), *Rural Settlement, Lifestyles and Social Change in the Later First Millennium AD: Anglo-Saxon Flixborough in it Wider Context*, Excavations at Flixborough, 4 (Oxford, 2007).

Loyn, H. R., *Anglo-Saxon England and the Norman Conquest* (2nd edn, 1991).

McCormick, M., *Origins of the European Economy: Communications and Commerce, AD 300–900* (Cambridge, 2001).

McGrail, S., *Ancient Boats and Ships* (2nd edn, Princes Risborough, 2006).

Mackenzie, D., *Goat Husbandry* (3rd edn, 1970).

McKerracher, M. J., 'Agricultural Development in Mid Saxon England' (unpublished DPhil thesis, Oxford University, 2013).

Maclean, M., *Hedges and Hedgelaying: A Guide to Planting, Management and Conservation* (Ramsbury, 2006).

Magennis, H., *Anglo-Saxon Appetites: Food and Drink and their Consumption in Old English and Related Literatures* (Dublin, 1999).

Maitland, F. W., *Domesday Book and Beyond: Three Essays in the Early History of England* (repr. 1960).

Manolson, F., and A. Fraser, 'Cattle', in Thear and Fraser (eds), *The Complete Book of Raising Livestock and Poultry*, 159–95.

Martin, E., and M. Satchell, *'Wheare most Enclosures be': East Anglian Fields: History, Morphology, Management* (Ipswich, 2008).

Mason, I. L., 'Goat', in I. L. Mason (ed.), *Evolution of Domesticated Animals*, 85–99.

Mason, I. L. (ed.), *Evolution of Domesticated Animals* (1984).

Mason, L., and C. Brown, *Traditional Foods of Britain: An Inventory* (Totnes, 1999).

Masschaele, J., *Peasants, Merchants and Markets: Inland Trade in Medieval England, 1150–1350* (Basingstoke, 1997).

Meens, R., 'A penitential diet', in M. Rubin (ed.), *Medieval Christianity in Practice* (Princeton, 2009), 144–50.

Metcalf, M., 'The coins from the *wics*', in D. Hill and Cowie (eds), *Wics*, 50–3, 90.

Metcalf, M., 'The coins', in P. Andrews (ed.), *Southampton Finds*, i: *The Coins and Pottery from Hamwic*, Southampton Archaeology Monographs, 4 (Southampton, 1998), 17–59.

Metcalf, M., 'Variations in the composition of the currency at different places in England', in T. Pestell, and K. Ulmschneider (eds), *Markets in Early Medieval Europe: Trading and 'Productive' Sites, 650–850* (Macclesfield, 2003), 37–47.

Miller, E. (ed.), *The Agrarian History of England and Wales*, iii: *1348–1500* (Cambridge, 1991).

Millett, M., *The Romanization of Britain: An Essay in Archaeological Interpretation* (Cambridge, 1990).

Mills, A. D., *A Dictionary of English Place-Names* (2nd edn, Oxford, 1998).

Mills, O., *Practical Sheep Dairying: The Care and Milking of the Dairy Ewe* (Wellingborough, 1989).

Moffett, L., 'Charred cereals from some ovens/kilns in late Saxon Stafford and the botanical evidence for the pre-*burh* economy', in J. Rackham (ed.), *Environment and Economy in Anglo-Saxon England*, 55–64.

Moffett, L., 'Food plants on archaeological sites: the nature of the archaeobotanical record', in Hamerow, Hinton, and Crawford (eds), *Oxford Handbook of Anglo-Saxon Archaeology*, 346–60.

Moffett, L., 'The archaeology of medieval food plants', in Woolgar, Serjeantson, and Waldron (eds), *Food in Medieval England*, 41–55.

Monk, M., 'Post-Roman drying kilns and the problem of function: a preliminary statement', in D. O'Corrain (ed.), *Irish Antiquity* (Cork, 1981), 216–30.

Morgan, D. H., *Harvesters and Harvesting 1840–1900: A Study of the Rural Proletariat* (1982).

Morris, C. A., 'Anglo-Saxon and Medieval Woodworking Crafts: The Manufacture and Use of Domestic and Utilitarian Wooden Artifacts in the British Isles, c. 400–1500 AD' (unpublished PhD dissertation, University of Cambridge, 1984).

Morris, C. A., *Craft, Industry and Everyday Life: Wood and Woodworking in Anglo-Scandinavian and Medieval York*, The Archaeology of York, 17.13 (York, 2000)

Morton, A. D., *Excavations at Hamwic*, i: *Excavations 1946–83, excluding Six Dials and Melbourne Street*, CBA Research Report, 84 (1992).

Morton, A. J., and L. Avanzo, 'Executive decision-making in the domestic sheep', *PloS ONE*, 6.1 (2011), 1–8.

Murphy, D. P., *People, Plants and Genes: The Story of Crops and Humanity* (Oxford, 2007).

Murphy, P., 'Iron Age to late Saxon land-use in the Breckland', in M. Jones (ed.), *Integrating the Subsistence Economy*, BAR, International Series, 181 (Oxford, 1983), 177–209.

Museum of London, *The Prittlewell Prince: The Discovery of a Rich Anglo-Saxon Burial in Essex* (2004).

Myrdal, J., 'The agricultural transformation of Sweden, 1000–1300', in Astill and Langdon (eds), *Medieval Farming and Technology*, 147–71.

Myrdal, J., 'Source pluralism and a package of methods: medieval tending of livestock as an example', in M. Lamberg et al. (eds), *Methods and the Medievalist: Current Approaches in Medieval Studies* (Newcastle upon Tyne, 2008), 134–58.

Naismith, R., *Money and Power in Anglo-Saxon England: The Southern English Kingdoms, 757–865* (Cambridge, 2012).

Napier, A. S., 'Altenglische Miscellen', *Archiv für das Studium der neueren Sprachen und Literaturen*, 84 (1890), 323–7.

Napier, A. S., and W. H. Stevenson, *The Crawford Collection of Early Charters and Documents now in the Bodleian Library* (Oxford, 1895).

Neidorf, L., 'Scribal errors of proper names in the *Beowulf* manuscript', *Anglo-Saxon England*, 42 (2014), 249–69.

Neuk, B. S., 'Medieval Britain and Ireland in 1991', *Medieval Archaeology*, 36 (1992), 184–308.

Newman, P., *The Field Archaeology of Dartmoor* (Swindon, 2011).

Nicholson, J. R., *Traditional Life in Shetland* (1978).

O'Brien, C., 'The early medieval shires of Yeavering, Breamish and Bamburgh', *Archaeologia Æliana*, 5th ser., 30 (2002), 53–73.

O'Brien O'Keeffe, K. (ed.), *The Anglo-Saxon Chronicle: MS A*, The Anglo-Saxon Chronicle: A Collaborative Edition, 5 (Cambridge, 2001).

O'Connor, T., 'Animal bones from Anglo-Scandinavian York', in R. A. Hall (ed.), *Aspects of Anglo-Scandinavian York*, 427–45.

O'Connor, T., 'The house mouse', in O'Connor and Sykes (eds), *Extinctions and Invasions*, 127–33.

O'Connor, T., 'Making themselves at home: the archaeology of commensal vertebrates', in D. Campana, P. Crabtree, S. D. deFrance, J. Lev-Tov, and A. M. Choyke (eds), *Anthropological Approaches to Zooarchaeology: Colonialism, Complexity and Animal Transformations* (Oxford, 2010), 270–4.

O'Connor, T., 'Animal husbandry', in Hamerow, Hinton, and Crawford (eds), *Oxford Handbook of Anglo-Saxon Archaeology*, 361–76.

O'Connor, T., and N. Sykes (eds), *Extinctions and Invasions: A Social History of British Fauna* (Oxford, 2010).

O'Connor, T. P., *The Analysis of Urban Bone Assemblages: A Handbook for Archaeologists*, The Archaeology of York, 19.2 (York, 2003).

Ohlgren, T. H., *Anglo-Saxon Textual Illustration: Photographs of Sixteen Manuscripts* (Kalamazoo, MI, 1992).

Oosthuizen, S., 'Anglo-Saxon fields', in Hamerow, Hinton, and Crawford (eds), *The Oxford Handbook of Anglo-Saxon Archaeology*, 377–401.

Oosthuizen, S., 'Medieval field systems and settlement nucleation: common or separate origins?' in Higham and Ryan (eds), *The Landscape Archaeology of Anglo-Saxon England*, 107–31.

Oosthuizen, S., 'Medieval greens and commons in the Central Province: evidence from the Bourn Valley, Cambridgeshire', *Landscape History*, 24 (2002), 73–89.

Oosthuizen, S., *Landscapes Decoded: The Origins and Development of Cambridgeshire's Medieval Fields* (Hatfield, 2006).

Oosthuizen, S., 'Archaeology, common rights and the origins of Anglo-Saxon identity', *Early Medieval Europe*, 19 (2011), 153–81.

Oosthuizen, S., *Tradition and Transformation in Anglo-Saxon England: Archaeology, Common Rights and Landscape* (2013).

Orchard, A., *Pride and Prodigies: Studies in the Monsters of the Beowulf Manuscript* (Woodbridge, 1995).

Orosius, Paulus, see Bately (ed.), *The Old English Orosius*.

Orwin, C. S., *A History of English Farming* (1949).

Orwin, C. S., and C. S. Orwin, *The Open Fields* (Oxford, 1938).

Oswald, A., 'A new earthwork survey of Wharram Percy', in Wrathmell (ed.), *A History of Wharram Percy*, 23–44.

Ottaway, P., 'Agricultural tools', in D. H. Evans and Loveluck (eds), *Life and Economy at Early Medieval Flixborough*, 245.

Ottaway, P., L. Barber, and G. Thomas, 'Cultivation, crop processing, and food procurement', in G. Thomas, *The Later Anglo-Saxon Settlement at Bishopstone*, 130–3.

Owen, A. E. B., 'Romans and roads in south-east Lindsey: the place-name evidence', in A. Rumble and A. D. Mills (eds), *Names, Places and People: An Onomastic Miscellany for John McNeal Dodgson* (Stamford, 1997), 254–68.

Padel, O., 'Place-names', in J. Kain and R. J. P. Ravenhill, *Historical Atlas of South-West England* (Exeter, 1999), 88–99.

Padel, O., 'Ancient and medieval administrative divisions of Cornwall', *Proceedings of the Dorset Natural History and Archaeological Society*, 131 (2010), 211–14.

Padel, O. J., and D. N. Parsons (eds), *A Commodity of Good Names: Essays in Honour of Margaret Gelling* (Donington, 2008).

Page, M., *The Pipe Rolls of the Bishopric of Winchester 1301–2* (Winchester, 1996).

Page, R. I., '*Gerefa*: some problems of meaning', in A. Bammesberger (ed.), *Problems of Old English Lexicography: Studies in Memory of Angus Cameron*, Eichstätter Beiträge, 15 (Eichstätt, 1985), 211–28.

Pantos, A., 'The location and form of Anglo-Saxon assembly-places: some "moot points"', in A. Pantos and S. Semple (eds), *Assembly Places and Practices in Medieval Europe* (Dublin, 2003), 155–80.

Parry, S., *Raunds Area Survey: An Archaeological Study of the Landscape of Raunds, Northamptonshire, 1985–94* (Oxford, 2006).

Pearce, S., 'Early medieval land-use on Dartmoor and its flanks', *Devon Archaeology*, 3: *Dartmoor Issue* (1985), 13–19.

Pearce, S., *South-West Britain in the Early Middle Ages* (Leicester, 2004).

Pelling, R., 'Archaeobotanical remains', in Hardy, Dodd, and Keevil, *Ælfric's Abbey*, 439–48.

Pelteret, D. A. E., *Slavery in Early Mediaeval England: From the Reign of Alfred until the Twelfth Century* (Woodbridge, 1995).

Pettit, E. (ed.), *Anglo-Saxon Remedies, Charms and Prayers from British Library MS Harley 585: The Lacnunga*, 2 vols (Lampeter, 2001).

Phillips, A. D. M., *The Underdraining of Farmland in England in the Nineteenth Century*, Cambridge Studies in Historical Geography, 15 (Cambridge, 1989).

Phythian-Adams, C., *Land of the Cumbrians: A Study in British Provincial Origins, A.D. 400–1120* (Aldershot, 1996).

Plummer, C. (ed.), *Venerabilis Bedae Opera historica* (Oxford, 1896).

Pluskowski, A., 'The wolf', in O'Connor and Sykes (eds), *Extinctions and Invasions*, 68–74.

Pluskowski, A., 'The archaeology of paganism', in Hamerow, Hinton, and Crawford (eds), *Oxford Handbook of Anglo-Saxon Archaeology*, 764–78.

Poole, K., 'Bird introductions', in O'Connor and Sykes (eds), *Extinctions and Invasions*, 156–65.

Porter, D. W., *The Antwerp–London Glossaries*, i: *Texts and Indices*, Publications of the Dictionary of Old English, 8 (Toronto, 2011).

Powlesland, D., 'West Heslerton settlement mobility: a case of static development', in H. Geake and J. Kenny (eds), *Early Deira: Archaeological Studies of the East Riding in the Fourth to Ninth Centuries* (Oxford and Oakville, CT, 2000), 19–26.

Price, L., *The Plan of St Gall in Brief* (Berkeley, 1982).

Pryor, F., *Farmers in Prehistoric Britain* (Stroud, 1998).

Rackham, J. (ed.), *Environment and Economy in Anglo-Saxon England* (York, 1994).

Rackham, O., *Ancient Woodland: Its History, Vegetation and Uses in England* (1980).

Rackham, O., *The History of the Countryside* (1986).

Rahtz, P., *The Saxon and Medieval Places at Cheddar: Excavations 1960–62*, BAR, British Series, 65 (Oxford, 1979).

Randell, A., *Fenland Memories*, ed. Enid Porter (1969).

Reaney, P. H., *The Place-Names of Essex*, English Place-Name Society, 12 (Cambridge, 1935).

Reilly, K., 'The black rat', in O'Connor and Sykes (eds), *Extinctions and Invasions*, 134–45.

Reynolds, P. J., *Iron-Age Farm: The Butser Experiment* (1979).

Reynolds, P. J., 'The medieval fence', in *Occasional Papers by Dr Peter J. Reynolds*, 3 ([Waterlooville], n.d.), 37–42.

Reynolds, P. J., and J. Langley, 'Romano-British corn drying oven; an experiment', *Archaeological Journal*, 136 (1980 for 1979), 27–42.

Riddler, I., and N. Trzaska-Nartowski, 'Chanting upon a dunghill: working skeletal materials', in Hyer and Owen-Crocker (eds), *The Material Culture of Daily Living*, 116–41.

Rippon, S., 'Landscape change in the "long eighth century" in southern England', in Higham and Ryan (eds), *The Landscape Archaeology of Anglo-Saxon England*, 39–64.

Rippon, S., *The Transformation of Coastal Wetlands: Exploitation and Management of Marshland Landscapes in Northwest Europe during the Roman and Medieval Periods* (Oxford, 2000).

Rippon, S., *Beyond the Medieval Village: The Diversification of Landscape Character in Southern Britain* (Oxford, 2008).

Rixson, D., *The History of Meat Trading* (Nottingham, 2000).

Roberts, B. K., and S. Wrathmell, *Region and Place: A Study of English Rural Settlement* (2002).

Roberts, E., 'Notes on the history of the landscape of Tichborne, Cheriton and Beaworth', Typescript, Hampshire Record Office, Pamphlets, Box 7, HP 112.

Roberts, E., 'The Saxon Bounds of Ticceburn', *Hampshire Field Club and Archaeological Society Newsletter*, NS, 18 (1992), 29–33.

Roberts, E., and G. Allam, 'Saxon Alresford and Bighton', *Hampshire Field Club and Archaeological Society Newsletter*, NS, 20 (1993), 9–13.

Roberts, I., R. Carlton, and A. Rushworth, *Drove Roads of Northumberland* (Stroud, 2010).

Robertson, A. J. (ed. and tr.), *The Laws of the Kings of England from Edmund to Henry I* (Cambridge, 1925).

Robertson, A. J. (ed. and tr.), *Anglo-Saxon Charters* (2nd edn, Cambridge, 1956).

Robinson, M., 'The charred honeybees', in Leary et al., *Tatberht's Lundenwic*, 38–9.

Roden, D., 'Field systems of the Chiltern Hills and their environs', in Baker and Butlin (eds), *Studies of Field Systems*, 325–76.

Rodwell, W. J. and K. A., *Rivenhall: Investigation of a Roman Villa, Church and Village 1950–1977*, 2 vols, CBA Research Report, 55 and 80 (London, 1985–93).

Roffe, D., *Decoding Domesday* (Woodbridge, 2007).

Roud, S., *The English Year: A Month-by-Month Guide to the Nation's Customs and Festivals, from May Day to Mischief Night* (2006).

Round, J. H., 'The Domesday Survey', in H. A. Doubleday (ed.), *Victoria History of the County of Essex*, i (1903), 368–74.

Rowley, R. T. (ed.), *The Origins of Open-Field Agriculture* (1981).

Rowley-Conwy, P., and K. Dobney, 'Wild boar and domestic pigs in Mesolithic and Neolithic southern Scandinavia', in Albarella, Dobney, Ervynck, and Rowley-Conwy (eds), *Pigs and Humans*, 131–55.

Ryder, M. L., *Sheep & Man* (1983).

Sambraus, H. H., *A Colour Atlas of Livestock Breeds* (1992).

Samuel, R., '"Quarry roughs": life and labour in Headington Quarry, 1860–1920; an essay in oral history', in R. Samuel (ed.), *Village Life and Labour* (1975), 139–263.

Saunders, T., 'Early medieval emporia and the tributary social function', in D. Hill and Cowie (eds), *Wics*, 7–13.

Sawyer, P., *Anglo-Saxon Charters: An Annotated List and Bibliography* (1968), revised version by S. E. Kelly et al., online at <http://www.esawyer.org.uk/>.

Sayer, K., 'Eggs, an underesearched [*sic*] topic', *Rural History Today*, 23 (2012), 1 and 8.

Seebohm F., *The English Village Community* (4th edn, 1896).

Serjeantson, D., 'Birds: food and a mark of status', in Woolgar, Serjeantson, and Waldron (eds), *Food in Medieval England*, 131–47.

Serjeantson, D., 'Extinct birds', in O'Connor and Sykes (eds), *Extinctions and Invasions*, 148–55.

Serjeantson, D., 'Goose husbandry in medieval Europe, and the problem of ageing goose bones', *Acta zoologica Cracoviensia*, 45 (2002), 39–54.

Serjeantson, D., *Birds*, Cambridge Manuals in Archaeology (Cambridge, 2009).

Serpell, J. (ed.), *The Domestic Dog: Its Evolution, Behaviour, and Interactions with People* (Cambridge, 1995).

Seymour, J. and S., *Self-Sufficiency* (1973).

Sheppard, J. A., 'Field systems of Yorkshire' in Baker and Butlin (eds), *Studies of Field Systems*, 145–87.

Shiel, R., 'Science and practice: the ecology of manure in historical retrospect', in R. Jones (ed.), *Manure Matters*, 13–23.

Short, B., 'The evolution of settlement and open-field topography in north Arden down to 1300', in Rowley (ed.), *The Origins of Open-Field Agriculture*, 163–83.

Short, B., 'Forests and wood-pasture in lowland England', in Thirsk (ed.), *The English Rural Landscape*, 129–49.

Sillitoe, P., 'Pigs in the New Guinea Highlands: an ethnographic example', in Albarella, Dobney. Ervynck, and Rowley-Conwy (eds), *Pigs and Humans*, 330–56.

Silvester, R., and J. Kissock, 'Wales: medieval settlements, nucleated and dispersed, permanent and seasonal', in Christie and Stamper (eds), *Medieval Rural Settlement*, 151–71.

Skeat, W. W., *The Holy Gospels in Anglo-Saxon, Northumbrian and Old Mercian Versions* (1871–87) [each gospel separately paginated].

Skipp, V., *Medieval Yardley: The Origin and Growth of a West Midland Community* (London and Chichester, 1970).

Smartt, J., and N. W. Simmonds (eds), *Evolution of Crop Plants* (2nd edn, Harlow, 1995).

Smith, A. H., *English Place-Name Elements*, 2 vols, English Place-Name Society, 25–6 (Cambridge, 1956).

Smith, A. H., *The Place-Names of Gloucestershire, Part 4*, English Place-Name Society, 41 (1963–4).

Spencer, C., *British Food: An Extraordinary Thousand Years of History* (2002).

Spray, Martin, 'Holly as a fodder in England', *Agricultural History Review*, 29 (1981), 97–110.

Stenton, F. M., *Anglo-Saxon England* (3rd edn, Oxford, 1971).

Stephens, H., *Stephens' Book of the Farm* (Edinburgh, 1844).

Stephenson, M. J., 'Wool yields in the medieval economy', *Economic History Review*, 2nd ser., 41 (1988), 368–91.

Stevens, C., 'Lentils as climatic indicators', *The Archaeologist*, 66 (2007), 46.

Stevenson, W. H., 'A contemporary description of the Domesday survey', *EHR*, 22 (1907), 72–84.

Stoertz, C., *Ancient Landscapes of the Yorkshire Wolds* (1997).

Stone, D. J., 'The consumption and supply of birds in late medieval England', in Woolgar, Serjeantson, and Waldron (eds), *Food in Medieval England*, 148–61.

Stone, D. J., 'The consumption of field crops in late medieval England', in Woolgar, Serjeantson, and Waldron (eds), *Food in Medieval England*, 11–26.

Stryker, W. G., 'The Latin–Old English Glossary in MS Cotton Cleopatra A. iii' (unpublished PhD thesis, Stanford University, 1951).

Sturt, G., *Change in the Village* (Firle, 1984).

Svensson, Ö., 'The Worthy-names of Devon', *Nomina* 15 (1991–2), 53–9.

Sykes, N., 'The animal bone', in S. Preston, 'Bronze Age occupation and Saxon feature at the Wolverton Turn enclosure, near Stony Stratford, Milton Keynes', *Records of Buckinghamshire*, 47 (2007), 81–117, at 103–9.

Sykes, N. J., 'From *cu* and *sceap* to *beffe* and *motton*: the management, distribution, and consumption of cattle and sheep in medieval England', in Woolgar, Serjeantson, and Waldron (eds), *Food in Medieval England*, 56–71.

Sykes, N. J., *The Norman Conquest: A Zoological Perspective*, BAR, International Series, 1656 (Oxford, 2007).

Taylor, C., *Dorset* (1970).

Taylor, C., *Fields in the English Landscape* (1975).

Taylor, C., *Roads and Tracks of Britain* (1979).

Thear, K., *Home and Farm Dairying* (Saffron Walden, 1988).

Thear, K., *The Smallholder's Manual* (Marlborough, 2002).

Thear, K., and A. Fraser (eds), *The Complete Book of Raising Livestock and Poultry: A Smallholder's Guide* (1980).

Thirsk, J., 'The origins of the common fields', *Past and Present*, no. 33 (1966), 142–7.

Thirsk, J. (ed.), *The English Rural Landscape* (Oxford, 2000).

Thomas, G., 'The symbolic life of later Anglo-Saxon settlements: a cellared structure and iron hoard from Bishopstone, East Sussex', *Archaeological Journal*, 165 (2008), 334–98.

Thomas, G., *The Later Anglo-Saxon Settlement at Bishopstone: A Downland Manor in the Making*, CBA Research Report, 163 (York, 2010).

Thomas, G., 'Ploughs, Kent and the Anglo-Saxon conversion', *Medieval Archaeology Newsletter*, 47 (2012), 1–2.

Thomas, G., 'The prehistory of medieval farms and villages: from Saxons to Scandinavians', in Christie and Stamper (eds), *Medieval Rural Settlement*, 43–62.

Thomas, H., 'Oats', in Smartt and Simmonds (eds), *Evolution of Crop Plants*, 132–6.

Thompson, F., *Lark Rise to Candleford* (Oxford, 1945).

Thorburn, M., *Mostly Rodmell: A Parish in the Lower Ouse Valley, Sussex* (Lewes, 2009).

Todd, M., *The South-West to AD 1000* (1987).

Townley, E., *Fieldwork on the Forest Shore: Stroat to Woolaston, Glos.*, Severn Estuary Levels Research Reports, 9 (1998).

Trow-Smith, R., *A History of British Livestock Husbandry to 1700* (1957).

Trow-Smith, R., *A History of British Livestock Husbandry, 1700–1900* (1959).

Turner, S., *Ancient Country: The Historic Character of Rural Devon*, Devon Archaeological Society Occasional Paper, 20 (Exeter, 2007).

Turner, S., *Making a Christian Landscape: The Countryside in Early Medieval Cornwall, Devon and Wessex* (Exeter, 2006).

Turner, S. (ed.), *Medieval Devon and Cornwall: Shaping an Ancient Countryside* (Macclesfield, 2006).

Turner, S., and B. Sylvester (eds), *Life in Medieval Landscapes: People and Places in the Middle Ages: Papers in Memory of H. S. A. Fox* (Oxford, 2012).

Tusser, T., *Five Hundred Points of Good Husbandry*, ed. G. Grigson (Oxford, 1984).

Ulmschneider, K., *Markets, Minsters and Metal-Detectors: The Archaeology of Middle Saxon Lincolnshire and Hampshire Compared*, BAR, British Series, 307 (Oxford, 2000).

Unwin, T., 'Towards a model of Anglo-Scandinavian rural settlement in England', in Hooke (ed.), *Anglo-Saxon Settlements*, 77–98.

van der Veen, M., *Crop Husbandry Regimes: An Archaeobotanical Study of Farming in Northern England, 1000 BC–AD 500*, Sheffield Archaeological Monographs, 3 (Sheffield, 1992).

van Doesburg, J., 'Archaeological evidence for pest control in medieval rural settlements in the Netherlands', in Klápště and Sommer (eds), *Processing, Storage, Distribution*, 119–211.

van Zeist, W., and W. A. Casparie (eds), *Plants and Ancient Man* (Rotterdam, 1984).

Vera, F. W. M., *Grazing, Ecology and Forest History* (Wallingford, 2000).

Wade-Martins, Susanna, 'Oxen ploughing, 1952', *Rural History Today*, 21 (2011), 1.

Wager, S. J., *Woods, Wolds and Groves: The Woodland of Medieval Warwickshire* (Oxford, 1984).

Walton Rogers, P., *Cloth and Clothing in Early Anglo-Saxon England*, CBA Research Report, 145 (York, 2007).

Walton Rogers, P., 'Textile production', in D. H. Evans and Loveluck (ed.), *Life and Economy at Early Medieval Flixborough*, 281–316.

Ward, C., *Cotters and Squatters: Housing's Hidden History* (Nottingham, 2002).

Warner, P., *The Origins of Suffolk* (Manchester, 1996).

Wasserschleben, H. (ed.), *Die Bussordnungen der abendländischen Kirche* (Halle, 1851).

Waters, B., *Severn Tide: A Study of the Upper Part of the Tidal Estuary of the Severn, its Inshore Fishing, Cider-making and Shipping, History, Local Life and Lore* (1947).

Watts, M., *Working Oxen* (Princes Risborough, 1999).

Welch, M., 'Rural settlement patterns in the early and middle Anglo-Saxon periods', *Landscape History*, 7 (1985), 13–25.

West, S., *West Stow, the Anglo-Saxon Village*, East Anglian Archaeology, 24 (Ipswich, 1985).

Wexler, J., and P. Harper, 'The lay of the land', *Clean Slate*, 76 (2010), 14–15.

White, K. D., *Roman Farming* (1970).

White, L., Jr., *Medieval Technology and Social Change* (Oxford, 1962).

White, N. A., 'Anglo-Saxon finds from three sites in Lincolnshire', *Lincolnshire History and Archaeology*, 23 (1988), 87–8.

Whitelock, D. (ed.), *Anglo-Saxon Wills* (Cambridge, 1930).

Whitelock, D. (ed.), *English Historical Documents*, i: c. 500–1042 (1955).

Wibberley, E. J., *Cereal Husbandry* (Ipswich, 1989).

Wickham, C., *Framing the Middle Ages: Europe and the Mediterranean, 400–800* (Oxford, 2005).

Wilkie, T., I. Mainland, U. Albarella, K. Dobney, and P. Rowley-Conwy, 'A dental micro-wear study of pig diet and management in Iron Age, Romano-British, Anglo-Scandinavian and medieval contexts in England', in Albarella, Dobney, Ervynck, and Rowley-Conwy (eds), *Pigs and Humans*, 241–54.

Wilkinson, T., *Archaeology and Environment in South Essex: Rescue Archaeology along the Grays By-Pass*, East Anglian Archaeology, 42 (Ipswich, 1988).

Williams, A., *The Backyard Cow* (Dorchester, 1979).

Williams, H., 'Animals, ashes and ancestors', in A. Pluskowski (ed.), *Just Skin and Bones? New Perspectives on Human–Animal Relations in the Historical Past*, BAR, International Series, 1410 (Oxford, 2005), 19–40.

Williams, P., and R. Newman, *Market Lavington, Wiltshire: An Anglo-Saxon Cemetery and Settlement* (Salisbury, 2006).

Williamson, T., 'The development of settlement in North West Essex: the results of a recent field survey', *Essex Archaeology and History*, 17 (1986), 120–32.

Williamson, T., 'Settlement, hierarchy and economy: a case study in northwest Essex', in K. Branigan and D. Miles (eds), *Villa Economies: Economic Aspects of Romano-British Villas* (Sheffield, [1989]), 73–87.

Williamson, T., *Shaping Medieval Landscapes: Settlement, Society, Environment* (Macclesfield, 2003).

Williamson, T., *Sandlands: The Suffolk Coasts and Heaths* (Macclesfield, 2005).

Williamson, T., *Sutton Hoo and its Landscape: The Context of the Monuments* (Oxford, 2008).

Williamson, T., *The Origins of Hertfordshire* (2nd edn, Manchester, 2010).

Williamson, T., *Environment, Society and Landscape in Early Medieval England: Time and Topography* (Woodbridge, 2013).

Wilson, C. A., *Food and Drink in Britain* (1973).

Wilson, D. M., *The Bayeux Tapestry: The Complete Tapestry in Colour* (1985).

Wilson, P., and M. King, *Arable Plants: A Field Guide* (Old Basing, 2003).

Winchester, A., *Discovering Parish Boundaries* (2nd edn, Princes Risborough, 2000).

Winchester, A. J. L., 'Seasonal settlement in Northern England: shieling place-names revisited', in Turner and Sylvester (eds), *Life in Medieval Landscapes*, 125–49.

Winchester, A. J. L., *England's Landscape: The North West* (2006).

Wiseman, J., *The Pig: A British History* (2000).

Witney, K. P., *The Jutish Forest: A Study of the Weald of Kent from 450–1380 AD* (1976).

Woolgar, C. M., D. Serjeantson, and T. Waldron (eds), *Food in Medieval England: Diet and Nutrition* (Oxford, 2006).

Wormald, P., 'Courts', in Lapidge et al. (eds), *The Wiley Blackwell Encyclopedia of Anglo-Saxon England*, 129.

Wormald, P., *The Making of English Law: King Alfred to the Twelfth Century*, i: *Legislation and its Limits* (Oxford, 1999).

Wrathmell, S. (ed.), *A History of Wharram Percy and its Neighbours*, Wharram: A Study of Settlement on the Yorkshire Wolds, 13, York University Archaeological Publications, 15 (York, 2012).

Wright, T., *Anglo-Saxon and Old English Vocabularies*, ed. R. P. Wülcker (2nd edn, 1884).

Yalden, D., 'Conclusion', in O'Connor and Sykes (eds), *Extinctions and Invasions*, 190–6.

Yalden, D., with U. Albarella, *The History of British Birds* (Oxford, 2009).

Yorke, B., *Wessex in the Early Middle Ages* (1995).

Zohary, D., and M. Hopf, *Domestication of Plants in the Old World* (2nd edn, Oxford, 1993).

Zupitza, J. (ed.), *Ælfrics Grammatik und Glossar* (Berlin, 1880).

Index